# Contents

# Acknowledgments

This book has been a joyous collaboration. We are eager to thank our editor, Jill Bialosky, for her encouragement, patience, tact, and generosity. We also wish to pay tribute to the rich field of studies in the sonnet form. We have gained from a tremendous number of poets, readers, critics, and scholars from different countries, who have thought about the form over the centuries. We have included a wide range of sonnets—our earliest poet was born around 1255, our most recent in 1956—but we have also had to exclude much that we value. We have had to limit the number of poems by individual poets and exclude others for reasons of space. We have also had to comply, reluctantly, with the current difficult climate of permissions. We have, in the process, lost poems we loved, or reduced the representation of cherished poets.

We are indebted to many period anthologies, such as *Elizabethan Sonnets*, edited by Maurice Evans and revised by Roy J. Booth, and *A Century of Sonnets*, edited by Paula R. Feldman and Daniel Robinson. We have gained from general anthologies, such as Phillis Levin's *The Penguin Book of the Sonnet*, as well as from national ones, such as Geoff Page's *The Indigo Book of Modern Australian Sonnets*. Paul Kane also made recommendations about the Australian sonnet. Our section "The Sonnet Under the Lamp" owes something to *A Book of the Sonnet: Poems and Criticism*, edited by Martin Kallich, Jack C. Gray, and Robert M. Rodney. Sonnets.org is a useful resource. Thanks to our employers, the

John Simon Guggenheim Memorial Foundation and Stanford University. Thanks especially to Pat O'Sullivan at the Guggenheim and to Mary Popek, Rita Mae Reese, and Sara Michas-Martin at Stanford. André Bernard provided indispensable help. We would also like to thank Chris Ahn and Paul Whitlatch at Norton and Sapna Mehta for their terrific work. Edward Hirsch would also like to thank Lauren Watel; Eavan Boland would like to thank Kevin Casey. Finally, as poets, editors, and friends, we are delighted to be able to thank each other for our inspiring and deeply rewarding collaborative work. Our work together is a sustained tribute to "a moment's monument."

—*Edward Hirsch*
*Eavan Boland*

# Editors' Note

This is a personal book. It has been a joy to compile, but it has also raised some rich complications and textual difficulties. We faced excitements, challenges, and frustrations. The frustrations we are eager to account for. Because this anthology is a close-up of a single form—the extraordinary history of which is best shown through the poets who encountered and deployed it over time— we wanted to include more sonnets by more poets than we could possibly accommodate. We especially regretted having to include only one or two instances of the form from poets whose work often constituted a lifetime's discovery and exploration of it. These, however, are the limitations of the editing process. We can only hope that the sonnets we have chosen prompt the reader to look for more. The door is open.

The power of the sonnet is in the way meaning is developed and determined by its strategies, its formal constraints. Each poet individually comes up against the massive determinants of the form. We decided that we could best tell the larger story of the sonnet by dividing our collection into centuries. We grouped poets chronologically as best we could. We felt, for example, that Colonel David Humphreys, the first American sonneteer, really belonged to the eighteenth century, whereas William Blake, who was born just a few years later, looked forward to the nineteenth century. We have also tried to enrich the story of the sonnet by including a range of other sections. We think our book demonstrates that the sonnet is both the most traditional and the most experimental of forms. Our lively section of historical comments makes clear that it is also highly controversial.

The sonnet has had such an international standing that we especially regret that we couldn't include more sonnets by poets from all over the world. Some of the poems we have included in this section are fairly literal translations, whereas others are free adaptations. We have listed these adaptations under the original poet who spurred the later work. Thus Ezra Pound's adaptation of a poem by Cavalcanti is listed under the Italian poet who helped to create the American one. Sir Thomas Wyatt's reworkings of Petrarch are really new poems that nonetheless take their impetus from the greatest sonneteer of all time. The reader can find Wyatt's work both at the start of the sixteenth century and in our selection of sonnets from around the world.

One of our most extraordinary examples is the poem by the late French writer Raymond Queneau. This poem comes from his book *Cent mille milliard de poèmes*, which consists of ten poems that could be read in any one of thousands of combinations. As Harry Matthews writes, "A book exists which contains so many sonnets that someone reading for a million years, at five minutes per sonnet, would never read the same sonnet twice."

Throughout this book, we have relied mostly on original texts. However, for clarity and ease of reading, a modern version has been used for some of the older poems and quotations. Our goal has been to create a friendly, decisive, readable, and imaginative book. We think it is filled with surprises. We hope it brings you as much happiness and consolation as it has given us.

# THE
# MAKING
# OF A
# SONNET

*A Norton Anthology*

# Personal Essays on
# Encountering the Sonnet

---

## MY OWN ACQUAINTANCE
### *Edward Hirsch*

The fourteen-line rhyming poem was invented in southern Italy around 1235 or so ("Eternal glory to the inventor of the sonnet," Paul Valéry proclaimed) and has had an astonishingly durable life ever since. The word *sonnet* derives from the Italian *sonetto*, meaning "a little sound" or "a little song," but the stateliness of the form belies the modesty of the word's derivation. The sonnet is a small vessel capable of plunging tremendous depths. It is one of the enabling forms of human inwardness.

The sonnet is an obsessive form—compact, expansive—that travels remarkably well. It crosses between countries and languages. It adapts to different meters and reverberates down the centuries. There must be something hardwired into its machinery —a heartbeat, a pulse—that keeps it breathing. How many times over the decades has it been pronounced dead and then somehow revitalized, deconstructed, and then constructed again, refashioned, remade? It darkens and then lightens again. It thinks on its feet.

Something about the spaciousness and brevity of the fourteen-line poem seems to suit the contours of rhetorical argument, especially when the subject is erotic love. The form becomes a medium for the poet to explore his or her capacity to bring together the heart and the head, feeling and thought, the lyrical and the discursive. It is conducive to calculation and experiment—a closed form that keeps opening up. It is generational. It keeps finding poets in places far from its sun-struck origins, in provincial enclaves and outposts, in the suburbs of distant cities, for example, such as Dublin and Chicago.

My own acquaintance with the sonnet came to me in a roundabout way. The form snuck on up me without my knowing it—a stealth music—and insinuated itself inside of me: a little sound, a little song. It carried me away. "I have been one acquainted with the night," I used to hum to myself under my breath. The pace of the lines—the sound of the sentences—mesmerized me. "I have walked out in rain—and back in rain. / I have outwalked the furthest city light."

At seventeen, I had begun to write poetry with great energy and determination. I was overwhelmed by feelings I couldn't understand. I seemed to be perpetually stunned—desolate, exuberant. I needed vessels and containers. I was probably grief-stricken over the loss of my childhood, but I wouldn't have understood that then. My brain was teeming with ideas, but there couldn't have been more than two clear thoughts in my head. I was intoxicated by poetry but I didn't know a single other person who wrote or read the stuff. How could one devote oneself to poetry in a culture that seemed to care so little about it? I had no way of knowing that this question would be one of the recurring agons of American poetry—from Anne Bradstreet to John Berryman.

I was devastated by loneliness, and reading lonely poems somehow made me feel less alone. That's when I discovered Robert Frost's "Acquainted with the Night." I didn't much like the cracker-barrel Yankee image of Frost that we had picked up at school, but this poem seemed to have been written out of a darker inner spirit. It had a kind of directness, a moody undertow, that appealed to me. There was something respectful about the word "acquainted" paired with the word "night." It had dignity. It wasn't overly familiar. It kept its privacy, its wit. I liked the way the speaker of the poem walked out into the night, the way he confronted and coped with darkness. He didn't explain his feelings away, or apologize for them. I liked the solitary music. I read "Acquainted with the Night" so often that I memorized it without knowing that I was learning it. I used to say it to myself as I walked through the park at night. I remember lying on my back in the forlorn darkness of my teenage room and reciting it aloud.

## Acquainted with the Night

I have been one acquainted with the night.
I have walked out in rain—and back in rain.
I have outwalked the furthest city light.

I have looked down the saddest city lane.
I have passed by the watchman on his beat
And dropped my eyes, unwilling to explain.

I have stood still and stopped the sound of feet
When far away an interrupted cry
Came over houses from another street,

But not to call me back or say good-bye;
And further still at an unearthly height,
One luminary clock against the sky

Proclaimed the time was neither wrong nor right.
I have been one acquainted with the night.

I was putting myself to school on Whitman and Ginsberg, and if someone had asked me, I probably would have said that American poetry shunned traditional forms, such as sonnets. I was filled with unearned opinions. This one was partly right, but only partly, since the evidence also suggests otherwise. There has always been a countercurrent of American poets expanding and rethinking traditional forms, sometimes in inherited meters, sometimes in free verse. They tend to think of these forms as organically as possible. A wide range of American poets are included in this book—from Ralph Waldo Emerson to Gwendolyn Brooks, from a homemade modernist like E. E. Cummings to an open field poet like Robert Duncan, from Elinor Wylie to James Merrill, from Edwin Arlington Robinson to Sterling Brown, from Robert Lowell to Ted Berrigan. It was also true that I didn't at first recognize the form of Frost's poem. It worked on me before I worked on it.

I wanted to write a poem like Frost's, a poem with a kind of massive American loneliness at the core, a deep center of solitude, which I also recognized in the paintings of Edward Hopper. I'd still like to write that poem. It occurred to me to count the lines— I was stumbling into becoming a maker—and thus discovered a different kind of sonnet structure. It wasn't Petrarchan or Shakespearean, the two main types of sonnet form in English. In fact, Frost had borrowed the rhyme scheme from Dante (*aba bcb cdc*) and written a terza rima sonnet, as Shelley had done in the five sections of "Ode to the West Wind." The poem was a walk. The rhythm and the rhymes gave the feeling of that walk, of moving forward while looking back. I felt that the music of the poem— the poem itself—had sent me out to the edge of myself and then reeled me back in. It circled back on itself. There was a kind of submission in it—a coping mechanism—that consoled me. It seemed to go beyond right and wrong. It was surrounded by a vast silence. It raised me to an unearthly height and then brought me gently back to earth.

"There are two absorbing facts," as Emerson formulated it: "I and the Abyss." The sonnet can be the vessel of that confrontation. Soon I would follow my discovery of the darker Frost and encounter the English Romantic sonnets of John Keats ("When I have fears that I may cease to be / Before my pen has glean'd my teeming brain") and John Clare ("I feel I am—I only know I am"), the so-called terrible sonnets of Gerard Manley Hopkins ("I wake and feel the fell of dark, not day"). These poems helped seal my vocation. They were written from the margins. The terrible loneliness at the heart of them was inscribed in fourteen lines, the social realm of a prescribed form. This was the great lesson that I learned as an isolated teenager in Chicago. Poetry counts; language mediates. I felt then—and I still feel—that poetry can embody loneliness and bring us into the human community in a fuller way. That loneliness, the feeling of solitude, can be thought through; it can be developed and delivered by a simple form that sacramentalizes a moment in time, a moment out of time—a little sound, a little song.

—*Edward Hirsch*
*New York City, 2006*

# DISCOVERING THE SONNET
## *Eavan Boland*

The sunny Italian court that created the sonnet also christened it: *Sonetto. A small song.* In the courtly world of Sicily, in the thirteenth century, it came into its own. Its features were set from the start: fourteen lines with a narrow turning space for wit and argument. From that moment, the sonnet would fulfill and defy the expectations of its origins in almost equal parts.

In other parts of this book, we chart both origin and expectation. The first location for any poetic form is in its own tradition and history. But every poetic form has a secondary and vital existence through the personal encounter—by poet and reader, both. This piece is about such an encounter. I found the sonnet for myself far from its home, in the gray and often sunless surroundings of the Dublin of my teenage years. No city, no country, and no young poet was a less likely candidate for that discovery.

At seventeen, I was a freckle-faced know-it-all, certain of my views on almost everything. I was newly returned from a childhood away from Ireland. I was trying to put together some foundation for my hope of being a poet. I wanted to belong to Irish poetry; I wanted Irish poetry to belong to me. The sonnet, I believed, could have no role in that. I had read it at school and resisted writing it. I was sure it was un-Irish, un-local, too courtly for a new republic, too finished to ever find a new beginning in the literature I was trying to understand.

In some ways, I was going on the evidence. From what I could see—which meant my scattershot reading—the nineteenth century in England had been rich in sonnets. This in itself was a black mark. I was sure the flourishing, musical industry of British sonnet-making—as I saw it, a factory of epigram, couplet, summary—must have been a sideshow of empire. I was equally sure it could never come to Ireland—to a new country, tense at the memory of its struggle with a larger one. Let alone to an untried and doubting Irish poet.

Dublin was a small city then. The streets near the center were filled with little bookshops, generous to browsers. Further up, beside the Liffey were long barrows laid out on sunny mornings, where readers gathered in an almost balletic movement: lifting, page-turning, setting down, lifting, page-turning. And there one day, without warning, I joined this jagged urban dance and stumbled on a poem that changed my mind. In order to describe that change, I will have go back, shift a scene or two, and describe how that poem came to be written.

The writer of the poem was Patrick Kavanagh, a poet from Monaghan. In a year or so, I would meet him, just at the edge of my twenties. I would sit opposite him in a small café on Grafton Street and watch a man in his sixties, plainly ill, speak through his rough breathing on a wintry day. For years afterward that meeting would be a fresh and unsettling memory. But at that moment, leaning over the book barrow, the Liffey glinting at my right shoulder, he was unknown to me.

"Shakespeare, I feel," said Robert Lowell, "wrote the couplets to his sonnets in a single reckless afternoon." The poem in front of me, by Patrick Kavanagh and titled "Epic," was carefully made. But the air of recklessness was there all the same—not exactly in a throwaway dazzle of craft, but in a boldness that was at once wrenching and touching.

This was not the poem of the frail man I met a year before his death. He had written it as a rangy, defiant young countryman. He had left his homelands in Monaghan in 1939, the year of the

Munich accords, and had come to an inhospitable Dublin. Shy, homesick, at odds with his surroundings, he had had to listen to metropolitan condescension and crisis politics all at once, and for the first time. As he did so, his own home must have seemed farther and farther away: the quarrels of his neighbors, the frost-blue potato pits.

Later, when I read and reread the poem, I would try to explain to myself why it so moved me. Yes, it had a defiant tone. Yes, it had reach and ambition. But it was more than that. It had to do with the event itself: the fact that when a marginal—in historical terms, at least—and powerless Irish poet looked for expression, what came to his aid was the swift-footed, fourteen-line strategy that had bent to empires and loitered in courts. It came to his assistance to remember and confirm a life far away from the form's own origins. It was this that made me realize that a great form can discover a poet just as much and as often as a poet discovers a form.

"Epic" opens in the townland Kavanagh came from—the borderlands of Inniskeen, with its potato pits and small farms. "No man," wrote Patrick Kavanagh of his townland, "ever loved that landscape and even some of the people more than I." And yet the first lines, with their shallow bragging and deep irony, put us right down in the marsh of reference and inference:

> I have lived in important places, times
> When great events were decided. . . .

Now here, we think for a moment—getting ourselves ready for it—is the start of a public sonnet. Here is a man living in the twentieth century, with Europe at the edge of war. But no. Not at all. If ever there was proof that the sonnet is a form that is nimble and always at the ready for quirks and surprises of tone, this is it. The important places and great events turn out to be something quite different.

The delight the reader might feel at that difference comes with the drop of the enjambed second line, which sends everything—sound, sense, the reader also—tumbling into a microworld, a landscape where all the signs point back the title of the poem, which of course is "Epic."

I have lived in important places, times
When great events were decided, who owned
That half a rood of rock, a no-man's land
Surrounded by our pitchfork-armed claims.

In an article he once wrote for a newspaper, Kavanagh made a distinction between provincialism and parochialism. Parochialism, he suggested, was a blind conviction that you were at the center of things: it could be the summer crossroads where he first made up ballads. It could be a place that talked about itself endlessly: Joyce's city, with draped curtains, a glittering coastline, and endless malice. Provincialism was different and lesser. It was the hankering for an elsewhere, an anxious measuring of the local against a distant standard. Parochialism was essential; provincialism was disabling.

Yet by this measure, Kavanagh should never have used the sonnet for "Epic." The sonnet, after all—certainly in my first prejudices this seemed so—is hardly a form of the parish. Its origins were at the centers of power and in the neighborhood of princes. "Epic" is about the neighborly and unrehearsed rituals of an Irish townland. It takes the center of the earth to be the fulcrum of the world. Above all, it is about the way poetry comes whispering and ready to the small situation as well as the splendid one.

I have lived in important places, times
When great events were decided, who owned
That half a rood of rock, a no-man's land
Surrounded by our pitchfork-armed claims.
I heard the Duffys shouting 'Damn your soul'
And old McCabe stripped to the waist, seen
Step the plot defying blue cast-steel—
'Here is the march along these iron stones'

The original form of the sonnet, the Petrarchan, made a shadow play of eight lines against six. Of all the form's claims, this may be the most ingenious. The octave sets out the problems, the perceptions, the wishes of the poet. The sestet does something different: It makes a swift, wonderfully compact turn on the hidden meanings of *but* and *yet* and *wait for a moment*. The sestet answers the octave, but neither politely nor smoothly. And this simple engine of proposition and rebuttal has allowed the sonnet over centuries, in the hands of vastly different poets, to replicate over and over again the magic of inner argument.

But there is something else about the sestet—some secret of propulsion, as if jet flight was discovered before its time. The octave gives it an undefined power. The sestet gathers a space, a territory for flight that could hardly be predicted or believed before the poem begins. Who would have thought that Kavanagh's eight lines, for all their deft irony, could introduce a poem that ends with a vast, wrenching claim? The shift between octave and sestet gives hardly any clue either. It is in the same almost deadpan tone:

> That was the year of the Munich bother; Which
> Was more important? . . .

This still has the plain-spoken insistence of the opening lines. Nothing here yet to make a sense of astonishment. But it's on its way.

> That was the year of the Munich bother; Which
> Was more important? I inclined
> To lose my faith in Ballyrush and Gortin
> Till Homer's ghost came whispering to my mind

Now for the first time, the ambition and reach of the poem are clear. Here, closed into a form that has helped to define the relation between power and poetry, is a radical suggestion about form itself. To the townlands, the quarreling voices, the theater of rural Ireland—all without power and far from definition—comes Homer with an exuberant claim about the art of origin and the origins of art.

> That was the year of the Munich bother; Which
> Was more important? I inclined
> To lose my faith in Ballyrush and Gortin

Till Homer's ghost came whispering to my mind
He said: I made the Iliad from such
A local row. Gods make their own importance.

I still remember the chill and reach of river light behind me, the noisy turning of buses at the corner of the quays, and my surprise at that closure: "Gods make their own importance." The idea that poetry would go anywhere to be renewed, that form would take up its habitation in the most unlikely place was—even at that age—thrilling and consoling. The poem was brave, serious, and devil-may-care. It was also, traditionally and scrupulously, a sonnet. The perfect exchange between the octave and sestet, the narrowing of the first and the sudden brilliant widening of the second showed the age-old resilience of the form.

It showed something else as well: It convinced me there and then that the sonnet is a form of true power—malleable, nomadic, humane. And that it can travel to any situation and to any uncertainty and offer its marvelous interior architecture to shelter the moment. This book is about those travels.

—*Eavan Boland*
*Stanford, Dublin,*
*2006*

# The Sonnet in Summary

- There are two main types of sonnet form in English. The first is the Italian or Petrarchan sonnet, so called because Petrarch was its greatest practitioner. The second is the English or Shakespearean sonnet, so called because Shakespeare was its greatest practitioner.

- The Petrarchan sonnet consists of an octave (eight lines rhyming *abbaabba*) and a sestet (six lines commonly rhyming *cdecde*).

- The Petrarchan sonnet probably developed out of the Sicilian *strambotto*, a popular song form consisting of two quatrains and two tercets.

- Italian readers coined the term *volta* (or "turn") to refer to the rhetorical division and shift between the opening eight lines and the concluding six.

- The Shakespearean sonnet consists of three quatrains and a couplet. The rhyme scheme is usually *abab, cdcd, efef, gg*. This sonnet characteristically closes with a summarizing couplet.

- The meter of the sonnet has tended to follow the prevalent meter of the language in which it is written. In English this is iambic pentameter.

# The Making of a Sonnet: A Formal Introduction

There is a sense of permanence and fragility, of spaciousness and constriction, about the sonnet form that has always had poets brooding about it, as in John Donne's lines from "The Canonization":

> We'll build in sonnets pretty rooms;
> As well a well-wrought urn becomes
> The greatest ashes, as half-acre tombs

The sonnet is a form with a past. It has seen all kinds of "pretty rooms"—many of them idealized, some of them less than ideal. It puts love on a pedestal (and takes it down again). It names names (Beatrice, Laura). The history of the sonnet is the history of its creations, its revisions and modifications, its distillations and expansions, its creative destructions.

The meter of the sonnet has tended to follow the prevalent meter of the language in which it is written. The bedrock meter in English has always been iambic pentameter, a five-stress, ten-syllable line. It is the traditional line closest to the form of our speech and thus has been especially favored for the sonnet—from Shakespeare and Milton to Wordsworth and Coleridge to Robinson and Millay. It has been estimated that three-fourths of all English language poetry from Chaucer to Frost has been written in rhymed or unrhymed iambic pentameter. So, too, the traditional French sonnet employs the alexandrine, a twelve-syllable line, often with a caesura—a hard cut—between the sixth and seventh syllables. The alexandrine reigned until the advent of vers libre (free verse) in the nineteenth century. Similarly, the classical Italian sonnet employs the hendecasyllable, an eleven-syllable line brilliantly exploited by both Dante and Petrarch. The alexandrine and the hendecasyllable have a striking role, and a formal structure, comparable to iambic pentameter in English.

There are two main types of sonnet form in English. The first is the Italian or Petrarchan sonnet (so called because Petrarch was its greatest practitioner), which consists of an octave (eight lines rhyming *abbaabba*) and a sestet (six lines commonly rhyming *cdecde*). Italian readers coined the term *volta* (or "turn") to refer to the rhetorical division and shift between the opening eight lines and the concluding six. The second type is the English or Shakespearean sonnet (so called because Shakespeare was its greatest practitioner), which consists of three quatrains and a couplet usually rhyming *abab, cdcd, efef, gg*. The couplet gives it a strong rhetorical close.

The Petrarchan sonnet probably developed out of the Sicilian *strambotto*, a popular song form consisting of two quatrains and two tercets. The sonnet was widely practiced throughout the later Middle Ages by all the Italian lyric poets, especially the *stilnovisti* —Guinizelli, Cavalcanti, and Dante, who used it to reinvent the love poem as a medium of quasi-religious devotion to a beloved lady, a *donna*. (Giosuè Carducci wrote that Dante gave the sonnet "the movement of cherubim, and surrounded it with gold and azure air.")

Petrarch's 317 sonnets to Laura are a kind of encyclopedia of passion. (Shelley called them "spells, which unseal the inmost enchanted fountains of the delight which is the grief of love.") The Petrarchan sonnet invites an asymmetrical two-part division of the argument. Its rhyming is impacted and it tends to build an obsessive feeling in the octave that is let loose in the sestet. "One of the emotional archetypes of the Petrarchan sonnet structure," as Paul Fussell puts it, "is the pattern of sexual pressure and release."

Sir Thomas Wyatt and Henry Howard, Earl of Surrey,

imported the Petrarchan form into England early in the sixteenth century. Surrey later established the rhyme scheme *abab, cdcd, efef, gg*. George Gascoigne described this new version of the sonnet in 1575:

> I . . . call those Sonnets which are of fourteen lines, every line containing ten syllables. The first twelve do rhyme in staves of four lines by cross meter, and the last two rhyming together do conclude the whole.

*SHAKE-SPEARE'S SONNETS. Neuer before Imprinted* appeared in 1609, and these 154 sonnets comprise one of the high-water marks of English poetry. The Shakespearean sonnet invites a more symmetrical division of thought into three equal quatrains and a summarizing couplet. It is well-balanced, well-suited to what Rosalie Colie calls Shakespeare's "particularly brainy, calculated incisiveness." The form enables a precision of utterance and freedom of forensic argument. It also offers more flexibility in rhyming, which is crucial since Italian is so much richer in rhyme than English. (Nonetheless, "Ryme is no impediment to his conceit," Samuel Daniel wrote in his 1603 *A Defence of Ryme*, "but rather gives him wings to mount and carries him, not out of his course, but as it were beyond his power to a farre happier flight.") The poet using this highly reasonable, toughly reasoning form can also create wild disturbances within the prescribed form. This seems to work especially well for closely reasoned and ultimately highly unreasonable and even obsessive subjects, like erotic love.

Over the centuries poets have proved ingenious at reinventing —reinscribing—the formal chamber of the sonnet. The Elizabethan poet Edmund Spenser developed an interlacing version of the sonnet called the *link* or Spenserian sonnet. It interlinks rhymes and concludes with a binding couplet (*abab, bcbc, cdcd, ee*). The Spenserian sonnet has a kind of deliberate and steady pace. "Sweet Spenser," Wordsworth wrote, "moving through his clouded heaven / With the moon's beauty and the moon's soft pace." Milton also put the sonnet to his own remarkable usages. He retained the octave rhyme scheme of the Petrarchan sonnet but didn't turn at the sestet and varied its rhyme scheme, thus opening up the form. He also firmly turned the sonnet away from love to occasional and political subjects.

Can the Petrarchan and Shakespearean sonnets be intermingled? The Russian poet Aleksandr Pushkin thought so. He invented a hybrid sonnet form that, most amazingly, can work either as an Italian or an English sonnet. His masterpiece, *Eugene Onegin* (1833), consists of 365 such sonnets with the rhyme scheme *ababccddeffegg*. Turn it one way and it looks Italian (*abab ccdd eff egg*). Turn it the other way and it looks English (*abab ccdd effe gg*). The form is a shape-shifter.

Sonnets reverberate with the memory of other sonnets. So, too, sonnet sequences reverberate with the memory of previous sequences. New sequences also revise—and rebel against—old ones. This is the history of the sonnet, then: a prescribed form with a long history, a closed form that somehow keeps changing and opening up.

# THE SONNET
# IN THE MIRROR

*These self-reflective sonnets about the sonnet, which are often witty
and light-hearted, are also a profound register of a truth about poetry.
They mark an engagement and chart a relationship. They show, above
all, that—for these poets as for so many others—this form was a pas-
sionate, deliberate choice and not an abstract exercise.*

# The Sonnet in the Mirror

*Look in my face . . .*

—DANTE GABRIEL ROSSETTI,
*The House of Life*, "A Superscription"

These self-reflective sonnets about the sonnet, which are often witty and light-hearted, register a profound truth about poetry. They illustrate that there are many ways of understanding a form. But one of the best may be the simplest: reflection. To see how it looks in the mirror of its time. To see how it appears at different moments, to different poets. To read how they described it through their own encounters with it.

Poets have written a number of stylish sonnets about the sonnet itself. The form becomes the muse of these poems. There are twenty-six poets in this section. All had strong opinions about the form. The sonnets here show them reflecting on it at the same time they are enacting it. This in itself suggests one of the charming and confirming properties of the sonnet: that—for all its history and tradition—each poet comes to it with a different and self-conscious sense of ownership. Each puts an individual stamp on the hard mathematics of the form. Each gives it a face.

The poets here come from different centuries and different continents. They are men and women, both. We include major and minor poets. Here are aristocrats and Scottish farmers, American sages, avant-garde Victorians, and jazz age icons. At first sight, it seems they have little in common. Take a closer look and they do; each wrote sonnets. Each of them wrote about the form they employed even as they employed it. A report from the frontier of a form, so to speak. Some of these sonnets-on-sonnets are humorous. Others are earnest. Some are aesthetic; many are political. But almost all, in one way or another, strike a note of wonder at how this small circumference, this bit of poetic real estate, could enclose such a large reach of feeling and expression. "I will put Chaos into fourteen lines," Edna St. Vincent Millay declared. She could be speaking for all of them.

The sonnet seems almost from the beginning to have engendered reflections about it. It is a self-conscious form. The major manuscripts of late thirteenth-century Italy, which preserve the very first sonnets, include layouts that graphically emphasize how the sonnet should "make its points." So, too, by the fourteenth century, the Italian poet Pieraccio Tedaldi was already amiably instructing novices in the art of sonnet writing. The continuance of the form has always been a matter of real enquiry for poets. It's to this mood of self-questioning and formal self-consciousness that we owe these poems.

These sonnets, then, mark an engagement and chart a relationship. They show, above all, that—for these poets as for so many others—this form was a passionate, deliberate choice and not an abstract exercise.

The sonnet has long been an irresistible subject for sonneteers. The form attracts unique feelings and strong reactions. What follows here can be read as a workbook of sorts. We begin with an emphasis on formal self-reflection because it marks a place where the sonnet strikes a pose and stakes a claim. These fourteen-line poems can be read as a rough, yet unique, journal kept through the ages, describing the reactions, the affections, the exasperations with this charged, complex, and provocative form.

We have taken the unusual step here of arranging the poems in nonchronological order. We invite the reader to view this chronicle out of time. These sonnets are in dialogue with each other across the ages. We believe there is something very real to be gained in reading them in this relationship to each other. Every sonnet has a kind of immediacy that places it in its time and also lifts it out of time. As Dante Gabriel Rossetti put it in the peerless prefatory sonnet in *The House of Life*:

> A Sonnet is a moment's monument,—
> Memorial from the Soul's eternity
> To one dead deathless hour. . . .

Every great sonnet is itself a moment's monument to the form itself. As Northrop Frye wrote about the Shakespearean sonnet, "The true father or shaping spirit of the poems is the form of the poem itself, and this form is a manifestation of the universal spirit of poetry."

EDNA ST. VINCENT MILLAY

## *"I will put Chaos into fourteen lines"*

I will put Chaos into fourteen lines
And keep him there; and let him thence escape
If he be lucky; let him twist, and ape
Flood, fire, and demon—his adroit designs
Will strain to nothing in the strict confines
Of this sweet Order, where, in pious rape,
I hold his essence and amorphous shape,
Till he with Order mingles and combines.
Past are the hours, the years, of our duress,
His arrogance, our awful servitude:
I have him. He is nothing more nor less
Than something simple not yet understood;
I shall not even force him to confess;
Or answer. I will only make him good.

ROBERT BURNS

## *A Sonnet upon Sonnets*

Fourteen, a sonneteer thy praises sings;
What magic myst'ries in that number lie!
Your hen hath fourteen eggs beneath her wings
That fourteen chickens to the roost may fly.
Fourteen full pounds the jockey's stone must be;
His age fourteen—a horse's prime is past.
Fourteen long hours too oft the Bard must fast;
Fourteen bright bumpers—bliss he ne'er must see!
Before fourteen, a dozen yields the strife;
Before fourteen—e'en thirteen's strength is vain.
Fourteen good years—a woman gives us life;
Fourteen good men—we lose that life again.
What lucubrations can be more upon it?
Fourteen good measur'd verses make a sonnet.

SIR PHILIP SIDNEY

## *"My Muse may well grudge at my heav'nly joy"*

My Muse may well grudge at my heav'nly joy,
If still I force her in sad rimes to creepe:
She oft hath drunke my teares, now hopes to enjoy
Nectar of Mirth, since I *Jove's* cup do keepe.
Sonnets be not bound prentise to annoy:
Trebles sing high, as well as bases deepe:
Griefe but *Love's* winter liverie is; the Boy
Hath cheeks to smile, as well as eyes to weepe.
  Come then my Muse, shew thou height of delight
In well raisde notes; my pen the best it may
Shall paint out joy, though but in blacke and white.
Cease, eager Muse; peace pen, for my sake stay;
    I give you here my hand for truth of this,
    Wise silence is best musicke unto blisse.

JOHN ADDINGTON SYMONDS

## *from* The Sonnet

**III**

The Sonnet is a world, where feelings caught
    In webs of phantasy, combine and fuse
    Their kindred elements 'neath mystic dews
    Shed from the ether round man's dwelling wrought;
Distilling heart's content, star-fragrance fraught
    With influences from the breathing fires
    Of heaven in everlasting endless gyres
    Enfolding and encircling orbs of thought.
Our Sonnet's world hath two fixed hemispheres:
    This, where the sun with fierce strength masculine
    Pours his keen rays and bids the noonday shine:
That, where the moon and stars, concordant powers,
    Shed milder rays, and daylight disappears
    In low melodious music of still hours.

WILLIAM WORDSWORTH

### "Scorn not the Sonnet; Critic, you have frowned"

Scorn not the Sonnet; Critic, you have frowned,
Mindless of its just honours; with this key
Shakespeare unlocked his heart; the melody
Of this small lute gave ease to Petrarch's wound;
A thousand times this pipe did Tasso sound;
With it Camöens soothed an exile's grief;
The Sonnet glittered a gay myrtle leaf
Amid the cypress with which Dante crowned
His visionary brow: a glow-worm lamp,
It cheered mild Spenser, called from Faeryland
To struggle through dark ways; and, when a damp
Fell round the path of Milton, in his hand
The Thing became a trumpet; whence he blew
Soul-animating strains—alas, too few!

WILLIAM WORDSWORTH

### "Nuns fret not at their convent's narrow room"

Nuns fret not at their convent's narrow room;
And hermits are contented with their cells;
And students with their pensive citadels;
Maids at the wheel, the weaver at his loom,
Sit blithe and happy; bees that soar for bloom,
High as the highest Peak of Furness-fells,
Will murmur by the hour in foxglove bells:
In truth the prison, into which we doom
Ourselves, no prison is: and hence for me,
In sundry moods, 'twas pastime to be bound
Within the Sonnet's scanty plot of ground;
Pleased if some Souls (for such there needs must be)
Who have felt the weight of too much liberty,
Should find brief solace there, as I have found.

JOHN KEATS

## *"If by dull rhymes our English must be chain'd"*

If by dull rhymes our English must be chain'd,
And, like Andromeda, the Sonnet sweet
Fetter'd, in spite of pained loveliness;
Let us find out, if we must be constrain'd,
Sandals more interwoven and complete
To fit the naked foot of Poesy:
Let us inspect the Lyre, and weigh the stress
Of every chord, and see what may be gain'd
By ear industrious, and attention meet;
Misers of sound and syllable, no less
Than Midas of his coinage, let us be
Jealous of dead leaves in the bay wreath crown;
So, if we may not let the Muse be free,
She will be bound with garlands of her own.

JOHN DOVASTON

## *from* Sonnets

### XXIX. Concluding Sonnet on the Sonnet

There are who say the sonnet's meted maze
    Is all too fettered for the poet's powers,
    Compelled to crowd his flush and airy flowers,
Like pots of tall imperials, ill at ease.
Or should some tiny thought his fancy seize,
    A violet on a vase's top it towers,
    And 'mid the mass of leaves he round it showers
Its little cap and tippet scarce can raise.
Others assert the sonnet's proper praise,
    Like petaled flowers, to each its due degree,
The king-cup five, the pilewort eight bright rays,
    The speedwell four, the green-tipped snowdrop
        three:
So 'mid the bard's all-petaled sorts is seen
The sonnet—simple flow'ret of fourteen.

DANTE GABRIEL ROSSETTI

## *from* The House of Life

A Sonnet is a moment's monument,—
   Memorial from the Soul's eternity
   To one dead deathless hour. Look that it be,
Whether for lustral rite or dire portent,
Of its own arduous fulness reverent:
   Carve it in ivory or in ebony,
   As Day or Night may rule; and let Time see
Its flowering crest impearled and orient.

A Sonnet is a coin: its face reveals
   The soul,—its converse, to what Power 'tis due:—
Whether for tribute to the august appeals
   Of Life, or dower in Love's high retinue,
It serve; or, 'mid the dark wharf's cavernous breath,
In Charon's palm it pay the toll to Death.

ANNA SEWARD

## *To Mr. Henry Cary, On the Publication of his Sonnets*

Praised be the poet, who the sonnet's claim,
   Severest of the orders that belong
   Distinct and separate to the Delphic Song,
   Shall venerate, nor its appropriate name
Lawless assume. Peculiar is its frame,
   From him derived, who shunned the city throng,
   And warbled sweet thy rocks and streams among,
   Lonely Valclusa!—and that heir of fame,
Our greater Milton, hath, by many a lay
   Formed on that arduous model, fully shown
   That English verse may happily display
Those strict energic measures, which alone
   Deserve the name of sonnet, and convey
   A grandeur, grace and spirit all their own.

EBENEZER ELLIOTT

## Powers of the Sonnet

Why should the tiny harp be chained to themes
In fourteen lines with pedant rigor bound?
The sonnet's might is mightier than it seems:
Witness the bard of Eden lost and found,
Who gave this lute a clarion's battle sound.
And, lo! another Milton calmly turns
His eyes within on light that ever burns,
Waiting till Wordsworth's second peer be found!
Meantime, Fitzadam's mournful music shows
That the scorned sonnet's charm may yet endear
Some long deep strain, or lay of well-told woes;
Such as, in Byron's couplet, brings a tear
To manly cheeks, or o'er his stanza throws
Rapture and grief, solemnity and fear.

CHRISTINA ROSSETTI

## "Sonnets are full of love, and this my tome"

Sonnets are full of love, and this my tome
    Has many sonnets: so here now shall be
  One sonnet more, a love sonnet, from me
To her whose heart is my heart's quiet home,
    To my first Love, my Mother, on whose knee
I learnt love-lore that is not troublesome;
    Whose service is my special dignity,
And she my loadstar while I go and come.
And so because you love me, and because
    I love you, Mother, I have woven a wreath
      Of rhymes wherewith to crown your honored
        name:
      In you not fourscore years can dim the flame
Of love, whose blessed glow transcends the laws
    Of time and change and mortal life and death.

FREDERICK WILLIAM FABER

## Sonnet-writing. To F. W. F.

Young men should not write sonnets, if they dream
Some day to reach the bright bare seats of fame:
To such, sweet thoughts and mighty feelings seem
As though, like foreign things, they rarely came.
Eager as men, when haply they have heard
Of some new songster, some gay-feathered bird,
That hath o'er blue seas strayed in hope to find
In our thin foliage here a summer home—
Fain would they catch the bright things in their mind,
And cage them into sonnets as they come.
No; they should serve their wants most sparingly,
Till the ripe time of song, when young thoughts fail,
Then their sad sonnets, like old bards, might be
Merry as youth, and yet gray-haired and hale.

THEODORE WATTS-DUNTON

## The Sonnet's Voice

Yon silvery billows breaking on the beach
Fall back in foam beneath the star-shine clear,
The while my rimes are murmuring in your ear
A restless lore like that the billows teach;
For on these sonnet waves my soul would reach
From its own depths, and rest within you, dear,
As through the billowy voices yearning here
Great nature strives to find a human speech.

A sonnet is a wave of melody;
From heaving waters of the impassioned soul
A billow of tidal music one and whole
Flows in the "octave"; then, returning free,
Its ebbing surges in the "sestet" roll
Back to the deeps of Life's tumultuous sea.

EUGENE LEE-HAMILTON

## What the Sonnet Is

Fourteen small broidered berries on the hem
   Of Circe's mantle, each of magic gold;
   Fourteen of lone Calypso's tears that rolled
Into the sea, for pearls to come of them;

Fourteen clear signs of omen in the gem
   With which Medea human fate foretold;
   Fourteen small drops, which Faustus, growing
     old,
Craved of the Fiend, to water Life's dry stem.

It is the pure white diamond Dante brought
   To Beatrice; the sapphire Laura wore
When Petrarch cut it sparkling out of thought;

The ruby Shakespeare hewed from his heart's core;
   The dark, deep emerald that Rossetti wrought
For his own soul, to wear for evermore.

EDGAR ALLAN POE

## An Enigma

"Seldom we find," says Solomon Don Dunce,
   "Half an idea in the profoundest sonnet.
Through all the flimsy things we see at once
   As easily as through a Naples bonnet—
   Trash of all trash!—how *can* a lady don it?
Yet heavier far than your Petrarchan stuff—
Owl-downy nonsense that the faintest puff
   Twirls into trunk-paper the while you con it."
And, veritably, Sol is right enough.
The general tuckermanities are arrant
Bubbles—ephemeral and *so* transparent—
   But *this* is, now,—you may depend upon it—
Stable, opaque, immortal—all by dint
Of the dear names that lie concealed within 't.

ELLA WHEELER WILCOX

## The Sonnet

Alone it stands in Poesy's fair land,
   A temple by the muses set apart;
   A perfect structure of consummate art,
By artists builded and by genius planned.
Beyond the reach of the apprentice hand,
   Beyond the ken of the untutored heart,
   Like a fine carving in a common mart,
Only the favored few will understand.
A *chef-d'œuvre* toiled over with great care,
   Yet which the unseeing careless crowd goes by,
A plainly set, but well-cut solitaire,
An ancient bit of pottery, too rare
   To please or hold aught save the special eye,
These only with the sonnet can compare.

EDWIN ARLINGTON ROBINSON

## Sonnet

The master and the slave go hand in hand,
Though touch be lost. The poet is a slave,
And there be kings do sorrowfully crave
The joyance that a scullion may command.
But, ah, the sonnet-slave must understand
The mission of his bondage, or the grave
May clasp his bones, or ever he shall save
The perfect word that is the poet's wand.

The sonnet is a crown, whereof the rhymes
Are for Thought's purest gold the jewel-stones;
But shapes and echoes that are never done
Will haunt the workshop, as regret sometimes
Will bring with human yearning to sad thrones
The crash of battles that are never won.

LORD ALFRED DOUGLAS

## *Sonnet on the Sonnet*

To see the moment holds a madrigal,
To find some cloistered place, some hermitage
For free devices, some deliberate cage
Wherein to keep wild thoughts like birds in thrall;
To eat sweet honey and to taste black gall,
To fight with form, to wrestle and to rage,
Till at the last upon the conquered page
The shadows of created Beauty fall.

This is the sonnet, this is all delight
Of every flower that blows in every Spring,
And all desire of every desert place;
This is the joy that fills a cloudy night
When, bursting from her misty following,
A perfect moon wins to an empty space.

SYLVIA TOWNSEND WARNER

## *"Farewell, I thought. How many sonnets have"*

Farewell, I thought. How many sonnets have
Begun or ended on these syllables.
Sooner or later chimes that seventh wave
Like a ground bell among a chime of bells.
Above that steadfast note the changes veer,
And through them their begetting ending clangs:
*Some time,* but never, *never. Next year. This year.*
Then on the air the rigid echo hangs;
And through it one looks round and sees the sky,
The trees, the houses where men live, the small
Mounds of the dead, and live men going by,
And everything is there, and that is all.
Only the echo cries the music's over.
So it is to have loved and lost the lover.

MERRILL MOORE

## *In Magic Words*

Wordsworth to the contrary notwithstanding,
Milton's and Shakespeare's statements also doubted:
A sonnet's force is not so easily routed
That flying one should not seek the safest landing.

As much as anything, a magic word
Is what a sonnet is, that quickly falls
If touched indelicately or shaken hard,
Or if it be reared too heavy or too tall.

Sonnets possess impertinence; they have bliss,
They require excitement in at least one line,
They need specific gravity and this
Especially is important—to be in focus;

Rarely a sonnet deserves to be exhibited;
Most of them should be (and they are) inhibited.

PETER DICKINSON

## *"Scorn not the sonnet" (Wordsworth)*

Scorn not the sonnet on the sonnet, critic;
   It is a bank where poets love to lie
   And praise each other's ingenuity
In finding such a form. The analytic
Reader may stigmatise as parasitic
   The mirror-image of a mystery,
   This echo of lost voices, find it dry,
And intellectually paralytic.
   Yet 'tis a child of Fancy, light and live,
A fragile veil of Nature, scarcely worn
    (Of Wordsworth's two, of Shakespeare's none,
      survive):
Empty not then the vials of scorn upon it.
   Nor, since we're on the subject, should you scorn
The sonnet on the sonnet on the sonnet.

GEOFF PAGE

## The Recipe

"A sonnet tells me nothing but itself,"
as William Carlos Williams liked to say—
somewhat perversely lifting from the shelf
a pattern even free verse must obey.
Your sonnet's eight and six are sacrosanct;
the greatest chef would hardly dare to alter
the ancient taste for eight lines neatly ranked
then six from what Italians call the *volta*.
A rhyme scheme down the side is *de rigeur*.
Elizabethan maybe—or Petrarchan.
And cooks from Spenser on will all concur
the sonnet is the dish to make your mark in.
By God, we're there and, yes, you're doing fine.
And now, like pepper, add the fourteenth line.


LOUISE BOGAN

## Single Sonnet

Now, you great stanza, you heroic mould,
Bend to my will, for I must give you love:
The weight in the heart that breathes, but cannot
    move,
Which to endure flesh only makes so bold.

Take up, take up, as it were lead or gold
The burden; test the dreadful mass thereof.
No stone, slate, metal under or above
Earth, is so ponderous, so dull, so cold.

Too long as ocean bed bears up the ocean,
As earth's core bears the earth, have I borne this;
Too long have lovers, bending for their kiss,
Felt bitter force cohering without motion.

Staunch meter, great song, it is yours, at length,
To prove how stronger you are than my strength.

GEORGE STARBUCK

## Sonnet with a Different Letter at the End of Every Line

*for Helen Vendler*

O for a muse of fire, a sack of dough,
Or both! O promissory notes of woe!
One time in Santa Fe N.M.
Ol' Winfield Townley Scott and I . . . But whoa.

One can exert oneself, *ff,*
Or architect a heaven like Rimbaud,
Or if that seems, how shall I say, *de trop,*
One can at least write sonnets, a propos
Of nothing save the do-re-mi-fa-sol
Of poetry itself. Is not the row
Of perfect rhymes, the terminal bon mot,
Obeisance enough to the Great O?

"Observe," said Chairman Mao to Premier
    Chou,
"On voyage à Parnasse pour prendre les eaux.
On voyage comme poisson, incog."

HAYDEN CARRUTH

## Late Sonnet

For that the sonnet no doubt was my own true
singing and suchlike other song, for that
I gave it up half-coldheartedly to set
my lines in a fashion that proclaimed its virtue
original in young arrogant artificers who
had not my geniality nor voice, and yet
their fashionableness was persuasive to me,—what
shame and sorrow I pay!
                            And that I knew
that beautiful hot old man Sidney Bechet
and heard his music often but not what he
was saying, that tone, phrasing, and free play
of feeling mean more than originality,
these being the actual qualities of song.
Nor is it essential to be young.

BILLY COLLINS

## Sonnet

All we need is fourteen lines, well, thirteen now,
and after this next one just a dozen
to launch a little ship on love's storm-tossed seas,
then only ten more left like rows of beans.
How easily it goes unless you get Elizabethan
and insist the iambic bongos must be played
and rhymes positioned at the ends of lines,
one for every station of the cross.
But hang on here while we make the turn
into the final six where all will be resolved,
where longing and heartache will find an end,
where Laura will tell Petrarch to put down his pen,
take off those crazy medieval tights,
blow out the lights, and come at last to bed.

# THE SIXTEENTH CENTURY

In a century in which poets were executed, suffered disgrace, and saw vast change, the sonnet changed as well. A form that had begun in Europe, chastened by ornament and the heraldry of romance, became a text of depth, power, and darkness. By the end of the sixteenth century the sonnet was established as a preeminent poetic form in the English language.

# The Sonnet in Its Century: The Sixteenth

*Then have you Sonnets...*

—GEORGE GASCOIGNE,

*"Certain Notes of Instruction...."* (1575)

The sonnet began in the English language in the sixteenth century. It migrated from the Mediterranean with an air of rush and drama, attaching itself to some of the most colorful and accomplished poets of the time.

Sir Thomas Wyatt wrote the first sonnets in English. Born in 1503, by the time he was thirty he had been Anne Boleyn's lover, had traveled widely, and had barely evaded execution for treason. His diplomatic missions to Spain and Italy exposed him to new poetic models, one of them the sonnet. He brought the *sonetto* back to the Tudor Court of England.

Wyatt's younger contemporary Henry Howard, Earl of Surrey, was a more gifted stylist but a lesser poet. Like Wyatt, he wrote in the shadow of the gallows. He was a soldier as well as a poet, but at the end of his twenties fell foul of the glittering menace of court politics. In 1547, at the age of thirty, he was executed for treason.

The sonnet in the English language begins with these two men. Both were innovators, but in different ways. Wyatt's metrics were awkward, distinctive. He borrowed Petrarch's octave and was reverent with its music—eight controlled and proposing lines. But he broke the sestet, revising the Italian form. Instead of the usual answering six lines, he chose to work with four lines and a couplet.

For the future of the sonnet in English, it was a momentous revision. That last couplet became an anvil: a place for the epigram to ring out its summary. It would become a signature of the English method. Surrey added another change, dismantling the octave as well as the sestet. He changed the eight lines into separate quatrains.

Now the English sonnet had a native model. And so began the rich, tense dialogue between foreign influence and native speech. This tension, as much as anything, was responsible for the energy and power of the Elizabethan sonnet. Undoubtedly, Petrarch was the presiding spirit—the exemplary presence. He imported well. Taking a different formal strategy, Edmund Spenser, influenced by French models, was also one of the key founders of the English sonnet. He created a sonnet drama, *Amoretti* (1595), that is one of the most sustained lyric performances of sixteenth-century poetry.

Only in the last decade of the sixteenth century did the sonnet become, at last, a dialect of the English poetic tradition. Then, suddenly, every major Elizabethan poet—Sidney, Spenser, Drayton, Shakespeare—tried his hand. A foreign model had become an English fashion. "The sonnet was the bow of Ulysses," as one scholar puts it, "which every established or would-be poet, every young man of the Inns of Court with a literary taste, felt it his duty to bend." Thus a rigid pattern loosened and became a fever chart of the age. Between them Wyatt and Surrey had opened the floodgates. By the time of Shakespeare the form had come into its own, a cornerstone of English poetry.

In a century in which poets were executed, suffered disgrace, and saw vast change, the sonnet changed as well. A form that had begun in Europe, chastened by ornament and the heraldry of romance, became a text of depth, power, and darkness. By the end of the sixteenth century the sonnet was established as a preeminent poetic form in the English language.

SIR THOMAS WYATT

## "The long love that in my thought doth harbor"

The long love that in my thought doth harbor,
And in mine heart doth keep his residence,
Into my face presseth with bold pretense
And therein campeth, spreading his banner.
She that me learneth to love and suffer
And will that my trust and lust's negligence
Be reined by reason, shame, and reverence,
With his hardiness taketh displeasure.
Wherewithal unto the heart's forest he fleeth,
Leaving his enterprise with pain and cry,
And there him hideth, and not appeareth.
What may I do, when my master feareth,
But in the field with him to live and die?
For good is the life ending faithfully.

SIR THOMAS WYATT

## "Whoso list to hunt, I know where is an hind"

Whoso list to hunt, I know where is an hind,
But as for me, alas, I may no more.
The vain travail hath wearied me so sore,
I am of them that farthest cometh behind.
Yet may I, by no means, my wearied mind
Draw from the deer, but as she fleeth afore,
Fainting I follow. I leave off, therefore,
Since in a net I seek to hold the wind.
Who list her hunt, I put him out of doubt,
As well as I, may spend his time in vain.
And graven with diamonds in letters plain
There is written, her fair neck round about,
"*Noli me tangere*, for Caesar's I am,
And wild for to hold, though I seem tame."

SIR THOMAS WYATT

### "My galley charged with forgetfulness"

My galley charged with forgetfulness
   Thorough sharp seas in winter nights doth pass
   'Tween rock and rock; and eke mine enemy, alas,
   That is my lord, steereth with cruelness;
And every oar a thought in readiness,
   As though that death were light in such a case.
   An endless wind doth tear the sail apace
   Of forced sighs and trusty fearfulness.
A rain of tears, a cloud of dark disdain,
   Hath done the wearied cords great hinderance;
   Wreathed with error and eke with ignorance.
The stars be hid that led me to this pain;
   Drowned is reason that should me consort,
   And I remain despairing of the port.

HENRY HOWARD, EARL OF SURREY

### "Love, that doth reign and live within my thought"

Love, that doth reign and live within my thought,
And built his seat within my captive breast,
Clad in the arms wherein with me he fought,
Oft in my face he doth his banner rest.
But she that taught me love and suffer pain,
My doubtful hope and eke my hot desire
With shamefast look to shadow and refrain,
Her smiling grace converteth straight to ire.
And coward Love then to the heart apace
Taketh his flight, where he doth lurk and plain,
His purpose lost, and dare not show his face.
For my lord's guilt thus faultless bide I pain,
Yet from my lord shall not my foot remove:
Sweet is the death that taketh end by love.

HENRY HOWARD, EARL OF SURREY

## "Norfolk sprang thee, Lambeth holds thee dead"

Norfolk sprang thee, Lambeth holds thee dead,
Clere, of the County of Cleremont, though hight.
Within the womb of Ormond's race thou bred,
And sawest thy cousin crownèd in thy sight.
Shelton for love, Surrey for Lord, thou chase;—
Ay me! while life did last that league was tender,
Tracing whose steps thou sawest Kelsall blaze,
Laundersey burnt, and battered Bullen render.
At Muttrel gates, hopeless of all recure,
Thine Earl, half dead, gave in thy hand his will,
Which cause did thee this pining death procure,
Ere summers four times seven thou could'st fulfil.
  Ah, Clere! if love had booted, care, or cost,
  Heaven had not won, nor earth so timely lost.

ANNE LOCKE

## *from* A Meditation of a Penitent Sinner, upon the 51. Psalme.

**Have mercie upon me (o God) after thy great merci**

Have mercy, God, for thy great mercies sake.
O God: my God, unto my shame I say,
Beynge fled from thee, so as I dred to take
Thy name in wretched mouth, and feare to pray
Or aske the mercy that I have abusde.
But, God of mercy, let me come to thee:
Not for justice, that justly am accusde:
Which selfe word Justice so amaseth me,
That scarce I dare thy mercy sound againe.
But mercie, Lord, yet suffer me to crave.
Mercie is thine: Let me not crye in vaine,
Thy great mercie for my great fault to have.
Have mercie, God, pitie my penitence
With greater mercie than my great offence.

GEORGE GASCOIGNE

### *"That self-same tongue which first did thee entreat"*

That self-same tongue which first did thee entreat
To link thy liking with my lucky love,
That trusty tongue must now these words repeat,
*I love thee still,* my fancy cannot move.
That dreadless heart which durst attempt the thought
To win thy will with mine for to consent,
Maintains that vow which love in me first wrought,
*I love thee still,* and never shall repent.
That happy hand which hardly did touch
Thy tender body to my deep delight,
Shall serve with sword to prove my passion such
*As loves thee still,* much more than it can write.
   Thus love I still with tongue, hand, heart and all,
   And when I change, let vengeance on me fall.

GILES FLETCHER, THE ELDER

### *from* Licia

**Sonnet XXVIII**

In time the strong and stately turrets fall.
In time the rose, and silver lilies die.
In time the monarchs captive are and thrall.
In time the sea and rivers are made dry.
   The hardest flint in time doth melt asunder.
Still living fame, in time doth fade away.
The mountains proud, we see in time come under:
And earth, for aye, we see in time decay.
   The sun in time forgets for to retire
From out the East, where he was wont to rise.
The basest thoughts, we see in time aspire.
And greedy minds, in time do wealth despise.
   Thus all, sweet Fair, in time must have an end:
   Except thy beauty, virtues, and thy friend.

EDMUND SPENSER

## *from* Amoretti

### Sonnet 1

Happy ye leaves when as those lilly hands,
Which hold my life in their dead doing might,
Shall handle you and hold in loves soft bands,
Lyke captives trembling at the victors sight.
And happy lines, on which with starry light,
Those lamping eyes will deigne sometimes to look
And reade the sorrowes of my dying spright,
Written with teares in harts close bleeding book.
And happy rymes bathed in the sacred brooke
Of Helicon whence she derivéd is,
When ye behold that Angels blesséd looke,
My soules long lackéd foode, my heavens blis.
Leaves, lines, and rymes, seeke her to please alone,
Whom if ye please, I care for other none.

EDMUND SPENSER

## *from* Amoretti

### Sonnet 8

More then most faire, full of the living fire
Kindled above unto the maker neere:
No eies but joyes, in which al powers conspire
That to the world naught else be counted deare.
Thrugh your bright beams doth not the blinded
    guest
Shoot out his darts to base affections wound?
But Angels come to lead fraile mindes to rest
In chast desires on heavenly beauty bound.
You frame my thoughts and fashion me within,
You stop my toung, and teach my hart to speake,
You calme the storme that passion did begin,
Strong thrugh your cause, but by your vertue weak.
Dark is the world where your light shinéd never;
Well is he borne that may behold you ever.

EDMUND SPENSER

## *from* Amoretti

Sonnet 30

My love is lyke to yse, and I to fyre;
How comes it then that this her cold so great
Is not dissolved through my so hot desyre,
But harder growes the more I her intreat?
Or how comes it that my exceeding heat
Is not delayd by her hart frosen cold:
But that I burne much more in boyling sweat,
And feele my flames augmented manifold?
What more miraculous thing may be told,
That fire which all thing melts, should harden yse:
And yse which is congeald with sencelesse cold,
Should kindle fyre by wonderfull devyse?
Such is the powre of love in gentle mind,
That it can alter all the course of kynd.

EDMUND SPENSER

## *from* Amoretti

Sonnet 75

One day I wrote her name upon the strand,
But came the waves and washéd it away:
Agayne I wrote it with a second hand,
But came the tyde, and made my paynes his pray.
"Vayne man," sayd she, "that doest in vaine assay
A mortall thing so to immortalize,
For I my selve shall lyke to this decay,
And eek my name bee wypéd out lykewize."
"Not so," quod I, "let baser things devize
To dy in dust, but you shall live by fame:
My verse your vertues rare shall eternize,
And in the hevens wryte your glorious name.
Where whenas death shall all the world subdew,
Our love shall live, and later life renew."

EDMUND SPENSER

## *from* Amoretti

**Sonnet 77**

Was it a dreame, or did I see it playne,
A goodly table of pure yvory:
All spred with juncats, fit to entertayne
The greatest Prince with pompous roialty?
Mongst which there in a silver dish did ly
Two golden apples of unvalewd price:
Far passing those which Hercules came by,
Or those which Atalanta did entice.
Exceeding sweet, yet voyd of sinfull vice,
That many sought yet none could ever taste,
Sweet fruit of pleasure brought from paradice
By Love himselfe and in his garden plaste.
Her brest that table was so richly spredd,
My thoughts the guests, which would thereon have
    fedd.


FULKE GREVILLE, LORD BROOKE

## *from* Cælica

**Sonnet LXXXVI**

The earth with thunder torn, with fire blasted,
With waters drowned, with windy palsy shaken,
Cannot for this with heaven be distasted,
Since thunder, rain and winds from earth are taken.
Man torn with love, with inward furies blasted,
Drown'd with despair, with fleshly lustings shaken,
Cannot for this with heaven be distasted;
Love, fury, lustings out of man are taken.
Then Man, endure thy self, those clouds will vanish;
Life is a top which whipping sorrow driveth;
Wisdom must bear what our flesh cannot banish;
The humble lead, the stubborn bootless striveth:
    Or Man, forsake thy self, to heaven turn thee;
    Her flames enlighten nature, never burn thee.

SIR WALTER RALEGH

## Sir Walter Ralegh to His Son

Three things there be that prosper up apace
And flourish, whilst they grow asunder far,
But on a day, they meet all in one place,
And when they meet, they one another mar;
And they be these: the wood, the weed, the wag.
The wood is that which makes the gallow tree;
The weed is that which strings the hangman's bag;
The wag, my pretty knave, betokeneth thee.
Mark well, dear boy, whilst these assemble not,
Green springs the tree, hemp grows, the wag is wild,
But when they meet, it makes the timber rot,
It frets the halter, and it chokes the child.
    Then bless thee, and beware, and let us pray
    We part not with thee at this meeting day.

SIR PHILIP SIDNEY

## *from* Astrophil and Stella

1

Loving in truth, and fain in verse my love to show,
That the dear She might take some pleasure of my
    pain,
Pleasure might cause her read, reading might make
    her know,
Knowledge might pity win, and pity grace obtain,
    I sought fit words to paint the blackest face of woe,
Studying inventions fine, her wits to entertain,
Oft turning others' leaves, to see if thence would flow
Some fresh and fruitful showers upon my sunburned
    brain.
    But words came halting forth, wanting Invention's
        stay;
Invention, Nature's child, fled step-dame Study's
    blows,
And others' feet still seemed but strangers in my way.

Thus great with child to speak, and helpless in my
 throes,
 Biting my trewand pen, beating myself for spite,
 "Fool," said my Muse to me, "look in thy heart and
 write."

SIR PHILIP SIDNEY

## *from* Astrophil and Stella

### 31

With how sad steps, O Moon, thou climb'st the skies,
 How silently, and with how wan a face!
 What, may it be that even in heavenly place
That busy archer his sharp arrows tries?
Sure, if that long-with-love-acquainted eyes
 Can judge of love, thou feel'st a lover's case;
 I read it in thy looks: thy languished grace,
To me that feel the like, thy state descries.
 Then even of fellowship, O Moon, tell me,
Is constant love deemed there but want of wit?
Are beauties there as proud as here they be?
Do they above love to be loved, and yet
 Those lovers scorn whom that love doth possess?
 Do they call virtue there ungratefulness?

SIR PHILIP SIDNEY

## *from* Astrophil and Stella

### 39

Come sleep! O sleep the certain knot of peace,
The baiting place of wit, the balm of woe,
The poor man's wealth, the prisoner's release,
Th' indifferent judge between the high and low;
 With shield of proof shield me from out the prease
Of those fierce darts Despair at me doth throw:
O make in me those civil wars to cease;
I will good tribute pay if thou do so.
 Take thou of me smooth pillows, sweetest bed,

A chamber deaf to noise and blind to light,
A rosy garland, and a weary head:
And if these things, as being thine by right,
    Move not thy heavy grace, thou shalt in me
    Livelier than elsewhere Stella's image see.

SIR PHILIP SIDNEY
### *from* Astrophil and Stella

**54**

Because I breathe not love to everyone,
    Nor do not use set colors for to wear,
    Nor nourish special locks of vowèd hair,
Nor give each speech a full point of a groan,
The courtly nymphs, acquainted with the moan
    Of them who in their lips Love's standard bear,
    "What, he?" say they of me, "now I dare swear
He cannot love; no, no, let him alone!"
    And think so still, so Stella know my mind.
Profess indeed I do not Cupid's art;
But you, fair maids, at length this true shall find,
That his right badge is but worn in the heart:
    Dumb swans, not chatt'ring pies, do lovers prove;
    They love indeed, who quake to say they love.

SIR PHILIP SIDNEY
### *from* Astrophil and Stella

**71**

Who will in fairest book of Nature know
    How Virtue may best lodged in beauty be,
    Let him but learn of Love to read in thee,
Stella, those fair lines, which true goodness show.
There shall he find all vices' overthrow,
    Not by rude force, but sweetest sovereignty
    Of reason, from whose light those night-birds fly;
That inward sun in thine eyes shineth so.
    And not content to be Perfection's heir

Thyself, dost strive all minds that way to move,
Who mark in thee what is in thee most fair.
So while thy beauty draws the heart to love,
   As fast thy Virtue bends that love to good;
   "But, ah," Desire still cries, "give me some food."

THOMAS LODGE
## *from* Phillis

**Sonnet XL**

Reſembling none, and none ſo poore as I,
Poore to the world, and poore in each eſteeme,
Whoſe firſt borne loues, at firſt obſcurd did die,
And bred no fame but flame of bace miſdeeme.
   Vnder the Enſigne of vvhoſe tyred pen,
Loues legions forth haue maskt, by others masked:
Thinke hovv I have lyue wronged by ill tonged men,
Not Maiſter of my ſelfe, to all wrongs tasked.
   Oh thou that canſt, and ſhe that may doe all things,
Support theſe languiſhing conceits that perriſh,
Looke on theyr growth: perhaps theſe ſillie ſmall things
May winne this worldly palme, ſo you doe cherriſh.
   *Homer* hath vowd, and I with him doe vowe thys,
   He vvill and ſhall reuiue, if you alowe thys.

GEORGE CHAPMAN
## *A Coronet for his Mistress Philosophy*

**1**

Muses that sing love's sensual empery,
   And lovers kindling your enragèd fires
   At Cupid's bonfires burning in the eye,
   Blown with the empty breath of vain desires,
You that prefer the painted cabinet
   Before the wealthy jewels it doth store ye,
   That all your joys in dying figures set,
   And stain the living substance of your glory,
Abjure those joys, abhor their memory,

And let my love the honoured subject be
Of love, and honour's complete history.
Your eyes were never yet let in to see
The majesty and riches of the mind,
But dwell in darkness, for your god is blind.


SAMUEL DANIEL

## *from* Delia

**49**

Care-charmer Sleep, son of the sable Night,
Brother to Death, in silent darkness born.
Relieve my languish and restore the light;
With dark forgetting of my cares, return.
And let the day be time enough to mourn
The shipwreck of my ill-adventured youth;
Let waking eyes suffice to wail their scorn
Without the torment of the night's untruth.
Cease, dreams, th' imagery of our day desires,
To model forth the passions of the morrow;
Never let rising sun approve you liars,
To add more grief to aggravate my sorrow.
Still let me sleep, embracing clouds in vain,
And never wake to feel the day's disdain.


MICHAEL DRAYTON

## *from* Idea

**61**

Since there's no help, come let us kiss and part;
Nay, I have done, you get no more of me,
And I am glad, yea glad with all my heart
That thus so cleanly I myself can free;
Shake hands forever, cancel all our vows,
And when we meet at any time again,
Be it not seen in either of our brows
That we one jot of former love retain.
Now at the last gasp of love's latest breath,
When, his pulse failing, Passion speechless lies,

When Faith is kneeling by his bed of death,
And Innocence is closing up his eyes,
    Now if thou wouldst, when all have given him over,
    From death to life thou mightst him yet recover.

HUGH HOLLAND

### Upon the Lines, and Life, of the famous Scenic Poet, Master William Shakespeare

Those hands which you so clapp'd, go now and
    wring,
You Britons brave; for done are Shakespeare's days:
His days are done that made the dainty plays,
    Which made the Globe of heaven and earth to ring.
    Dried is that vein, dried is the Thespian spring,
Turn'd all to tears, and Phœbus clouds his rays;
That corpse, that coffin, now bestick those bays,
    Which crown'd him poet first, then poet's king.
If tragedies might any prologue have,
    All those he made would scarce make one to this;
Where fame, now that he gone is to the grave,
    (Death's public tiring-house) the Nuntius is:
For, though his line of life went soon about,
The life yet of his lines shall never out.

MARK ALEXANDER BOYD

### Sonet

Fra banc to banc, fra wod to wod, I rin
    Owrhailit with my feble fantasie,
    Lyc til a leif that fallis from a trie
    Or til a reid owrblawin with the win'.
Twa gods gyds me: the ane of tham is blin',
    Ye, and a bairn brocht up in vanitie;
    The nixt a wyf ingenrit of the se,
    And lichter nor a dauphin with hir fin.
Unhappie is the man for evirmaire
    That teils the sand and sawis in the aire,
    Bot twyse unhappier is he, I lairn,

That feidis in his hairt a mad desyre,
    And follows on a woman throu the fyre,
    Led be a blind and teichit be a bairn.


WILLIAM SHAKESPEARE

### *from* Love's Labour's Lost *(act 4, scene 3)*

Did not the heavenly rhetoric of thine eye,
    'Gainst whom the world cannot hold argument,
Persuade my heart to this false perjury?
    Vows for thee broke deserve not punishment.
A woman I forswore, but I will prove,
    Thou being a goddess, I forswore not thee.
My vow was earthly, thou a heavenly love.
    Thy grace being gained cures all disgrace in me.
Vows are but breath, and breath a vapour is.
    Then thou, fair sun, which on my earth dost shine,
Exhal'st this vapour-vow; in thee it is.
    If broken then, it is no fault of mine.
If by me broke, what fool is not so wise
To lose an oath to win a paradise?


WILLIAM SHAKESPEARE

### *from* Romeo and Juliet *(act 1, scene 5)*

ROMEO  If I profane with my unworthiest hand
    This holy shrine, the gentler sin is this:
My lips, two blushing pilgrims, ready stand
    To smooth that rough touch with a tender kiss.
JULIET  Good pilgrim, you do wrong your hand too
        much,
    Which mannerly devotion shows in this.
For saints have hands that pilgrims' hands do touch,
    And palm to palm is holy palmers' kiss.
ROMEO  Have not saints lips, and holy palmers, too?
JULIET  Ay, pilgrim, lips that they must use in prayer.
ROMEO  O then, dear saint, let lips do what hands do:
    They pray; grant thou, lest faith turn to despair.

JULIET  Saints do not move, though grant for
    prayers' sake.
ROMEO  Then move not while my prayer's effect I
    take.

WILLIAM SHAKESPEARE

## Sonnet 18

Shall I compare thee to a summer's day?
Thou art more lovely and more temperate:
Rough winds do shake the darling buds of May,
And summer's lease hath all too short a date;
Sometime too hot the eye of heaven shines,
And often is his gold complexion dimmed;
And every fair from fair sometime declines,
By chance or nature's changing course untrimmed.
But thy eternal summer shall not fade,
Nor lose possession of that fair thou ow'st;
Nor shall death brag thou wander'st in his shade,
When in eternal lines to time thou grow'st:
    So long as men can breathe or eyes can see,
    So long lives this, and this gives life to thee.

WILLIAM SHAKESPEARE

## Sonnet 29

When, in disgrace with Fortune and men's eyes,
I all alone beweep my outcast state,
And trouble deaf heaven with my bootless cries,
And look upon myself and curse my fate,
Wishing me like to one more rich in hope,
Featured like him, like him with friends possessed,
Desiring this man's art and that man's scope,
With what I most enjoy contented least;
Yet in these thoughts myself almost despising,
Haply I think on thee, and then my state
(Like to the lark at break of day arising

From sullen earth) sings hymns at heaven's gate;
   For thy sweet love remembered such wealth brings
   That then I scorn to change my state with kings.


WILLIAM SHAKESPEARE
### Sonnet 94

They that have power to hurt and will do none,
That do not do the thing they most do show,
Who, moving others, are themselves as stone,
Unmovèd, cold, and to temptation slow;
They rightly do inherit heaven's graces
And husband nature's riches from expense;
They are the lords and owners of their faces,
Others but stewards of their excellence.
The summer's flower is to the summer sweet,
Though to itself it only live and die,
But if that flower with base infection meet,
The basest weed outbraves his dignity:
   For sweetest things turn sourest by their deeds;
   Lilies that fester smell far worse than weeds.


WILLIAM SHAKESPEARE
### Sonnet 116

Let me not to the marriage of true minds
Admit impediments; love is not love
Which alters when it alteration finds,
Or bends with the remover to remove:
O, no, it is an ever-fixèd mark,
That looks on tempests and is never shaken;
It is the star to every wand'ring bark,
Whose worth's unknown, although his highth be
   taken.
Love's not Time's fool, though rosy lips and cheeks
Within his bending sickle's compass come;
Love alters not with his brief hours and weeks,
But bears it out even to the edge of doom.

If this be error and upon me proved,
I never writ, nor no man ever loved.


WILLIAM SHAKESPEARE
### Sonnet 129

Th' expense of spirit in a waste of shame
Is lust in action; and till action, lust
Is perjured, murd'rous, bloody, full of blame,
Savage, extreme, rude, cruel, not to trust;
Enjoyed no sooner but despisèd straight:
Past reason hunted; and no sooner had,
Past reason hated, as a swallowed bait,
On purpose laid to make the taker mad:
Mad in pursuit, and in possession so;
Had, having, and in quest to have, extreme;
A bliss in proof and proved, a very woe;
Before, a joy proposed; behind, a dream.
   All this the world well knows; yet none knows well
   To shun the heaven that leads men to this hell.


WILLIAM SHAKESPEARE
### Sonnet 130

My mistress' eyes are nothing like the sun;
Coral is far more red than her lips' red;
If snow be white, why then her breasts are dun;
If hairs be wires, black wires grow on her head.
I have seen roses damasked, red and white,
But no such roses see I in her cheeks;
And in some perfumes is there more delight
Than in the breath that from my mistress reeks.
I love to hear her speak, yet well I know
That music hath a far more pleasing sound;
I grant I never saw a goddess go;
My mistress, when she walks, treads on the ground.
   And yet, by heaven, I think my love as rare
   As any she belied with false compare.

WILLIAM SHAKESPEARE
## Sonnet 138

When my love swears that she is made of truth,
I do believe her, though I know she lies,
That she might think me some untutored youth,
Unlearnèd in the world's false subtleties.
Thus vainly thinking that she thinks me young,
Although she knows my days are past the best,
Simply I credit her false-speaking tongue:
On both sides thus is simple truth suppressed.
But wherefore says she not she is unjust?
And wherefore say not I that I am old?
Oh, love's best habit is in seeming trust,
And age in love loves not to have years told.
   Therefore I lie with her and she with me,
   And in our faults by lies we flattered be.

WILLIAM SHAKESPEARE
## Sonnet 147

My love is as a fever, longing still
For that which longer nurseth the disease,
Feeding on that which doth preserve the ill,
Th' uncertain sickly appetite to please.
My reason, the physician to my love,
Angry that his prescriptions are not kept,
Hath left me, and I desperate now approve
Desire is death, which physic did except.
Past cure I am, now reason is past care,
And frantic mad with evermore unrest;
My thoughts and my discourse as madmen's are,
At random from the truth, vainly expressed.
   For I have sworn thee fair, and thought thee bright,
   Who art as black as hell, as dark as night.

JAMES I

## An Epitaph on Sir Philip Sidney

Thou mighty Mars, the god of soldiers brave,
And thou, Minerva, that does in wit excel,
And thou, Apollo, that does knowledge have
Of every art that from Parnassus fell,
With all the sisters that thereon do dwell,
Lament for him who duly served you all,
Whom-in you wisely all your arts did mell,—
Bewail, I say, his unexpected fall.
I need not in remembrance for to call
His youth, his race, the hope had of him aye,
Since that in him doth cruel death appall
Both manhood, wit, and learning every way.
   Now in the bed of honor doth he rest,
   And evermore of him shall live the best.

BARNABE BARNES

## from Parthenophil and Parthenophe

**Sonnet XLIIII**

Oh dart and thunder whose fierce violence
   Surmounting Rhetorickes dart and thunderboultes
   Can neuer be set out in eloquence,
   Whose might all mettles masse a sonder moultes:
Where be they famous Prophetes of ould Greece?
   Those anchiant Romaine Poetes of acompt,
   Musæus which went for the Golden Fleece
   With Iason, and did Heroes loues recompt,
And thou sweet Naso with thy golden vearse
   Whose louely spirite rauish't Cæsars daughter,
   And that sweet Tuskane Petrarke which did pearse
   His Laura with loue Sonnets when he saught her:
Where be these all? that all these might haue taught her
   That sainctes deuine are knowne sainctes by their
      mercy,
   And sainctlike bewtie should not rage with pearse
      eye.

SIR JOHN DAVIES

## "If you would know the love which I you bear"

If you would know the love which I you bear,
Compare it to the Ring which your fair hand
Shall make more precious when you shall it wear:
So my love's nature you shall understand.
Is it of metal pure? so you shall prove
My love, which ne'er disloyal thought did stain.
Hath it no end? so endless is my love,
Unless you it destroy with your disdain.
Doth it the purer wax the more 'tis tried?
So doth my love: yet herein they dissent,
That whereas gold, the more 'tis purified,
By waxing less doth show some part is spent,
My love doth wax more pure by your more trying,
And yet increaseth in the purifying.

# THE SEVENTEENTH CENTURY

By the start of the seventeenth century it appeared that the sonnet had taken root in English. That Wyatt, Surrey, and, later, Sidney and Shakespeare had succeeded in grafting this European form onto the English tree. An array of shaping spirits—Italian and French—was still in the air. But it was a homegrown influence that gave the form its true, early identity. By the end of the sixteenth century Shakespeare's sonnets were being circulated. Vital, headstrong, powerful—they gave the sonnet the one thing no Italian or French influence could provide: a local vernacular. Here was a poet equal to Dante and Petrarch. From now on, the sonnet would be adopted as an idiom by English poets. Samuel Daniel praised the form as "neither too long for the shortest project, nor too short for the longest."

# THE SONNET IN ITS CENTURY: THE SEVENTEENTH

*We'll build in sonnets pretty rooms*
                    —JOHN DONNE, *"The Canonization"*

"In 1600," Douglas Bush wrote, "the educated Englishman's mind and world were more than half medieval; by 1660 they were more than half modern." It was a century of whirling change and renewal. Of the introduction of tobacco and sugar. Of the execution of an English king. Of Shakespeare's sonnets. And, finally, of the decline of the sonnet as a viable form.

In the beginning none of this was clear. By the start of the seventeenth century it appeared that the sonnet had taken root in English. That Wyatt, Surrey, and, later, Sidney and Shakespeare had succeeded in grafting this European form onto the English tree. An array of shaping spirits—Italian and French—was still in the air. But it was a homegrown influence that gave the form its true, early identity. By the end of the sixteenth century Shakespeare's sonnets were being circulated. Vital, headstrong, powerful—they gave the sonnet the one thing no Italian or French influence could provide: a local vernacular. Here was a poet equal to Dante and Petrarch. From now on, the sonnet would be adopted as an idiom by English poets. Samuel Daniel praised the form as "neither too long for the shortest project, nor too short for the longest." The individual sonnet could bring the immediacy of the moment into a larger sequential whole.

In 1603 Queen Elizabeth died. In the same year James I was

crowned king. The new theater of public poetry was now religious rather than political. The king, a poet himself, who had a decided interest in theology, fostered this ethos. In "Basilikon Doron," his 1599 treatise on government, he advised poets, "If ye would write worthily, choose subjects worthy of you, that be not full of vanity, but of virtue."

And so the English sonneteer of the early part of the seventeenth century listened to sedition, saw the blue curl of tobacco, and knew that the devil and his works—and therefore God and his justice—were a fit subject for poetry. The sonnet expanded on love as its primary subject. John Donne's muscular religious sonnets are among the finest written. John Milton's political and occasional sonnets stand as great pillars of the form. They would become a primary model and inspiration for the Romantic poets.

But England was darkening. The Stuart dynasty was inept. When James I died his son Charles succeeded. He was executed in 1649. In an age of Puritanism and national strife, the Petrarchan decorums no longer seemed appropriate. Even earlier there had been complaints. In 1619 William Drummond, in his conversations published later, noted that Ben Jonson, Shakespeare's friend, had rebuked the form for being authoritarian: "He [Jonson] cursed Petrarch for redacting verses into sonnets; which he said were like that tyrant's bed, where some who were too short were racked, others too long cut short." A mood of anti-Petrarchanism was in the air.

The relation between a form and its moment is always a mystery. The execution of a king and a civil war in England, followed by the Restoration, proved inhospitable to the sonnet, though the turmoil of the Elizabethan age had not. The sonnet—despite the splendors of Donne and Milton—entered the shadows. For all its grace, innovation, and adaptation to English, it would become dormant. The critic George Saintsbury, writing about Philip Ayres, said: "Ayres loves the sonnet, and the sonnet was just about almost to disappear from English literature for the best part of a century." It would come back in the Romantic period with a vengeance.

BEN JONSON

## *A Sonnet to the Noble Lady, the Lady Mary Wroth*

I that have been a lover, and could show it,
    Though not in these, in rithmes not wholly dumb,
    Since I exscribe your sonnets, am become
A better lover, and much better poet.
Nor is my Muse or I ashamed to owe it
    To those true numerous graces, whereof some
    But charm the senses, others overcome
Both brains and hearts; and mine now best do
    know it:
For in your verse all Cupid's armory,
    His flames, his shafts, his quiver, and his bow,
    His very eyes are yours to overthrow.
But then his mother's sweets you so apply,
    Her joys, her smiles, her loves, as readers take
    For Venus' ceston every line you make.

RICHARD BARNFIELD

## *To his Friend Maister R. L.*
## *In Praise of Musique and Poetrie*

If Musique and sweet Poetrie agree,
As they must needes (the Sister and the Brother)
Then must the Love be great, twixt thee and mee,
    Because thou lov'st the one, and I the other.
*Dowland* to thee is deare; whose heavenly tuch
Upon the Lute, doeth ravish humaine sense:
*Spenser* to mee; whose deepe Conceit is such,
    As passing all Conceit, needs no defence.
    Thou lov'st to heare the sweete melodious sound,
That *Phoebus* Lute (the Queene of Musique) makes:
And I in deepe Delight am chiefly drownd,
    When as himselfe to singing he betakes.
    One God is God of Both (as Poets faigne)
    One Knight loves Both, and Both in thee
        remaine.

LADY MARY WROTH

## "*When everyone to pleasing pastime hies*"

When everyone to pleasing pastime hies,
    Some hunt, some hawk, some play, while some
        delight
    In sweet discourse, and music shows joy's might:
    Yet I my thoughts do far above these prize.
The joy which I take is, that free from eyes
    I sit and wonder at this day-like night,
    So to dispose themselves as void of right,
    And leave true pleasure for poor vanities.
When others hunt, my thoughts I have in chase;
    If hawk, my mind at wishèd end doth fly:
    Discourse, I with my spirit talk and cry;
    While others music choose as greatest grace.
O God say I, can these fond pleasures move,
Or music be but in sweet thoughts of love?

JOHN DONNE

## *from* Holy Sonnets

1

Thou hast made me, and shall thy work decay?
Repair me now, for now mine end doth haste;
I run to death, and death meets me as fast,
And all my pleasures are like yesterday.
I dare not move my dim eyes any way,
Despair behind, and death before doth cast
Such terror, and my feeble flesh doth waste
By sin in it, which it towards hell doth weigh.
Only thou art above, and when towards thee
By thy leave I can look, I rise again;
But our old subtle foe so tempteth me
That not one hour myself I can sustain.
Thy grace may wing me to prevent his art,
And thou like adamant draw mine iron heart.

JOHN DONNE

## *from* Holy Sonnets

5

I am a little world made cunningly
Of elements, and an angelic sprite;
But black sin hath betrayed to endless night
My world's both parts, and O, both parts must die.
You which beyond that heaven which was most high
Have found new spheres, and of new lands can write,
Pour new seas in mine eyes, that so I might
Drown my world with my weeping earnestly,
Or wash it if it must be drowned no more.
But O, it must be burnt! Alas, the fire
Of lust and envy have burnt it heretofore,
And made it fouler; let their flames retire,
And burn me, O Lord, with a fiery zeal
Of thee and thy house, which doth in eating heal.

JOHN DONNE

## *from* Holy Sonnets

7

At the round earth's imagined corners, blow
Your trumpets, angels; and arise, arise
From death, you numberless infinities
Of souls, and to your scattered bodies go:
All whom the flood did, and fire shall, o'erthrow,
All whom war, dearth, age, agues, tyrannies,
Despair, law, chance hath slain, and you whose eyes
Shall behold God, and never taste death's woe.
But let them sleep, Lord, and me mourn a space;
For, if above all these, my sins abound,
'Tis late to ask abundance of thy grace
When we are there. Here on this lowly ground,
Teach me how to repent; for that's as good
As if thou hadst sealed my pardon with thy blood.

JOHN DONNE

## *from* Holy Sonnets

### 10

Death, be not proud, though some have callèd thee
Mighty and dreadful, for thou art not so;
For those whom thou think'st thou dost overthrow
Die not, poor Death, nor yet canst thou kill me.
From rest and sleep, which but thy pictures be,
Much pleasure; then from thee much more must flow,
And soonest our best men with thee do go,
Rest of their bones, and soul's delivery.
Thou art slave to fate, chance, kings, and desperate
    men,
And dost with poison, war, and sickness dwell,
And poppy or charms can make us sleep as well
And better than thy stroke; why swell'st thou then?
One short sleep past, we wake eternally
And death shall be no more; Death, thou shalt die.

JOHN DONNE

## *from* Holy Sonnets

### 14

Batter my heart, three-personed God; for you
As yet but knock, breathe, shine, and seek to mend;
That I may rise and stand, o'erthrow me, and bend
Your force to break, blow, burn, and make me new.
I, like an usurped town, to another due,
Labor to admit you, but O, to no end;
Reason, your viceroy in me, me should defend,
But is captived, and proves weak or untrue.
Yet dearly I love you, and would be loved fain,
But am betrothed unto your enemy.
Divorce me, untie or break that knot again;
Take me to you, imprison me, for I,
Except you enthrall me, never shall be free,
Nor ever chaste, except you ravish me.

JOHN DONNE

## *from* Holy Sonnets

**19**

Oh, to vex me, contraries meet in one:
Inconstancy unnaturally hath begot
A constant habit; that when I would not
I change in vows, and in devotion.
As humorous is my contrition
As my profane love, and as soon forgot:
As riddlingly distempered, cold and hot,
As praying, as mute, as infinite, as none.
I durst not view heaven yesterday; and today
In prayers, and flattering speeches I court God:
Tomorrow I quake with true fear of his rod.
So my devout fits come and go away
Like a fantastic ague; save that here
Those are my best days, when I shake with fear.

EDWARD, LORD HERBERT OF CHERBURY

## *Epitaph of King James*

Here lies King James, who did ſo propagate
Unto the World that bleſt and quiet ſtate
Wherein his ſubjects liv'd, he ſeemed to give
That peace which Chriſt did leave; and did ſo live,
As once that King and Shepherd of his Sheep,
That whom God ſaved, here he ſeemed to keep,
Till with that innocent and ſingle heart
With which he firſt was crown'd he did depart,
To better life. Great Brittain, ſo lament
That Strangers more than thou may yet reſent
The ſad effects, and while they feel the harm
They muſt endure from the victorious arm
Of our King Charles, may they ſo long complain,
That tears in them force thee to weep again.

WILLIAM DRUMMOND OF HAWTHORNDEN

## Sonnet LXXIII

My lute, be as thou wert when thou didst grow
With thy green mother in some shady grove,
When immelodious winds but made thee move,
And birds their ramage did on thee bestow.
Since that dear voice which did thy sounds approve,
Which wont in such harmonious strains to flow,
Is reft from earth to tune those spheres above,
What art thou but a harbinger of woe?
Thy pleasing notes be pleasing notes no more,
But orphans' wailings to the fainting ear,
Each stroke a sigh, each sound draws forth a tear,
For which be silent as in woods before:
   Or if that any hand to touch thee deign,
   Like widow'd turtle still her loss complain.


GEORGE HERBERT

## Prayer (I)

Prayer the Church's banquet, Angels' age,
   God's breath in man returning to his birth,
   The soul in paraphrase, heart in pilgrimage,
The Christian plummet sounding heav'n and earth;
Engine against th' Almighty, sinners' tower,
   Reversed thunder, Christ-side-piercing spear,
   The six-days' world transposing in an hour,
A kind of tune, which all things hear and fear;
Softness, and peace, and joy, and love, and bliss,
   Exalted Manna, gladness of the best,
   Heaven in ordinary, man well drest,
The milky way, the bird of Paradise,
   Church bells beyond the stars heard, the soul's
      blood,
   The land of spices; something understood.

GEORGE HERBERT

## "My God, where is that ancient heat towards thee"

My God, where is that ancient heat towards thee,
   Wherewith whole shoals of *Martyrs* once did
      burn,
   Besides their other flames? Doth Poetry
Wear *Venus'* livery? only serve her turn?
Why are not *Sonnets* made of thee? and lays
   Upon thine Altar burnt? Cannot thy love
   Heighten a spirit to sound out thy praise
As well as any she? Cannot thy *Dove*
Outstrip their *Cupid* easily in flight?
   Or, since thy ways are deep, and still the same,
   Will not a verse run smooth that bears thy name!
Why doth that fire, which by thy power and might
   Each breast does feel, no braver fuel choose
   Than that, which one day, Worms may chance
      refuse?

GEORGE HERBERT

## Redemption

Having been tenant long to a rich Lord,
   Not thriving, I resolved to be bold,
   And make a suit unto him, to afford
A new small-rented lease, and cancel th'old.
In heaven at his manor I him sought:
   They told me there, that he was lately gone
   About some land, which he had dearly bought
Long since on earth, to take possession.
I straight returned, and knowing his great birth,
   Sought him accordingly in great resorts,
   In cities, theatres, gardens, parks, and courts:
At length I heard a ragged noise and mirth
   Of thieves and murderers: there I him espied,
   Who straight, *Your suit is granted*, said, and died.

GEORGE HERBERT

## "Sure Lord, there is enough in thee to dry"

Sure Lord, there is enough in thee to dry
   Ocean of *Ink*; for, as the Deluge did
   Cover the Earth, so doth thy Majesty:
Each Cloud distills thy praise, and doth forbid
*Poets* to turn it to another use.
   *Roses and Lilies* speak thee; and to make
   A pair of Cheeks of them, is thy abuse.
Why should I *Women's eyes* for Crystal take?
Such poor invention burns in their low mind
   Whose fire is wild, and doth not upward go
   To praise, and on thee Lord, some *ink* bestow.
Open the bones, and you shall nothing find
   In the best *face* but *filth*, when Lord, in thee
   The *beauty* lies, in the *discovery*.

THOMAS CAREW

## Song: Mediocrity in Love Rejected

Give me more love, or more disdain;
   The torrid or the frozen zone
Bring equal ease unto my pain,
   The temperate affords me none;
Either extreme, of love or hate,
Is sweeter than a calm estate.

Give me a storm; if it be love,
   Like Danaë in that golden shower,
I swim in pleasure; if it prove
   Disdain, that torrent will devour
My vulture-hopes; and he's possessed
Of heaven, that's but from hell released.
   Then crown my joys, or cure my pain;
   Give me more love, or more disdain.

ROBERT HERRICK

## The Bad Season Makes the Poet Sad

Dull to myself, and almost dead to these
My many fresh and fragrant mistresses,
Lost to all music now, since every thing
Puts on the semblance here of sorrowing;
Sick is the land to th'heart, and doth endure
More dangerous faintings by her desp'rate cure.
But if that golden age would come again,
And Charles here rule, as he before did reign;
If smooth and unperplexed the seasons were
As when the sweet Maria livéd here;
I should delight to have my curls half drowned
In Tyrian dews, and head with roses crowned,
And once more yet, ere I am laid out dead,
Knock at a star with my exalted head.


JOHN MILTON

## "How soon hath Time, the subtle thief of youth"

How soon hath Time, the subtle thief of youth,
    Stol'n on his wing my three and twentieth year!
    My hasting days fly on with full career,
    But my late spring no bud or blossom shew'th.
Perhaps my semblance might deceive the truth,
    That I to manhood am arrived so near,
    And inward ripeness doth much less appear,
    That some more timely-happy spirits endu'th.
Yet be it less or more, or soon or slow,
    It shall be still in strictest measure even
    To that same lot, however mean or high,
Toward which Time leads me, and the will of Heaven;
    All is, if I have grace to use it so,
    As ever in my great Taskmaster's eye.

JOHN MILTON

## "A book was writ of late called Tetrachordon"

A book was writ of late called *Tetrachordon*;
    And woven close, both matter, form and style;
    The subject new: it walked the town a while,
    Numb'ring good intellects; now seldom pored on.
Cries the stall-reader, Bless us! what a word on
    A title page is this! and some in file
    Stand spelling false, while one might walk to Mile-
End Green. Why is it harder sirs than Gordon,
Colkitto, or Macdonnel, or Galasp?
    Those rugged names to our like mouths grow sleek
    That would have made Quintilian stare and gasp.
Thy age, like ours, O soul of Sir John Cheke,
    Hated not learning worse than toad or asp,
    When thou taught'st Cambridge and King Edward
        Greek.

JOHN MILTON

## To the Lord General Cromwell, May 1652

Cromwell, our chief of men, who through a cloud
    Not of war only, but detractions rude,
    Guided by faith and matchless fortitude
    To peace and truth thy glorious way hast ploughed,
And on the neck of crownèd Fortune proud
    Hast reared God's trophies, and his work pursued,
    While Darwen stream with blood of Scots imbrued
    And Dunbar field resounds thy praises loud,
And Worcester's laureate wreath; yet much remains
    To conquer still; peace hath her victories
    No less renowned than war; new foes arise,
Threatening to bind our souls with secular chains:
    Help us to save free conscience from the paw
    Of hireling wolves whose gospel is their maw.

JOHN MILTON

## "Methought I saw my late espousèd saint"

Methought I saw my late espousèd saint
  Brought to me like Alcestis from the grave,
  Whom Jove's great son to her glad husband gave,
  Rescued from death by force though pale and
    faint.
Mine, as whom washed from spot of childbed taint,
  Purification in the old law did save,
  And such, as yet once more I trust to have
  Full sight of her in heaven without restraint,
Came vested all in white, pure as her mind.
  Her face was veiled, yet to my fancied sight
  Love, sweetness, goodness, in her person shined
So clear, as in no face with more delight.
  But O, as to embrace me she inclined,
  I waked, she fled, and day brought back my night.

JOHN MILTON

## On the Late Massacre in Piedmont

Avenge, O Lord, thy slaughtered saints, whose bones
  Lie scattered on the Alpine mountains cold;
  Even them who kept thy truth so pure of old
  When all our fathers worshipped stocks and
    stones,
Forget not: in thy book record their groans
  Who were thy sheep and in their ancient fold
  Slain by the bloody Piemontese that rolled
  Mother with infant down the rocks. Their moans
The vales redoubled to the hills, and they
  To heaven. Their martyred blood and ashes sow
  O'er all th' Italian fields, where still doth sway
The triple tyrant: that from these may grow
  A hundredfold, who having learnt thy way
  Early may fly the Babylonian woe.

JOHN MILTON

## "When I consider how my light is spent"

When I consider how my light is spent,
　　Ere half my days, in this dark world and wide,
　　And that one talent which is death to hide
　　Lodged with me useless, though my soul more
　　　bent
To serve therewith my Maker, and present
　　My true account, lest he returning chide;
　　"Doth God exact day-labor, light denied?"
　　I fondly ask; but Patience to prevent
That murmur, soon replies, "God doth not need
　　Either man's work or his own gifts; who best
　　Bear his mild yoke, they serve him best. His state
Is kingly. Thousands at his bidding speed
　　And post o'er land and ocean without rest:
　　They also serve who only stand and wait."

PHILIP AYRES

## *A Sonnet, of Petrarc, Shewing how long he had lov'd Madonna Laura*

Pleaſure in Thought, in Weeping Eaſe I find;
　　I catch at Shadows, graſp Air with my Hand;
　　On Seas I float are bounded with no Land;
　　Plow Water, ſow on Rocks, and reap the Wind.

The Sun I gaz'd ſo long at, I became
　　Struck with its Dazling Rays, and loſt my Eyes;
　　I chaſe a Nimble Doe that always flyes,
　　And hunt with a Dull Creature, Weak and Lame.

Heartleſs I live to all things but my Ill,
　　Which I'm ſollicitous to follow ſtill;
　　And only call on *Laura*, Love, and Death.

Thus Twenty Years I've ſpent in Miſery,
Whilſt only Sighs, and Tears, and Sobs I buy,
  Under ſuch hard Stars firſt I drew my Breath.


APHRA BEHN

### Epitaph on the Tombstone of a Child, the Last of Seven That Died Before

This little, silent, gloomy monument,
Contains all that was sweet and innocent;
The softest prattler that e'er found a tongue,
His voice was music and his words a song;
Which now each list'ning angel smiling hears,
Such pretty harmonies compose the spheres;
Wanton as unfledg'd cupids, ere their charms
Had learn'd the little arts of doing harms;
Fair as young cherubins, as soft and kind,
And though translated, could not be refin'd;
The seventh dear pledge the nuptial joys had given,
Toil'd here on Earth, retir'd to rest in Heaven;
Where they the shining host of angels fill,
Spread their gay wings before the throne, and smile.

# THE EIGHTEENTH CENTURY

*The relation of a form to a time is a fascinating study. The sonnet had flourished in the sunshine of Italian courts, in the shadow of the gallows in England, and even at the threshold of civil war. Now it was out of fashion and far from favor. The Augustan age that enshrined the routine simulation of wit in the rhyming couplet also honored regulation and reason—not especial purposes or strengths of the sonnet.*

# The Sonnet in Its Century: The Eighteenth

*A small poem.*

—SAMUEL JOHNSON,
*A Dictionary of the English Language* (1755)

The eighteenth century was the age of wit and science. It was also the era in which the sonnet fell on hard times. Some poets continued to write it, and some with real grace. But Augustan poets, such as John Dryden and Alexander Pope, either ignored or disdained it. Indeed, Pope could refer to a "starv'd hackney sonneteer" as if it were the commonly held view of practitioners of the form.

But why? The reasons are elusive. Hungry for reason rather than emotion, it seems that early eighteenth-century readers found the sonnet pedestrian. Pope mocked the form in his "Essay on Criticism": "What woful stuff this madrigal would be, / In some starv'd hackney sonneteer, or me?"

And yet only sixty years earlier the sonnet, in the hands of Donne and Milton, had achieved one of its finest moments. The eroticism of religious feeling and the power of political dissent had found there remarkable expression and compression. Now there was outright skepticism. Samuel Johnson, one of the authors of the Augustan literary ethos, was dismissive. "The fabric of a sonnet," he said, "however adapted to the Italian language, has never succeeded in ours." He also defined a "sonnetteer" as a term of contempt for "a small poet."

The relation of a form to a time is a fascinating study. The sonnet had flourished in the sunshine of Italian courts, in the shadow of the gallows in England, and even at the threshold of civil war. Now it was out of fashion and far from favor. The Augustan age that enshrined the routine simulation of wit in the rhyming couplet also honored regulation and reason—not especial purposes or strengths of the sonnet. An age in which Thomas Hobbes could say, "Science is the knowledge of Consequences, and dependance of one fact upon another," was unlikely to value the Petrarchan sigh and flourish.

The locus of writing and writers had shifted. In the years after the Restoration in 1660, the court became less important. Instead, writers gathered in the coffeehouses around the Royal Exchange and Cornhill. It was an ethos more conducive to forced literary survival and epigrammatic wit than to a Petrarchan world of rhetoric and arranged cadence.

Nevertheless, some sonnets were written. And, below the surface of neglect, the sonnet had survived and, indeed, would be strengthened when it reappeared. The gains made in the sixteenth and seventeenth centuries were not lost; they just had to wait for a later age to become applicable. The spare, stripped rhythms of the twenty-four sonnets Milton wrote, for example, would haunt the practice of the form in the English language. William Cowper, an important eighteenth-century poet, echoes Milton strongly in his sonnet on William Wilberforce, included here. The ability that poets like Donne and Milton displayed—to absorb the form into the spirit as well as the practice of English poetry—enabled the sonnet's resurgence in the Romantic era.

THOMAS EDWARDS
## *On a Family-Picture*

When pensive on that portraiture I gaze,
　Where my four brothers round about me stand,
　And four fair sisters smile with graces bland,
The goodly monument of happier days;

And think how soon insatiate Death, who preys
　On all, has cropped the rest with ruthless hand;
　While only I survive of all that band,
Which one chaste bed did to my father raise;

It seems that like a column left alone,
　The tottering remnant of some splendid fane,
　　'Scaped from the fury of the barbarous Gaul,
And wasting Time, which has the rest o'erthrown;
　Amidst our house's ruins I remain
　　Single, unpropped, and nodding to my fall.

THOMAS EDWARDS
## *On the Edition of Mr. Pope's Works with a Commentary and Notes*

In evil hour did Pope's declining age,
　Deceived and dazzled by the tinsel show
　Of wordy science and the nauseous flow
Of mean officious flatteries, engage

Thy venal quill to deck his laboured page
　With ribald nonsense, and permit to strew,
　Amidst his flowers, the baleful weeds that grow
In th'unblessed soil of rude and rancorous rage.

Yet this the avenging Muse ordainèd so,
　When, by his counsel or weak sufferance,
　　To thee were trusted Shakespeare's fame and fate.
She doom'd him down the stream of time to tow
　Thy foul, dirt-loaded hulk, or sink perchance,
　　Dragged to oblivion by the foundering weight.

THOMAS GRAY

## *On the Death of Mr. Richard West*

In vain to me the smiling mornings shine,
And redd'ning Phoebus lifts his golden fire:
The birds in vain their amorous descant join;
Or cheerful fields resume their green attire:
These ears, alas! for other notes repine,
A different object do these eyes require.
My lonely anguish melts no heart but mine;
And in my breast the imperfect joys expire.
Yet morning smiles the busy race to cheer,
And new-born pleasure brings to happier men:
The fields to all their wonted tribute bear:
To warm their little loves the birds complain:
I fruitless mourn to him, that cannot hear,
And weep the more, because I weep in vain.


THOMAS WARTON, THE YOUNGER

## *To the River Lodon*

Ah! what a weary race my feet have run
Since first I trod thy banks with alders crowned,
And thought my way was all through fairy ground,
Beneath thy azure sky and golden sun,
Where first my Muse to lisp her notes begun.
While pensive Memory traces back the round
Which fills the varied interval between,
Much pleasure, more of sorrow, marks the scene.
Sweet native stream, those skies and suns so pure
No more return to cheer my evening road,
Yet still one joy remains, that not obscure
Nor useless all my vacant days have flowed
From Youth's grey dawn to manhood's prime mature,
Nor with the Muse's laurel unbestowed.

WILLIAM COWPER

## Sonnet to William Wilberforce, Esquire

Thy country, Wilberforce, with just disdain,
Hears thee, by cruel men and impious call'd
Fanatic, for thy zeal to loose th' enthrall'd
From exile, public sale, and slav'ry's chain.
Friend of the poor, the wrong'd, the fetter-gall'd,
Fear not lest labour such as thine be vain.
Thou hast achiev'd a part; hast gain'd the ear
Of Britain's senate to thy glorious cause;
Hope smiles, joy springs, and though cold
    caution pause
And weave delay, the better hour is near
That shall remunerate thy toils severe
By peace for Afric, fenced with British laws.
    Enjoy what thou hast won, esteem and love
    From all the Just on earth, and all the Blest above.

WILLIAM COWPER

## To Mrs. Unwin

Mary! I want a lyre with other strings,
    Such aid from heaven as some have feigned
      they drew,
    An eloquence scarce given to mortals, new
And undebased by praise of meaner things;
That, ere through age or woe I shed my wings,
    I may record thy worth with honour due,
    In verse as musical as thou art true,
And that immortalizes whom it sings.
But thou hast little need. There is a Book
    By seraphs writ with beams of heavenly light,
On which the eyes of God not rarely look,
    A chronicle of actions just and bright;—
      There all thy deeds, my faithful Mary, shine;
      And since thou own'st that praise, I spare
        thee mine.

WILLIAM COWPER

## *To George Romney, Esq.*

*His picture of me in crayons, drawn at Eartham in the
sixty-first year of my age, and in the months of August
and September, 1792.*

Romney, expert infallibly to trace
On chart or canvas, not the form alone
And semblance, but, however faintly shown,
The mind's impression too on every face,
With strokes that time ought never to erase;
Thou hast so pencilled mine, that though I own
The subject worthless, I have never known
The artist shining with superior grace.
But this I mark,—that symptoms none of woe
In thy incomparable work appear.
Well; I am satisfied it should be so,
Since, on maturer thought, the cause is clear;
For in my looks what sorrow couldst thou see
When I was Hayley's guest, and sat to thee?

ANNA SEWARD

## *To a Friend, Who Thinks Sensibility a Misfortune*

Ah, thankless! canst thou envy him who gains
　　The Stoic's cold and indurate repose?
　　Thou! with thy lively sense of bliss and woes!—
　　From a false balance of life's joys and pains
Thou deem'st him happy.—Plac'd 'mid fair domains,
　　Where full the river down the valley flows,
　　As wisely might'st thou wish thy home had rose
On the parch'd surface of unwater'd plains,
For that, when long the heavy rain descends,
　　Bursts over guardian banks their whelming tide!—
　　Seldom the wild and wasteful flood extends,
But, spreading plenty, verdure, beauty wide,
　　The cool translucent stream perpetual bends,
　　And laughs the vale as the bright waters glide.

ANNA SEWARD
## To the Poppy

While summer roses all their glory yield
   To crown the votary of Love and Joy,
   Misfortune's victim hails, with many a sigh,
   Thee, scarlet poppy of the pathless field,
Gaudy, yet wild and lone; no leaf to shield
   Thy flaccid vest, that, as the gale blows high,
   Flaps, and alternate folds around thy head.—
So stands in the long grass a love-crazed maid
Smiling aghast; while stream to every wind
   Her garish ribbons, smeared with dust and rain;
   But brain-sick visions cheat her tortured mind,
And bring false peace. Thus, lulling grief and pain,
   Kind dreams oblivious from thy juice proceed,
   Thou flimsy, showy, melancholy weed.

ANNA MARIA JONES
## Sonnet to the Moon

Thou lovely Sorc'ress of the witching Night,
   Whose paly Charms thro' sombre Regions glide;
Lur'd by the Softness of thy silver Light,
   The Muse pathetic glows with conscious Pride.

On the gem'd Margin of the lustrous Flood,
   Whose ripling Waters glide so sweetly by;
Oft have I list'ning to its Murmurs stood,
   Trac'd thy pure Ray, and wing'd a lonely Sigh!

For *Thou*, chaste *Cynthia*, o'er my gentle Soul,
   Shed'st the mild Beam of Contemplation's Sway;
Thy fascinating Spell with proud Controul
   Sweeps the full Cadence of my trembling Lay:
Then gleam, bright Orb, from Midnight's velvet Vest,
And dart thy pearly Lustre o'er my pensive Breast.

CHARLOTTE SMITH

## "The partial Muse has from my earliest hours"

The partial Muse has from my earliest hours
　　Smiled on the rugged path I'm doomed to tread,
And still with sportive hand has snatched wild flowers,
　　To weave fantastic garlands for my head:
But far, far happier is the lot of those
　　Who never learned her dear delusive art;
Which, while it decks the head with many a rose,
　　Reserves the thorn to fester in the heart.
For still she bids soft pity's melting eye
　　Stream o'er the ills she knows not to remove,
Points every pang, and deepens every sigh
　　Of mourning friendship, or unhappy love.
Ah! then, how dear the Muse's favors cost,
*If those paint sorrow best—who feel it most!*


CHARLOTTE SMITH

## To the South Downs

Ah! hills beloved!—where once a happy child,
　　Your beechen shades, "your turf, your flowers
　　　　among,"
I wove your blue-bells into garlands wild,
　　And woke your echoes with my artless song.
Ah! hills beloved!—your turf, your flowers remain;
　　But can they peace to this sad breast restore;
For one poor moment soothe the sense of pain,
　　And teach a breaking heart to throb no more?
And you, Aruna!—in the vale below,
　　As to the sea your limpid waves you bear,
Can you one kind Lethean cup bestow,
　　To drink a long oblivion to my care?
Ah, no!—when all, e'en Hope's last ray is gone,
There's no oblivion—but in death alone!

CHARLOTTE SMITH

## To Night

I love thee, mournful, sober-suited Night!
    When the faint moon, yet lingering in her wane,
    And veiled in clouds, with pale uncertain light
        Hangs o'er the waters of the restless main.
In deep depression sunk, the enfeebled mind
        Will to the deaf cold elements complain,
        And tell the embosomed grief, however vain,
To sullen surges and the viewless wind.
Though no repose on thy dark breast I find,
    I still enjoy thee—cheerless as thou art;
        For in thy quiet gloom the exhausted heart
Is calm, though wretched; hopeless, yet resigned.
While to the winds and waves its sorrows given,
May reach—though lost on earth—the ear of
        Heaven!


CHARLOTTE SMITH

## To a nightingale

Poor melancholy bird—that all night long
    Tell'st to the Moon thy tale of tender woe;
        From what sad cause can such sweet sorrow flow,
And whence this mournful melody of song?

Thy poet's musing fancy would translate
    What mean the sounds that swell thy little breast,
        When still at dewy eve thou leavest thy nest,
Thus to the listening night to sing thy fate.

Pale Sorrow's victims wert thou once among,
    Tho' now released in woodlands wild to rove?
    Say—hast thou felt from friends some cruel
        wrong,
Or died'st thou—martyr of disastrous love?
Ah! songstress sad! that such my lot might be,
To sigh, and sing at liberty—like thee!

DAVID HUMPHREYS

### Addressed to His Royal Highness, The Prince of Brazil, On Taking Leave of the Court of Lisbon, July, 1797

Farewell, ye flowery fields! where Nature's hand
Profusely sheds her vegetable store,
Nurtured by genial suns and zephyrs bland!
Farewell, thou Tagus! and thy friendly shore:
Long shall my soul thy lost retreats deplore,
Thy haunts where shades of heroes met my eyes.
As oft I mused where Camoens trod before,
I saw the god-like form of Gama rise,
With chiefs renowned beneath your eastern skies.
O, long may peace and glory crown thy scene!
Farewell, just Prince! no sycophantic lay
Insults thy ear. Be what thy sires have been,
Thy great progenitors! who oped the way
Through seas unsailed before to climes of orient day.

JOHN CODRINGTON BAMPFYLDE

### On a Wet Summer

All ye who far from town in rural hall,
    Like me, were wont to dwell near pleasant field,
    Enjoying all the sunny day did yield,
    With me the change lament, in irksome thrall,
By rains incessant held; for now no call
    From early swain invites my hand to wield
    The scythe; in parlour dim I sit concealed,
    And mark the lessening sand from hour-glass fall,
Or 'neath my window view the wistful train
    Of dripping poultry, whom the vine's broad leaves
    Shelter no more.—Mute is the mournful plain,
Silent the swallow sits beneath the thatch,
    And vacant hind hangs pensive o'er his hatch,
    Counting the frequent drop from reeded eaves.

# THE NINETEENTH CENTURY

The nineteenth-century sonnet is a chameleon. It looks backward to the Renaissance and forward to the modern era. Boswell praised Shakespeare; Lamb praised Sidney. Keats mastered the Shakespearean sonnet even as he experimented with a combination of the Italian and English forms. John Clare's rural muse often expressed itself in sonnet form, as did Gerard Manley Hopkins's religious sensibility and radical formalism. Hopkins pushed the sonnet to new limits. During the nineteenth century, the sonnet also crossed the ocean to the New World.

Nineteenth-century American poetry is rightly known for its transcendental spirit, for sounding—in Whitman's phrase—its "barbaric yawp over the roofs of the world." Emerson called poets "liberating gods" and argued that "it is not meters, but a meter-making argument that makes a poem." The organicism of Whitman's free-verse catalogues and Dickinson's radically fragmented hymns suited—and still suits—the New World ethos. Yet the unlikely, lesser known countertruth is that the American spirit of invention also expressed itself through certain inherited forms, especially sonnets.

# THE SONNET IN ITS CENTURY: THE NINETEENTH

*The Sonnet then is a small poem, in which some lonely feeling is developed.*

—SAMUEL TAYLOR COLERIDGE,
*"A Sheet of Sonnets"* (1796)

The Romantic poets revitalized the sonnet form, which had become virtually extinct after 1650. They marked and internalized it. Every major Romantic poet wrote sonnets, with the possible exception of Blake (though he hesitated in the doorway and we have included a fourteen-line poem sometimes considered a sonnet). Some of the most loved poems of the nineteenth century are sonnets, including Wordsworth's "Composed Upon Westminster Bridge, September 3, 1802," Keats's "On First Looking into Chapman's Homer," and Shelley's "Ozymandias." The Romantic-era revival was an amazing turn for the rhyming fourteen-line poem. For the second time in English literary history, it became one of the primary staples of poetry.

The Romantic poets followed Milton's lead in taking the sonnet both tenderly inward and politically outward. As Francis Jeffrey remarked in 1807, "All English writers of sonnets have imitated Milton." Wordsworth confessed he had considered the sonnet form "egregiously absurd" until his sister happened to read him some of Milton's sonnets and he was "singularly struck with the style of harmony, and the gravity, and republican austerity of those compositions." He went on to become one of the major practitioners of the sonnet form in English. Like Milton himself, he ferried backward and forward between the private and the public sonnet with great ease and mastery.

The sonnet was often viewed as a form capable of tremendous inwardness, a key to emotion rather than reason. Coleridge considered the sonnet "a small poem, in which some lonely feeling is developed." William Hazlitt characterized it as "a sigh uttered from the fulness of the heart, an involuntary aspiration born and dying in the same moment." Wordsworth took Shakespeare's sonnets personally. "[W]ith this key / Shakespeare unlocked his heart." Later, Robert Browning would retort: "Did Shakespeare? If so, the less Shakespeare he!" Browning understood that the speaker of Shakespeare's sonnets is a construction, a personal mask, a persona. His sense of theatrical emotion is one of the hallmarks of the Victorian sonnet.

The sonnet also proved to be an important theater for women poets. Anna Seward spoke of "the Sonnet's claim," and, indeed, many women poets claimed the sonnet as their own. They used it to prove their poetic legitimacy. One thinks of Charlotte Smith, who was the first eighteenth-century female poet to publish a book of sonnets; Mary Robinson, who strictly adhered to what she considered the "legitimate" Petrarchan form; and Elizabeth Barrett Browning, who expanded the emotional range of the form in *Sonnets from the Portuguese.*

The nineteenth-century sonnet is a chameleon. It looks backward to the Renaissance and forward to the modern era. Boswell praised Shakespeare; Lamb praised Sidney. Keats mastered the Shakespearean sonnet even as he experimented with a combination of the Italian and English forms. John Clare's rural muse often expressed itself in sonnet form, as did Gerard Manley Hopkins's religious sensibility and radical formalism. Hopkins pushed the sonnet to new limits. During the nineteenth century, the sonnet also crossed the ocean to the New World.

Nineteenth-century American poetry is rightly known for its transcendental spirit, for sounding—in Whitman's phrase—its "barbaric yawp over the roofs of the world." Emerson called poets "liberating gods" and argued that "it is not meters, but a meter-making argument that makes a poem." The organicism of Whitman's free-verse catalogues and Dickinson's radically fragmented hymns suited—and still suits—the New World ethos. Yet the unlikely, lesser known countertruth is that the American spirit of invention also expressed itself through certain inherited forms, especially sonnets.

"The sonnet is indeed the most settled and traditional of forms," as David Bromwich puts it. "Yet there have been so many good and memorable sonnets by Americans that F. O. Matthiessen, the editor of the great *Oxford Book of American Verse*, confessed one of his leading principles in choosing poems for that anthology had been 'not too many sonnets.'" The nineteenth-century American sonnet has an unorthodox intensity—an untamable spirit—that has been unleashed in a small space.

WILLIAM BLAKE

## To the Evening Star

Thou fair-hair'd angel of the evening,
Now, while the sun rests on the mountains, light
Thy bright torch of love; thy radiant crown
Put on, and smile upon our evening bed!
Smile on our loves; and, while thou drawest the
Blue curtains of the sky, scatter thy silver dew
On every flower that shuts its sweet eyes
In timely sleep. Let thy west wind sleep on
The lake; speak silence with thy glimmering eyes,
And wash the dusk with silver. Soon, full soon,
Dost thou withdraw; then the wolf rages wide,
And the lion glares thro' the dun forest:
The fleeces of our flocks are cover'd with
Thy sacred dew: protect them with thine influence.

MARY ROBINSON

## *from* Sappho and Phaon

### I. Sonnet Introductory

Favored by Heaven are those, ordained to taste
    The bliss supreme that kindles fancy's fire;
    Whose magic fingers sweep the muses' lyre,
In varying cadence, eloquently chaste!
Well may the mind, with tuneful numbers graced,
    To Fame's immortal attributes aspire,
    Above the treacherous spells of low desire,
That wound the sense, by vulgar joys debased.
    For thou, blest Poesy! with godlike powers
To calm the miseries of man wert given;
    When passion rends, and hopeless love devours,
By memory goaded, and by frenzy driven,
    'Tis thine to guide him 'midst Elysian bowers,
And show his fainting soul,—a glimpse of Heaven.

JANE WEST

## Sonnet to May

Come May, the empire of the earth aſſume,
  Be crown'd with flowers as univerſal queen;
  Take from freſh budded groves their tender green,
Beſpangled with Pomona's richeſt bloom,
And form thy veſture. Let the ſun illume
  The dew-drops glittering in the blue ſerene,
  And let them hang, like orient pearls, between
Thy locks beſprent with Flora's beſt perfume.
Attend your ſovereign's ſteps, ye balmy gales!
  O'er her ambroſial floods of fragrance pour;
Let livelier verdure animate the vales,
    And brighter hues embelliſh every flower;
And hark, the concert of the woodland hails,
    All gracious May! thy preſence, and thy power.

ROBERT BURNS

## Sonnet

*Written on the 25th January, 1793, the Birthday of the Author,*
*on hearing a Thrush sing in a morning Walk.*

Sing on, sweet thrush, upon the leafless bough,
  Sing on, sweet bird, I listen to thy strain;
  See aged Winter 'mid his surly reign,
At thy blithe carol clears his furrow'd brow.

So in lone Poverty's dominion drear,
  Sits meek Content with light unanxious heart,
  Welcomes the rapid moments, bids them part,
Nor asks if they bring ought to hope or fear.

I thank thee, Author of this opening day!
  Thou whose bright sun now gilds yon orient skies!
  Riches denied, thy boon was purer joys,
What wealth could never give nor take away!

Yet come, thou child of poverty and care,
The mite high Heaven bestow'd, that mite with thee
    I'll share.


WILLIAM LISLE BOWLES

## To the River Itchin, Near Winton

Itchin, when I behold thy banks again,
    Thy crumbling margin, and thy silver breast,
    On which the self-same tints still seem to rest,
Why feels my heart the shivering sense of pain?
    Is it—that many a summer's day has past
Since, in life's morn, I caroled on thy side?
Is it—that oft, since then, my heart has sighed,
    As youth, and hope's delusive gleams, flew fast?
Is it—that those, who circled on thy shore,
Companions of my youth, now meet no more?
    Whate'er the cause, upon thy banks I bend
Sorrowing, yet feel such solace at my heart,
    As at the meeting of some long-lost friend,
From whom, in happier hours, we wept to part.


JOHN QUINCY ADAMS

## To the Sun-Dial

*Under the Window of the Hall of the House of Representatives
of the United States*

Thou silent herald of Time's silent flight!
    Say, could'st thou speak, what warning voice were
        thine?
    Shade, who canst only show how others shine!
Dark, sullen witness of resplendent light
In day's broad glare, and when the noontide bright
    Of laughing fortune sheds the ray divine,
    Thy ready favors cheer us—but decline
The clouds of morning and the gloom of night.

Yet are thy counsels faithful, just, and wise;
    They bid us seize the moments as they pass—
Snatch the retrieveless sunbeam as it flies,
    Nor lose one sand of life's revolving glass—
Aspiring still, with energy sublime,
By virtuous deeds to give eternity to Time.


WILLIAM WORDSWORTH

## Composed Upon Westminster Bridge, September 3, 1802

Earth has not any thing to show more fair:
Dull would he be of soul who could pass by
A sight so touching in its majesty:
This city now doth like a garment wear
The beauty of the morning; silent, bare,
Ships, towers, domes, theaters, and temples lie
Open unto the fields, and to the sky;
All bright and glittering in the smokeless air.
Never did sun more beautifully steep
In his first splendor valley, rock, or hill;
Ne'er saw I, never felt, a calm so deep!
The river glideth at his own sweet will:
Dear God! the very houses seem asleep;
And all that mighty heart is lying still!


WILLIAM WORDSWORTH

## "It is a beauteous evening, calm and free"

It is a beauteous evening, calm and free;
The holy time is quiet as a nun
Breathless with adoration; the broad sun
Is sinking down in its tranquillity;
The gentleness of heaven is on the Sea:
Listen! the mighty Being is awake,
And doth with his eternal motion make
A sound like thunder—everlastingly.

Dear Child! dear Girl! that walkest with me here,
If thou appear'st untouched by solemn thought,
Thy nature is not therefore less divine:
Thou liest in Abraham's bosom all the year;
And worshipp'st at the Temple's inner shrine,
God being with thee when we know it not.


WILLIAM WORDSWORTH

## To Toussaint L'Ouverture

Toussaint, the most unhappy Man of Men!
Whether the rural milk-maid by her cow
Sing in thy hearing, or thou liest now
Alone in some deep dungeon's earless den,
O miserable chieftain! where and when
Wilt thou find patience? Yet die not; do thou
Wear rather in thy bonds a cheerful brow:
Though fallen thyself, never to rise again,
Live, and take comfort. Thou hast left behind
Powers that will work for thee; air, earth, and skies;
There's not a breathing of the common wind
That will forget thee; thou has great allies;
Thy friends are exultations, agonies,
And love, and Man's unconquerable mind.


WILLIAM WORDSWORTH

## London, 1802

Milton! thou should'st be living at this hour:
England hath need of thee: she is a fen
Of stagnant waters: altar, sword and pen,
Fireside, the heroic wealth of hall and bower,
Have forfeited their ancient English dower
Of inward happiness. We are selfish men;
Oh! raise us up, return to us again;
And give us manners, virtue, freedom, power.
Thy soul was like a star and dwelt apart:
Thou hadst a voice whose sound was like the sea;
Pure as the naked heavens, majestic, free,

So didst thou travel on life's common way,
In cheerful godliness; and yet thy heart
The lowliest duties on itself did lay.


WILLIAM WORDSWORTH

## "The world is too much with us; late and soon"

The world is too much with us; late and soon,
Getting and spending, we lay waste our powers:
Little we see in Nature that is ours;
We have given our hearts away, a sordid boon!
This sea that bares her bosom to the moon;
The winds that will be howling at all hours
And are up-gathered now like sleeping flowers;
For this, for every thing, we are out of tune;
It moves us not—Great God! I'd rather be
A Pagan suckled in a creed outworn;
So might I, standing on this pleasant lea,
Have glimpses that would make me less forlorn
Have sight of Proteus coming from the sea;
Or hear old Triton blow his wreathed horn.


WILLIAM WORDSWORTH

## "Surprised by joy—impatient as the wind"

Surprised by joy—impatient as the wind
I turned to share the transport—Oh! with whom
But thee, long buried in the silent tomb,
That spot which no vicissitude can find?
Love, faithful love, recalled thee to my mind—
But how could I forget thee?—Through what power,
Even for the least division of an hour,
Have I been so beguiled as to be blind
To my most grievous loss?—That thought's return
Was the worst pang that sorrow ever bore,
Save one, one only, when I stood forlorn,
Knowing my heart's best treasure was no more;
That neither present time, nor years unborn
Could to my sight that heavenly face restore.

WILLIAM WORDSWORTH

## Mutability

From low to high doth dissolution climb,
And sinks from high to low, along a scale
Of awful notes, whose concord shall not fail;
A musical but melancholy chime,
Which they can hear who meddle not with crime,
Nor avarice, nor over-anxious care.
Truth fails not; but her outward forms that bear
The longest date do melt like frosty rime,
That in the morning whitened hill and plain
And is no more; drop like the tower sublime
Of yesterday, which royally did wear
Its crown of weeds, but could not even sustain
Some casual shout that broke the silent air,
Or the unimaginable touch of Time.

SAMUEL TAYLOR COLERIDGE

## To the River Otter

Dear native brook! wild streamlet of the west!
　How many various-fated years have past,
　What blissful and what anguished hours, since last
I skimmed the smooth thin stone along thy breast,
　Numbering its light leaps! Yet so deep impressed
　Sink the sweet scenes of childhood, that mine eyes
I never shut amid the sunny blaze,
　But straight with all their tints thy waters rise,
Thy crossing plank, thy margin's willowy maze,
　And bedded sand that veined with various dyes
Gleamed through thy bright transparence to the gaze!
　Visions of childhood! oft have ye beguiled
Lone manhood's cares, yet waking fondest sighs,
　Ah! that once more I were a careless child!

SAMUEL TAYLOR COLERIDGE
## *Work Without Hope*

*Lines Composed on a Day in February*

All Nature seems at work. Slugs leave their lair—
The bees are stirring—birds are on the wing—
   And Winter slumbering in the open air,
Wears on his smiling face a dream of Spring!
And I, the while, the sole unbusy thing,
Nor honey make, nor pair, nor build, nor sing.

Yet well I ken the banks where amaranths blow,
Have traced the fount whence streams of nectar flow.
Bloom, O ye amaranths! bloom for whom ye may—
For me ye bloom not! Glide, rich streams, away!
With lips unbrightened, wreathless brow, I stroll:
And would you learn the spells that drowse my soul?
Work without Hope draws nectar in a sieve,
And Hope without an object cannot live.


SAMUEL TAYLOR COLERIDGE
## *Pantisocracy*

No more my visionary soul shall dwell
On joys that were; no more endure to weigh
The shame and anguish of the evil day,
Wisely forgetful! O'er the ocean swell
Sublime of Hope, I seek the cottag'd dell
Where Virtue calm with careless step may stray,
And dancing to the moonlight roundelay,
The wizard Passions weave an holy spell.
Eyes that have ach'd with Sorrow! Ye shall weep
Tears of doubt-mingled joy, like theirs who start
From Precipices of distemper'd sleep,
On which the fierce-eyed Fiends their revels keep,
And see the rising Sun, and feel it dart
New rays of pleasance trembling to the heart.

MARY TIGHE

## Sonnet Addressed to My Mother

Oh, thou! whose tender smile most partially
　　Hath ever bless'd thy child: to thee belong
　　The graces which adorn my first wild song,
If aught of grace it knows: nor thou deny
Thine ever prompt attention to supply.
　　But let me lead thy willing ear along,
　　Where virtuous love still bids the strain prolong
His innocent applause; since from thine eye
　　The beams of love first charm'd my infant breast,
And from thy lip Affection's soothing voice
　　That eloquence of tenderness express'd,
Which still my grateful heart confess'd divine:
Oh! ever may its accents sweet rejoice
The soul which loves to own whate'er it has is thine!

ROBERT SOUTHEY

## *from* Poems on the Slave Trade

VI

High in the air exposed the slave is hung
　　To all the birds of Heaven, their living food!
He groans not, though awaked by that fierce sun
　　New tortures live to drink their parent blood!
He groans not, though the gorging vulture tear
　　The quivering fiber! Hither gaze O ye
　　Who tore this man from peace and liberty!
Gaze hither ye who weigh with scrupulous care
The right and prudent; for beyond the grave
　　There is another world! and call to mind,
　　Ere your decrees proclaim to all mankind
Murder is legalized, that there the slave
Before the Eternal, "thunder-tongued shall plead
Against the deep damnation of your deed."

WALTER SAVAGE LANDOR
## To Robert Browning

There is delight in singing, tho' none hear
Beside the singer; and there is delight
In praising, tho' the praiser sit alone
And see the prais'd far off him, far above.
Shakespeare is not our poet, but the world's,
Therefore on him no speech! and brief for thee,
Browning! Since Chaucer was alive and hale,
No man hath walkt along our roads with step
So active, so inquiring eye, or tongue
So varied in discourse. But warmer climes
Give brighter plumage, stronger wing: the breeze
Of Alpine highths thou playest with, borne on
Beyond Sorrento and Amalfi, where
The Siren waits thee, singing song for song.

LEIGH HUNT
## To the Grasshopper and the Cricket

Green little vaulter in the sunny grass,
   Catching your heart up at the feel of June,
   Sole voice that's heard amidst the lazy noon,
When even the bees lag at the summoning brass
And you, warm little housekeeper, who class
   With those who think the candles come too
      soon,
   Loving the fire, and with your tricksome tune
Nick the glad silent moments as they pass;

Oh sweet and tiny cousins, that belong,
   One to the fields, the other to the hearth,
Both have your sunshine; both, though small, are
   strong
   At your clear hearts; and both seem given to
     earth
To ring in thoughtful ears this natural song—
   Indoors and out, summer and winter, Mirth.

GEORGE GORDON, LORD BYRON

## Sonnet on Chillon

Eternal spirit of the chainless mind!
    Brightest in dungeons, Liberty! thou art,
    For there thy habitation is the heart—
The heart which love of thee alone can bind;
And when thy sons to fetters are consigned—
    To fetters, and the damp vault's dayless gloom,
    Their country conquers with their martyrdom,
And Freedom's fame finds wings on every wind.
Chillon! thy prison is a holy place,
    And thy sad floor an altar—for 'twas trod,
Until his very steps have left a trace
    Worn, as if thy cold pavement were a sod,
By Bonnivard!—May none those marks efface!
    For they appeal from tyranny to God.


GEORGE GORDON, LORD BYRON

## "Rousseau—Voltaire—our Gibbon—and de Staël"

Rousseau—Voltaire—our Gibbon—and de Staël—
    Leman! these names are worthy of thy shore,
    Thy shore of names like these! wert thou no more,
Their memory thy remembrance would recall:
To them thy banks were lovely as to all,
    But they have made them lovelier, for the lore
    Of mighty minds doth hallow in the core
Of human hearts the ruin of a wall
    Where dwelt the wise and wondrous; but by *thee*
How much more, Lake of Beauty! do we feel,
    In sweetly gliding o'er thy crystal sea,
The wild glow of that not ungentle zeal,
    Which of the heirs of immortality
Is proud, and makes the breath of glory real!

MARY LOCKE

## "I hate the Spring in parti-colored vest"

I hate the Spring in parti-colored vest,
    What time she breathes upon the opening rose,
When every vale in cheerfulness is dressed,
    And man with grateful admiration glows.
Still may he glow, and love the sprightly scene,
    Who ne'er has felt the iron hand of Care;
But what avails to me a sky serene,
    Whose mind is torn with Anguish and Despair?
Give me the Winter's desolating reign,
    The gloomy sky in which no star is found;
Howl, ye wild winds, across the desert plain;
    Ye waters roar, ye falling woods resound!
Congenial horrors, hail! I love to see
All Nature mourn, and share my misery.

PERCY BYSSHE SHELLEY

## Ozymandias

I met a traveler from an antique land
Who said: Two vast and trunkless legs of stone
Stand in the desert. Near them, on the sand,
Half sunk, a shattered visage lies, whose frown,
And wrinkled lip, and sneer of cold command,
Tell that its sculptor well those passions read
Which yet survive, stamped on these lifeless things,
The hand that mocked them and the heart that fed;
And on the pedestal these words appear:
"My name is Ozymandias, king of kings:
Look on my works, ye Mighty, and despair!"
Nothing beside remains. Round the decay
Of that colossal wreck, boundless and bare,
The lone and level sands stretch far away.

PERCY BYSSHE SHELLEY

## *England in 1819*

An old, mad, blind, despised, and dying king,—
Princes, the dregs of their dull race, who flow
Through public scorn—mud from a muddy spring,—
Rulers, who neither see, nor feel, nor know,
But leech-like to their fainting country cling,
Till they drop, blind in blood, without a blow,—
A people starved and stabbed in the untilled field,—
An army, which liberticide and prey
Makes as a two-edged sword to all who wield,
Golden and sanguine laws which tempt and slay,—
Religion Christless, Godless—a book sealed;
A Senate—Time's worst statute unrepealed,—
Are graves, from which a glorious Phantom may
Burst, to illumine our tempestuous day.


PERCY BYSSHE SHELLEY

## *Ode to the West Wind*

I

O wild West Wind, thou breath of Autumn's being,
Thou, from whose unseen presence the leaves dead
Are driven, like ghosts from an enchanter fleeing,

Yellow, and black, and pale, and hectic red,
Pestilence-stricken multitudes: O, thou,
Who chariotest to their dark wintry bed

The winged seeds, where they lie cold and low,
Each like a corpse within its grave, until
Thine azure sister of the spring shall blow

Her clarion o'er the dreaming earth, and fill
(Driving sweet buds like flocks to feed in air)
With living hues and odors plain and hill:

Wild Spirit, which art moving everywhere;
Destroyer and preserver; hear, O hear!

II

Thou on whose stream, 'mid the steep sky's
   commotion,
Loose clouds like earth's decaying leaves are shed,
Shook from the tangled boughs of Heaven and Ocean,

Angels of rain and lightning: there are spread
On the blue surface of thine aery surge,
Like the bright hair uplifted from the head

Of some fierce Mænad, even from the dim verge
Of the horizon to the zenith's height
The locks of the approaching storm. Thou Dirge

Of the dying year, to which this closing night
Will be the dome of a vast sepulchre,
Vaulted with all thy congregated might

Of vapours, from whose solid atmosphere
Black rain and fire and hail will burst: O, hear!

III

Thou who didst waken from his summer dreams
The blue Mediterranean, where he lay,
Lulled by the coil of his crystalline streams,

Beside a pumice isle in Baiæ's bay,
And saw in sleep old palaces and towers
Quivering within the wave's intenser day,

All overgrown with azure moss and flowers
So sweet, the sense faints picturing them! Thou
For whose path the Atlantic's level powers

Cleave themselves into chasms, while far below
The sea-blooms and the oozy woods which wear
The sapless foliage of the ocean, know

Thy voice, and suddenly grow grey with fear,
And tremble and despoil themselves: O, hear!

IV

If I were a dead leaf thou mightest bear;
If I were a swift cloud to fly with thee;
A wave to pant beneath thy power, and share

The impulse of thy strength, only less free
Than thou, O Uncontrollable! If even
I were as in my boyhood, and could be

The comrade of thy wanderings over Heaven,
As then, when to outstrip thy skiey speed
Scarce seemed a vision; I would ne'er have striven

As thus with thee in prayer in my sore need.
Oh! lift me as wave, a leaf, a cloud!
I fall upon the thorns of life! I bleed!

A heavy weight of hours has chained and bowed
One too like thee: tameless, and swift, and proud.

V

Make me thy lyre, even as the forest is:
What if my leaves are falling like its own!
The tumult of thy mighty harmonies

Will take from both a deep, autumnal tone,
Sweet though in sadness. Be thou, Spirit fierce,
My spirit! Be thou me, impetuous one!

Drive my dead thoughts over the universe
Like withered leaves to quicken a new birth!
And, by the incantation of this verse,

Scatter, as from an unextinguished hearth
Ashes and sparks, my words among mankind!
Be through my lips to unawakened Earth

The trumpet of a prophecy! O Wind,
If Winter comes, can Spring be far behind?

JOHN CLARE

## Schoolboys in Winter

The schoolboys still their morning rambles take
To neighbouring village school with playing speed,
Loitering with pastimes' leisure till they quake,
Oft looking up the wild geese droves to heed,
Watching the letters which their journeys make,
Or plucking 'awes on which the fieldfares feed,
And hips and sloes—and on each shallow lake
Making glib slides where they like shadows go
Till some fresh pastimes in their minds awake
And off they start anew and hasty blow
Their numbed and clumpsing fingers till they glow,
Then races with their shadows wildly run
That stride, huge giants, o'er the shining snow
In the pale splendour of the winter sun.

JOHN CLARE

## To John Clare

Well, honest John, how fare you now at home?
The spring is come and birds are building nests,
The old cock robin to the sty is come
With olive feathers and its ruddy breast,
And the old cock with wattles and red comb
Struts with the hens and seems to like some best,

Then crows and looks about for little crumbs
Swept out by little folks an hour ago;
The pigs sleep in the sty, the book man comes,
The little boy lets home-close nesting go
And pockets tops and taws where daisies bloom
To look at the new number just laid down
With lots of pictures and good stories too
And Jack-the-giant-killer's high renown.

JOHN CLARE

### To Wordsworth

Wordsworth I love, his books are like the fields,
   Not filled with flowers, but works of human kind;
The pleasant weed a fragrant pleasure yields,
   The briar and broomwood shaken by the wind,
The thorn and bramble o'er the water shoot
   A finer flower than gardens e'er gave birth,
The aged huntsman grubbing up the root—
   I love them all as tenants of the earth:
Where genius is, there often die the seeds;
   What critics throw away I love the more;
I love to stoop and look among the weeds,
   To find a flower I never knew before;
Wordsworth, go on—a greater poet be;
Merit will live, though parties disagree!

JOHN CLARE

### Sonnet: "I Am"

I feel I am—I only know I am
And plod upon the earth as dull and void:
Earth's prison chilled my body with its dram
Of dullness and my soaring thoughts destroyed,
I fled to solitudes from passion's dream,
But strife pursued—I only know I am,
I was a being created in the race
Of men disdaining bounds of place and time—

A spirit that could travel o'er the space
Of earth and heaven like a thought sublime,
Tracing creation, like my maker, free—
A soul unshackled—like eternity,
Spurning earth's vain and soul-debasing thrall.
But now I only know I am—that's all.

JOHN KEATS

## On first looking into Chapman's Homer

Much have I travell'd in the realms of gold,
    And many goodly states and kingdoms seen;
    Round many western islands have I been
Which bards in fealty to Apollo hold.
Oft of one wide expanse had I been told,
    That deep-brow'd Homer ruled as his demesne:
    Yet did I never breathe its pure serene
Till I heard Chapman speak out loud and bold:
Then felt I like some watcher of the skies
    When a new planet swims into his ken;
Or like stout Cortez when with eagle eyes
    He stared at the Pacific—and all his men
Look'd at each other with a wild surmise—
    Silent, upon a peak in Darien.

JOHN KEATS

## On seeing the Elgin Marbles

My spirit is too weak—mortality
    Weighs heavily on me like unwilling sleep,
    And each imagined pinnacle and steep
Of godlike hardship, tells me I must die
Like a sick eagle looking at the sky.
    Yet 'tis a gentle luxury to weep
    That I have not the cloudy winds to keep,
Fresh for the opening of the morning's eye.
Such dim-conceived glories of the brain
    Bring round the heart an undescribable feud;

So do these wonders a most dizzy pain,
    That mingles Grecian grandeur with the rude
Wasting of old time—with a billowy main—
    A sun—a shadow of a magnitude.

JOHN KEATS

### *"When I have fears that I may cease to be"*

When I have fears that I may cease to be
    Before my pen has glean'd my teeming brain,
Before high-piled books, in charactery,
    Hold like rich garners the full ripen'd grain;
When I behold, upon the night's starr'd face,
    Huge cloudy symbols of a high romance,
And think that I may never live to trace
    Their shadows, with the magic hand of chance;
And when I feel, fair creature of an hour,
    That I shall never look upon thee more,
Never have relish in the faery power
    Of unreflecting love;—then on the shore
Of the wide world I stand alone, and think
Till love and fame to nothingness do sink.

JOHN KEATS

### *To Sleep*

O soft embalmer of the still midnight!
    Shutting, with careful fingers and benign,
Our gloom-pleased eyes, embower'd from the light,
    Enshaded in forgetfulness divine;
O soothest Sleep! if so it please thee, close,
    In midst of this thine hymn, my willing eyes,
Or wait the amen, ere thy poppy throws
    Around my bed its lulling charities;
Then save me, or the passèd day will shine
Upon my pillow, breeding many woes;
    Save me from curious conscience, that still lords
Its strength in darkness, burrowing like a mole;

Turn the key deftly in the oilèd wards,
And seal the hushèd casket of my soul.

JOHN KEATS

## *"Bright Star, would I were stedfast as thou art"*

Bright Star, would I were stedfast as thou art—
    Not in lone splendor hung aloft the night
And watching, with eternal lids apart,
    Like nature's patient, sleepless Eremite,
The moving waters at their priestlike task
    Of pure ablution round earth's human shores,
Or gazing on the new soft-fallen masque
    Of snow upon the mountains and the moors.
No—yet still stedfast, still unchangeable,
    Pillow'd upon my fair love's ripening breast,
To feel for ever its soft swell and fall,
    Awake for ever in a sweet unrest,
Still, still to hear her tender-taken breath,
And so live ever—or else swoon to death.

JOHN KEATS

## *To Fanny*

I cry your mercy—pity—love!—ay, love!
    Merciful love that tantalises not
One-thoughted, never-wandering, guileless love,
    Unmask'd, and being seen—without a blot!
O! let me have thee whole,—all—all—be mine!
    That shape, that fairness, that sweet minor zest
Of love, your kiss,—those hands, those eyes divine,
    That warm, white, lucent, million-pleasured
        breast,—
Yourself—your soul—in pity give me all,
    Withhold no atom's atom or I die,
Or living on, perhaps, your wretched thrall,
    Forget, in the mist of idle misery,
Life's purposes,—the palate of my mind
Losing its gust, and my ambition blind!

ELIZABETH BARRETT BROWNING

## *from* Sonnets from the Portuguese

### XVIII

I never gave a lock of hair away
To a man, Dearest, except this to thee,
Which now upon my fingers thoughtfully
I ring out to the full brown length and say
"Take it." My day of youth went yesterday;
My hair no longer bounds to my foot's glee,
Nor plant I it from rose- or myrtle-tree,
As girls do, any more: it only may
Now shade on two pale checks the mark of tears,
Taught drooping from the head that hangs aside
Through sorrow's trick. I thought the funeral-shears
Would take this first, but Love is justified,—
Take it thou,—finding pure, from all those years,
The kiss my mother left here when she died.


ELIZABETH BARRETT BROWNING

## *from* Sonnets from the Portuguese

### XLIII

How do I love thee? Let me count the ways.
I love thee to the depth and breadth and height
My soul can reach, when feeling out of sight
For the ends of Being and ideal Grace.
I love thee to the level of everyday's
Most quiet need, by sun and candlelight.
I love thee freely, as men strive for Right;
I love thee purely, as they turn from Praise.
I love thee with the passion put to use
In my old griefs, and with my childhood's faith.
I love thee with a love I seemed to lose
With my lost saints,—I love thee with the breath,
Smiles, tears, of all my life!—and, if God choose,
I shall but love thee better after death.

JOHN GREENLEAF WHITTIER
## To a Cape Ann Schooner

Luck to the craft that bears this name of mine,
Good fortune follow with her golden spoon
The glazèd hat and tarry pantaloon;
And wheresoe'er her keel shall cut the brine,
Cod, hake and haddock quarrel for her line.
Shipped with her crew, whatever wind may blow,
Or tides delay, my wish with her shall go,
Fishing by proxy. Would that it might show
At need her course, in lack of sun and star,
Where icebergs threaten, and the sharp reefs are;
Lift the blind fog on Anticosti's lee
And Avalon's rock; make populous the sea
Round Grand Manan with eager finny swarms,
Break the long calms, and charm away the storms.

HENRY WADSWORTH LONGFELLOW
## Mezzo Cammin

Half of my life is gone, and I have let
    The years slip from me and have not fulfilled
    The aspiration of my youth, to build
    Some tower of song with lofty parapet.
Not indolence, nor pleasure, nor the fret
    Of restless passions that would not be stilled,
    But sorrow, and a care that almost killed,
    Kept me from what I may accomplish yet;
Though, half-way up the hill, I see the Past
    Lying beneath me with its sounds and sights,—
    A city in the twilight dim and vast,
With smoking roofs, soft bells, and gleaming lights,—
    And hear above me on the autumnal blast
    The cataract of Death far thundering from the
        heights.

HENRY WADSWORTH LONGFELLOW
## Night

Into the darkness and the hush of night
   Slowly the landscape sinks, and fades away,
   And with it fade the phantoms of the day,
   The ghosts of men and things, that haunt the
      light.
The crowd, the clamor, the pursuit, the flight,
   The unprofitable splendor and display,
   The agitations, and the cares that prey
   Upon our hearts, all vanish out of sight.
The better life begins; the world no more
   Molests us; all its records we erase
   From the dull common-place book of our lives,
That like a palimpsest is written o'er
   With trivial incidents of time and place,
   And lo! the ideal, hidden beneath, revives.


HENRY WADSWORTH LONGFELLOW
## The Cross of Snow

In the long, sleepless watches of the night,
   A gentle face—the face of one long dead—
   Looks at me from the wall, where round its head
   The night-lamp casts a halo of pale light.
Here in this room she died; and soul more white
   Never through martyrdom of fire was led
   To its repose; nor can in books be read
   The legend of a life more benedight.
There is a mountain in the distant West
   That, sun-defying, in its deep ravines
   Displays a cross of snow upon its side.
Such is the cross I wear upon my breast
   These eighteen years, through all the changing
      scenes
   And seasons, changeless since the day she died.

EDGAR ALLAN POE

## Sonnet—To Science

Science! true daughter of Old Time thou art!
   Who alterest all things with thy peering eyes.
Why preyest thou thus upon the poet's heart,
   Vulture, whose wings are dull realities?
How should he love thee? or how deem thee wise,
   Who wouldst not leave him in his wandering
To seek for treasure in the jewelled skies,
   Albeit he soared with an undaunted wing?
Hast thou not dragged Diana from her car?
   And driven the Hamadryad from the wood
To seek a shelter in some happier star?
   Hast thou not torn the Naiad from her flood,
The Elfin from the green grass, and from me
The summer dream beneath the tamarind tree?

ALFRED, LORD TENNYSON

## "How thought you that this thing could captivate?"

How thought you that this thing could captivate?
   What are those graces that could make her dear,
   Who is not worth the notice of a sneer
To rouse the vapid devil of her hate?
A speech conventional, so void of weight
   That after it has buzzed about one's ear,
   'Twere rich refreshment for a week to hear
The dentist babble or the barber prate;

A hand displayed with many a little art;
   An eye that glances on her neighbour's dress;
   A foot too often shown for my regard;
An angel's form—a waiting-woman's heart;
   A perfect-featured face, expressionless,
   Insipid, as the Queen upon a card.

MARGARET FULLER

## Flaxman

We deemed the secret lost, the spirit gone,
Which spake in Greek simplicity of thought,
And in the forms of gods and heroes wrought
Eternal beauty from the sculptured stone,—
A higher charm than modern culture won
With all the wealth of metaphysic lore,
Gifted to analyze, dissect, explore.
A many-colored light flows from one sun;
Art, 'neath its beams, a motley thread has spun;
The prism modifies the perfect day;
But thou hast known such mediums to shun,
And cast once more on life a pure, white ray.
Absorbed in the creations of thy mind,
Forgetting daily self, my truest self I find.

ROBERT BROWNING

## Why I Am a Liberal

"Why?" Because all I haply can and do,
    And that I am now, all I hope to be,—
    Whence comes it save from fortune setting
        free
Body and soul the purpose to pursue,
God traced for both? If letters not a few,
    Of prejudice, convention, fall from me,
    These shall I bid men—each in his degree
Also God-guided—bear, and gaily, too?
But little do or can the best of us:
    That little is achieved through Liberty.
Who, then, dares hold, emancipated thus,
    His fellow shall continue bound? Not I,
Who live, love, labor freely, nor discuss
    A brother's right to freedom. That is "Why."

EDWARD LEAR

## Cold Are the Crabs

Cold are the crabs that crawl on yonder hills,
Colder the cucumbers that grow beneath,
And colder still the brazen chops that wreathe
    The tedious gloom of philosophic pills!
For when the tardy film of nectar fills
The ample bowls of demons and of men,
There lurks the feeble mouse, the homely hen,
    And there the porcupine with all her quills.
Yet much remains—to weave a solemn strain
That lingering sadly—slowly dies away,
Daily departing with departing day.
A pea-green gamut on a distant plain
When wily walruses in congress meet—
    Such such is life—

JONES VERY

## The New Birth

'Tis a new life—thoughts move not as they did
With slow uncertain steps across my mind,
In thronging haste fast pressing on they bid
The portals open to the viewless wind;
That comes not, save when in the dust is laid
The crown of pride that gilds each mortal brow,
And from before man's vision melting fade
The heavens and earth—Their walls are falling now—
Fast crowding on each thought claims utterance
    strong,
Storm-lifted waves swift rushing to the shore
On from the sea they send their shouts along,
Back through the cave-worn rocks their thunders
    roar,
And I a child of God by Christ made free
Start from death's slumbers to eternity.

JONES VERY

## The Dead

I see them crowd on crowd they walk the earth
Dry, leafless trees no Autumn wind laid bare;
And in their nakedness find cause for mirth,
And all unclad would winter's rudeness dare;
No sap doth through their clattering branches flow,
Whence springing leaves and blossoms bright
    appear;
Their hearts the living God have ceased to know,
Who gives the spring time to th'expectant year;
They mimic life, as if from him to steal
His glow of health to paint the livid cheek;
They borrow words for thoughts they cannot feel,
That with a seeming heart their tongue may speak;
And in their show of life more dead they live
Than those that to the earth with many tears they
    give.

JONES VERY

## Yourself

'Tis to yourself I speak; you cannot know
Him whom I call in speaking such an one,
For thou beneath the earth liest buried low,
Which he alone as living walks upon;
Thou mayst at times have heard him speak to you,
And often wished perchance that you were he;
And I must ever wish that it were true,
For then thou couldst hold fellowship with me;
But now thou hearst us talk as strangers, met
Above the room wherein thou liest abed;
A word perhaps loud spoken thou mayst get,
Or hear our feet when heavily they tread;
But he who speaks, or him who's spoken to,
Must both remain as strangers still to you.

WALT WHITMAN

## *Patroling Barnegat*

Wild, wild the storm, and the sea high running,
Steady the roar of the gale, with incessant undertone
    muttering,
Shouts of demoniac laughter fitfully piercing and
    pealing,
Waves, air, midnight, their savagest trinity lashing,
Out in the shadows there milk-white combs careering,
On beachy slush and sand spirts of snow fierce
    slanting,
Where through the murk the easterly death-wind
    breasting,
Through cutting swirl and spray watchful and firm
    advancing,
(That in the distance! is that a wreck? is the red signal
    flaring?)
Slush and sand of the beach tireless till daylight
    wending,
Steadily, slowly, through hoarse roar never remitting,
Along the midnight edge by those milk-white combs
    careering,
A group of dim, weird forms, struggling, the night
    confronting,
That savage trinity warily watching.


FREDERICK GODDARD TUCKERMAN

## *from* Sonnets, First Series

X

An upper chamber in a darkened house,
Where, ere his footsteps reached ripe manhood's
    brink,
Terror and anguish were his cup to drink,—
I cannot rid the thought, nor hold it close;
But dimly dream upon that man alone;—
Now though the autumn clouds most softly pass;

The cricket chides beneath the doorstep stone,
And greener than the season grows the grass.
Nor can I drop my lids, nor shade my brows,
But there he stands beside the lifted sash;
And, with a swooning of the heart, I think
Where the black shingles slope to meet the boughs,
And—shattered on the roof like smallest snows—
The tiny petals of the mountain-ash.


FREDERICK GODDARD TUCKERMAN

### *from* Sonnets, Second Series

**VII**

His heart was in his garden; but his brain
Wandered at will among the fiery stars:
Bards, heroes, prophets, Homers, Hamilcars,
With many angels, stood, his eye to gain;
The devils, too, were his familiars.
And yet the cunning florist held his eyes
Close to the ground,—a tulip-bulb his prize,—
And talked of tan and bone-dust, cutworms, grubs,
As though all Nature held no higher strain;
Or, if he spoke of Art, he made the theme
Flow through box-borders, turf, and flower-tubs;
Or, like a garden-engine's, steered the stream,—
Now spouted rainbows to the silent skies;
Now kept it flat, and raked the walks and shrubs.


FREDERICK GODDARD TUCKERMAN

### *from* Sonnets, Third Series

**X**

Sometimes I walk where the deep water dips
Against the land. Or on where fancy drives
I walk and muse aloud, like one who strives
To tell his half-shaped thought with stumbling lips,
And view the ocean sea, the ocean ships,
With joyless heart: still but myself I find

And restless phantoms of my restless mind:
Only the moaning of my wandering words,
Only the wailing of the wheeling plover,
And this high rock beneath whose base the sea
Has wormed long caverns, like my tears in me;
And hard like this I stand, and beaten and blind,
This desolate rock with lichens rusted over,
Hoar with salt-sleet and chalkings of the birds.


MATTHEW ARNOLD

## Shakespeare

Others abide our question. Thou art free.
We ask and ask—Thou smilest and art still,
Out-topping knowledge. For the loftiest hill,
Who to the stars uncrowns his majesty,

Planting his steadfast footsteps in the sea,
Making the heaven of heavens his dwelling-place,
Spares but the cloudy border of his base
To the foiled searching of mortality;

And thou, who didst the stars and sunbeams know,
Self-schooled, self-scanned, self-honoured, self-secure,
Didst tread on earth unguessed at.—Better so!

All pains the immortal spirit must endure,
All weakness which impairs, all griefs which bow,
Find their sole speech in that victorious brow.


WILLIAM ALLINGHAM

## In Snow

O English mother, in the ruddy glow
Hugging your baby closer when outside
You see the silent, soft, and cruel snow
Falling again, and think what ills betide
Unshelter'd creatures,—your sad thoughts may go

Where War and Winter now, two spectre-wolves,
Hunt in the freezing vapour that involves
Those Asian peaks of ice and gulfs below.
Does this young Soldier heed the snow that fills
His mouth and open eyes? or mind, in truth,
To-night, *his* mother's parting syllables?
Ha! is't a red coat?—Merely blood. Keep ruth
For others; this is but an Afghan youth
Shot by the stranger on his native hills.

GEORGE MEREDITH

## Lucifer in Starlight

On a starred night Prince Lucifer uprose.
Tired of his dark dominion swung the fiend
Above the rolling ball in cloud part screened,
Where sinners hugged their spectre of repose.
Poor prey to his hot fit of pride were those.
And now upon his western wing he leaned,
Now his huge bulk o'er Afric's sands careened,
Now the black planet shadowed Arctic snows.
Soaring through wider zones that pricked his scars
With memory of the old revolt from Awe,
He reached a middle height, and at the stars,
Which are the brain of heaven, he looked, and sank.
Around the ancient track marched, rank on rank,
The army of unalterable law.

DANTE GABRIEL ROSSETTI

## *from* The House of Life

### XVIII. Genius in Beauty

Beauty like hers is genius. Not the call
   Of Homer's or of Dante's heart sublime,—
   Not Michael's hand furrowing the zones of time,—
Is more with compassed mysteries musical;
Nay, not in Spring's or Summer's sweet footfall
   More gathered gifts exuberant Life bequeathes

Than doth this sovereign face, whose love-spell
    breathes
Even from its shadowed contour on the wall.

As many men are poets in their youth,
    But for one sweet-strung soul the wires prolong
    Even through all change the indomitable song;
So in like wise the envenomed years, whose tooth
Rends shallower grace with ruin void of ruth,
    Upon this beauty's power shall wreak no wrong.

DANTE GABRIEL ROSSETTI

### *from* The House of Life

#### XLVII. Broken Music

The mother will not turn, who thinks she hears
    Her nursling's speech first grow articulate;
    But breathless with averted eyes elate
She sits, with open lips and open ears,
That it may call her twice. 'Mid doubts and fears
    Thus oft my soul has hearkened; till the song,
    A central moan for days, at length found tongue,
And the sweet music welled and the sweet tears.

But now, whatever while the soul is fain
    To list that wonted murmur, as it were
The speech-bound sea-shell's low importunate
    strain,—
    No breath of song, thy voice alone is there,
O bitterly beloved! and all her gain
    Is but the pang of unpermitted prayer.

DANTE GABRIEL ROSSETTI

### *from* The House of Life

#### LXXXIII. Barren Spring

Once more the changed year's turning wheel returns:
    And as a girl sails balanced in the wind,

And now before and now again behind
Stoops as it swoops, with cheek that laughs and
    burns,—
So Spring comes merry towards me here, but earns
    No answering smile from me, whose life is twin'd
    With the dead boughs that winter still must bind,
And whom to-day the Spring no more concerns.

Behold, this crocus is a withering flame;
    This snowdrop, snow; this apple-blossom's part
    To breed the fruit that breeds the serpent's art.
Nay, for these Spring-flowers, turn thy face from
    them,
Nor stay till on the year's last lily-stem
    The white cup shrivels round the golden heart.

DANTE GABRIEL ROSSETTI

## *from* The House of Life

### XCVII. A Superscription

Look in my face; my name is Might-have-been;
    I am also called No-more, Too-late, Farewell;
    Unto thine ear I hold the dead-sea shell
Cast up thy Life's foam-fretted feet between;
Unto thine eyes the glass where that is seen
    Which had Life's form and Love's, but by my spell
    Is now a shaken shadow intolerable,
Of ultimate things unuttered the frail screen.

Mark me, how still I am! But should there dart
    One moment through thy soul the soft surprise
    Of that winged Peace which lulls the breath of
        sighs,—
Then shalt thou see me smile, and turn apart
Thy visage to mine ambush at thy heart
    Sleepless with cold commemorative eyes.

CHRISTINA ROSSETTI

## Remember

Remember me when I am gone away,
  Gone far away into the silent land;
  When you can no more hold me by the hand,
Nor I half turn to go yet turning stay.
Remember me when no more day by day
  You tell me of our future that you planned:
  Only remember me; you understand
It will be late to counsel then or pray.
Yet if you should forget me for a while
  And afterwards remember, do not grieve:
  For if the darkness and corruption leave
A vestige of the thoughts that once I had,
Better by far you should forget and smile
  Than you should remember and be sad.

CHRISTINA ROSSETTI

## In an Artist's Studio

One face looks out from all his canvasses,
  One selfsame figure sits or walks or leans;
  We found her hidden just behind those screens,
That mirror gave back all her loveliness.
A queen in opal or in ruby dress,
  A nameless girl in freshest summer greens,
  A saint, an angel;—every canvas means
The same one meaning, neither more nor less.
He feeds upon her face by day and night,
  And she with true kind eyes looks back on him
Fair as the moon and joyful as the light:
  Not wan with waiting, not with sorrow dim;
Not as she is, but was when hope shone bright;
  Not as she is, but as she fills his dream.

ALGERNON CHARLES SWINBURNE

## On the Russian persecution of the Jews

O son of man, by lying tongues adored,
   By slaughterous hands of slaves with feet red-shod
   In carnage deep as ever Christian trod
Profaned with prayer and sacrifice abhorred
And incense from the trembling tyrant's horde,
   Brute worshippers or wielders of the rod,
   Most murderous even of all that call thee God,
Most treacherous even that ever called thee Lord;
Face loved of little children long ago,
   Head hated of the priests and rulers then,
      If thou see this, or hear these hounds of thine
      Run ravening as the Gadarean swine,
Say, was not this thy Passion, to foreknow
   In death's worst hour the works of Christian men?

WILFRID SCAWEN BLUNT

## St. Valentine's Day

Today, all day, I rode upon the down,
With hounds and horsemen, a brave company;
On this side in its glory lay the sea,
On that the Sussex weald, a sea of brown.
The wind was light, and brightly the sun shone,
And still we gallop'd on from gorse to gorse:
And once, when check'd, a thrush sang, and my horse
Prick'd his quick ears as to a sound unknown.
I knew the Spring was come. I knew it even
Better than all by this, that through my chase
In bush and stone and hill and sea and heaven
I seem'd to see and follow still your face.
Your face my quarry was. For it I rode,
My horse a thing of wings, myself a god.

THOMAS HARDY

## *Hap*

If but some vengeful god would call to me
From up the sky, and laugh: "Thou suffering thing,
Know that thy sorrow is my ecstasy,
That thy love's loss is my hate's profiting!"

Then would I bear it, clench myself, and die,
Steeled by the sense of ire unmerited;
Half-eased in that a Powerfuller than I
Had willed and meted me the tears I shed.

But not so. How arrives it joy lies slain,
And why unblooms the best hope ever sown?
—Crass Casualty obstructs the sun and rain,
And dicing Time for gladness casts a moan. . . .
These purblind Doomsters had as readily strown
Blisses about my pilgrimage as pain.

THOMAS HARDY

## *from* She, to Him

I

When you shall see me in the toils of Time,
My lauded beauties carried off from me,
My eyes no longer stars as in their prime,
My name forgot of Maiden Fair and Free;

When in your being heart concedes to mind,
And judgement, though you scarce its process know,
Recalls the excellences I once enshrined,
And you are irk'd that they have wither'd so;

Remembering mine the loss is, not the blame,
That Sportsman Time but rears his brood to kill,
Knowing me in my soul the very same—
One who would die to spare you touch of ill!—

Will you not grant to old affection's claim
The hand of friendship down Life's sunless hill?

THOMAS HARDY

## *from* She, to Him

II

Perhaps, long hence, when I have passed away,
Some other's feature, accent, thought like mine,
Will carry you back to what I used to say,
And bring some memory of your love's decline.

Then you may pause awhile and think, "Poor jade!"
And yield a sigh to me—as ample due,
Not as the tittle of a debt unpaid
To one who could resign her all to you—

And thus reflecting, you will never see
That your thin thought, in two small words conveyed,
Was no such fleeting phantom-thought to me,
But the Whole Life wherein my part was played;
And you amid its fitful masquerade
A Thought—as I in your life seem to be!

THOMAS HARDY

## *The Pity of It*

I walked in loamy Wessex lanes, afar
From rail-track and from highway, and I heard
In field and farmstead many an ancient word
Of local lineage like 'Thu bist', 'Er war',

'Ich woll', 'Er sholl', and by-talk similar,
Nigh as they speak who in this month's moon gird
At England's very loins, thereunto spurred
By gangs whose glory threats and slaughters are.

Then seemed a Heart crying: 'Whosoever they be
At root and bottom of this, who flung this flame
Between kin folk kin tongued even as are we,

'Sinister, ugly, lurid, be their fame;
May their familiars grow to shun their name,
And their brood perish everlastingly.'

GERARD MANLEY HOPKINS

## God's Grandeur

The world is charged with the grandeur of God.
    It will flame out, like shining from shook foil;
    It gathers to a greatness, like the ooze of oil
Crushed. Why do men then now not reck his rod?
Generations have trod, have trod, have trod;
    And all is seared with trade; bleared, smeared with toil;
    And wears man's smudge and shares man's smell:
        the soil
Is bare now, nor can foot feel, being shod.

And for all this, nature is never spent;
    There lives the dearest freshness deep down things;
And though the last lights off the black West went
    Oh, morning, at the brown brink eastward, springs—
Because the Holy Ghost over the bent
    World broods with warm breast and with ah!
        bright wings.

GERARD MANLEY HOPKINS

## The Windhover

*To Christ our Lord*

I caught this morning morning's minion, king-
    dom of daylight's dauphin, dapple-dawn-drawn
        Falcon, in his riding

Of the rolling level underneath him steady air, and
  striding
High there, how he rung upon the rein of a
  wimpling wing
In his ecstasy! then off, off forth on swing,
  As a skate's heel sweeps smooth on a bow-bend:
  the hurl and gliding
Rebuffed the big wind. My heart in hiding
Stirred for a bird,—the achieve of, the mastery of
  the thing!

Brute beauty and valour and act, oh, air, pride,
  plume, here
  Buckle! AND the fire that breaks from thee then, a
  billion
Times told lovelier, more dangerous. O my chevalier!

No wonder of it: shéer plód makes plough down
  sillion
Shine, and blue-bleak embers, ah my dear,
  Fall, gall themselves, and gash gold-vermilion.

GERARD MANLEY HOPKINS

### "As kingfishers catch fire, dragonflies draw flame"

As kingfishers catch fire, dragonflies draw flame;
As tumbled over rim in roundy wells
Stones ring; like each tucked string tells, each hung
  bell's
Bow swung finds tongue to fling out broad its name;
Each mortal thing does one thing and the same:
Deals out that being indoors each one dwells;
Selves—goes itself; *myself* it speaks and spells,
Crying *Whát I dó is me: for that I came.*

I say móre: the just man justices;
Keeps gráce: thát keeps all his goings graces;

Acts in God's eye what in God's eye he is—
Christ—for Christ plays in ten thousand places,
Lovely in limbs, and lovely in eyes not his
To the Father through the features of men's faces.

GERARD MANLEY HOPKINS

### "Not, I'll not, carrion comfort, Despair, not feast on thee"

Not, I'll not, carrion comfort, Despair, not feast on
      thee;
Not untwist—slack they may be—these last
      strands of man
In me ór, most weary, cry *I can no more.* I can;
Can something, hope, wish day come, not choose
      not to be.
But ah, but O thou terrible, why wouldst thou rude
      on me
Thy wring-world right foot rock? lay a lionlimb
      against me? scan
With darksome devouring eyes my bruisèd bones?
      and fan,
O in turns of tempest, me heaped there; me frantic
      to avoid thee and flee?
      Why? That my chaff might fly; my grain lie, sheer
         and clear.
Nay in all that toil, that coil, since (seems) I kissed
      the rod,
Hand rather, my heart lo! lapped strength, stole joy,
      would laugh, chéer.
Cheer whom though? the hero whose heaven-
      handling flung me, fóot tród
Me? or me that fought him? O which one? is it each
      one? That night, that year
Of now done darkness I wretch lay wrestling with
      (my God!) my God.

GERARD MANLEY HOPKINS

## *"I wake and feel the fell of dark, not day."*

I wake and feel the fell of dark, not day.
What hours, O what black hours we have spent
This night! what sights you, heart, saw; ways you went!
And more must, in yet longer light's delay.
  With witness I speak this. But where I say
Hours I mean years, mean life. And my lament
Is cries countless, cries like dead letters sent
To dearest him that lives alas! away.

  I am gall, I am heartburn. God's most deep decree
Bitter would have me taste: my taste was me;
Bones built in me, flesh filled, blood brimmed the
    curse.
  Selfyeast of spirit a dull dough sours. I see
The lost are like this, and their scourge to be
As I am mine, their sweating selves; but worse.

GERARD MANLEY HOPKINS

## *"Thou art indeed just, Lord, if I contend"*

*Justus quidem tu es, Domine, si disputem tecum; verumtamen
justa loquar ad te: Quare via impiorum prosperatur? &c.*

Thou art indeed just, Lord, if I contend
With thee; but, sir, so what I plead is just.
Why do sinners' ways prosper? and why must
Disappointment all I endeavour end?
  Wert thou my enemy, O thou my friend,
How wouldst thou worse, I wonder, than thou dost
Defeat, thwart me? Oh, the sots and thralls of lust
Do in spare hours more thrive than I that spend,
Sir, life upon thy cause. See, banks and brakes
Now, leavèd how thick! lacèd they are again
With fretty chervil, look, and fresh wind shakes
Them; birds build—but not I build; no, but strain,

Time's eunuch, and not breed one work that wakes.
Mine, O thou lord of life, send my roots rain.

EMMA LAZARUS
## The New Colossus

Not like the brazen giant of Greek fame,
With conquering limbs astride from land to land;
Here at our sea-washed, sunset gates shall stand
A mighty woman with a torch, whose flame
Is the imprisoned lightning, and her name
Mother of Exiles. From her beacon-hand
Glows world-wide welcome; her mild eyes command
The air-bridged harbor that twin cities frame.
"Keep, ancient lands, your storied pomp!" cries she
With silent lips. "Give me your tired, your poor,
Your huddled masses yearning to breathe free,
The wretched refuse of your teeming shore.
Send these, the homeless, tempest-tost to me,
I lift my lamp beside the golden door!"

EMMA LAZARUS
## Long Island Sound

I see it as it looked one afternoon
In August,—by a fresh soft breeze o'erblown.
The swiftness of the tide, the light thereon,
A far-off sail, white as a crescent moon,
The shining waters with pale currents strewn,
The quiet fishing-smacks, the Eastern cove,
The semi-circle of its dark, green grove.
The luminous grasses, and the merry sun
In the grave sky; the sparkle far and wide,
Laughter of unseen children, cheerful chirp
Of crickets, and low lisp of rippling tide,
Light summer clouds fantastical as sleep
Changing unnoted while I gazed thereon.
All these fair sounds and sights I made my own.

EMMA LAZARUS

## 1492

Thou two-faced year, Mother of Change and Fate,
Didst weep when Spain cast forth with flaming sword,
The children of the prophets of the Lord,
Prince, priest, and people, spurned by zealot hate.
Hounded from sea to sea, from state to state,
The West refused them, and the East abhorred.
No anchorage the known world could afford,
Close-locked was every port, barred every gate.

Then smiling, thou unveil'dst, O two-faced year,
A virgin world where doors of sunset part,
Saying, "Ho, all who weary, enter here!
There falls each ancient barrier that the art
Of race or creed or rank devised, to rear
Grim bulwarked hatred between heart and heart!"

ELLA WHEELER WILCOX

## Friendship After Love

After the fierce midsummer all ablaze
     Has burned itself to ashes, and expires
     In the intensity of its own fires,
There come the mellow, mild, St. Martin days
Crowned with the calm of peace, but sad with haze.
     So after Love has led us, till he tires
     Of his own throes, and torments, and desires,
Comes large-eyed friendship: with a restful gaze,
He beckons us to follow, and across
     Cool verdant vales we wander free from care.
     Is it a touch of frost lies in the air?
Why are we haunted with a sense of loss?
We do not wish the pain back, or the heat;
And yet, and yet, these days are incomplete.

LIZETTE WOODWORTH REESE

## *April in Town*

Straight from the east the wind blows sharp with rain,
  That just now drove its wild ranks down the street,
  And westward rushed into the sunset sweet.
Spouts brawl, boughs drip and cease and drip again,
Bricks gleam; keen saffron glows each window-pane,
  And every pool beneath the passing feet
  Innumerable odors fine and fleet
Are blown this way from blossoming lawn and lane.
Wet roofs show black against a tender sky;
    The almond bushes in the lean-fenced square,
      Beaten to the walks, show all their draggled
      white.
A troop of laborers comes slowly by;
    One bears a daffodil, and seems to bear
      A new-lit candle through the fading light.

OSCAR WILDE

## *On the Sale by Auction of Keats' Love Letters*

These are the letters which Endymion wrote
To one he loved in secret, and apart.
And now the brawlers of the auction mart
Bargain and bid for each poor blotted note,
Ay! for each separate pulse of passion quote
The merchant's price. I think they love not art
Who break the crystal of a poet's heart
That small and sickly eyes may glare and gloat.
Is it not said that many years ago,
In a far Eastern town, some soldiers ran
With torches through the midnight, and began
To wrangle for mean raiment, and to throw
Dice for the garments of a wretched man,
Not knowing the God's wonder, or His woe?

LOUISE IMOGEN GUINEY

## The Lights of London

The evenfall, so slow on hills, hath shot
Far down into the valley's cold extreme,
Untimely midnight; spire and roof and stream
Like fleeing spectres, shudder and are not.
The Hampstead hollies, front their sylvan plot
Yet cloudless, lean to watch as in a dream,
From chaos climb with many a sudden gleam,
London, one moment fallen and forgot.

Her booths begin to flare; and gases bright
Prick door and window; all her streets obscure
Sparkle and swarm with nothing true nor sure,
Full as a marsh of mist and winking light;
Heaven thickens over, Heaven that cannot cure
Her tear by day, her fevered smile by night.

GEORGE SANTAYANA

## On a Piece of Tapestry

Hold high the woof, dear friends, that we may see
The cunning mixture of its colours rare.
Nothing in nature purposely is fair,—
Her beauties in their freedom disagree;
But here all vivid dyes that garish be,
To that tint mellowed which the sense will bear,
Glow, and not wound the eye that, resting there,
Lingers to feed its gentle ecstasy.
Crimson and purple and all hues of wine,
Saffron and russet, brown and sober green
Are rich the shadowy depths of blue between;
While silver threads with golden intertwine,
To catch the glimmer of a fickle sheen,—
All the long labour of some captive queen.

# THE TWENTIETH CENTURY

In the twentieth century, the sonnet's appeal extends to traditionalists and experimentalists. Tradition had to be summoned up, authorized, challenged, and reinvigorated. It is a touchstone and a rallying cry. The form has been lit and shadowed by modernism and postmodernism. It is a stay against confusion (every New Formalist bleeds in sonnets) and an opportunity for innovation. There are ardent modernists who wrote sonnets, such as Marianne Moore, and equally fervent anti-modernists, such as Philip Larkin. There are masters of traditional form, such as James Merrill and Anthony Hecht, and committed improvisers, such as John Ashbery and Ted Berrigan. The sonnet is both a contained space and a poetic battleground.

# THE SONNET IN ITS CENTURY: THE TWENTIETH

Now, you great stanza, you heroic mould,
Bend to my will . . .

      —LOUISE BOGAN, *"Single Sonnet"*

"On or about December 1910," Virginia Woolf declared, "human character changed." So did poetry. Modernism was a literature in crisis, a literature that responded to a breakdown in the nineteenth-century consensus of values. The old rules no longer seemed to apply. Yet the sonnet, unlikely chameleon, archetypal form, proved adaptable to the new world of the twentieth century. It survived in an era of science and technology. It flourished in a radically changed world.

Throughout the twentieth century, poets continued to find and redefine the sonnet form. At times, the history of the sonnet and the sonnet as history came together with dramatic results. For example, the sonnets of Rupert Brooke and Wilfred Owen stand on two sides of World War I. They divide the centuries. The sonnet could reify old values or foster subversion and dissent. On the threshold of the Jazz age, in the work, say, of Edna St. Vincent Millay and E. E. Cummings, it sounded a defiant note of personal freedom. In the cunning hands of Robert Frost, it became both a shockingly pessimistic lyric ("Design") and a richly affirmative love poem ("The Silken Tent").

The twentieth century turned out to be a proving ground for the sonnet. It had both its advocates and its detractors. Sometimes they were one and the same. For example, Ezra Pound attacked the sonnet, even as he wrote many fourteen-line poems as part of his poetic apprenticeship. In his youth, he wrote a series of sonnets for Hilda Doolittle, which he bound together as "Hilda's Book." So, too, his adaptations of Cavalcanti's sonnets stand as one of the cornerstones of modernism. T. S. Eliot also dismissed the sonnet, yet modeled his own difficult poetry on the knotty poetic structures—some of them sonnets—of the Metaphysical poets. His archrival William Carlos Williams thought that we don't live in a sonnet world. He said that writing a sonnet in modern America was like "putting a crab into a square box. You've got to cut his legs off to make him fit." Yet he changed his mind reading the sonnets of Merrill Moore: "The sonnet, I see now, is not and has never been a form at all in any fixed sense other than that incident upon a certain turn of the mind. It is the extremely familiar dialogue unit upon which all dramatic writing is founded."

In the twentieth century, the sonnet's appeal extends to traditionalists and experimentalists. Tradition had to be summoned up, authorized, challenged, and reinvigorated. It is a touchstone and a rallying cry. The form has been lit and shadowed by modernism and postmodernism. It is a stay against confusion (every New Formalist bleeds in sonnets) and an opportunity for innovation. There are ardent modernists who wrote sonnets, such as Marianne Moore, and equally fervent antimodernists, such as Philip Larkin. There are masters of traditional form, such as James Merrill and Anthony Hecht, and committed improvisers, such as John Ashbery and Ted Berrigan. The sonnet is both a contained space and a poetic battleground.

It is something of a mystery why the sonnet has thrived through different centuries. The history of poetry is filled with the corpses of once popular forms. Yet the sonnet continues to fascinate us. It seems to suit the peculiarly human need for making forms, for singing and thinking, for engaging passion, for passionate argument, for talking to ourselves, to lovers, to other people. It speaks to something that is deep within us. It turns us both inward and outward. It is both timely and timeless.

W. B. YEATS

## Leda and the Swan

A sudden blow: the great wings beating still
Above the staggering girl, her thighs caressed
By the dark webs, her nape caught in his bill,
He holds her helpless breast upon his breast.

How can those terrified vague fingers push
The feathered glory from her loosening thighs?
And how can body, laid in that white rush,
But feel the strange heart beating where it lies?

A shudder in the loins engenders there
The broken wall, the burning roof and tower
And Agamemnon dead.
                              Being so caught up,
So mastered by the brute blood of the air,
Did she put on his knowledge with his power
Before the indifferent beak could let her drop?

CHARLOTTE MEW

## Not for that City

Not for that city of the level sun,
    Its golden streets and glittering gates ablaze—
    The shadeless, sleepless city of white days,
White nights, or nights and days that are as one—
We weary, when all is said, all thought, all done.
    We strain our eyes beyond this dusk to see
    What, from the threshold of eternity
We shall step into. No, I think we shun
The splendour of that everlasting glare,
    The clamour of that never-ending song.
    And if for anything we greatly long,
It is for some remote and quiet stair
    Which winds to silence and a space of sleep
    Too sound for waking and for dreams too deep.

EDWIN ARLINGTON ROBINSON

## Reuben Bright

Because he was a butcher and thereby
Did earn an honest living (and did right),
I would not have you think that Reuben Bright
Was any more a brute than you or I;
For when they told him that his wife must die,
He stared at them, and shook with grief and fright,
And cried like a great baby half that night,
And made the women cry to see him cry.

And after she was dead, and he had paid
The singers and the sexton and the rest,
He packed a lot of things that she had made
Most mournfully away in an old chest
Of hers, and put some chopped-up cedar boughs
In with them, and tore down the slaughter house.

EDWIN ARLINGTON ROBINSON

## George Crabbe

Give him the darkest inch your shelf allows,
Hide him in lonely garrets, if you will,—
But his hard, human pulse is throbbing still
With the sure strength that fearless truth endows.
In spite of all fine science disavows,
Of his plain excellence and stubborn skill
There yet remains what fashion cannot kill,
Though years have thinned the laurel from his
    brows.

Whether or not we read him, we can feel
From time to time the vigor of his name
Against us like a finger for the shame
And emptiness of what our souls reveal
In books that are as altars where we kneel
To consecrate the flicker, not the flame.

EDWIN ARLINGTON ROBINSON
## How Annandale Went Out

"They called it Annandale—and I was there
To flourish, to find words, and to attend:
Liar, physician, hypocrite, and friend,
I watched him; and the sight was not so fair
As one or two that I have seen elsewhere:
An apparatus not for me to mend—
A wreck, with hell between him and the end,
Remained of Annandale; and I was there.

"I knew the ruin as I knew the man;
So put the two together, if you can,
Remembering the worst you know of me.
Now view yourself as I was, on the spot—
With a slight kind of engine. Do you see?
Like this . . . You wouldn't hang me? I thought not."

EDWIN ARLINGTON ROBINSON
## The Sheaves

Where long the shadows of the wind had rolled,
Green wheat was yielding to the change assigned;
And as by some vast magic undivined
The world was turning slowly into gold.
Like nothing that was ever bought or sold
It waited there, the body and the mind;
And with a mighty meaning of a kind
That tells the more the more it is not told.

So in a land where all days are not fair,
Fair days went on till on another day
A thousand golden sheaves were lying there,
Shining and still, but not for long to stay—
As if a thousand girls with golden hair
Might rise from where they slept and go away.

EDWIN ARLINGTON ROBINSON

## Why He Was There

Much as he left it when he went from us
Here was the room again where he had been
So long that something of him should be seen,
Or felt—and so it was. Incredulous,
I turned about, loath to be greeted thus,
And there he was in his old chair, serene
As ever, and as laconic and as lean
As when he lived, and as cadaverous.

Calm as he was of old when we were young,
He sat there gazing at the pallid flame
Before him. "And how far will this go on?"
I thought. He felt the failure of my tongue,
And smiled: "I was not here until you came;
And I shall not be here when you are gone."

JAMES WELDON JOHNSON

## Mother Night

Eternities before the first-born day,
 Or ere the first sun fledged his wings of flame,
 Calm Night, the everlasting and the same,
 A brooding mother over chaos lay.
And whirling suns shall blaze and then decay,
 Shall run their fiery courses and then claim
 The haven of the darkness whence they came;
 Back to Nirvanic peace shall grope their way.

So when my feeble sun of life burns out,
 And sounded is the hour for my long sleep,
 I shall, full weary of the feverish light,
Welcome the darkness without fear or doubt,
 And heavy-lidded, I shall softly creep
 Into the quiet bosom of the Night.

PAUL LAURENCE DUNBAR
## Robert Gould Shaw

Why was it that the thunder voice of Fate
    Should call thee, studious, from the classic groves,
    Where calm-eyed Pallas with still footsteps roves,
And charge thee seek the turmoil of the State?
What bade thee hear the voice and rise elate,
    Leave home and kindred and thy spicy loaves,
    To lead th' unlettered and despised droves
To manhood's home and thunder at the gate?

Far better the slow blaze of Learning's light,
    The cool and quiet of her dearer fane,
Than this hot terror of a hopeless fight,
    This cold endurance of the final pain,—
Since thou and those who with thee died for right
    Have died, the Present teaches, but in vain!

PAUL LAURENCE DUNBAR
## Douglass

Ah, Douglass, we have fall'n on evil days,
    Such days as thou, not even thou didst know,
    When thee, the eyes of that harsh long ago
Saw, salient, at the cross of devious ways,
And all the country heard thee with amaze.
    Not ended then, the passionate ebb and flow,
    The awful tide that battled to and fro;
We ride amid a tempest of dispraise.

Now, when the waves of swift dissension swarm,
    And Honor, the strong pilot, lieth stark,
Oh, for thy voice high-sounding o'er the storm,
    For thy strong arm to guide the shivering bark,
The blast-defying power of thy form,
    To give us comfort through the lonely dark.

TRUMBULL STICKNEY

## *"Live blindly and upon the hour. The Lord"*

Live blindly and upon the hour. The Lord,
Who was the Future, died full long ago.
Knowledge which is the Past is folly. Go,
Poor child, and be not to thyself abhorred.
Around thine earth sun-wingèd winds do blow
And planets roll; a meteor draws his sword;
The rainbow breaks his seven-coloured chord
And the long strips of river-silver flow:
Awake! Give thyself to the lovely hours.
Drinking their lips, catch thou the dream in flight
About their fragile hairs' aërial gold.
Thou art divine, thou livest,—as of old
Apollo springing naked to the light,
And all his island shivered into flowers.

TRUMBULL STICKNEY

## *Six O'Clock*

Now burst above the city's cold twilight
The piercing whistles and the tower-clocks:
For day is done. Along the frozen docks
The workmen set their ragged shirts aright.
Thro' factory doors a stream of dingy light
Follows the scrimmage as it quickly flocks
To hut and home among the snow's gray blocks.—
I love you, human labourers. Good-night!
Good-night to all the blackened arms that ache!
Good-night to every sick and sweated brow,
To the poor girl that strength and love forsake,
To the poor boy who can no more! I vow
The victim soon shall shudder at the stake
And fall in blood: we bring him even now.

ROBERT FROST

## Design

I found a dimpled spider, fat and white,
On a white heal-all, holding up a moth
Like a white piece of rigid satin cloth—
Assorted characters of death and blight
Mixed ready to begin the morning right,
Like the ingredients of a witches' broth—
A snow-drop spider, a flower like a froth,
And dead wings carried like a paper kite.

What had that flower to do with being white,
The wayside blue and innocent heal-all?
What brought the kindred spider to that height,
Then steered the white moth thither in the night?
What but design of darkness to appall?—
If design govern in a thing so small.

ROBERT FROST

## The Silken Tent

She is as in a field a silken tent
At midday when a sunny summer breeze
Has dried the dew and all its ropes relent,
So that in guys it gently sways at ease,
And its supporting central cedar pole,
That is its pinnacle to heavenward
And signifies the sureness of the soul,
Seems to owe naught to any single cord,
But strictly held by none, is loosely bound
By countless silken ties of love and thought
To everything on earth the compass round,
And only by one's going slightly taut
In the capriciousness of summer air
Is of the slightest bondage made aware.

ROBERT FROST

## Never Again Would Birds' Song Be the Same

He would declare and could himself believe
That the birds there in all the garden round
From having heard the daylong voice of Eve
Had added to their own an oversound,
Her tone of meaning but without the words.
Admittedly an eloquence so soft
Could only have had an influence on birds
When call or laughter carried it aloft.
Be that as may be, she was in their song.
Moreover her voice upon their voices crossed
Had now persisted in the woods so long
That probably it never would be lost.
Never again would birds' song be the same.
And to do that to birds was why she came.

RUPERT BROOKE

## Sonnet Reversed

Hand trembling towards hand; the amazing lights
Of heart and eye. They stood on supreme heights.

Ah, the delirious weeks of honeymoon!
    Soon they returned, and, after strange adventures,
Settled at Balham by the end of June.
    Their money was in Can. Pacs. B. Debentures,
And in Antofagastas. Still he went
    Cityward daily; still she did abide
At home. And both were really quite content
    With work and social pleasures. Then they died.
They left three children (besides George, who
        drank):
    The eldest Jane, who married Mr. Bell,
William, the head-clerk in the County Bank,
    And Henry, a stock-broker, doing well.

RUPERT BROOKE

## The Soldier

If I should die, think only this of me;
    That there's some corner of a foreign field
That is for ever England. There shall be
    In that rich earth a richer dust concealed;
A dust whom England bore, shaped, made aware,
    Gave, once, her flowers to love, her ways to roam,
A body of England's breathing English air,
    Washed by the rivers, blessed by suns of home.

And think, this heart, all evil shed away,
    A pulse in the eternal mind, no less
        Gives somewhere back the thoughts by England
        given;
Her sights and sounds; dreams happy as her day;
    And laughter, learned of friends; and gentleness,
        In hearts at peace, under an English heaven.

EDWARD THOMAS

## February Afternoon

Men heard this roar of parleying starlings, saw,
    A thousand years ago even as now,
        Black rooks with white gulls following the plough
So that the first are last until a caw
Commands that last are first again,—a law
    Which was of old when one, like me, dreamed how
    A thousand years might dust lie on his brow
Yet thus would birds do between hedge and shaw.

Time swims before me, making as a day
    A thousand years, while the broad ploughland oak
    Roars mill-like and men strike and bear the stroke
    Of war as ever, audacious or resigned,
And God still sits aloft in the array
    That we have wrought him, stone-deaf and
        stone-blind.

WALLACE STEVENS

## *The Poem That Took the Place of a Mountain*

There it was, word for word,
The poem that took the place of a mountain.

He breathed its oxygen,
Even when the book lay turned in the dust of his
    table.

It reminded him how he had needed
A place to go to in his own direction,

How he had recomposed the pines,
Shifted the rocks and picked his way among clouds,

For the outlook that would be right,
Where he would be complete in an unexplained
    completion:

The exact rock where his inexactnesses
Would discover, at last, the view toward which
    they had edged,

Where he could lie and, gazing down at the sea,
Recognize his unique and solitary home.


WILLIAM CARLOS WILLIAMS

## *Sonnet in Search of an Author*

Nude bodies like peeled logs
sometimes give off a sweetest
odor, man and woman

under the trees in full excess
matching the cushion of

aromatic pine-drift fallen
threaded with trailing woodbine
a sonnet might be made of it

Might be made of it! odor of excess
odor of pine needles, odor of
peeled logs, odor of no odor
other than trailing woodbine that

has no odor, odor of a nude woman
sometimes, odor of a man.


ELINOR WYLIE

## Self-portrait

A lens of crystal whose transparence calms
Queer stars to clarity, and disentangles
Fox-fires to form austere refracted angles:
A texture polished on the horny palms
Of vast equivocal creatures, beast or human:
A flint, a substance finer-grained than snow,
Graved with the Graces in intaglio
To set sarcastic sigil on the woman.

This for the mind, and for the little rest
A hollow scooped to blackness in the breast,
The simulacrum of a cloud, a feather:
Instead of stone, instead of sculptured strength,
This soul, this vanity, blown hither and thither
By trivial breath, over the whole world's length.


SARA TEASDALE

## Crowned

I wear a crown invisible and clear,
  And go my lifted royal way apart
  Since you have crowned me softly in your heart
With love that is half ardent, half austere;
And as a queen disguised might pass anear
  The bitter crowd that barters in a mart,
  Veiling her pride while tears of pity start,
I hide my glory thru a jealous fear.
My crown shall stay a sweet and secret thing

Kept pure with prayer at evensong and morn,
   And when you come to take it from my head,
   I shall not weep, nor will a word be said,
But I shall kneel before you, oh my king,
   And bind my brow forever with a thorn.


EZRA POUND

## A Virginal

No, no! Go from me. I have left her lately.
I will not spoil my sheath with lesser brightness,
For my surrounding air hath a new lightness;
Slight are her arms, yet they have bound me straitly
And left me cloaked as with a gauze of æther;
As with sweet leaves; as with subtle clearness.
Oh, I have picked up magic in her nearness
To sheathe me half in half the things that sheathe her.
No, no! Go from me. I have still the flavour,
Soft as spring wind that's come from birchen bowers.
Green come the shoots, aye April in the branches,
As winter's wound with her sleight hand she staunches,
Hath of the trees a likeness of the savour:
As white their bark, so white this lady's hours.


SIEGFRIED SASSOON

## Dreamers

Soldiers are citizens of death's grey land,
   Drawing no dividend from time's tomorrows.
In the great hour of destiny they stand,
   Each with his feuds, and jealousies, and sorrows.

Soldiers are sworn to action; they must win
   Some flaming, fatal climax with their lives.
Soldiers are dreamers, when the guns begin
   They think of firelit homes, clean beds, and wives.

I see them in foul dug-outs, gnawed by rats,
   And in the ruined trenches, lashed with rain,

Dreaming of things they did with balls and bats,
   And mocked by hopeless longing to regain
Bank-holidays, and picture shows, and spats,
   And going to the office in the train.


SIEGFRIED SASSOON
## Trench Duty

Shaken from sleep, and numbed and scarce awake,
Out in the trench with three hours' watch to take,
I blunder through the splashing mirk; and then
Hear the gruff muttering voices of the men
Crouching in cabins candle-chinked with light.
Hark! There's the big bombardment on our right
Rumbling and bumping; and the dark's a glare
Of flickering horror in the sectors where
We raid the Boche; men waiting, stiff and chilled,
Or crawling on their bellies through the wire.
'What? Stretcher-bearers wanted? Some one killed?'
Five minutes ago I heard a sniper fire:
Why did he do it? . . . Starlight overhead—
Blank stars. I'm wide-awake; and some chap's dead.


SIEGFRIED SASSOON
## Banishment

I am banished from the patient men who fight
They smote my heart to pity, built my pride.
Shoulder to aching shoulder, side by side,
They trudged away from life's broad wealds of light.
Their wrongs were mine; and ever in my sight
They went arrayed in honour. But they died,—
Not one by one: and mutinous I cried
To those who sent them out into the night.

The darkness tells how vainly I have striven
To free them from the pit where they must dwell
In outcast gloom convulsed and jagged and riven
By grappling guns. Love drove me to rebel.

Love drives me back to grope with them through hell;
And in their tortured eyes I stand forgiven.

ROBINSON JEFFERS
## Love the Wild Swan

"I hate my verses, every line, every word,
Oh pale and brittle pencils ever to try
One grass-blade's curve, or the throat of one bird
That clings to twig, ruffled against white sky.
Oh cracked and twilight mirrors ever to catch
One color, one glinting flash, of the splendor of
        things.
Unlucky hunter, Oh bullets of wax,
The lion beauty, the wild-swan wings, the storm of
        the wings."
—This wild swan of a world is no hunter's game.
Better bullets than yours would miss the white breast,
Better mirrors than yours would crack in the flame.
Does it matter whether you hate your . . . self? At least
Love your eyes that can see, your mind that can
Hear the music, the thunder of the wings. Love the
        wild swan.

MARIANNE MOORE
## No Swan So Fine

"No water so still as the
        dead fountains of Versailles." No swan,
with swart blind look askance
and gondoliering legs, so fine
        as the chintz china one with fawn-
brown eyes and toothed gold
collar on to show whose bird it was.

Lodged in the Louis Fifteenth
        candelabrum-tree of cockscomb-
tinted buttons, dahlias,

sea urchins, and everlastings,
  it perches on the branching foam
of polished sculptured
flowers—at ease and tall. The king is dead.

EDWIN MUIR

## Milton

Milton, his face set fair for Paradise,
And knowing that he and Paradise were lost
In separate desolation, bravely crossed
Into his second night and paid his price.
There towards the end he to the dark tower came
Set square in the gate, a mass of blackened stone
Crowned with vermilion fiends like streamers blown
From a great funnel filled with roaring flame.

Shut in his darkness, these he could not see,
But heard the steely clamour known too well
On Saturday nights in every street in Hell.
Where, past the devilish din, could Paradise be?
A footstep more, and his unblinded eyes
Saw far and near the fields of Paradise.

JOHN CROWE RANSOM

## Piazza Piece

—I am a gentleman in a dustcoat trying
To make you hear. Your ears are soft and small
And listen to an old man not at all,
They want the young men's whispering and sighing.
But see the roses on your trellis dying
And hear the spectral singing of the moon;
For I must have my lovely lady soon,
I am a gentleman in a dustcoat trying.

—I am a lady young in beauty waiting
Until my truelove comes, and then we kiss.

But what grey man among the vines is this
Whose words are dry and faint as in a dream?
Back from my trellis, Sir, before I scream!
I am a lady young in beauty waiting.


T. S. ELIOT

### from *The Fire Sermon*

The river's tent is broken; the last fingers of leaf
Clutch and sink into the wet bank. The wind
Crosses the brown land, unheard. The nymphs are
    departed.
Sweet Thames, run softly, till I end my song.
The river bears no empty bottles, sandwich papers,
Silk handkerchiefs, cardboard boxes, cigarette ends
Or other testimony of summer nights. The nymphs
    are departed.
And their friends, the loitering heirs of City directors;
Departed, have left no addresses.
By the waters of Leman I sat down and wept . . .
Sweet Thames, run softly till I end my song,
Sweet Thames, run softly, for I speak not loud or long.
But at my back in a cold blast I hear
The rattle of the bones, and chuckle spread from ear
    to ear.


IVOR GURNEY

### *Strange Hells*

There are strange hells within the minds war made
Not so often, not so humiliatingly afraid
As one would have expected—the racket and fear
    guns made
One hell the Gloucester soldiers they quite put out:
Their first bombardment, when in combined black
    shout

Of fury, guns aligned, they ducked lower their heads
And sang with diaphragms fixed beyond all dreads,

That tin and stretched-wire tinkle, that blither of tune:
"Après la guerre fini," till hell all had come down,
Twelve-inch, six-inch, and eighteen pounders
    hammering hell's thunders.

Where are they now, on state-doles, or showing
    shop-patterns
Or walking town to town sore in borrowed tatterns
Or begged. Some civic routine one never learns.
The heart burns—but has to keep out of face how
    heart burns.

CLAUDE MCKAY

## The Lynching

His spirit in smoke ascended to high heaven.
His father, by the cruellest way of pain,
Had bidden him to his bosom once again:
The awful sin remained still unforgiven.
All night a bright and solitary star
(Perchance the one that ever guided him,
Yet gave him up at last to Fate's wild whim)
Hung pitifully o'er the swinging char.
Day dawned, and soon the mixed crowds came to view
The ghastly body swaying in the sun:
The women thronged to look, but never a one
Showed sorrow in her eyes of steely blue;
And little lads, lynchers that were to be,
Danced round the dreadful thing in fiendish glee.

CLAUDE MCKAY

## If We Must Die

If we must die, let it not be like hogs
Hunted and penned in an inglorious spot,
While round us bark the mad and hungry dogs,
Making their mock at our accursèd lot.
If we must die, O let us nobly die,
So that our precious blood may not be shed

In vain; then even the monsters we defy
Shall be constrained to honor us though dead!
O kinsmen! we must meet the common foe!
Though far outnumbered let us show us brave,
And for their thousand blows deal one death-blow!
What though before us lies the open grave?
Like men we'll face the murderous, cowardly pack,
Pressed to the wall, dying, but fighting back!

CLAUDE MCKAY

## America

Although she feeds me bread of bitterness,
And sinks into my throat her tiger's tooth,
Stealing my breath of life, I will confess
I love this cultured hell that tests my youth!
Her vigor flows like tides into my blood,
Giving me strength erect against her hate.
Her bigness sweeps my being like a flood.
Yet as a rebel fronts a king in state,
I stand within her walls with not a shred
Of terror, malice, not a word of jeer.
Darkly I gaze into the days ahead,
And see her might and granite wonders there,
Beneath the touch of Time's unerring hand,
Like priceless treasures sinking in the sand.

EDNA ST. VINCENT MILLAY

## "What lips my lips have kissed, and where, and why"

What lips my lips have kissed, and where, and why,
I have forgotten, and what arms have lain
Under my head till morning; but the rain
Is full of ghosts tonight, that tap and sigh
Upon the glass and listen for reply,
And in my heart there stirs a quiet pain
For unremembered lads that not again

Will turn to me at midnight with a cry.
Thus in the winter stands the lonely tree,
Nor knows what birds have vanished one by one,
Yet knows its boughs more silent than before:
I cannot say what loves have come and gone,
I only know that summer sang in me
A little while, that in me sings no more.

WILFRED OWEN

## Anthem for Doomed Youth

What passing-bells for these who die as cattle?
　　—Only the monstrous anger of the guns.
　　Only the stuttering rifles' rapid rattle
Can patter out their hasty orisons.
No mockeries now for them; no prayers nor bells;
　　Nor any voice of mourning save the choirs,—
The shrill, demented choirs of wailing shells;
　　And bugles calling for them from sad shires.

What candles may be held to speed them all?
　　Not in the hands of boys but in their eyes
Shall shine the holy glimmers of goodbyes.
　　The pallor of girls' brows shall be their pall;
Their flowers the tenderness of patient minds,
And each slow dusk a drawing-down of blinds.

WILFRED OWEN

## Dulce et Decorum Est

Bent double, like old beggars under sacks,
Knock-kneed, coughing like hags, we cursed
　　through sludge,
Till on the haunting flares we turned our backs
And towards our distant rest began to trudge.
Men marched asleep. Many had lost their boots
But limped on, blood-shod. All went lame; all
　　blind;

Drunk with fatigue; deaf even to the hoots
Of tired, outstripped Five-Nines that dropped
　　behind.

Gas! GAS! Quick, boys!—An ecstasy of fumbling,
Fitting the clumsy helmets just in time:
But someone still was yelling out and stumbling,
And flound'ring like a man in fire or lime . . .
Dim, through the misty panes and thick green
　　light,
As under a green sea, I saw him drowning.

In all my dreams, before my helpless sight,
He plunges at me, guttering, choking, drowning.

If in some smothering dreams you too could pace
Behind the wagon that we flung him in,
And watch the white eyes writhing in his face,
His hanging face, like a devil's sick of sin;
If you could hear, at every jolt, the blood
Come gargling from the froth-corrupted lungs,
Obscene as cancer, bitter as the cud
Of vile, incurable sores on innocent tongues,—
My friend, you would not tell with such high zest
To children ardent for some desperate glory,
The old Lie: Dulce et decorum est
Pro patria mori.

WILFRED OWEN
### *Futility*

Move him into the sun—
Gently its touch awoke him once,
At home, whispering of fields half-sown.
Always it woke him, even in France,
Until this morning and this snow.
If anything might rouse him now
The kind old sun will know.

Think how it wakes the seeds—
Woke once the clays of a cold star.
Are limbs, so dear achieved, are sides
Full-nerved, still warm, too hard to stir?
Was it for this the clay grew tall?
—O what made fatuous sunbeams toil
To break earth's sleep at all?

DOROTHY PARKER

## I Shall Come Back

I shall come back without fanfaronade
Of wailing wind and graveyard panoply;
But, trembling, slip from cool Eternity—
A mild and most bewildered little shade.
I shall not make sepulchral midnight raid,
But softly come where I had longed to be
In April twilight's unsung melody,
And I, not you, shall be the one afraid.

Strange, that from lovely dreamings of the dead
I shall come back to you, who hurt me most.
You may not feel my hand upon your head,
I'll be so new and inexpert a ghost.
Perhaps you will not know that I am near,—
And that will break my ghostly heart, my dear.

E. E. CUMMINGS

## *from* Two

### III

"next to of course god america i
love you land of the pilgrims' and so forth oh
say can you see by the dawn's early my
country 'tis of centuries come and go
and are no more what of it we should worry
in every language even deafanddumb
thy sons acclaim your glorious name by gorry

by jingo by gee by gosh by gum
why talk of beauty what could be more beaut-
iful than these heroic happy dead
who rushed like lions to the roaring slaughter
they did not stop to think they died instead
then shall the voice of liberty be mute?"

He spoke.   And drank rapidly a glass of water

E. E. CUMMINGS

### *from* One Times One

XIV

pity this busy monster,manunkind,

not.   Progress is a comfortable disease:
your victim(death and life safely beyond)

plays with the bigness of his littleness
—electrons deify one razorblade
into a mountainrange;lenses extend

unwish through curving wherewhen till unwish
returns on its unself.
          A world of made
is not a world of born—pity poor flesh

and trees,poor stars and stones,but never this
fine specimen of hypermagical

ultraomnipotence.   We doctors know

a hopeless case if—listen:there's a hell
of a good universe next door;let's go

ROBERT GRAVES
## *In Her Praise*

This they know well: the Goddess yet abides.
Though each new lovely woman whom she rides,
Straddling her neck a year or two or three,
Should sink beneath such weight of majesty
And, groping back to humankind, gainsay
The headlong power that whitened all her way
With a broad track of trefoil—leaving you,
Her chosen lover, ever again thrust through
With daggers, your purse rifled, your rings gone—
Nevertheless they call you to live on
To parley with the pure, oracular dead,
To hear the wild pack whimpering overhead,
To watch the moon tugging at her cold tides.
Woman is mortal woman. She abides.


EDMUND BLUNDEN
## *Vlamertinghe: Passing the Chateau, July 1917*

"And all her silken flanks with garlands drest"—
But we are coming to the sacrifice.
Must those have flowers who are not yet gone West?
May those have flowers who live with death and
    lice?
This must be the floweriest place
That earth allows; the queenly face
Of the proud mansion borrows grace for grace
Spite of those brute guns lowing at the skies.

Bold great daisies, golden lights,
Bubbling roses' pinks and whites—
Such a gay carpet! poppies by the million;
Such damask! such vermilion!
But if you ask me, mate, the choice of color
Is scarcely right; this red should have been much
    duller.

HART CRANE

## To Emily Dickinson

You who desired so much—in vain to ask—
Yet fed your hunger like an endless task,
Dared dignify the labor, bless the quest—
Achieved that stillness ultimately best,

Being, of all, least sought for: Emily, hear!
O sweet, dead Silencer, most suddenly clear
When singing that Eternity possessed
And plundered momently in every breast;

—Truly no flower yet withers in your hand,
The harvest you descried and understand
Needs more than wit to gather, love to bind.
Some reconcilement of remotest mind—

Leaves Ormus rubyless, and Ophir chill.
Else tears heap all within one clay-cold hill.

ALLEN TATE

## *from* Sonnets at Christmas

### I

This is the day His hour of life draws near,
Let me get ready from head to foot for it
Most handily with eyes to pick the year
For small feed to reward a feathered wit.
Some men would see it an epiphany
At ease, at food and drink, others at chase;
Yet I, stung lassitude, with ecstasy
Unspent argue the season's difficult case
So: Man, dull creature of enormous head,
What would he look at in the coiling sky?
But I must kneel again unto the Dead
While Christmas bells of paper white and red,
Figured with boys and girls spilt from a sled,
Ring out the silence I am nourished by.

LÉONIE ADAMS

## A Gull Goes Up

Gulls when they fly move in a liquid arc,
Still head, and wings that bend above the breast,
Covering its glitter with a cloak of dark,
Gulls fly. So as at last toward balm and rest,
Remembering wings, the desperate leave their earth,
Bear from their earth what there was ruinous-crossed,
Peace from distress, and love from nothing-worth,
Fast at the heart, its jewels of dear cost.
Gulls go up hushed to that entrancing flight,
With never a feather of all the body stirred.
So in an air less rare than longing might
The dream of flying lift a marble bird.
Desire it is that flies; then wings are freight
That only bear the feathered heart no weight.

JANET LEWIS

## At Carmel Highlands

Below the gardens and the darkening pines
The living water sinks among the stones,
Sinking yet foaming, till the snowy tones
Merge with the fog drawn landward in dim lines.
The cloud dissolves among the flowering vines,
And now the definite mountain-side disowns
The fluid world, the immeasurable zones.
Then white oblivion swallows all designs.

But still the rich confusion of the sea,
Unceasing voice, sombre and solacing,
Rises through veils of silence past the trees;
In restless repetition bound, yet free,
Wave after wave in deluge fresh releasing
An ancient speech, hushed in tremendous ease.

YVOR WINTERS

## To Emily Dickinson

Dear Emily, my tears would burn your page,
But for the fire-dry line that makes them burn—
Burning my eyes, my fingers, while I turn
Singly the words that crease my heart with age.
If I could make some tortured pilgrimage
Through words or Time or the blank pain of Doom
And kneel before you as you found your tomb,
Then I might rise to face my heritage.

Yours was an empty upland solitude
Bleached to the powder of a dying name;
The mind, lost in a word's lost certitude
That faded as the fading footsteps came
To trace an epilogue to words grown odd
In that hard argument which led to God.

STERLING BROWN

## Salutamus

*O Gentlemen the time of Life is short.*
        —HENRY IV, PART 1

The bitterness of days like these we know;
Much, much we know, yet cannot understand
What was our crime that such a searing brand
Not of our choosing, keeps us hated so.
Despair and disappointment only grow,
Whatever seeds are planted from our hand,
What though some roads wind through a gladsome
        land?
It is a gloomy path that we must go.

And yet we know relief will come some day
For these seared breasts; and lads as brave again
Will plant and find a fairer crop than ours.

It must be due our hearts, our minds, our powers;
These are the beacons to blaze out the way.
*We must plunge onward; onward, gentlemen.* . . .


ROBERT FRANCIS

## The Gardener

I watch an old man working in his garden
Dealing life to plant and death to weed.
Of one he saves, of one destroys the seed.
He knows the weeds and not one will he pardon.
He bids the pea vines bloom and they obey.
He teaches them to climb. He tests a pod.
Much that another man might throw away
He saves, he forks it under for decay
To be another generation's need.
This is his work to do. This is his day.
He makes all birth and growth and death his deed.
Slowly he moves, but slow is not delay.
He has all time to work. I watch him plod.
Old man, old man, who told you you were God?


COUNTEE CULLEN

## Yet Do I Marvel

I doubt not God is good, well-meaning, kind,
And did He stoop to quibble could tell why
The little buried mole continues blind,
Why flesh that mirrors Him must some day die,
Make plain the reason tortured Tantalus
Is baited by the fickle fruit, declare
If merely brute caprice dooms Sisyphus
To struggle up a never-ending stair.
Inscrutable His ways are, and immune
To catechism by a mind too strewn
With petty cares to slightly understand
What awful brain compels His awful hand.
Yet do I marvel at this curious thing:
To make a poet black, and bid him sing!

COUNTEE CULLEN

## From the Dark Tower

*(To Charles S. Johnson)*

We shall not always plant while others reap
The golden increment of bursting fruit,
Not always countenance, abject and mute,
That lesser men should hold their brothers cheap;
Not everlastingly while others sleep
Shall we beguile their limbs with mellow flute,
Not always bend to some more subtle brute;
We were not made eternally to weep.

The night whose sable breast relieves the stark,
White stars is no less lovely being dark,
And there are buds that cannot bloom at all
In light, but crumple, piteous, and fall;
So in the dark we hide the heart that bleeds,
And wait, and tend our agonizing seeds.

LANGSTON HUGHES

## Christ in Alabama

Christ is a nigger,
Beaten and black:
Oh, bare your back!

Mary is His mother:
Mammy of the South,
Silence your mouth.

God is His father:
White Master above
Grant Him your love.

Most holy bastard
Of the bleeding mouth,
  Nigger Christ
  On the cross
  Of the South.

EDWIN DENBY

### The Subway

The subway flatters like the dope habit,
For a nickel extending peculiar space:
You dive from the street, holing like a rabbit,
Roar up a sewer with a millionaire's face.

Squatting in the full glare of the locked express
Imprisoned, rocked, like a man by a friend's death,
O how the immense investment soothes distress,
Credit laps you like a huge religious myth.

It's a sound effect. The trouble is seeing
(So anaesthetized) a square of bare throat
Or the fold at the crotch of a clothed human
  being:
You'll want to nuzzle it, crop at it like a goat.

That's not in the buy. The company between stops
Offers you security, and free rides to cops.

CECIL DAY-LEWIS

### from O Dreams, O Destinations

**4**

Our youthtime passes down a colonnade
Shafted with alternating light and shade.
All's dark or dazzle there. Half in a dream
Rapturously we move, yet half afraid
Never to wake. That diamond-point, extreme
Brilliance engraved on us a classic theme:

The shaft of darkness had its lustre too,
Rising where earth's concentric mysteries gleam.
Oh youth-charmed hours, that made an avenue
Of fountains playing us on to love's full view,
A cypress walk to some romantic grave—
Waking, how false in outline and in hue
We find the dreams that flickered on our cave:
Only your fire, which cast them, still seems true.

PATRICK KAVANAGH

## Epic

I have lived in important places, times
When great events were decided, who owned
That half a rood of rock, a no-man's land
Surrounded by our pitchfork-armed claims.
I heard the Duffys shouting 'Damn your soul'
And old McCabe stripped to the waist, seen
Step the plot defying blue cast-steel—
'Here is the march along these iron stones'
That was the year of the Munich bother. Which
Was more important? I inclined
To lose my faith in Ballyrush and Gortin
Till Homer's ghost came whispering to my mind
He said: I made the Iliad from such
A local row. Gods make their own importance.

STANLEY KUNITZ

## So Intricately Is This World Resolved

So intricately is this world resolved
Of substance arched on thrust of circumstance,
The earth's organic meaning so involved
That none may break the pattern of his dance;
Lest, deviating, he confound the line
Of reason with the destiny of race,
And, altering the perilous design,
Bring ruin like a rain on time and space.

Lover, it is good to lie in the sweet grass
With a dove-soft nimble girl. But O lover,
Lift no destroying hand; let fortune pass
Unchallenged, beauty sleep; dare not to cover
Her mouth with kisses by the garden wall,
Lest, cracking in bright air, a planet fall.


R. A. K. MASON
### Sonnet of Brotherhood

Garrisons pent up in a little fort
  with foes who do but wait on every side
  knowing the time soon comes when they shall ride
  triumphant over those trapped and make sport
  of them: when those within know very short
  is now their hour and no aid can betide:
  such men as these not quarrel and divide
  but friend and foe are friends in their hard sort

And if these things be so oh men then what
  of these beleaguered victims this our race
  betrayed alike by Fate's gigantic plot
  here in this far-pitched perilous hostile place
  this solitary hard-assaulted spot
  fixed at the friendless outer edge of space.


PHYLLIS MCGINLEY
### View from a Suburban Window

When I consider how my light is spent,
  Also my sweetness, ditto all my power,
Papering shelves or saving for the rent
  Or prodding grapefruit while the grocers glower,
Or dulcetly persuading to the dentist
  The wailing young, or fitting them for shoes,
Beset by menus and my days apprenticed
  Forever to a grinning household muse;

And how I might, in some tall town instead,
From nine to five be furthering a Career,
Dwelling unfettered in my single flat,
My life my own, likewise my daily bread—
When I consider this, it's very clear
I might have done much worse. I might, at that.

ROBERT PENN WARREN
## Milton: A Sonnet

No doubt he could remember how in the past
Late carmine had bathed the horizon with its wide
kindness.
Not now. In darkness he prayed, and at the last
Moved through the faithful brilliance they called
blindness,
Knew burgeoning Space in which old space
hummed like a fly,
And Time that devoured itself to defecate
A nobler dimension of that self whereby
The past and future are intrinsicate
To form a present in which the blessèd heart
May leap like a gleaming fish from water into
Sunlight before the joy-flashed curve may dart
Back to the medium of deep wisdom through
A pavane of bubbles like pearls, again to slash
Upward, and upward again, and, in joy, flash.

WILLIAM EMPSON
## The Ants

We tunnel through your noonday out to you.
We carry our tube's narrow darkness there
Where, nostrum-plastered, with prepared air,
With old men running and trains whining through

We ants may tap your aphids for your dew.
You may not wish their sucking or our care;

Our all-but freedom, too, your branch must bear,
High as roots' depth in earth, all earth to view.

No, by too much this station the air nears.
How small a chink lets in how dire a foe.
What though the garden in one glance appears?

Winter will come and all her leaves will go.
We do not know what skeleton endures.
Carry at least her parasites below.

LOUIS MACNEICE

### Sunday Morning

Down the road someone is practicing scales,
The notes like little fishes vanish with a wink of tails,
Man's heart expands to tinker with his car
For this is Sunday morning, Fate's great bazaar,
Regard these means as ends, concentrate on this Now,
And you may grow to music or drive beyond
    Hindhead anyhow,
Take corners on two wheels until you go so fast
That you can clutch a fringe or two of the windy past,
That you can abstract this day and make it to the
    week of time
A small eternity, a sonnet self-contained in rhyme.

But listen, up the road, something gulps, the church
    spire
Opens its eight bells out, skulls' mouths which will
    not tire
To tell how there is no music or movement which
    secures
Escape from the weekday time. Which deadens and
    endures.

W. H. AUDEN

## *from* Sonnets from China

### XII

Here war is harmless like a monument:
A telephone is talking to a man;
Flags on a map declare that troops were sent;
A boy brings milk in bowls. There is a plan

For living men in terror of their lives,
Who thirst at nine who were to thirst at noon,
Who can be lost and are, who miss their wives
And, unlike an idea, can die too soon.

Yet ideas can be true, although men die:
For we have seen a myriad faces
Ecstatic from one lie,

And maps can really point to places
Where life is evil now.
Nanking. Dachau.

HELENE JOHNSON

## *Sonnet to a Negro in Harlem*

You are disdainful and magnificent—
Your perfect body and your pompous gait,
Your dark eyes flashing solemnly with hate,
Small wonder that you are incompetent
To imitate those whom you so despise—
Your shoulders towering high above the throng,
Your head thrown back in rich, barbaric song,
Palm trees and mangoes stretched before your
    eyes.
Let others toil and sweat for labor's sake
And wring from grasping hands their meed of
    gold.
Why urge ahead your supercilious feet?

Scorn will efface each footprint that you make.
I love your laughter arrogant and bold.
You are too splendid for this city street!

A. D. HOPE

## Pasiphae

There stood the mimic cow; the young bull kept
Fast by the nose-ring, trampling in his pride,
Nuzzled her flanks and snuffed her naked side.
She was a queen: to have her will she crept

In that black box; and when her lover leapt
And fell thundering on his wooden bride,
When straight her fierce, frail body crouched
    inside
Felt the wet pizzle pierce and plunge, she wept.

She wept for terror, for triumph; she wept to know
Her love unable to embrace its bliss
So long imagined, waking and asleep.
But when within she felt the pulse, the blow,
The burst of copious seed, the burning kiss
Fill her with monstrous life, she did not weep.

THEODORE ROETHKE

## For an Amorous Lady

*Most mammals like caresses, in the sense in which we
usually take the word, whereas other creatures, even tame
snakes, prefer giving to receiving them.*
—FROM A NATURAL-HISTORY BOOK

The pensive gnu, the staid aardvark,
Accept caresses in the dark;
The bear, equipped with paw and snout;
Would rather take than dish it out.

But snakes, both poisonous and garter,
In love are never known to barter;
The worm, though dank, is sensitive:
His noble nature bids him *give*.

But you, my dearest, have a soul
Encompassing fish, flesh, and fowl.
When amorous arts we would pursue,
You can, with pleasure, bill *or* coo.
You are, in truth, one in a million,
At once mammalian and reptilian.


KATHLEEN RAINE

## Angelus

I see the blue, the green, the golden and the red,
I have forgotten all the angel said.

The flower, the leaf, the meadow and the tree,
But of the words I have no memory.

I hear the swift, the martin, and the wren,
But what was told me, past all thought is gone.

The dove, the rainbow, echo, and the wind,
But of the meaning, all is out of mind.

Only I know he spoke the word that sings its way
In my blood streaming, over rocks to sea,

A word engraved in the bone, that burns within
To apotheosis the substance of a dream,

That living I shall never hear again,
Because I pass, I pass, while dreams remain.

JAMES AGEE

## *from* Sonnets

I

So it begins. Adam is in his earth
Tempted, and fallen, and his doom made sure
Oh, in the very instant of his birth:
Whose deathly nature must all things endure.
The hungers of his flesh, and mind, and heart,
That governed him when he was in the womb,
These ravenings multiply in every part:
And shall release him only to the tomb.
Meantime he works the earth, and builds up nations,
And trades, and wars, and learns, and worships
    chance,
And looks to God, and weaves the generations
Which shall his many hungerings advance
When he is sunken dead among his sins.
Adam is in this earth. So it begins.

STEPHEN SPENDER

## *Daybreak*

At dawn she lay with her profile at that angle
Which, when she sleeps, seems the carved face of an
    angel.
Her hair a harp, the hand of a breeze follows
And plays, against the white cloud of the pillows.
Then, in a flush of rose, she woke, and her eyes that
    opened
Swam in blue through her rose flesh that dawned.
From her dew of lips, the drop of one word
Fell like the first of fountains: murmured
"Darling," upon my ears the song of the first bird.
"My dream becomes my dream," she said, "come true.
I waken from you to my dream of you."
Oh, my own wakened dream then dared assume
The audacity of her sleep. Our dreams
Poured into each other's arms, like streams.

MALCOLM LOWRY

### *Christ Walks in This Infernal District Too*

Beneath the Malebolge lies Hastings Street,
The province of the pimp upon his beat,
Where each in his little world of drugs or crime
Drifts helplessly or, hopeful, begs a dime
Wherewith to purchase half a pint of piss—
Although he will be cheated, even in this.
I hope, although I doubt it, God knows
This place where chancres blossom like the rose,
For in each face is such a hard despair
That nothing like a grief finds entrance there.
And on this scene from all excuse exempt
The mountains gaze in absolute contempt,
Yet this, yet this is Canada, my friend,
Yours to absolve of ruin, or make an end.

DOROTHEA TANNING

### *Report from the Field*

Sublimation, a new version of piety,
Hovers the paint and gets her going.
Everything drifts, a barely heard sigh is the

Sound of wind in the next room blowing
Dust from anxiety. A favorite receptacle
Holds her breath and occasional sewing.

Only the artist will be held responsible
For something so far unsaid but true,
For having the crust to let the hysterical

Earnest of genuine feeling show through,
And watching herself in the glassy eyeing
Of *Art as seen through a hole in her shoe.*

Painter and poet, sometimes said to be lying,
Agonizingly know it is more like dying.

ELIZABETH BISHOP

## *The Prodigal*

The brown enormous odor he lived by
was too close, with its breathing and thick hair,
for him to judge. The floor was rotten; the sty
was plastered halfway up with glass-smooth dung.
Light-lashed, self-righteous, above moving snouts,
the pigs' eyes followed him, a cheerful stare—
even to the sow that always ate her young—
till, sickening, he leaned to scratch her head.
But sometimes mornings after drinking bouts
(he hid the pints behind a two-by-four),
the sunrise glazed the barnyard mud with red;
the burning puddles seemed to reassure.
And then he thought he almost might endure
his exile yet another year or more.

But evenings the first star came to warn.
The farmer whom he worked for came at dark
to shut the cows and horses in the barn
beneath their overhanging clouds of hay,
with pitchforks, faint forked lightnings, catching
    light,
safe and companionable as in the Ark.
The pigs stuck out their little feet and snored.
The lantern—like the sun, going away—
laid on the mud a pacing aureole.
Carrying a bucket along a slimy board,
he felt the bats' uncertain staggering flight,
his shuddering insights, beyond his control,
touching him. But it took him a long time
finally to make his mind up to go home.

J. V. CUNNINGHAM

## The Aged Lover Discourses in the Flat Style

There are, perhaps, whom passion gives a grace,
Who fuse and part as dancers on the stage,
But that is not for me, not at my age,
Not with my bony shoulders and fat face.
Yet in my clumsiness I found a place
And use for passion: with it I ignore
My gaucheries and yours, and feel no more
The awkwardness of the absurd embrace.

It is a pact men make, and seal in flesh,
To be so busy with their own desires
Their loves may be as busy with their own,
And not in union. Though the two enmesh
Like gears in motion, each with each conspires
To be at once together and alone.

PAUL GOODMAN

## *from* Sonnets, 1

3

Foster excellence. If I do not
who will do it? The vulgarity
of this country makes my spirit faint, what we
have misdone to our history and what
to the landscape. The tasteless food we eat,
the music, how we waste day after day
child, woman, and man have stunned me to
    dismay
like an ox bludgeoned, swaying on his feet.

John, rescue me by becoming. I have well
deserved of the Republic, though it has
rewarded me with long oblivion.
Make you me proud and famous as the one
who thought that we could be what Florence was
when angry men made rough rocks beautiful.

JOSEPHINE MILES

## Luncheon 2

We met for luncheon to exchange views,
Soviet authors and ours, two Armenians
And a writer of children's stories,
Beef stew and jello, but no shared language,
So we say, Pasternak? No, no, their anger.
Gogol? More kindly, shake hands.
Sroyán? Aha! You happy people,
He walks among the pomegranate rows.

Dear friends, we exchange cards,
Minor titles and their authorship.
How much we know each other, drink our tea.
Then comes the tardy interpreter, checks all round
In Russian, and then asks us,
Why did you drop the bomb on Hiroshima?

KENNETH PATCHEN

## Religion Is That I Love You

As time will turn our bodies straight
In single sleep, the hunger fed, heart broken
Like a bottle used by thieves

Beloved, as so late our mouths meet, leaning
Our faces close, eyes closed
Out there

      outside this window where branches toss
      in soft wind, where birds move sudden
        wings
Within that lame air, love, we are dying

Let us watch that sleep come, put our fingers
Through the breath falling from us

Living, we can love though dying comes near
It is its desperate singing that we must not hear

It is that we cling together, not dying near each
    other now

DELMORE SCHWARTZ
### *The Beautiful American Word, Sure*

The beautiful American word, Sure,
As I have come into a room, and touch
The lamp's button, and the light blooms with such
Certainty where the darkness loomed before,

As I care for what I do not know, and care
Knowing for little she might not have been,
And for how little she would be unseen,
The intercourse of lives miraculous and dear.

Where the light is, and each thing clear,
Separate from all others, standing in its place,
I drink the time and touch whatever's near,

And hope for day when the whole world has that face:
For what assures her present every year?
In dark accidents the mind's sufficient grace.

MURIEL RUKEYSER
### *from* Letter to the Front

7

To be a Jew in the twentieth century
Is to be offered a gift.    If you refuse,
Wishing to be invisible, you choose
Death of the spirit, the stone insanity.
Accepting, take full life.    Full agonies:

Your evening deep in labyrinthine blood
Of those who resist, fail, and resist; and God
Reduced to a hostage among hostages.

The gift is torment.        Not alone the still
Torture, isolation; or torture of the flesh.
That may come also.        But the accepting wish,
The whole and fertile spirit as guarantee
For every human freedom, suffering to be free,
Daring to live for the impossible.

ROBERT HAYDEN

## Those Winter Sundays

Sundays too my father got up early
and put his clothes on in the blueblack cold,
then with cracked hands that ached
from labor in the weekday weather made
banked fires blaze. No one ever thanked him.

I'd wake and hear the cold splintering, breaking.
When the rooms were warm, he'd call,
and slowly I would rise and dress,
fearing the chronic angers of that house,

Speaking indifferently to him,
who had driven out the cold
and polished my good shoes as well.
What did I know, what did I know
of love's austere and lonely offices?

GEORGE BARKER

## To My Mother

Most near, most dear, most loved and most far,
Under the window where I often found her
Sitting as huge as Asia, seismic with laughter,

Gin and chicken helpless in her Irish hand,
Irresistible as Rabelais, but most tender for
The lame dogs and hurt birds that surround her,—
She is a procession no one can follow after
But be like a little dog following a brass band.

She will not glance up at the bomber, or condescend
To drop her gin and scuttle to a cellar,
But lean on the mahogany table like a mountain
Whom only faith can move, and so I send
O all my faith, and all my love to tell her
That she will move from mourning into morning.


KARL SHAPIRO

### *Jew*

The name is immortal but only the name, for the rest
Is a nose that can change in the weathers of time or
  persist
Or die out in confusion or model itself on the best.

But the name is a language itself that is whispered
  and hissed
Through the houses of ages, and ever a language the
  same,
And ever and ever a blow on our heart like a fist.

And this last of our dream in the desert, O curse of
  our name,
Is immortal as Abraham's voice in our fragment of
  prayer
Adonai, Adonai, for our bondage of murder and
  shame!

And the word for the murder of God will cry out on
  the air
Though the race is no more and the temples are
  closed of our will

And the peace is made fast on the earth and the
    earth is made fair;

Our name is impaled in the heart of the world
    on a hill
Whether we suffer to die by the hands of ourselves,
    and to kill.


DYLAN THOMAS

## "When all my five and country senses see"

When all my five and country senses see,
The fingers will forget green thumbs and mark
How, through the halfmoon's vegetable eye,
Husk of young stars and handfull zodiac,
Love in the frost is pared and wintered by,
The whispering ears will watch love drummed
    away
Down breeze and shell to a discordant beach,
And, lashed to syllables, the lynx tongue cry
That her fond wounds are mended bitterly.
My nostrils see her breath burn like a bush.

My one and noble heart has witnesses
In all love's countries, that will grope awake;
And when blind sleep drops on the spying senses,
The heart is sensual, though five eyes break.


WELDON KEES

## For My Daughter

Looking into my daughter's eyes I read
Beneath the innocence of morning flesh
Concealed, hintings of death she does not heed.
Coldest of winds have blown this hair, and mesh
Of seaweed snarled these miniatures of hands;
The night's slow poison, tolerant and bland,

Has moved her blood. Parched years that I have
   seen
That may be hers appear: foul, lingering
Death in certain war, the slim legs green.
Or, fed on hate, she relishes the sting
Of others' agony; perhaps the cruel
Bride of a syphilitic or a fool.
These speculations sour in the sun.
I have no daughter. I desire none.

JOHN BERRYMAN

## *from* Sonnets to Chris

117

All we were going strong last night this time,
the *mots* were flying & the frozen daiquiris
were downing, supine on the floor lay Lise
listening to Schubert grievous & sublime,
my head was frantic with a following rime:
it was a good evening, an evening to please,
I kissed her in the kitchen—ecstasies—
among so much good we tamped down the crime.

The weather's changing. This morning was cold,
as I made for the grove, without expectation,
some hundred Sonnets in my pocket, old,
to read her if she came. Presently the sun
yellowed the pines & my lady came not
in blue jeans & a sweater. I sat down & wrote.

WILLIAM STAFFORD

## *A Stared Story*

Over the hill came horsemen, horsemen whistling.
They were all hard-driven, stamp, stamp, stamp.
Legs withdrawn and delivered again like pistons,
down they rode into the winter camp,
and while earth whirled on its forgotten center

those travelers feasted till dark in the lodge of their
   chief.
Into the night at last on earth their mother
they drummed away; the farthest hoofbeat ceased.

Often at cutbanks where roots hold dirt together
survivors pause in the sunlight, quiet, pretending
that stared story—and gazing at earth their mother:
all journey far, hearts beating, to some such ending.
And all, slung here in our cynical constellation,
whistle the wild world, live by imagination.

JUDITH WRIGHT

## Sonnet

Now let the draughtsman of my eyes be done
marking the line of petal and of hill.
Let the long commentary of the brain
be silent. Evening and the earth are one,
and bird and tree are simple and stand still.
Now, fragile heart swung in your webs of vein,
and perilous self won hardly out of clay,
gather the harvest of last light, and reap
the luminous fields of sunset for your bread.
Blurs the laborious focus of the day
and shadow brims the hillside slow as sleep.
Here is the word that, when all words are said,
shall compass more than speech. The sun is gone;
draws on the night at last; the dream draws on.

GAVIN EWART

## Sonnet: Afterwards

When I am gone, the whole satirical setup
will carry on as before—into the foreseeable future
the world will fill itself like a basin of water
with all the archetypes. The lonely, the mother-fixated,
the psychopaths, the deviants. The big superstitious
   religions

will enrol from birth their thousands and tens of
    thousands.
The smug, the respected, the cheer-leaders, the
    purse-proud.
People will still believe it is right to kill people.

I shall have done little enough to improve the
    cosmos—
my political influence nil, my personal kindness
only a drop in an ocean where already the children
are born who will commit the next century's
    murders,
my love so transient it's pathetic. They'll say (if I'm
    lucky):
He wrote some silly poems, and some of them were
    funny.


JAMES MCAULEY

### Pietà

A year ago you came
Early into the light.
You lived a day and night,
Then died; no-one to blame.

Once only, with one hand,
Your mother in farewell
Touched you. I cannot tell,
I cannot understand

A thing so dark and deep,
So physical a loss:
One touch, and that was all

She had of you to keep.
Clean wounds, but terrible,
Are those made with the Cross.

ROBERT LOWELL

## Words for Hart Crane

"When the Pulitzers showered on some dope
or screw who flushed our dry mouths out with
   soap,
few people would consider why I took
to stalking sailors, and scattered Uncle Sam's
phoney gold-plated laurels to the birds.
Because I knew my Whitman like a book,
stranger in America, tell my country: I,
*Catullus redivivus*, once the rage
of the Village and Paris, used to play my role
of homosexual, wolfing the stray lambs
who hungered by the Place de la Concorde.
My profit was a pocket with a hole.
Who asks for me, the Shelley of my age,
must lay his heart out for my bed and board."

ROBERT LOWELL

## History

History has to live with what was here,
clutching and close to fumbling all we had—
it is so dull and gruesome how we die,
unlike writing, life never finishes.
Abel was finished; death is not remote,
a flash-in-the-pan electrifies the skeptic,
his cows crowding like skulls against high-voltage
   wire,
his baby crying all night like a new machine.
As in our Bibles, white-faced, predatory,
the beautiful, mist-drunken hunter's moon
   ascends—
a child could give it a face: two holes, two holes,
my eyes, my mouth, between them a skull's no-
   nose—
O there's a terrifying innocence in my face
drenched with the silver salvage of the mornfrost.

GWENDOLYN BROOKS

## Gay Chaps at the Bar

*... and guys I knew in the States, young officers, return
from the front crying and trembling. Gay chaps at the
bar in Los Angeles, Chicago, New York. ...*
—LIEUTENANT WILLIAM COUCH
IN THE SOUTH PACIFIC

We knew how to order. Just the dash
Necessary. The length of gaiety in good taste.
Whether the raillery should be slightly iced
And given green, or served up hot and lush.
And we knew beautifully how to give to women
The summer spread, the tropics, of our love.
When to persist, or hold a hunger off.
Knew white speech. How to make a look an omen.
But nothing ever taught us to be islands.
And smart, athletic language for this hour
Was not in the curriculum. No stout
Lesson showed how to chat with death. We
    brought
No brass fortissimo, among our talents,
To holler down the lions in this air.

WILLIAM MEREDITH

## The Illiterate

Touching your goodness, I am like a man
Who turns a letter over in his hand
And you might think this was because the hand
Was unfamiliar but, truth is, the man
Has never had a letter from anyone;
And now he is both afraid of what it means
And ashamed because he has no other means
To find out what it says than to ask someone.

His uncle could have left the farm to him,
Or his parents died before he sent them word,
Or the dark girl changed and want him for beloved.
Afraid and letter-proud, he keeps it with him.
What would you call his feeling for the words
That keep him rich and orphaned and beloved?

AMY CLAMPITT

### The Cormorant in Its Element

That bony potbellied arrow, wing-pumping along
implacably, with a ramrod's rigid adherence,
airborne, to the horizontal, discloses talents
one would never have guessed at. Plummeting

waterward, big black feet splayed for a landing
gear, slim head turning and turning, vermilion-
strapped, this way and that, with a lightning glance
over the shoulder, the cormorant astounding-

ly, in one sleek involuted arabesque, a vertical
turn on a dime, goes into that inimitable
vanishing-and-emerging-from-under-the-briny-

deep act which, unlike the works of Homo Houdini,
is performed for reasons having nothing at all
to do with ego, guilt, ambition, or even money.

GWEN HARWOOD

### In the Park

She sits in the park. Her clothes are out of date.
Two children whine and bicker, tug her skirt.
A third draws aimless patterns in the dirt.
Someone she loved once passes by—too late

to feign indifference to that casual nod.
'How nice,' et cetera. 'Time holds great surprises.'

From his neat head unquestionably rises
a small balloon . . .'but for the grace of God . . .'

They stand a while in flickering light, rehearsing
the children's names and birthdays. 'It's so sweet
to hear their chatter, watch them grow and thrive,'
she says to his departing smile. Then, nursing
the youngest child, sits staring at her feet.
To the wind she says, 'They have eaten me alive.'

EDWIN MORGAN

## The Coin

We brushed the dirt off, held it to the light.
The obverse showed us *Scotland*, and the head
of a red deer; the antler-glint had fled
but the fine cut could still be felt. All right:
we turned it over, read easily *One Pound*,
but then the shock of Latin, like a gloss,
*Respublica Scotorum*, sent across
such ages as we guessed but never found
at the worn edge where once the date had been
and where as many fingers had gripped hard
as hopes their silent race had lost or gained.
The marshy scurf crept up to our machine,
sucked at our boots. Yet nothing seemed ill-starred.
And least of all the realm the coin contained.

HOWARD NEMEROV

## A Primer of the Daily Round

A peels an apple, while B kneels to God,
C telephones to D, who has a hand
On E's knee, F coughs, G turns up the sod
For H's grave, I do not understand
But J is bringing one clay pigeon down
While K brings down a nightstick on L's head,
And M takes mustard, N drives into town,

O goes to bed with P, and Q drops dead,
R lies to S, but happens to be heard
By T, who tells U not to fire V
For having to give W the word
That X is now deceiving Y with Z,
   Who happens just now to remember A
   Peeling an apple somewhere far away.


GEORGE MACKAY BROWN

## Chapel Between Cornfield and Shore

Above the ebb, that gray uprooted wall
Was arch and chancel, choir and sanctuary,
A solid round of stone and ritual.
Knox brought all down in his wild hogmanay.

The wave turns round. New ceremonies will thrust
From the thrawn acre where those good stones bleed
Like corn compelling sun and rain and dust
After the crucifixion of the seed.

Restore to that maimed rockpool, when the flood
Sounds all her lucent strings, its ocean dance;
And let the bronze bell nod and cry above
Ploughshare and creel; and sieged with hungry sins
A fisher priest offer our spindrift bread
For the hooked hands and harrowed heart of love.


MARIE PONSOT

## Out of Eden

Under the May rain over the dug grave
my mother is given canticles and I who believe
in everything watch flowers stiffen to new bloom.

Behind us the rented car fabricates a cave.
My mother nods: Is he? He is. But, is? Nods.
Angels shoo witches from this American tomb.

The nod teaches me. It is something I can save.
He left days ago. We, so that we too may leave,
install his old belongings in a bizarre new room.
I want to kneel indignantly anywhere and rave.

Well, God help us, now my father's will is God's.
At games and naming he beat Adam. He loved
    his Eve.
I knew him and his wicked tongue. What he
    had, he gave.

I do not know where to go to do it, but I grieve.


RICHARD WILBUR

## O

The idle dayseye, the laborious wheel,
The osprey's tours, the pointblank matin sun
Sanctified first the circle; thence for fun
Doctors deduced a shape, which some called real
(So all games spoil), a shape of spare appeal,
Cryptic and clean, and endlessly spinning unspun.
Now I go backward, filling by one and one
Circles with hickory spokes and rich soft shields
Of petalled dayseyes, with herehastening steel
Volleys of daylight, writhing white looks of sun;
And I toss circles skyward to be undone
By actual wings, for wanting this repeal
I should go whirling a thin Euclidean reel,
No hawk or hickory to true my run.


PHILIP LARKIN

## Whatever Happened?

At once whatever happened starts receding.
Panting, and back on board, we line the rail

With trousers ripped, light wallets, and lips
  bleeding.

Yes, gone, thank God! Remembering each detail
We toss for half the night, but find next day
All's kodak-distant. Easily, then (though pale),

'Perspective brings significance,' we say,
Unhooding our photometers, and, snap!
What can't be printed can be thrown away.

Later, it's just a latitude: the map
Points out how unavoidable it was:
'Such coastal bedding always means mishap.'

Curses? The dark? Struggling? Where's the source
Of these yarns now (except in nightmares, of
  course)?

HOWARD MOSS

## The Snow Weed

Last summer's weed sprang from my window box,
A perseverant marvel; I let it hatch
Into a lyre-branch of small sunflowers
That never quite turned gold. Today, for hours
It snowed, and when it stopped, the sun came out,
Ghostly, at first, like a dim parachute,
Then its summer self, hotheaded, prodigal,
Blazing at the cold. The weed stood tall,
Thrust up from a snowbank, with more snow to
  come,
A fan-shaped skeleton, or wide whisk broom,
A peacock tail but colorless. All form,
Adaptable to cold as it was to warm,
It swayed upon its root, remaining firm,
And bore a second blossoming of storm.

DONALD DAVIE

## *Jacob's Ladder*

It was agreed we would not mount by those
Platonic ladders planted on the heart,
Minds that abide the body and its throes,
Reluctantly, and only for a start.
But Jacob's is a ladder we ascend
Without our knowing any sense of strain,
To upland air that we need not expend
One gulp of carnal breathing to attain.
So here we are upon the heights, my love,
Although in habit's level pastures still.
We want, and yet we do not want, the skill
To scale the peaks that others tell us of,
Where breathing gets so difficult, and the will
Kicks back the ground it tries to rise above.

CONSTANCE URDANG

## from *To Live with a Landscape*

1

Take your boulevards, your Locust Street,
Your Chestnut, Pine, your Olive,
Take your Forest Park and Shaw's Garden,
Your avenues that lead past street-corner violence,
Past your West End, past your Limit,
To shabby suburban crime,
Vandalism in the parking-lot,
Abductions from the shopping mall—
Like making the same mistake over and over
On the piano or typewriter keys,
Always hitting the wrong note—
How "very alive, very American"
They are, how chockfull of metaphysics,
Hellbent to obliterate the wilderness.

ALAN ANSEN

## Tennyson

The lawns darken, evening broods in the black.
Juiceless heroic phantoms wander in pain
Whispering, sighing threnodies for a lack,
For a luck, for a look, for a likeness they sought in
    vain
As they slithered and wraithed over a rotting plain
To the Faceless City where kindly exorcists
By playing house banish the hoarse refrain
Of a vatic Sybil ululating in mists
Woe, woe, woe to the bowler hats and the spats.
The Muse, a Fury with her nine-lashed whip,
Beats us in tears of refusal to the acid vats
Where the decomposing somatic lies steadily
    fulsomely drip.
Oh you who in spite of yourself have shown us the
    end,
Help us to break like oaks in the soughing bacterial
    wind.

ELIZABETH BREWSTER

## Death by Drowning

Plunging downward through the slimy water
He discovered, as the fear grew worse,
That life, not death, was what he had been after:
Ironic to die in life's symbol and source.

Drowning was not so easy as it looked from shore.
He had thought of sinking down through layers of
    peace
To depths where mermaids sang. He would be
    lapped over
By murmuring waves that lulled him into rest.

But all death is a kind of strangulation,
He had been told once and remembered now,
Choking on water like a rope, and coughing
Its bloody taste from his mouth. He had not
    known
Before how the body struggled to survive
And must be forced, and forced again, to die.

ANTHONY HECHT

## Naming the Animals

Having commanded Adam to bestow
Names upon all the creatures, God withdrew
To empyrean palaces of blue
That warm and windless morning long ago,
And seemed to take no notice of the vexed
Look on the young man's face as he took thought
Of all the miracles the Lord had wrought,
Now to be labeled, dubbed, yclept, indexed.

Before an addled mind and puddle brow,
The feathered nation and the finny prey
Passed by; there went biped and quadruped.
Adam looked forth with bottomless dismay
Into the tragic eyes of his first cow,
And shyly ventured, "Thou shalt be called 'Fred.'"

DANIEL HOFFMAN

## Violence

After I'd read my poem about a brawl
between two sidewalk hustlers—one,
insulted, throws the other down and nearly
kills him—over coffee and cookies a grave

senior citizen reproved me: *How
could you see such violence and you*

*didn't try to stop them?*—Oh, I explained,
it wasn't like that, really—I saw

two guys in a shoving match and thought
I'd write about aggression, what
anger really feels like. . . . *Yes,*

*and if the one got killed*
*it would be on your head.*
*You should've stopped them,* he said.

EDGAR BOWERS

## In the Last Circle

You spoke all evening hatred and contempt,
The ethical distorted to a fury
Of self-deception, malice, and conceit,
Yourself the judge, the lawyer, and the jury.
I listened, but, instead of proof, I heard,
As if the truth were merely what you knew,
Wrath cry aloud its wish and its despair
That all would be and must be false to you.

You are the irresponsible and damned,
Alone in final cold athwart your prey.
Your passion eats his brain. Compulsively,
The crime which is your reason eats away
Compassion, as they both have eaten you,
Till what you are is merely what you do.

JANE COOPER

## from After the Bomb Tests

1

The atom bellies like a cauliflower,
Expands, expands, shoots up again, expands
Into ecclesiastical curves and towers
We pray to with our cupped and empty hands.

This is the old Hebraic-featured fear
We nursed before humility began,
Our crown-on-crown or phallic parody
Begat by man on the original sea.

The sea's delivered. Galvanized and smooth
She kills a tired ship left in her lap
—Transfiguration—with a half-breath
Settling like an animal in sleep.
So godhead takes the difficult form of love.
Where is the little myth we used to have?

DONALD JUSTICE

## Mrs. Snow

Busts of the great composers glimmered in niches,
Pale stars. Poor Mrs. Snow, who could forget her,
Calling the time out in that hushed falsetto?
(How early we begin to grasp what kitsch is!)
But when she loomed above us like an alp,
We little towns below could feel her shadow.
Somehow her nods of approval seemed to matter
More than the stray flakes drifting from her scalp.
Her etchings of ruins, her mass-production Mings
Were our first culture: she put us in awe of things.
And once, with her help, I composed a waltz,
Too innocent to be completely false,
Perhaps, but full of marvelous clichés.
She beamed and softened then.

Ah, those were the days.

DONALD JUSTICE

## The Pupil

Picture me, the shy pupil at the door,
One small, tight fist clutching the dread Czerny.
Back then time was still harmony, not money,
And I could spend a whole week practicing for

That moment on the threshold.
                    Then to take courage,
And enter, and pass among mysterious scents,
And sit quite straight, and with a frail confidence
Assault the keyboard with a childish flourish!

Only to lose my place, or forget the key,
And almost doubt the very metronome
(Outside, the traffic, the laborers going home),
And still to bear on across Chopin or Brahms,
Stupid and wild with love equally for the storms
Of C♯ minor and the calms of C.


KENNETH KOCH

### *from* Our Hearts

1

All hearts should beat when Cho Fu's orchestra plays
    "Love"
And then all feet should start to move in the dance.
The dancing should be very quick and all step lightly.
Everyone should be moving around, all hearts
    beating—
Tip tap tip tap. The heart is actually beating all the
    time
And with almost the same intensity. The difference is
    not in our hearing
Which is also almost always the same. The difference
    must be really
Then in our consciousness, which they say is
    variegated.
Black-and-white shoes, red dress, an eye of flame,
A teeth of pearl, a hose of true, a life of seethings.
    Would
You like to dance? The excitement, it is there all the
    time.
Is human genius there all the time? With the analogy
    of dreams,

Which supposedly we have every night, one is
    tempted
To say, The seething is always there, and with it
    the possibility for great art.

CAROLYN KIZER

### Reunion

For more than thirty years we hadn't met.
I remembered the bright query of your face,
That single-minded look, intense and stern,
Yet most important—how could I forget?—
Was what you taught me inadvertently
(Tutored by books and parents, even more
By my own awe at what was yet to learn):
The finest intellect can be a bore.

At this, perhaps our final interview,
Still luminous with your passion to instruct,
You speak to that recalcitrant pupil who
Inhaled the chalk-dust of your rhetoric.
I nod, I sip my wine, I praise your view,
Grateful, my dear, that I escaped from you.

FRANK O'HARA

### from A City Winter

1

I understand the boredom of the clerks
fatigue shifting like dunes within their eyes
a frightful nausea gumming up the works
that once was thought aggression in disguise.
Do you remember? then how lightly dead
seemed the moon when over factories
it languid slid like a barrage of lead
above the heart, the fierce inventories
of desire. Now women wander our dreams
carrying money and to our sleep's shame

our hands twitch not for swift blood-sunk triremes
nor languorous white horses nor ill fame,
    but clutch the groin that clouds a pallid sky
    where tow'rs are sinking in their common eye.

JAMES K. BAXTER

### *from* Jerusalem Sonnets

**10**

Dark night—or rather, only the stars
Somebody called 'those watchfires in the sky'—

Too cold for me the thoughts of God—I crossed
The paddock on another errand,

And the cows were slow to move outside the gate
Where they sleep at night—nevertheless I came

As it were by accident into the church
And knelt again in front of the tabernacle,

His fortress—man, His thoughts are not cold!
I dare not say what fire burned then, burns now

Under my breastbone—but He came back with me
To my own house, and let this madman eat,

And shared my stupid prayer, and carried me up
As the mother eagle lifts her fluttering young with
    her wings.

JAMES MERRILL

### *Marsyas*

I used to write in the café sometimes:
Poems on menus, read all over town
Or talked out before ever written down.
One day a girl brought in his latest book.

I opened it—stiff rhythms, gorgeous rhymes—
And made a face. Then crash! my cup upset.
Of twenty upward looks mine only met
His, that gold archaic lion's look

Wherein I saw my wiry person skinned
Of every skill it labored to acquire
And heard the plucked nerve's elemental twang.
They found me dangling where his golden wind
Inflicted so much music on the lyre
That no one could have told you what he sang.


ALLEN GINSBERG

### from *Two Sonnets*

I

*After Reading Kerouac's Manuscript*
The Town and the City

I dwelled in Hell on earth to write this rhyme,
I live in stillness now, in living flame;
I witness Heaven in unholy time,
I room in the renownèd city, am
Unknown. The fame I dwell in is not mine,
I would not have it. Angels in the air
Serenade my senses in delight.
Intelligence of poets, saints and fair
Characters converse with me all night.
But all the streets are burning everywhere.
The city is burning these multitudes that climb
Her buildings. Their inferno is the same
I scaled as a stupendous blazing stair.
They vanish as I look into the light.

W. D. SNODGRASS

μῆτις ... οὖτις *(Not any man ... No Man)*

*For R. M. Powell*

He fed them generously who were his flocks,
Picked, shatterbrained, for food. Passed as a goat
Among his sheep, I cast off. Though hurled rocks
And prayers deranged by torment tossed our boat,
I could not silence, somehow, this defiant
Mind. From my fist into the frothed wake ran
The white eye's gluten of the living giant
I had escaped, by trickery, as no man.

Unseen where all seem stone blind, pure disguise
Has brought me home alone to No Man's land
To look at nothing I dare recognize.
My dead blind guide, you lead me here to claim
Still waters that will never wash my hand,
To kneel by my old face and know my name.

JOHN ASHBERY

### Sonnet

Each servant stamps the reader with a look.
After many years he has been brought nothing.
The servant's frown is the reader's patience.
The servant goes to bed.
The patience rambles on
Musing on the library's lofty holes.

His pain is the servant's alive.
It pushes to the top stain of the wall
Its tree-top's head of excitement:
Baskets, birds, beetles, spools.
The light walls collapse next day.
Traffic is the reader's pictured face.
Dear, be the tree your sleep awaits;
Worms be your words, you not safe from ours.

WILLIS BARNSTONE
## The Secret Reader

I write my unread book for you who in
a life or day will find it in a box
or cave or dead man's pocket or the inn
of mountain light where we awake while cocks
of twilight scream our solitude. Our fate
is to be free. No public ink. No hot
or cold inferno of the private wait.
Just this apocryphon which I forgot
for you, the secret friend. You are like me:
one soul fleshed out for ecstasy and night,
this planet's only birth and death, unknown
like everything. Saul lied about the light,
for no one rose again. We are alone,
alive with secret words. Then blackly free.

GALWAY KINNELL
## Blackberry Eating

I love to go out in late September
among the fat, overripe, icy, black blackberries
to eat blackberries for breakfast,
the stalks very prickly, a penalty
they earn for knowing the black art
of blackberry making; and as I stand among
    them
lifting the stalks to my mouth, the ripest berries
fall almost unbidden to my tongue,
as words sometimes do, certain peculiar words
like *strengths* or *squinched* or *broughamed*,
many-lettered, one-syllabled lumps,
which I squeeze, squinch open, and splurge
    well
in the silent, startled, icy, black language
of blackberry eating in late September.

W. S. MERWIN

## Sonnet

Where it begins will remain a question
for the time being at least which is to
say for this lifetime and there is no
other life that can be this one again
and where it goes after that only one
at a time is ever about to know
though we have it by heart as one and though
we remind each other on occasion

How often may the clarinet rehearse
alone the one solo before the one
time that is heard after all the others
telling the one thing that they all tell of
it is the sole performance of a life
come back I say to it over the waters

JAMES WRIGHT

## My Grandmother's Ghost

She skimmed the yellow water like a moth,
Trailing her feet across the shallow stream;
She saw the berries, paused and sampled them
Where a slight spider cleaned his narrow tooth.
Light in the air, she fluttered up the path,
So delicate to shun the leaves and damp,
Like some young wife, holding a slender lamp
To find her stray child, or the moon, or both.

Even before she reached the empty house,
She beat her wings ever so lightly, rose,
Followed a bee where apples blew like snow;
And then, forgetting what she wanted there,
Too full of blossom and green light to care,
She hurried to the ground, and slipped below.

R. F. BRISSENDEN
## Samuel Johnson Talking

*Two things he was afraid of—madness and death . . .*

His great body shambled, groaned and stank,
Kicked stones, climbed mountains, rolled through
  London streets;
Or snorted in clumsy joy between the sheets
With ageing Tetty. When he ate and drank
Sweat dewed the straining forehead. Every breath
With every year grew harder: the huge frame,
Always ungovernable, in the end became
An enemy he hated more than death.

But words he loved and mastered: when he talked
Confusion died; the world grew still to hear
His voice commanding chaos into art.
Language became the tight-rope which he walked
Above the mindless rush of guilt and fear
That thundered like Niagara in his heart.

THOMAS KINSELLA
## Wedding Morning

Down the church gravel where the bridal car
  Gleams at the gate among the waifs and strays
And women of Milewater, formal wear
  And Fashion's joker hats wink in the breeze.

Past, the hushed progress under sprays of broom
  And choirs of altar lilies, when all eyes
Went brimming with her and the white-lipped
    groom
  Brought her to kneel beside him. Past, the sighs;

Ahead lies the gaiety of her father's hall
  Thrown open to the chatter of champagne,

The poised photographer, the flying veil,
  The motors crowded on the squandered lawn.

Down the bright gravel stroll the families
  With Blood, the trader, profiting in their peace.

PHILIP LEVINE
### Llanto

*for Ernesto Trejo*

Plum, almond, cherry have come and gone,
the wisteria has vanished in
the dawn, the blackened roses rusting
along the barbed-wire fence explain

how April passed so quickly into
this hard wind that waited in the west.
Ahead is summer and the full sun
riding at ease above the stunned town

no longer yours. Brother, you are gone,
that which was earth gone back to earth,
that which was human scattered like rain
into the darkened wild eyes of herbs

that see it all, into the valley oak
that will not sing, that will not even talk.

ANNE SEXTON
### To a Friend Whose Work Has Come to Triumph

Consider Icarus, pasting those sticky wings on,
testing that strange little tug at his shoulder blade,
and think of that first flawless moment over the
    lawn
of the labyrinth. Think of the difference it made!

There below are the trees, as awkward as camels;
and here are the shocked starlings pumping past
and think of innocent Icarus who is doing quite well:
larger than a sail, over the fog and the blast
of the plushy ocean, he goes. Admire his wings!
Feel the fire at his neck and see how casually
he glances up and is caught, wondrously tunneling
into that hot eye. Who cares that he fell back to the
    sea?
See him acclaiming the sun and come plunging
    down
while his sensible daddy goes straight into town.

BURNS SINGER

## *from* Sonnets for a Dying Man

### XLIX

The life I die moves through the death I live
Corrupting even evil with the lie
Of the undying towards eternity:
It lives in fear that is life's negative.
I do not want to go. I will not give
The death I live in to the life I die;
Or trust it will reveal what I deny:
And will not die although I cannot live.
'Take courage, singer,' say your silent limbs,
'You sing of silence but the song that dims
All songs, it washes you and me asleep
And leaves no rumour where a doubt can creep.'
I stop my songs, and stop beside your bed,
And cover up your eyes—for you are dead.

THOM GUNN

## *High Fidelity*

I play your furies back to me at night,
The needle dances in the grooves they made,
For fury is passion like love, and fury's bite,

These grooves, no sooner than a love mark fade;
Then all swings round to nightmare: from the rim,
To prove the guilt I don't admit by day,
I duck love as a witch to sink or swim
Till in the ringed and level I survey
The tuneless circles that succeed a voice.
They run, without distinction, passion, rage,
Around a soloist's merely printed name
That still turns, from the impetus not choice,
Surrounded in that played-out pose of age
By notes he was, but cannot be again.


JOHN MONTAGUE

## from *She Writes*

I

'Dear one, no news from you so long.
I went and came back from the Alps,
I went and came back from the Vosges.
The boy you liked, the forester's son,
Who kept a yellow fox cub in the house
Now has a tame deer, which bumps wildly
Against the furniture, on bony stilts.
More news of shooting in the North.
Did you go to Enniskillen, as you said?
Lying alone at night, I see your body
Like Art O'Leary, that elegy you translated,
*Lying in a ditch before me, dead.*
The cherry tree is alight in the garden.
Come back to our little courtyard,' she said.


ADRIENNE RICH

## *Final Notations*

it will not be simple, it will not be long
it will take little time, it will take all your thought
it will take all your heart, it will take all your breath
it will be short, it will not be simple

it will touch through your ribs, it will take all your
    heart
it will not be long, it will occupy your thought
as a city is occupied, as a bed is occupied
it will take all your flesh, it will not be simple

You are coming into us who cannot withstand you
you are coming into us who never wanted to
    withstand you
you are taking parts of us into places never
    planned
you are going far away with pieces of our lives

it will be short, it will take all your breath
it will not be simple, it will become your will

DEREK WALCOTT

## *Homage to Edward Thomas*

Formal, informal, by a country's cast
topography delineates its verse,
erects the classic bulk, for rigid contrast
of sonnet, rectory or this manor house
dourly timbered against these sinuous
Downs, defines the formal and informal prose
of Edward Thomas's poems, which make this
    garden
return its subtle scent of Edward Thomas
in everything here hedged or loosely grown.
Lines which you once dismissed as tenuous
because they would not howl or overwhelm,
as crookedly grave-bent, or cuckoo-dreaming,
seeming dissoluble as this Sussex down
harden in their indifference, like this elm.

RUTH FAINLIGHT

## High Pressure Zone

Smoke from the bonfires and fireworks of Guy
    Fawkes night
combined with a high pressure zone and a clear calm
    sky
doesn't seem to add up to much, and yet was enough
to cover the whole country next morning with fog.

Your changes of mood, or mine, consume days
as the foulness bounces back and forth like claps of
    thunder
between curdling clouds. You say: 'You get rid of
    your hurt
by passing it on to me.' I think you do the same.

It's something like: 'For want of a nail the battle was
    lost'.
Every thing affects everything else, and the truisms
become truer. We walked to the square to watch the
    fires.
When I saw the children waving sparklers to make
    patterns
against the dark, I knew that we were in the last part
of our lives. But if nothing ends, how can we two
    die?

SYLVIA PLATH

## Conversation Among the Ruins

Through portico of my elegant house you stalk
With your wild furies, disturbing garlands of fruit
And the fabulous lutes and peacocks, rending the net
Of all decorum which holds the whirlwind back.
Now, rich order of walls is fallen; rooks croak
Above the appalling ruin; in bleak light

Of your stormy eye, magic takes flight
Like a daunted witch, quitting castle when real days
    break.

Fractured pillars frame prospects of rock;
While you stand heroic in coat and tie, I sit
Composed in Grecian tunic and psyche-knot,
Rooted to your black look, the play turned tragic:
With such blight wrought on our bankrupt estate,
What ceremony of words can patch the havoc?

GEOFFREY HILL

## Requiem for the Plantagenet Kings

For whom the possessed sea littered, on both shores,
Ruinous arms; being fired, and for good,
To sound the constitution of just wars,
Men, in their eloquent fashion, understood.

Relieved of soul, the dropping-back of dust,
Their usage, pride, admitted within doors;
At home, under caved chantries, set in trust,
With well-dressed alabaster and proved spurs
They lie; they lie; secure in the decay
Of blood, blood-marks, crowns hacked and coveted,
Before the scouring fires of trial-day
Alight on men; before sleeked groin, gored head,
Budge through the clay and gravel, and the sea
Across daubed rock evacuates its dead.

C. K. STEAD

## *from* Twenty-two Sonnets

### 16

Xuan Loc fallen, Danang fallen, we wait for the fall of
    Saigon.
Nobody weeps or cheers, nobody puts on sack-cloth

For the thousand thousand lives we took or broke
To get our own sweet way. We didn't get it.

Does Lyndon Johnnie underground sleep sound
Dreaming light at the end of a tunnel? Holyoake
    hasn't been told.

Harold Holt went swimming, and all those airy
    ministers
Of canister bombs and body counts took jobs

With the World Bank, UNESCO, the Ford
    Foundation.
Washington, Wellington, leather chairs, inflatable
    arses

'Peace with Honour'—and last night, walking
    home,
I saw in a darkened house a fish tank glowing

With purple lights. There's no God. We don't answer
    for
Our violences, nor even for our sense of beauty.


STEPHEN BERG

### My Bohemian Life

I jammed my fists into my torn pockets and took off,
my coat was beginning to look just right,
a big hole near my ass in my one pair of pants shone
    like a coin.
Muse, I was your slave, I wore the sky like a crown.
A dazed midget, I slept in the Big Dipper,
blew endless rhymes on the wind as I went.
What amazing torch-like loves scorched my dreams!
My own stars spoke to me like softly clashing reeds—
I listened to them sitting on the grassy
roadside stones those cool September nights

when dew graced my forehead like a strong
   Burgundy,
I wrote among unreal shadows, an unreal shadow
myself, and plucked the black elastics of my
wounded shoes like a lyre, one foot pulled up
   against my heart!


WENDELL BERRY

## *The Venus of Botticelli*

I knew her when I saw her
in the vision of Botticelli, riding
shoreward out of the waves,
and afterward she was in my mind

as she had been before, but changed,
so that if I saw her here, near
nightfall, striding off the gleam
of the Kentucky River as it darkened

behind her, the willows touching
her with little touches laid
on breast and arm and thigh, I

would rise as after a thousand
years, as out of the dark grave,
alight, shaken, to remember her.


MARK STRAND

## *One Winter Night*

I showed up at a party of Hollywood stars
Who milled about, quoted their memoirs, and
   drank.
The prettiest one stepped out of her dress, fell
To her knees and said that only her husband had
   glimpsed
The shadowy flower of her pudendum, and he
   was a prince.

A slip of sunlight rode the swell of her breasts
Into the blinding links of her necklace, and
    crashed.
Out on the lawn, The Platters were singing
    TWILIGHT TIME.
"Heavenly shades of night are falling . . ." This
    was a dream.

Later, I went to the window and gazed at a bull,
    huge and pink,
In a field of snow. Moonlight poured down his
    back, and the damp
Of his breath spread until he was wreathed in a
    silver steam.
When he lifted his head, he loosed a bellow that
    broke and rolled
Like thunder in the rooms below. This, too, was a
    dream.

SANDRA GILBERT

### *October 29, 1991: 4 PM,*
### *outside Saratoga Springs*

My shadow, facing east, is twice my size,
a long dull path through glittering, frost-bitten
blades of grayish green. A hasty glaze
of cold October sun gives it a sudden outline,
and there, on the chilly ground, I guess I am,
a thinning blurring shape that might be a woman
with a walking stick (no, really a cane) and a dim
sort of knob at the top—a head, if it's human!

I move, and this vague road slides forward too,
weaving a little as I do, trying to hide
under dragging branches, shadow under shadow,
then in a clearing pulling into the lead
as if to prove that at this late hour I have
nothing to track but the dark drift of myself.

JUNE JORDAN

## Sunflower Sonnet Number Two

Supposing we could just go on and on as two
voracious in the days apart as well as when
we side by side (the many ways we do
that) well! I would consider then
perfection possible, or else worthwhile
to think about. Which is to say
I guess the costs of long term tend to pile
up, block and complicate, erase away
the accidental, temporary, near
thing/pulsebeat promises one makes
because the chance, the easy new, is there
in front of you. But still, perfection takes
some sacrifice of falling stars for rare.
And there are stars, but none of you, to spare.

FREDERICK SEIDEL

## Robert Kennedy

I turn from Yeats to sleep, and dream of Robert
    Kennedy,
Assassinated ten years ago tomorrow.
Ten years ago he was alive—
Asleep and dreaming at this hour, dreaming
His wish-fulfilling dreams.
He reaches from the grave.

Shirtsleeves rolled up, a boy's brown hair, ice eyes
Softened by the suffering of others, and doomed;
Younger brother of a murdered president,
Senator and candidate for president;
Shy, compassionate and fierce
Like a figure out of Yeats;
The only politician I have loved says *You're*
    *dreaming* and says
*The gun is mightier than the word.*

C. K. WILLIAMS

## The Doe

Near dusk, near a path, near a brook,
we stopped, I in disquiet and dismay
for the suffering of someone I loved,
the doe in her always incipient alarm.

All that moved was her pivoting ear
the reddening sun shining through
transformed to a color I'd only seen
in a photo of a child in a womb.

Nothing else stirred, not a leaf,
not the air, but she startled and bolted
away from me into the crackling brush.

The part of my pain which sometimes
releases me from it fled with her, the rest,
in the rake of the late light, stayed.

ALICIA OSTRIKER

## Sonnet. To Tell the Truth

To tell the truth, those brick Housing Authority
    buildings
For whose loveliness no soul had planned,
Like random dominoes stood, worn out and
    facing each other,
Creating the enclosure that was our home.

Long basement corridors connected one house
    to another
And had a special smell, from old bicycles and
    baby carriages
In the storage rooms. The elevators
Were used by kissing teenagers.

The playground—iron swingchains, fences, iron
   monkey bars,
Iron seesaw handles, doubtless now rusted—
Left a strong iron smell on my hands and in the
   autumn air
And rang with cries. To me it is even precious

Where they chased the local Mongoloid, yelling
   "Stupid Joey! Stupid Joey!"
Now I've said everything nice I can about this.

LES MURRAY

## Performance

I starred last night, I shone:
I was footwork and firework in one,

a rocket that wriggled up and shot
darkness with a parasol of brilliants
and a peewee descant on a flung bit;
I was busters of glitter-bombs expanding
to mantle and aurora from a crown,
I was fouettés, falls of blazing paint,
para-flares spot-welding cloudy heaven,
loose gold off fierce toeholds of white,
a finale red-tongued as a haka leap:
that too was a butt of all right!

As usual after any triumph, I was
of course inconsolable.

CHARLES SIMIC

## History

On a gray evening
Of a gray century,
I ate an apple
While no one was looking.

A small, sour apple
The color of woodfire,
Which I first wiped
On my sleeve.

Then I stretched my legs
As far as they'd go,
Said to myself
Why not close my eyes now

Before the Late
World News and Weather.

FRANK BIDART

## Self-Portrait, 1969

He's *still* young—; thirty, but looks younger—
or does he? . . . In the eyes and cheeks, tonight,
turning in the mirror, he saw his mother,—
puffy; angry; bewildered . . . Many nights
now, when he stares there, he gets angry:—
something *unfulfilled* there, something dead
to what he once thought he surely could be—
Now, just the glamour of habits . . .
                                    Once, instead,
he thought insight would remake him, he'd reach
—what? The thrill, the exhilaration
unravelling disaster, that seemed to teach
necessary knowledge . . . became just jargon.

Sick of being decent, he craves another
crash. What *reaches* him except disaster?

KENNETH FIELDS
## *Poetic*

*with a line from Basil Bunting*

> *"It might be from a handbook on recorders."*

For one thing, it's on the air, you can hear music,
Knowing inflected by the ear. Not *wood,*
Not even *mouthpiece,* but the lovely *fipple*
("Hey, that's like nipple," my little daughter laughs),
And the conveyer of this joy's a player,
Whose breathing tunes the hollow that she fills,
Empties and fills again. I am caught up
In the roll of the hull, this ecstasy of naming,
This gathering up of more than fifty years
In a wide harbor, a life made up of words,
All of them here before we finally heard them,
And consolation rolling upon the tide:
*As the player's breath warms the fipple the tone clears.*
Ardor, attend us as our stars descend.

SEAMUS HEANEY
## *Fireside*

Always there would be stories of lights
hovering among bushes or at the foot
of a meadow; maybe a goat with cold horns
pluming into the moon; a tingle of chains

on the midnight road. And then maybe
word would come round of that watery
art, the lamping of fishes, and I'd be
mooning my flashlamp on the licked black pelt

of the stream, my left arm splayed to take
a heavy pour and run of the current

occluding the net. Was that the beam
buckling over an eddy or a gleam

of the fabulous? Steady the light
and come to your senses, they're saying good-night.

SEAMUS HEANEY

## Requiem for the Croppies

The pockets of our greatcoats full of barley—
No kitchens on the run, no striking camp—
We moved quick and sudden in our own country.
The priest lay behind ditches with the tramp.
A people, hardly marching—on the hike—
We found new tactics happening each day:
We'd cut through reins and rider with the pike
And stampede cattle into infantry,
Then retreat through hedges where cavalry must be
    thrown.
Until, on Vinegar Hill, the fatal conclave.
Terraced thousands died, shaking scythes at cannon.
The hillside blushed, soaked in our broken wave.
They buried us without shroud or coffin
And in August the barley grew up out of the grave.

MICHAEL LONGLEY

## Ceasefire

I

Put in mind of his own father and moved to tears
Achilles took him by the hand and pushed the old king
Gently away, but Priam curled up at his feet and
Wept with him until their sadness filled the building.

II

Taking Hector's corpse into his own hands Achilles
Made sure it was washed and, for the old king's sake,
Laid out in uniform, ready for Priam to carry
Wrapped like a present home to Troy at daybreak.

III

When they had eaten together, it pleased them
        both
To stare at each other's beauty as lovers might,
Achilles built like a god, Priam good-looking still
And full of conversation, who earlier had sighed:

IV

'I get down on my knees and do what must be
        done
And kiss Achilles' hand, the killer of my son.'

BILL KNOTT

## *Suicidal (or Simply Drunken) Thoughts on Being Refused a Guggenheim Grant for the 11th Time*

War headlines/peace tailstanzas don't
Like to feel real. Scare tactics take practice
So that, institutionally, a wine corked
By the horn of a charging unicorn might?

The fur opens and my face ain't.
The fur closes: eyes lips nose resume
The wretched perfection of feature-ifice
The dumbpan plan, identity, lack of choice.—

I cling to virgin, this veil scraped surface
Where our scars are an armor of absence
What knight attains: ignore

That pig-bladder matter, life, that failure
Dangled in whiskey like a longshot tooth.
The night has no thoughts heavier than itself.

Note:
Do I sound bitter? I have no right to be bitter, do I, because
I'm not really a real poet, am I. No. I'm a—a poet-biscuit.

ROBERT PINSKY

## Sonnet

Afternoon sun on her back,
calm irregular slap
of water against a dock.

Thin pines clamber
over the hill's top—
nothing to remember,

only the same lake
that keeps making the same
sounds under her cheek

and flashing the same color.
No one to say her name,
no need, no one to praise her,

only the lake's voice—over
and over, to keep it before her.


TOM CLARK

## Sonnet

Five A.M. on East Fourteenth I'm out to eat
The holiday littered city by my feet a jewel
In the mire of the night waits for the light
Getting and spending and day's taxi cry      The
    playful

Waves of the East River move toward their date
With eternity down the street, the slate sky
In Tompkins Square Park prepares for the break
Through of lean horses of morning      I

Move through these streets like a lamplighter
Touch ragged faces with laughter by my
    knowledge

Of tragic color on a pavement at the edge
Of the city      Softly in the deep East River water

Of dreams in which my long hair flows
Slow waves move      Of my beginnings, pauses

DEREK MAHON

## Grandfather

They brought him in on a stretcher from the world,
Wounded but humorous; and he soon recovered.
Boiler-rooms, row upon row of gantries rolled
Away to reveal the landscape of a childhood
Only he can recapture. Even on cold
Mornings he is up at six with a block of wood
Or a box of nails, discreetly up to no good
Or banging round the house like a four-year-old—

Never there when you call. But after dark
You hear his great boots thumping in the hall
And in he comes, as cute as they come. Each night
His shrewd eyes bolt the door and set the clock
Against the future, then his light goes out.
Nothing escapes him; he escapes us all.

ELIZABETH SMITHER

## Visiting Juliet Street

All the streets are named after Shakespeare.
Hamlet and Juliet are separated by an intersection
Down which floats Ophelia Street, very sleepy.
They are all such demanding people
Which lends the town an air of tragedy
As though Mercutio coming home after a party
Failed to dip his lights and ran over
Polonius Street right up onto the sidewalk.
Even Shakespeare thought it best to keep them
     separated.
At the end of long girlish Juliet Street

With limbs like Twiggy the air grows
Sleepier and sleepier as though
Juliet had anorexia nervosa and could hardly bear
A morsel of blossoms or any sap.

MARILYN HACKER

## Fourteen

We shopped for dresses which were always wrong:
sweatshop approximations of the lean-
lined girls' wear I studied in *Seventeen.*
The armholes pinched, the belt didn't belong,
the skirt drooped forward (I'd be told at school).
Our odd-lot bargains deformed the image,
but she and I loved Saturday rummage.
One day she listed outside Loehmann's. Drool
wet her chin. Stumbling, she screamed at me.
Dropping
our parcels on the pavement, she fell in
what looked like a fit. I guessed: insulin.
The cop said, "Drunk," and called an ambulance
while she cursed me and slapped away my hands.
When I need a mother, I still go shopping.

EILÉAN NÍ CHUILLEANÁIN

## The Angel in the Stone

Trampled in the causeway, the stone the builders
    passed over
Calls out: 'Bone of the ranked heights, from darkness
Where moss and spiders never venture.
You know what ways I plumbed, past what hard
    threshold;

'You see our affliction, you know
How we were made and how we decay. At hand
When the backbone splintered in the sea tide, you
    have heard
The twang of the waves breaking our bones.

'You look down where the high peaks are ranging,
You see them flickering like flames—
They are like a midge dancing at evening.

'Give me rest for one long day of mourning;
Let me lie on the stone bench above the tree-line
And drink water for one whole day.'

WILLIAM MATTHEWS

## Cheap Seats, the Cincinnati Gardens, Professional Basketball, 1959

The less we paid, the more we climbed. Tendrils
of smoke lazed just as high and hung there, blue,
particulate, the opposite of dew.
We saw the whole court from up there. Few girls
had come, few wives, numerous boys in molt
like me. Our heroes leapt and surged and looped
and two nights out of three, like us, they'd lose.
But "like us" is wrong: we had no result
three nights out of three: so we had heroes.
And "we" is wrong, for I knew none by name
among that hazy company unless
I brought her with me. This was loneliness
with noise, unlike the kind I had at home
with no clock running down, and mirrors.

DOUGLAS DUNN

## Modern Love

It is summer, and we are in a house
That is not ours, sitting at a table
Enjoying minutes of a rented silence,
The upstairs people gone. The pigeons lull
To sleep the under-tens and invalids,
The tree shakes out its shadows to the grass,
The roses rove through the wilds of my neglect.
Our lives flap, and we have no hope of better

Happiness than this, not much to show for love
Than how we are, or how this evening is,
Unpeopled, silent, and where we are alive
In a domestic love, seemingly alone,
All other lives worn down to trees and sunlight,
Looking forward to a visit from the cat.


SUSAN MITCHELL

## from *From a Book of Prophets*

### 3. Boca Raton, 1990

Say the night was a cliff, a huge expectancy
the car climbed at right angles to a sky
floating its jets and fountains, its flimsy
chiffons of spray. I'm a sucker for beauty.
Besides, the seekers after comfort had gone
to the bar for daiquiris and drinks that foam.
Sometimes I dare myself to swim alone
where wind swells the imagination
black and something big as an ocean
takes a long drag, then heaves itself back.
When it happens, I don't want to come back.
Maybe I don't want to be believed.
Whatever it hisses into my ear, for me
only—unshared, undiluted, unsheathed.


DAVE SMITH

## *The Spring Poem*

*Everyone should write a Spring poem*
—LOUISE GLÜCK


Yes, but we must be sure of verities
such as proper heat and adequate form.
That's what poets are for, is my theory.
This then is a Spring poem. A car warms
its rusting hulk in a meadow; weeds slog

up its flanks in martial weather. April
or late March is our month. There is a fog
of spunky mildew and sweaty tufts spill
from the damp rump of a back seat. A spring
thrusts one gleaming tip out, a brilliant tooth
uncoiling from Winter's tension, a ring
of insects along, working out the Truth.
Each year this car, melting around that spring,
hears nails trench from boards and every squeak sing.


LOUISE GLÜCK

### Earthly Terror

I stood at the gate of a rich city.
I had everything the gods required;
I was ready; the burdens
of preparation had been long.
And the moment was the right moment,
the moment assigned to me.

Why were you afraid?

The moment was the right moment;
response must be ready.
On my lips,
the words trembled that were
the right words. Trembled—

and I knew that if I failed to answer
quickly enough, I would be turned away.

MICHAEL PALMER

## Pre-Petrarchan Sonnet

*(after Peter Altenberg)*

Someone identical with Dante
sits beside a stone. Enough
is enough is enough of.
It's odd that your hand feels warm
(snow carefully falling).
It's odd that the page was torn
just where the snow had begun.
There was never very much.
There is more (less) than there was.
Today it is 84, 74 and 12
and light and dark.
We are nowhere else.
His smile fell to one side.
Here and there it was very light and dark.


ELLEN BRYANT VOIGT

## *from* Kyrie

Who said the worst was past, who knew
such a thing? Someone writing history,
someone looking down on us
from the clouds. Down here, snow and wind:
cold blew through the clapboards,
our spring was frozen in the frozen ground.
Like the beasts in their holes,
no one stirred—if not sick
exhausted or afraid. In the village,
the doctor's own wife died in the night
of the nineteenth, 1919.
But it was true: at the window,
every afternoon, toward the horizon,
a little more light before the darkness fell.

W. S. DI PIERO

## *Starlings*

Snarls, bread trucks, yeast
breathing inside huddled bags,
and sleepers completing lives
behind their gray windows.

A whistle on the phonewires,
feathers, twitches, whistling
down to the hot loaves.

Reeds everywhere, pulse,
flesh, flutes, and wakened sighs.
An answer. Radio news

and breathers behind our windows,
birds' new voices changing,
*changed,* to the unforgiving
hunger screech of immigrants.

J. D. MCCLATCHY

## *from* Kilim

1

The force of habit takes order to its heart,
As when a nurse, her basket filled with the dead
Child's toys, has put it by the head
Of her tomb, unwittingly on an acanthus root.

Kallimachos, they say, made his capital
Of it, when around that basket the thorny leaf
Sprang up, nature pressed down by grief
Into shapes that made the loss a parable,

His idea to change the shallow bead and reel
For an imprint of afterlife apparent to all,
Bringing down to earth an extravagance.

So skill gives way to art, or a headstone
To history—the body by now left alone,
As if bodies were the soul's ornaments.

### Sonnet

The late Gracie Allen was a very lucid comedienne,
Especially in the way that lucid means shining and
    bright.
What her husband George Burns called her illogical
    logic
Made a halo around our syntax and ourselves as we
    laughed.

George Burns most often was her artful inconspicuous
    straight man.
He could move people about stage, construct skits
    and scenes, write
And gather jokes. They were married as long as
    ordinary magic
Would allow, thirty-eight years, until Gracie Allen's
    death.

In her fifties Gracie Allen developed a heart
    condition.
She would call George Burns when her heart felt
    funny and fluttered
He'd give her a pill and they'd hold each other till the
    palpitation
Stopped—just a few minutes, many times and pills.
    As magic fills
Then fulfilled must leave a space, one day Gracie
    Allen's heart fluttered
And hurt and stopped. George Burns said
    unbelievingly to the doctor, "But I still have some
    of the pills."

KAY RYAN

## *Full Measure*

You will get your full measure.
But, as when asking fairies for favors,
there is a trick: it comes in a block.
And of course one block is not
like another. Some respond to water,
giving everything wet a little flavor.
Some succumb to heat like butter.
Others give to steady pressure.
Others shatter at a tap. But
some resist; nothing in nature softens up
their bulk and no personal attack works.
People whose gift will not break
live by it all their lives; it shadows
every empty act they undertake.


MARILYN NELSON

## *Beauty Shoppe*

Yes, girl, he was fine. All night he'd groan I love you
baby, marry me, let me do it to you: Girl, he made
      my toes
curl. Then he got transferred. I quit my job, put my
furniture in storage, took my son out of school like a
      fool,
and waited for him to come back and get me. After a
      couple
of weeks, I got worried. Come a month of his silence,
I was praying he hadn't got himself killed. I called
his barracks every night, but they always said he was
      out.
After nights of calling I'd got to know the voice
of this white boy who said I'm sorry to tell you this,
Alberta, but he's been here every time you've called.
He won't come to the phone. All of the other Negro
guys are laughing at you. You shouldn't call again;
he's not worth it. Girl, that nigger broke my heart.

IAN WEDDE

## *from* Earthly: Sonnets for Carlos

### 20. a sonnet for Carlos

His new blue eyes see everything    to live
with the dream & have the world come on in!
because I believe it's happened again . . .
O their perfect intentions, all that love,
indifference he'll lose the knack of.
There's no date on the precious token
but I know it (huh!) november nineteen-
seventy-two, in time . . . while the dream heaves,
tilting heart true again on its fulcrum
among the unruly facts & fragments.
My fumbling voices clap their hands & shout
out, a swampy stink of old terrapin,
& for thanks, within this small settlement,
earthly & difficult & full of doubt!

DAVID LEHMAN

### *Like a Party*

You throw a war and hope people will come.
They do, and they bring signs, they bring rifles,
They make speeches, they build bombs,
And they fight the last war, or protest its arrival.
But this is now. One myth of war is that it takes
A lot of careful planning. Bunk. All you need is a cake
With a roll of film inside, or a briefcase full of germs.
Another myth stars Vulcan the smith,
Limping husband of Venus, mistress of Mars,
Who says: The bully broke my nose and what was I
To do, cry in the corner and ask him why
He didn't like me, or punch him back harder than he
Hit me? The war was not a play, not a movie but a mess;
Not a work of art; and if a game of chess, blind chess.

ALAN GOULD

## An Interrogator's Opening Remarks

We have no wish to lead you anywhere.
If anything we'd like to do you good.
The facts, of course, will shine like silverware,
but you must feel secure; that's understood.

A good rapport is what we're really after.
By all means keep the things you know concealed.
We know you know, behind the tea and laughter,
your secrets are a gravitational field.

We're falling in toward them very fast.
This happens by your simply being here
subtracted from the household of your past,
naked with what we think you think is dear.

So now let's chat, old son. You're not alone.
Your time is ours. Your choices are your own.

DENIS JOHNSON

## Passengers

The world will burst like an intestine in the sun,
the dark turn to granite and the granite to a name,
but there will always be somebody riding the bus
through these intersections strewn with broken glass
among speechless women beating their little ones,
always a slow alphabet of rain
speaking of drifting and perishing to the air,
always these definite jails of light in the sky
at the wedding of this clarity and this storm
and a woman's turning—her languid flight of hair
traveling through frame after frame of memory
where the past turns, its face sparking like emery,
to open its grace and incredible harm
over my life, and I will never die.

PHILIP NEILSEN

## Vermouth

One day she said to her husband, something is
missing from my life, and two weeks later she said
you know we haven't had sex for three months
and he said sex isn't everything. This is a doorway
out there light plays on the trees, small animals
sheath claws: isn't that your Women's Weekly reflex—
fall and the carpet cradles you: you finger dirty glasses
like a coroner, searching for the hidden cause.

She enrolled for an adult course in cocktail mixing,
the class full of divorcees took her by the hand,
stand and talk: you should tell yourself
woman, this is one of the doorways: you can't
just toss Vermouth in with Gin and expect them
to set up house. Here, give me your glass.

SHEROD SANTOS

## Ghost Sonnet

The offshore rains had come early to the headlands,
   the pools
of standing water quickly filling into streams, the
   wind
green-scented with the high grass thickening the
   margins
of the road. For a day and a half I'd slogged up
   through it
circling the bog beneath Queen Maeve's cairn. But
   just toward
dusk of that second day, as when a jostled memory's
   loosed
from some dark mooring in the head, the wet mist
   lifted, the last
thin wisps drawn off like topsails from the ditchbacks
   and ferns.

And then the wind whistled, in Yeats's phrase, history-
    haunted round the Mareotic Lake, and the sun-
    scrubbed windows
of the drying sheds gave back that last clear-
    vowelled light,
their canted roofs afloat in the hills like those
    storied stone boats
idling on the tide—or like the scatter of his
    unsettling swans,
which I now know can neither be found nor
    forgotten.

EDITH SPEERS

## *from* Love Sonnets

### Sonnet 9

Darling! I have to see you! Can you come?
Not right now, of course—I'm up to my bum
In boring things I have to do. Why not
Next month? Not Thursday because I work that
    day;
And what with this and that, all Wednesday's
    shot;
Tuesdays are so awkward, too. Let's say
A long weekend. But warn me in advance—
it won't be wise to leave it all to chance.

It's such a pity I'm not on the phone,
But call me at my job, that's quite okay,
Otherwise you mightn't find me home—
A shame if you drove down here all that way
For nothing. Which reminds me—I can't cook,
So bring some coleslaw and a barbecued chook.

JULIA ALVAREZ
## from 33

Let's make a modern primer for our kids:
A is for Auschwitz; B for Biafra;
Chile; Dachau; El Salvador; F is
the Falklands; Grenada; Hiroshima
stands for H; Northern Ireland for I;
J is for Jonestown; K for Korea;
L for massacres in Lidice; My Lai;
N, Nicaragua; O, Okinawa;
P is the Persian Gulf and Qatar, Q;
R wanda; Sarajevo—this year's hell;
T is Treblinka and Uganda U;
Vietnam and Wounded Knee. What's left to spell?
An X to name the countless disappeared
when they are dust in Yemen or Zaire.


DANA GIOIA
## Sunday Night in Santa Rosa

The carnival is over. The high tents,
the palaces of light, are folded flat
and trucked away. A three-time loser yanks
the Wheel of Fortune off the wall. Mice
pick through the garbage by the popcorn stand.
A drunken giant falls asleep beside
the juggler, and the Dog-Faced Boy sneaks off
to join the Serpent Lady for the night.
Wind sweeps ticket stubs along the walk.
The Dead Man loads his coffin on a truck.
Off in a trailer by the parking lot
the radio predicts tomorrow's weather
while a clown stares in a dressing mirror,
takes out a box, and peels away his face.

T. R. HUMMER

## *Telepathic Poetics*

To enter them all in darkness, over and over, coming
    through rear windows or baffled front-door locks,
Not worried about patrol cars or neighborhood
      watch, subverting
    streetlights, yard dogs, flowers or any lack of flowers:

To touch whatever is there—jewelry, shells, old letters,
    broken combs, dirty rag dolls, a saxophone on a
    stand—
Tenderly, as if to steal but not stealing, indiscriminate,
    while the righteous married breathe each other's
    sleep

In adjoining bedrooms: all this trouble just to be
      somewhere,
    anywhere, among furniture however polished or
    broken down,
Among bills, bank statements, death certificates (but
    none of them
    stamped with our names): in extinguished
    basements

With fuse boxes, rusted switches invisible but offering
    at least the possibility of ordinary light.

MEDBH MCGUCKIAN

## *Shelmalier*

Looked after only by the four womb-walls,
if anything curved in the ruined city his last hour
it was his human hands, bituminous, while all laws
were aimed at him, returning to the metre of a star:
like a century about to be over, a river trying
to film itself, detaching its voice from itself,
he qualified the air of his own dying,

his brain in folds like the semi-open rose of grief.
His eyes recorded calm and keen this exercise,
deep-seated, promising avenues, they keep their
   kingdom:
it is I who am only just left in flight, exiled
into an outline of time, I court his speech, not him.
This great estrangement has the destination of a
   rhyme.
The trees of his heart breathe regular, in my dream.

PAUL MULDOON

## *from* The Old Country

I

Where every town was a tidy town
and every garden a hanging garden.
A half could be had for half a crown.
Every major artery would harden

since every meal was a square meal.
Every clothesline showed a line of undies
yet no house was in dishabille.
Every Sunday took a month of Sundays

till everyone got it off by heart
every start was a bad start
since all conclusions were foregone.

Every wood had its twist of woodbine.
Every cliff its herd of fatalistic swine.
Every runnel was a Rubicon.

RITA DOVE

## *Sonnet in Primary Colors*

This is for the woman with one black wing
swept over her eyes: lovely Frida, erect
among parrots, in the stern petticoats of the peasant,

who painted herself a present—
wildflowers entwining the plaster corset
her spine resides in, that flaming pillar—
this priestess in the romance of mirrors.

Each night she lay down in pair and rose
to the celluloid butterflies of her Beloved Dead,
Lenin and Marx and Stalin arrayed at the footstead.
And rose to her easel, the hundred dogs panting
like children along the graveled walks of the garden,
until Diego appeared as a skull in the circular window
of the thumbprint searing her immutable brow.

SUSAN STEWART

## *from* Slaughter

5

Now let us go back to the stunning,
to the meeting of a human and animal mind, let us
go back and begin again where the function
overwhelms all hesitation and seems like
an act of nature. But they were tired and had no time
for me; the immense weight of memory dragged up
and brought back into the present was, too, like a
   great
beast, beached and spoiled. I finally grasped
what had happened, how the real could not
be evoked except in a spell of longing for
the past or the mime that would be, after all,
another occasion for suffering.
There would be no more instruction,
no more, in the end, hand guiding the hand.

TOM SLEIGH

## *from* **The Work**

*for my father*

### 1. Today

Today, this moment, speechlessly in pain,
He fights the terror of being poured out,
The fall into darkness unquenchably long
So that even as he hurtles he keeps holding

Back like a dam the flood overtops—but
   nothing now
Can stop that surge, already he swirls
To the source of Voices, the many throats inside
   the one
Throat, each swallowing the unstoppable
   flood . . .

And as if that, all along, were what he'd wanted,
He hears the Voices begin to die down
The way a marsh in spring pulsing and shrilling
Sunup to sundown falls gradually still

—Unappeasable, the silence that will follow
When his every last drop has been poured out.

ROSANNA WARREN

### *Alps*

The mountains taught us speechlessness.
A snowshoe hare loped to its place

in silence, through powder. We spoke
only below, in the village, and then
of merely human absences, as when
G. departed, taken sick,

or when we had to conclude affairs
that had not been love, or even,
often, affairs—conclude them in
haste, with our hats on, there by the stairs:

for whatever they'd been, they had
at least composed the bleak-
ness. And hard enough it had been to speak
of those un-mountainous matters, in few words,
    without fraud.


DAVID WOJAHN

## *from* Mystery Train

### 1. Homage: Light from the Hall

It is Soul Brother Number One, James Brown,
Chanting, "It wouldn't be nothing,
    noth-iiiinnnnnggg. . . ."
Dismembering the notes until everything hangs
On his mystical half-screech, notes skidding 'round
Your brain as you listen, rapt, thirteen,
Transistor and its single earphone tucked
With you beneath the midnight covers, station WKED,
Big Daddy Armand, The Ragin' Cajun,
"Spinning out the *bossest* platters for you all,"
Golden age trance, when New Orleans stations
Traveling two thousand miles shaped distance
Into alchemy. Beneath the door, a light from the hall
Bathing the bedroom in its stammering glow:
Cooke and Redding risen, James Brown quaking the
    Apollo.


DAVID BAKER

## *from* Sonnets from One State West

### 1. Inside the Covered Bridge Historic Site

Nothing about this is right. I have torn
my way down the old path, overgrown, thicker

than I had thought with ivy, brush, stickers
as long as safety pins—and all to mourn

a sway-backed bridge, a relic as forlorn
as the bone-dry creek bed strung with liquor

bottles that it spans. No mushroom picker,
squirrel hunter, or arrowhead collector born

with common sense would come out of his way
as far as I have to get here. So much

for history. Getting back out, I know,
will be worse. I see just one of two ways:

to battle the green wall of brush from which
this path has come—

                or there, into which it goes.


PHILLIS LEVIN

### On the Other Hand

The leaves of the ivy
Are heavy today.
Even we are too heavy,  .
Their shadows say:

Nothing moves us,
We cannot stray
Across a walkway.
But glory is still green.

Whoever leaned
Against a screen
Unlatches the door,

Whoever said
There, there, now
Doesn't anymore.

MARY JO SALTER

## Half a Double Sonnet

*for Ben*

Their ordeal over, now the only trouble
was conveying somehow to a boy of three
that for a week or two he'd be seeing double.
Surely he wouldn't recall the surgery
years later, but what about the psychic scars?
And so, when the patch came off, they bought the toy
he'd wanted most. He held it high. "Two cars!"
he cried; and drove himself from joy to joy.
Two baby sisters . . . One was enough of Clare,
but who could complain?—considering that another
woman had stepped forward to take care
of the girls, which left him all alone with Mother.
Victory! Even when he went to pee,
he was seconded in his virility.

CAROL ANN DUFFY

## Prayer

Some days, although we cannot pray, a prayer
utters itself. So, a woman will lift
her head from the sieve of her hands and stare
at the minims sung by a tree, a sudden gift.

Some nights, although we are faithless, the truth
enters our hearts, that small familiar pain;
then a man will stand stock-still, hearing his youth
in the distant Latin chanting of a train.

Pray for us now. Grade I piano scales
console the lodger looking out across
a Midlands town. Then dusk, and someone calls
a child's name as though they named their loss.

Darkness outside. Inside, the radio's prayer—
Rockall. Malin. Dogger. Finisterre.

KIMIKO HAHN

## *from* Reckless Sonnets

8

My father, as a boy in Milwaukee, thought
the cicada's cry was the whir from a live wire—
not from muscles on the sides of an insect
vibrating against an outer membrane. Strange though
that, because they have no ears, no one knows why
the males cry so doggedly into the gray air.
Not strange that the young live underground sucking
    sap from tree roots
for seventeen years. A long, charmed childhood
not unlike one in a Great Lake town where at dusk
you'd pack up swimsuit, shake sand off your towel
and head back to the lights in the two-family houses
lining the streets. Where the family sat around the
    radio.
And parents argued over their son and daughter
until each left for good. To cry in the air.

PAULA MEEHAN

## *Queen*

Go then. Don't let me stand in your way.
I hope you'll be very happy. She's quite
pretty if you like that type. Not a hair astray,
all that jangly jewellery, teeth so white
and even. Are they real? She's like a queen,
you a subject yoked to plod her wake.
I who spurn vanity admit
a fascination with her nails, long, sharp,
red as rosehips flashing in autumn dusk.
That dress—lotus flowers on a field of green,
just the thing to swan around your bedsit

in. Forgive me if I harp.
I never meant to nag you, act the wife,
it's just your cringing wounds me like a knife.


ROBIN ROBERTSON

### Swimming in the Woods

Her long body in the spangled shade of the wood
was a swimmer moving through a pool:
fractal, finned by leaf and light;
the loose plates of lozenge and rhombus
wobbling coins of sunlight.
When she stopped, the water stopped,
and the sun re-made her as a tree,
banded and freckled and foxed.

Besieged by symmetries, condemned
to these patterns of love and loss,
I stare at the wet shape on the tiles
till it fades; when she came and sat next to me
after her swim and walked away
back to the trees, she left a dark butterfly.


HENRI COLE

### Black Camellia

*[after Petrarch]*

Little room, with four and a half tatami mats
and sliding paper doors, that used to be
a white, translucent place to live in refined
     poverty,
what are you now but scalding water in a
     bath?
Little mattress, that used to fold around me
at sunrise as unfinished dreams were fading,
what are you now but a blood-red palanquin

of plucked feathers and silk airing in the sun?
Weeding the garden, paring a turnip, drinking
    tea
for want of wine, I flee from my secret love
and from my mind's worm—This is a poem.
Is this a table? No, this is a poem. Am I a girl?—
seeking out the meat-hook crowd I once
    loathed,
I'm so afraid to find myself alone.

# THE SONNET GOES TO
# DIFFERENT LENGTHS

The truth is that there have always been meaningful variations on the fourteen-line standard. Almost every one of the poems here defines itself as a sonnet. It relates an experience, develops a thought, makes a case, an argument. It takes a turn. The poets here have gone to great lengths to give the sonnet a different length. There have been extensions and reductions, departures, rebellions. The full story of the sonnet ought to include them.

# THE SONNET GOES TO
# DIFFERENT LENGTHS

*The Sonnet Form is not a matter of 14 lines...*
—LOUIS ZUKOFSKY, *A Test of Poetry* (1948)

The sonnet, which has had such a long life as a prescribed form, is essentially a fourteen-line poem. That is its core, its basic sound. That is its formal identity. These fourteen lines comprise what was originally considered the "normal sonnet." Yet even in the thirteenth century, the time of its origins, there was also a large number of alternative sonnet forms.

From the beginning, poets have tinkered with the fourteen-line formula. Some added lines, which led to the *sonnetto caudato* or "tailed sonnet." This form, wonderfully represented by a poem that Michelangelo wrote while he was painting the Sistine Chapel, was first imported by Milton into English ("On the New Forcers of Conscience under the Long Parliament"). Geoffrey Chaucer adapted one of Petrarch's sonnets (*Rime* 132) and turned it into three seven-line stanzas of rhyme royal, which are embedded in *Troilus and Criseyde* (lines 400–421). Other poets reduced the number of syllables in various lines; they moved from, say, eleven to seven syllables. In the mid-thirteenth century, the poet Guittone d'Arezzo did both; he created a twenty-two-line sonnet that used long and short lines. He most likely also invented the double sonnet, a poem with two sextets followed by two quatrains. Dante used this form, which is analogous to fourteen-line sonnets, to great effect in the two poems from *La Vita Nuova (The New Life),* which lead off our section. He was the first major practitioner of the sonnet form.

The sonnet originated as a short lyric. It made its first appearance in English through Chaucer's adaptation of Petrarch's *Canzoniere* 132. The word *sonnet* was initially used in English to describe almost any short poem, which can be seen, say, in John Donne's *Songs and Sonets*. It was only after the Elizabethan period that the word *sonnet* came to stand for the fourteen-line norm we recognize today.

Poets have also invoked the sonnet to engage—and sometimes to refute—its sentimental history. Thus George Meredith composed *Modern Love*, an autobiographical sequence of fifty sixteen-line "sonnets." These symmetrically shaped poems critique the Petrarchan tradition and dissect "the sentimental passion of these days." Meredith's sequence is a formal way of responding to the sonnet's historical take on love.

Poets like Meredith have sometimes kept the forensic strategies of the sonnet—it is often an argumentative form—but varied its length. Ralph Waldo Emerson eliminated lines altogether in his poem "Woods," which he subtitled "A Prose Sonnet." It seems to be a particularly American pleasure (Karl Shapiro did say that there is something "un-American" about the sonnet) to explode the form, an impulse that can be seen in a range of modern and contemporary sonnet sequences—from E. E. Cummings to Ted Berrigan and Gerald Stern. Yet these sequences also reflect the sonnet's long grip and history. Even the French poet Blaise Cendrars's *Unnatural Sonnets* gets something of its riotous power by playing off the "natural" sonnets of the past.

Many poets have also been interested in the mathematical proportions of the sonnet form. That was especially true for Gerard Manley Hopkins, who invented the "Curtal Sonnet." The term *curtal* applies to an animal that has had its tail docked, and Hopkins aptly borrowed it to describe his foreshortened version of the sonnet, which, one could say, is the opposite of the "tailed sonnet." His ten-and-a-half-line poem is literally a curtailed or contracted sonnet. It consists of three-fourths of a Petrarchan sonnet shrunk proportionately. Hopkins also experimented with metrics in "Spelt from Sibyl's Leaves" ("the longest sonnet," Hopkins contended, "ever made"), which employs eight-stress lines and begins:

> Earnest, earthless, equal, attuneable, ' vaulty,
>     voluminous, . . . stupendous
> Evening strains to be tíme's vást, ' womb-of-all,
>     home-of-all, hearse-of-all night.

Poetry is a precise art, and the mathematical possibilities of the sonnet form incite certain formally minded poets. Thus W. H. Auden expanded the sonnet in the proportion 12:9 in the third section of his sonnet sequence "The Quest." And John Brooks Wheelwright ingeniously came up with a twelve-line sonnet in alexandrines that has the same number of overall feet as a fourteen-line sonnet in iambic pentameter.

Other poets have also worked hard to expand (Millay) and contract (Bishop) the sonnet horizontally. The lines lengthen and shorten according to the new formula. Rimbaud's poem "Drunk Driver," which confines itself to one syllable per line, was probably the first "truly emaciated sonnet" (Anthony Hecht). Mona Van Duyn invented a short fourteen-line poem she called the "minimalist sonnet" and the "extended minimalist sonnet." "Of all the forms," she writes, "the sonnet seems most available to poets for deconstruction." In his poem "Post-Coitum Tristesse: A Sonnet," Brad Leithauser strips the form down to fourteen rhyming syllables (one per line) and, in so doing, takes the love poem all the way back to a sigh ("Hm. . .").

The truth is that there have always been meaningful variations on the fourteen-line standard. Almost every one of these poems defines itself as a sonnet. It relates an experience, develops a thought, makes a case, an argument. It takes a turn. The poets here have gone to great lengths to give the sonnet a different length. There have been extensions and reductions, departures, rebellions. The full story of the sonnet ought to include them.

DANTE ALIGHIERI (TRANS. DANTE GABRIEL ROSSETTI)
## *from* La Vita Nuova (The New Life)

Death, alway cruel, Pity's foe in chief,
Mother who brought forth grief,
   Merciless judgement and without appeal!
   Since thou alone hast made my heart to feel
   This sadness and unweal,
My tongue upbraideth thee without relief.

And now (for I must rid thy name of ruth)
Behoves me speak the truth
   Touching thy cruelty and wickedness:
   Not that they be not known; but ne'ertheless
   I would give hate more stress
With them that feed on love in very sooth.

Out of this world thou hast driven courtesy,
   And virtue, dearly prized in womanhood;
   And out of youth's gay mood
The lovely lightness is quite gone through thee.

Whom now I mourn, no man shall learn from me
   Save by the measure of these praises given.
   Whoso deserves not Heaven
May never hope to have her company.

DANTE ALIGHIERI (TRANS. DANTE GABRIEL ROSSETTI)
## *from* La Vita Nuova (The New Life)

All ye that pass along Love's trodden way,
Pause ye awhile and say
   If there be any grief like unto mine:
I pray you that you hearken a short space
Patiently, if my case
   Be not a piteous marvel and a sign.

Love (never, certes, for my worthless part,
But of his own great heart),
    Vouchsafed to me a life so calm and sweet
That oft I heard folk question as I went
What such great gladness meant:—
    They spoke of it behind me in the street.

But now that fearless bearing is all gone
    Which with Love's hoarded wealth was given me;
    Till I am grown to be
So poor that I have dread to think thereon.

And thus it is that I, being like as one
    Who is ashamed and hides his poverty,
    Without seem full of glee,
And let my heart within travail and moan.

GEOFFREY CHAUCER

## *from* Troilus and Criseyde

**Canticus Troili**

"If no love is, O God, what fele I so?
And if love is, what thing and which is he?
If love be good, from whennes cometh my woo?
If it be wikke, a wonder thynketh me,
When every torment and adversite
That cometh of hym, may to me savory thinke,
For ay thurst I, the more that ich it drynke.

"And if that at myn owen lust I brenne,
From whennes cometh my waillynge and my pleynte?
If harm agree me, wherto pleyne I thenne?
I noot, ne whi unwary that I feynte.
O quike deth, O swete harm so queynte,
How may of the in me swich quantite,
But if that I consente that it be?

"And if that I consente, I wrongfully
Compleyne, iwis. Thus possed to and fro,
Al stereless withinne a boot am I
Amydde the see, bitwixen wyndes two,
That in contrarie stonden evere mo.
Allas! what is this wonder maladie?
For hete of cold, for cold of hete, I dye."

MICHELANGELO BUONARROTI (TRANS. GAIL MAZUR)

## *from* Sonnets

### V. To Giovanni da Pistoia When the Author was Painting the Vault of the Sistine Chapel

I've already grown a goiter from this torture,
hunched up here like a cat in Lombardy
(or anywhere else where the stagnant water's
    poison).
My stomach's squashed under my chin, my
    beard's
pointing at heaven, my brain's crushed in a casket,
my breast twists like a harpy's. My brush,
above me all the time, dribbles paint
so my face makes a fine floor for droppings!

My haunches are grinding into my guts,
my poor ass strains to work as a counterweight,
every gesture I make is blind and aimless.
My skin hangs loose below me, my spine's
all knotted from folding over itself.
I'm bent taut as a Syrian bow.

Because I'm stuck like this, my thoughts
are crazy, perfidious tripe:
anyone shoots badly through a crooked
    blowpipe.
My painting is dead.
Defend it for me, Giovanni, protect my honor.
I am not in the right place—I am not a painter.

GEORGE PEELE

## *from* Polyhymnia

**Farewell to Arms**

His golden locks time hath to silver turned;
    O time too swift, O swiftness never ceasing!
His youth 'gainst time and age hath ever spurned,
    But spurned in vain; youth waneth by increasing:
Beauty, strength, youth, are flowers but fading seen;
Duty, faith, love, are roots, and ever green.

His helmet now shall make a hive for bees,
    And, lovers' sonnets turned to holy psalms,
A man-at-arms must now serve on his knees,
    And feed on prayers, which are age his alms:
But though from court to cottage he depart,
His saint is sure of his unspotted heart.

And when he saddest sits in homely cell,
    He'll teach his swains this carol for a song,—
"Blessed be the hearts that wish my sovereign well,
    Cursed be the souls that think her any wrong."
Goddess, allow this aged man his right,
To be your beadsman now that was your knight.

THOMAS WATSON

## *from* Hekatompathia,
## A Passionate Century of Love

**XIX**

If Cupid were a child, as poets feign,
How comes it then that Mars doth fear his might?
If blind, how chance so many to their pain
Whom he hath hit can witness of his sight?
If he have wings to fly where thinks him best,
How haps he lurketh still within my breast?
If bow and shafts should be his chiefest tools,
Why doth he set so many hearts on fire?

If he were mad, how could he further fools
To whet their wits as place and time require?
If wise, how could so many lose their wits
Or dote through love and die in frantic fits?
If naked, still he wander to and fro,
How doth not sun or frost offend his skin?
If that a god he be, how falls it so
That all wants end which he doth once begin?
Oh wondrous thing, that I whom love hath
    spent
Can scarcely know himself or his intent.

THOMAS LODGE

## *from* Rosalynde

**Montanus's Sonnet**

Phoebe sat,
Sweet she sat,
    Sweet sat Phoebe when I saw her,
White her brow,
Coy her eye:
    Brow and eye how much you please me.
Words I spent,
Sighs I sent;
    Sighs and words could never draw her.
Oh my love,
Thou art lost,
    Since no sight could ever ease thee.

Phoebe sat
By a fount,
    Sitting by a fount I spied her:
Sweet her touch,
Rare her voice:
    Touch and voice what may distain you?
As she sung,
I did sigh,

And by sighs whilst that I tried her,
Oh mine eyes,
You did lose
  Her first sight and whose want did pain you.

Phoebe's flocks,
White as wool,
  Yet were Phoebe's locks more whiter.
Phoebe's eyes
Dovelike mild,
  Dovelike eyes, both mild and cruel.
Montan swears,
In your lamps
  He will die for to delight her.
Phoebe yield,
Or I die:
  Shall true hearts be fancy's fuel?

WILLIAM SHAKESPEARE

## Sonnet 126

O thou, my lovely boy, who in thy power
Dost hold Time's fickle glass, his sickle Hour;
Who hast by waning grown, and therein show'st
Thy lovers withering as thy sweet self grow'st:
If Nature, sovereign mistress over wrack,
As thou goest onwards, still will pluck thee back,
She keeps thee to this purpose, that her skill
May Time disgrace, and wretched Minute kill.
Yet fear her, O thou minion of her pleasure:
She may detain, but not still keep, her treasure.
Her audit, though delayed, answered must be,
And her quietus is to render thee.

## *from* Parthenophil and Parthenophe

### 36

And thus continuing with outrageous fier,
   My Sunne proceeding forward to my sorrow
   Tooke up his court, but willing to retier
   Within the Lyon's denne, his rage did borrow:
But whiles within that mansion he remayned,
   How cruell was Parthenophe to me,
   And when of my great sorrowes I complained,
   She Lyon-like wish't they might tenfold be.
Then did I rage and in unkindly passions
   I rent mine heare, and rac'd my tender skinne,
   And raving in such frantique fashions
   That with such crueltie she did beginne
To feede the fier which I was burned in.
   Can women brooke to deale so sore with men?
   She manne's woe learn'd it in the Lyon's denne.

## *Sonnet. The Token*

Send me some token, that my hope may live,
   Or that my easeless thoughts may sleep and rest;
Send me some honey to make sweet my hive,
   That in my passions I may hope the best.
I beg no riband wrought with thine own hands,
   To knit our loves in the fantastic strain
Of new-touched youth; nor ring to shew the stands
   Of our affection, that, as that's round and plain,
So should our loves meet in simplicity;
   No, nor the corals which thy wrist enfold,
Laced up together in congruity,
   To shew our thoughts should rest in the same
     hold;
No, nor thy picture, though most gracious,
   And most desired, because best like the best;

Nor witty lines, which are most copious
   Within the writings which thou hast addressed.

Send me nor this nor that to increase my store,
   But swear thou think'st I love thee, and no more.

GEORGE HERBERT

### A Wreath

A wreathed garland of deserved praise,
Of praise deserved, unto thee I give,
I give to thee, who knowest all my ways,
My crooked winding ways, wherein I live,
Wherein I die, not live: for life is straight,
Straight as a line, and ever tends to thee,
To thee, who art more far above deceit,
Than deceit seems above simplicity.
Give me simplicity, that I may live,
So live and like, that I may know thy ways,
Know them and practise them: then shall I give
For this poor wreath, give thee a crown of praise.

JOHN MILTON

### On the New Forcers of Conscience
### under the Long Parliament

Because you have thrown off your prelate lord,
   And with stiff vows renounced his liturgy
   To seize the widowed whore plurality
From them whose sin ye envied, not abhorred,
Dare ye for this adjure the civil sword
   To force our consciences that Christ set free,
   And ride us with a classic hierarchy
Taught ye by mere A. S. and Rutherford?
Men whose life, learning, faith and pure intent
   Would have been held in high esteem with Paul
   Must now be named and printed heretics
By shallow Edwards and Scotch What-d'ye-call:

But we do hope to find out all your tricks,
    Your plots and packing worse than those of
        Trent,
        That so the Parliament
May with their wholesome and preventive shears
Clip your phylacteries, though balk your ears,
        And succour our just fears
When they shall read this clearly in your charge,
New *Presbyter* is but old *Priest* writ large.


SIR JOHN SUCKLING

## *from* Sonnets

I

Dost see how unregarded now
    That piece of beauty passes?
There was a time when I did vow
    To that alone;
    But mark the fate of faces;
The red and white works now no more on me,
Than if it could not charm, or I not see.

And yet the face continues good,
    And I have still desires,
And still the self-same flesh and blood,
    As apt to melt,
    And suffer from those fires;
O, some kind power unriddle where it lies:
Whether my heart be faulty, or her eyes?

She every day her man does kill,
    And I as often die;
Neither her power then nor my will
    Can question'd be;
    What is the mystery?
Sure beauty's empires, like to greater states,
Have certain periods set, and hidden fates.

RICHARD LOVELACE
## Sonnet

I.

When I by thy faire shape did sweare,
And mingled with each Vowe a teare,
   I lov'd, I lov'd thee best,
   I swore as I profest;
For all the while you lasted warme and pure,
   My Oathes too did endure;
But once turn'd faithlesse to thy selfe, and Old,
They then with thee incessantly grew Cold.

II.

I swore my selfe thy sacrifice
By th' *Ebon* Bowes that guard thine eyes,
   Which now are alter'd White,
   And by the glorious Light
Of both those Stars, of which their spheres bereft,
   Only the Gellie's left:
Then changed thus, no more I'm bound to you,
Then swearing to a Saint that proves untrue.

ANN RADCLIFFE
## Storied Sonnet

The weary traveler, who, all night long,
Has climbed among the Alps' tremendous steeps,
Skirting the pathless precipice, where throng
Wild forms of danger; as he onward creeps
If, chance, his anxious eye at distance sees
The mountain-shepherd's solitary home,
Peeping from forth the moon-illumined trees,
What sudden transports to his bosom come!
But, if between some hideous chasm yawn,
Where the cleft pine a doubtful bridge displays,
In dreadful silence, on the brink, forlorn
He stands, and views in the faint rays

Far, far below, the torrent's rising surge,
And listens to the wild impetuous roar;
Still eyes the depth, still shudders on the verge,
Fears to return, nor dares to venture o'er.
Desperate, at length the tottering plank he tries,
His weak steps slide, he shrieks, he sinks—he dies!


WILLIAM WORDSWORTH

## *"It is no Spirit who from Heaven hath flown"*

It is no Spirit who from Heaven hath flown,
And is descending on his embassy;
Nor Traveller gone from Earth the Heavens to
    espy!
'Tis Hesperus—there he stands with glittering
    crown,
First admonition that the sun is down!
For yet it is broad day-light: clouds pass by;
A few are near him still—and now the sky,
He hath it to himself—'tis all his own.
O most ambitious Star! an inquest wrought
Within me when I recognised thy light;
A moment I was startled at the sight:
And, while I gazed, there came to me a thought
That I might step beyond my natural race
As thou seem'st now to do; might one day trace
Some ground not mine; and, strong her strength
    above,
My Soul, an Apparition in the place,
Tread there, with steps that no one shall reprove!


JOHN KEATS

## *"Nature withheld Cassandra in the skies"*

Nature withheld Cassandra in the skies
    For meet adornment a full thousand years;
She took their cream of beauty, fairest dyes,
    And shaped and tinted her above all peers.

Love meanwhile held her dearly with his wings,
  And underneath their shadow charm'd her eyes
To such a richness, that the cloudy kings
  Of high Olympus utter'd slavish sighs.
When I beheld her on the earth descend,
  My heart began to burn—and only pains,
They were my pleasures, they my sad life's end;
  Love pour'd her beauty into my warm veins.


RALPH WALDO EMERSON

## Woods: A Prose Sonnet

Wise are ye, O ancient woods! wiser than man. Whoso goeth in your paths or into your thickets where no paths are, readeth the same cheerful lesson whether he be a young child or a hundred years old. Comes he in good fortune or bad, ye say the same things, & from age to age. Ever the needles of the pine grow & fall, the acorns on the oak, the maples redden in autumn, & at all times of the year the ground pine & the pyrola bud & root under foot. What is called fortune & what is called Time by men—ye know them not. Men have not language to describe one moment of your eternal life. This I would ask of you, o sacred Woods, when ye shall next give me somewhat to say, give me also the tune wherein to say it. Give me a tune of your own like your winds or rains or brooks or birds; for the songs of men grow old when they have been often repeated, but yours, though a man have heard them for seventy years, are never the same, but always new, like time itself, or like love.


EDGAR ALLAN POE

## Sonnet—Silence

There are some qualities—some incorporate things,
  That have a double life, which thus is made
A type of that twin entity which springs

From matter and light, evinced in solid and
   shade.
There is a two-fold *Silence*—sea and shore—
   Body and soul. One dwells in lonely places,
   Newly with grass o'ergrown; some solemn
     graces,
Some human memories and tearful lore,
Render him terrorless: his name's "No More."
He is the corporate Silence: dread him not!
   No power hath he of evil in himself;
But should some urgent fate (untimely lot!)
   Bring thee to meet his shadow (nameless elf,
That haunteth the lone regions where hath trod
No foot of man,) commend thyself to God!

ALFRED, LORD TENNYSON

## The Kraken

Below the thunders of the upper deep;
Far, far beneath in the abysmal sea,
His ancient, dreamless, uninvaded sleep
The Kraken sleepeth: faintest sunlights flee
About his shadowy sides: above him swell
Huge sponges of millennial growth and height;
And far away into the sickly light,
From many a wondrous grot and secret cell
Unnumbered and enormous polypi
Winnow with giant arms the slumbering green.
There hath he lain for ages and will lie
Battening upon huge seaworms in his sleep,
Until the latter fire shall heat the deep;
Then once by man and angels to be seen,
In roaring he shall rise and on the surface die.

MARY BRYAN

## The Maniac (2)

"My own MARIA!—Ah my own—my own!"
Withheld my steps in such entreating tone,
I turn'd—so meek a form I could not fear,
I prest th' extended hand and bath'd it with a
    tear.—
I stood as I could never leave that place,
Yet would have spoken, would have turn'd
    away:—
"My own MARIA!"—gazing on my face,
As one long lost to him, did that lorn maniac say.
I could not speak—so lovely was the joy
The maniac shew'd, 'twere cruel to destroy;
And I had seen him look so lost in woe,
That if I were not his—I could not tell him so.
"My own MARIA!"—with such tender grace,
Repeated oft—that now the maniac grew
Dear and more dear; till urged to leave the place,
I could not speak—I could not *look* adieu—
Lest I had seen him in his wild despair,
And hasten'd to that prison'd maniac's cell,
And left the world to dwell for ever there—
Few in that sordid world I lov'd so well:
And often since that hour, thou poor unknown,
In mem'ry's tenderest thoughts, I have been all thine
    own!

GEORGE MEREDITH

## *from* Modern Love

I

By this he knew she wept with waking eyes:
That, at his hand's light quiver by her head,
The strange low sobs that shook their common bed,
Were called into her with a sharp surprise,
And strangled mute, like little gaping snakes,

Dreadfully venomous to him. She lay
Stone-still, and the long darkness flowed away
With muffled pulses. Then, as midnight makes
Her giant heart of Memory and Tears
Drink the pale drug of silence, and so beat
Sleep's heavy measure, they from head to feet
Were moveless, looking through their dead black
    years,
By vain regret scrawled over the blank wall.
Like sculptured effigies they might be seen
Upon their marriage-tomb, the sword between;
Each wishing for the sword that severs all.

GEORGE MEREDITH

### *from* Modern Love

**XXV**

You like not that French novel? Tell me why.
You think it quite unnatural. Let us see.
The actors are, it seems, the usual three:
Husband, and wife, and lover. She—but fie!
In England we'll not hear of it. Edmond,
The lover, her devout chagrin doth share;
Blanc-mange and absinthe are his penitent fare,
Till his pale aspect makes her over-fond:
So, to preclude fresh sin, he tries rosbif.
Meantime the husband is no more abused:
Auguste forgives her ere the tear is used.
Then hangeth all on one tremendous IF:—
*If* she will choose between them. She does
    choose;
And takes her husband, like a proper wife.
Unnatural? My dear, these things are life:
And life, some think, is worthy of the Muse.

GEORGE MEREDITH

## *from* Modern Love

### XXX

What are we first? First, animals; and next
Intelligences at a leap; on whom
Pale lies the distant shadow of the tomb,
And all that draweth on the tomb for text.
Into which state comes Love, the crowning sun:
Beneath whose light the shadow loses form.
We are the lords of life, and life is warm.
Intelligence and instinct now are one.
But Nature says: 'My children most they seem
When they least know me: therefore I decree
That they shall suffer.' Swift doth young Love flee,
And we stand wakened, shivering from our dream.
Then if we study Nature we are wise.
Thus do the few who live but with the day:
The scientific animals are they.—
Lady, this is my sonnet to your eyes.

GEORGE MEREDITH

## *from* Modern Love

### L

Thus piteously Love closed what he begat:
The union of this ever-diverse pair!
These two were rapid falcons in a snare,
Condemned to do the flitting of the bat.
Lovers beneath the singing sky of May,
They wandered once; clear as the dew on flowers:
But they fed not on the advancing hours:
Their hearts held cravings for the buried day.
Then each applied to each that fatal knife,
Deep questioning, which probes to endless dole.
Ah, what a dusty answer gets the soul
When hot for certainties in this our life!—
In tragic hints here see what evermore

Moves dark as yonder midnight ocean's force,
Thundering like ramping hosts of warrior horse,
To throw that faint thin line upon the shore!


GERARD MANLEY HOPKINS
### Pied Beauty

Glory be to God for dappled things—
   For skies of couple-colour as a brinded cow;
      For rose-moles in all stipple upon trout that
      swim;
Fresh-firecoal chestnut-falls; finches' wings;
      Landscape plotted and pieced—fold, fallow,
      and plough;
        And áll trádes, their gear and tackle and trim.
All things counter, original, spare, strange;
      Whatever is fickle, freckled (who knows how?)
        With swift, slow; sweet, sour; adazzle, dim;
He fathers-forth whose beauty is past change:
          Praise him.


GERARD MANLEY HOPKINS
### Peace

When will you ever, Peace, wild wooddove, shy
   wings shut,
Your round me roaming end, and under be my
   boughs?
When, when, Peace, will you, Peace? I'll not play
   hypocrite
To own my heart: I yield you do come sometimes; but
That piecemeal peace is poor peace. What pure
   peace allows
Alarms of wars, the daunting wars, the death of it?


O surely, reaving Peace, my Lord should leave in lieu
Some good! And so he does leave Patience exquisite,
That plumes to Peace thereafter. And when Peace
   here does house

He comes with work to do, he does not come to coo,
He comes to brood and sit.


GERARD MANLEY HOPKINS
### Felix Randal

Felix Randal the farrier, O is he dead then? my duty
all ended,
Who have watched his mould of man, big-boned and
hardy-handsome
Pining, pining, till time when reason rambled in it
and some
Fatal four disorders, fleshed there, all contended?

Sickness broke him. Impatient, he cursed at first, but
mended
Being anointed and all; though a heavenlier heart
began some
Months earlier, since I had our sweet reprieve and
ransom
Tendered to him. Ah well, God rest him all road ever he
offended!

This seeing the sick endears them to us, us too it
endears.
My tongue had taught thee comfort, touch had
quenched thy tears,
Thy tears that touched my heart, child, Felix, poor
Felix Randal;

How far from then forethought of, all thy more
boisterous years,
When thou at the random grim forge, powerful
amidst peers,
Didst fettle for the great grey drayhorse his bright
and battering sandal!

GERARD MANLEY HOPKINS

## Spelt from Sibyl's Leaves

Earnest, earthless, equal, attuneable, ' vaulty,
    voluminous, . . . stupendous
Evening strains to be time's vást, ' womb-of-all,
    home-of-all, hearse-of-all night.
Her fond yellow hornlight wound to the west, ' her
    wild hollow hoarlight hung to the height
Waste; her earliest stars, earl-stars, ' stárs principal,
    overbend us,
Fíre-féaturing heaven. For earth ' her being has
    unbound, her dapple is at an end, as-
tray or aswarm, all throughther, in throngs; ' self ín
    self steepèd and páshed—qúite
Disremembering, dísmémbering ' áll now. Heart, you
    round me right
With: Óur évening is over us; óur night ' whélms,
    whélms, ánd will end us.
Only the beak-leaved boughs dragonish ' damask the
    tool-smooth bleak light; black,
Ever so black on it. Óur tale, O óur oracle! ' Lét life,
    wáned, ah lét life wind
Off hér once skéined stained véined varíety ' upon, áll
    on twó spools; párt, pen, páck
Now her áll in twó flocks, twó folds—black, white; '
    right, wrong; reckon but, reck but, mind
But thése two; wáre of a wórld where bút these ' twó
    tell, each off the óther; of a rack
Where, selfwrung, selfstrung, sheathe- and shelterless,
    ' thóughts agaínst thoughts ín groans grínd.


GERARD MANLEY HOPKINS

## That Nature Is a Heraclitean Fire and
## of the Comfort of the Resurrection

Cloud-puffball, torn tufts, tossed pillows ' flaunt
    forth, then chevy on an air-
built thoroughfare: heaven-roysterers, in gay-gangs '
    they throng; they glitter in marches.

Down roughcast, down dazzling whitewash, '
   wherever an elm arches,
Shivelights and shadowtackle in long ' lashes lace,
   lance, and pair.
Delightfully the bright wind boisterous ' ropes,
   wrestles, beats earth bare
Of yestertempest's creases; ' in pool and rut peel
   parches
Squandering ooze to squeezed ' dough, crust, dust;
   stanches, starches
Squadroned masks and manmarks ' treadmire toil
   there
Footfretted in it. Million-fuelèd, ' nature's bonfire
   burns on.
But quench her bonniest, dearest ' to her, her
   clearest-selvèd spark
Man, how fast his firedint, ' his mark on mind, is gone!
Both are in an unfathomable, all is in an enormous
   dark
Drowned. O pity and indig ' nation! Manshape, that
   shone
Sheer off, disseveral, a star, ' death blots black out;
   nor mark
      Is any of him at all so stark
But vastness blurs and time ' beats level. Enough! the
   Resurrection,
A heart's-clarion! Away grief's gasping, ' joyless days,
   dejection.
      Across my foundering deck shone
A beacon, an eternal beam. ' Flesh fade, and mortal
   trash
Fall to the residuary worm; ' world's wildfire, leave
   but ash:
      In a flash, at a trumpet crash,
I am all at once what Christ is, ' since he was what I
   am, and
This Jack, joke, poor potsherd, ' patch, matchwood,
   immortal diamond,
      Is immortal diamond.

ARTHUR RIMBAUD (TRANS. WYATT MASON)

## *from* Nonsense, Part 2

### I. Drunk Driver

Dirtbag
Drinks:
Mother-of pearl
Watches;

Bitter
Law,
Carriage
Topples!

Woman
Falls:
Thigh

Bleeds:
Moan
Groan.

ROBERT FROST

## Hyla Brook

By June our brook's run out of song and speed.
Sought for much after that, it will be found
Either to have gone groping underground
(And taken with it all the Hyla breed
That shouted in the mist a month ago,
Like ghost of sleigh-bells in a ghost of snow)—
Or flourished and come up in jewel-weed,
Weak foliage that is blown upon and bent
Even against the way its waters went.
Its bed is left a faded paper sheet
Of dead leaves stuck together by the heat—
A brook to none but who remember long.
This as it will be seen is other far
Than with brooks taken otherwise in song.
We love the things we love for what they are.

BLAISE CENDRARS (TRANS. RON PADGETT)

## *from* Unnatural Sonnets

**OpOetic**

to Jean COctO

what crimes are
not cOmmitted
in   thy   name!

Once upon a time there were pOets who spOke with rOund
    mOuths
Round as salami her beautiful eyes and smOke
Ophelia's hair Or the lyre Orpheus strOked
You belch up rOund hats to find a strOke-of-genius rhyme
    sharp as teeth that would nibble your lines    .
Open-mouthed
Since you like smOke rings why don't you repeat *smOke*
It's too easy or too hard
The 7 pawns and the Queens are there as commas
Oh POEtry
Ah! Oh!
COcOa
Since you like cowboys why don't you write *cowpOke*
It's a written grOan that'll make the French crOak
The English clOwn did it with his legs
The way AretinO made love
The Mind envies the circus poster and the alphabetical
    pOsitions of the Snake Man
Where are the pOets who spOke with rOund mOuths?

We have to loosen up their b  z enfant

nes

h

# *POETRY*

BLAISE CENDRARS (TRANS. RON PADGETT)

## Académie Médrano

*To Conrad Moricand*

Dance with your tongue, Poet, do an entrechat
Once around the ring
                        on a tiny black basset hound
                                        or old gray mare
Measure the lovely measures and fix the fixed forms
Which are the BELLES LETTRES you learn
Look:
            **The billboards are bored** with you bite
                        you with their colored teeth
                        between your toes
The director's daughter has electric lights
The jugglers also fly through the air
            pael suoregnaD
        pihw eht fo kcarC
taht sserpxE
The clown is in the mixing barrel
                        ⎧ go to the box office
        Your tongue must ⎨                        on nights when
                        ⎩ do the orchestra

No **Free Passes** are accepted.


EDNA ST. VINCENT MILLAY

## Rendezvous

Not for these lovely blooms that prank your
        chambers did I come. Indeed,
I could have loved you better in the dark;
That is to say, in rooms less bright with roses, rooms
        more casual, less aware
Of History in the wings about to enter with
        benevolent air
On ponderous tiptoe, at the cue "Proceed."

Not that I like the ash-trays over-crowded and the
    place in a mess,
Or the monastic cubicle too unctuously austere and
    stark,
But partly that these formal garlands for our Eighth
    Street Aphrodite are a bit too Greek,
And partly that to make the poor walls rich with our
    unaided loveliness
Would have been more *chic.*
Yet here I am, having told you of my quarrel with the
    taxi-driver over a line of Milton, and you laugh;
    and you are you, none other.
Your laughter pelts my skin with small delicious
    blows.
But I am perverse: I wish you had not scrubbed—with
    pumice, I suppose—
The tobacco stains from your beautiful fingers. And I
    wish I did not feel like your mother.


E. E. CUMMINGS

## *from* Sonnets—Actualities

**XVI**

i have found what you are like
the rain,

      (Who feathers frightened fields
with the superior dust-of-sleep.  wields

easily the pale club of the wind
and swirled justly souls of flower strike

the air in utterable coolness

deeds of green thrilling light
                 with thinned
newfragile yellows
             lurch and.press

—in the woods
              which
                   stutter
                        and


                                   sing
And the coolness of your smile is
stirringofbirds between my arms;but
i should rather than anything
have(almost when hugeness will shut
quietly)almost,
                   your kiss


JOHN BROOKS WHEELWRIGHT

### Father

An East Wind asperges Boston with Lynn's
    sulphurous brine.
Under the bridge of turrets my father built,—from
    turning sign
of CHEVROLET, out-topping our gilt State House
    dome
to burning sign of CARTER'S INK,—drip multitudes
of checker-board shadows. Inverted turreted
    reflections
sleeting over axle-grease billows, through all
    directions
cross-cut parliamentary gulls, who toss like gourds.

    Speak. Speak to me again, as fresh saddle leather
    (Speak; talk again) to a hunter smells of heather.
    Come home. Wire a wire of warning without
        words.
    Come home and talk to me again, my first friend.
        Father,
        come home, dead man, who made your mind my
        home.

W. H. AUDEN

## *from* The Quest

### III

Two friends who met here and embraced are gone,
Each to his own mistake; one flashes on
To fame and ruin in a rowdy lie,
A village torpor holds the other one,
Some local wrong where it takes time to die:
This empty junction glitters in the sun.

So at all quays and crossroads: who can tell
These places of decision and farewell
To what dishonour all adventure leads,
What parting gift could give that friend protection,
So orientated his vocation needs
The Bad Lands and the sinister direction?

All landscapes and all weathers freeze with fear,
But none have ever thought, the legends say,
The time allowed made it impossible;
For even the most pessimistic set
The limit of their errors at a year.
What friends could there be left then to betray,
What joy take longer to atone for; yet
Who would complete without the extra day
The journey that should take no time at all?

ELIZABETH BISHOP

## *Sonnet*

Caught—the bubble
in the spirit-level,
a creature divided;
and the compass needle
wobbling and wavering,
undecided.
Freed—the broken

thermometer's mercury
running away;
and the rainbow-bird
from the narrow bevel
of the empty mirror,
flying wherever
it feels like, gay!

ROY FULLER

## *from* Meredithian Sonnets

I

To suffer, yes, but suffer and not create
The compensations that will cancel out
The thing: to crawl alone in the redoubt
Of suffering, like an animal—too late!
Even the ruined life deceives itself.
He looks in the glass: the handsome features show
Nothing of that foul spell cast long ago
By some malicious uninvited elf
Who ordered him to love a purple flower.
Even desire re-touches what it bares,
Removing all that's human—creases, hairs
And likelihood.  A poet in a tower
With rapture watched an army dye the ford
And paper swans upon the stormy glooms:
Man's love is more primeval than a bloom's,
Another wrote, slain by a rose's sword.

ROBERT DUNCAN

## *Sonnet 4*

He's given me his *thee* to keep,
secret, alone, in Love's name,
for what sake I have only in faith.

Where it is . . . ? How it is near . . . ?
I would recognize him by the way he walks.
But it was so long ago and I was never sure

except in his regard and then
sure as the rose scattering its petals to prepare is sure
for the ripeness near to the perfection of the rose.

I would know the red *thee* of the enclosure
where thought too curls about, opens
out from, what's hid,

until it falls away, all the profuse allusion let go,
the rose-hip persistence of the truth hid therein from
   me

enduring.

ROBERT DUNCAN

### 5th Sonnet

Love too delighting in His numbers
keeps time so that our feet
dance to be true to the count,
repeating the hesitation, the

slight bow to His will in each change,
the giving up, His syncopation,
the receiving      an other
measure again.

      You were not there,
but in love with you I danced
this round, my feet
willingly sped to its numbers,

my glance wed to the glance exchanged,
      for the design's sake,
in Love's calling. As if
in the exchange of lives,

that music that most moves us,
unknowing and true to what

I do not know, where other
lovers in intermingling figures

come and go, there were a constant
First Caller of the Dance
Who moves me, First Partner, He
      in Whom
you are most you.


MONA VAN DUYN

## Double Sonnet for Minimalists

The spiral shell
apes creamhorns of smog,
Dalmation, quenelle
or frosted hedgehog,
yet is obsessed
by a single thought
that its inner guest
is strictly taught.

When the self that grew
to follow its rule
is gone, and it's through,
vacant, fanciful,

its thought will find
Fibonacci's mind.

That fragile slug,
bloodless, unborn,
till it knows the hug
of love's tutoring form,
whose life, upstart
in deep, is to learn
to follow the art
of turn and return,

when dead, for the dense
casts up no clue
to the infinite sequence
it submitted to.

May its bright ghost reach
the right heart's beach.

GERALD STERN

## *American Heaven*

A salt water pond in the Hamptons near David
Ignatow's house, the water up to my chest,
an American Heaven, a dog on the shore, this time
his mouth closed, his body alert, his ears
up, a dog *belongs* in heaven, at least our
kind. An egret skidding to a stop, I'm sure
water snakes and turtles, grasses and weeds,
and close to the water sycamores and locusts,
and pitch pine on the hill and sand in the distance,
and girls could suckle their babies standing in water,
so that was our place of origin, that was
the theory in 1982—David
had his own larder, Rose had hers, he brought
tuna fish into her kitchen, it was a triptych,
the centerpiece was the pond, the left panel
was his, his study, and he was stepping naked
across the frame into the pond holding an
open can and hers was the right, her arms had
entered the pond, holding a bowl, it was her
studio, we ate on a dry stone
and talked about James Wright and Stanley Kunitz,
and there was a star of the fourth magnitude
surrounded by planets, shining on all of us.

JOHN HOLLANDER

## *from* Powers of Thirteen

That other time of day when the chiming of Thirteen
Marks the hour in truth comes after midnight has
     made
Its unseen appearance. Then the whole trembling
     house starts
Gathering itself together in sudden fear, creaks
On the stairs grow tacit, and, even outside, the wind
In the lindens has been hushed. Unlike the time
     beyond
Noon, when your visitations shape that original
Hour, when we pull the shades down in our space
     between
Moments totally contiguous in the clocked world,
This black gap between days is no place for us:
     should you
Creep into my bed then you would find me
     shuddering
As at the opening of a secret whose shadowed
Power unbroken lay in coupling day unto day.

JOHN UPDIKE

## *Love Sonnet*

In Love's rubber armor I come to you,

                                    b
                    oo
                                      b.

              c,
                      d
                      c
                        d:

              e
          f———
              e
            f.
                    g
                  g.

JEAN VALENTINE

# X

*I have decorated this banner to honor my brother. Our parents
did not want his name used publicly.*

—FROM AN UNNAMED CHILD'S BANNER
IN THE AIDS MEMORIAL QUILT

The boatpond, broken off, looks back at the sky.
I remember looking at you, X, this way,
taking in your red hair, your eyes' light, and I miss you
so. I know,
you are you, and real, standing there in the doorway,
whether dead or whether living, real.—Then Y
said, "Who will remember me three years after I die?
What is there for my eye
to read then?"
The lamb should not have given
his wool.
He was so small. At the end, X, you were so small.
Playing with a stone
on your bedspread at the edge of the ocean.

TED BERRIGAN

## *from* The Sonnets

L

I like to beat people up
absence of passion, principles, love. She murmurs
What just popped into my eye was a fiend's umbrella
and if you should come and pinch me now
as I go out for coffee
. . . as I was saying winter of 18 lumps
Days produce life locations to banish 7 up
Nomads, my babies, where are you? Life's
My dream which is gunfire in my poem
Orange cavities of dreams stir inside "The Poems"
Whatever is going to happen is already happening

Some people prefer "the interior monologue"
I like to beat people up


TED BERRIGAN

## *from* The Sonnets

### LXXII. A Sonnet for Dick Gallup

The logic of grammar is not genuine    it shines forth
From The Boats    We fondle the snatches of virgins
    aching to be fucked
And O, I am afraid!    Our love has red in it    and
I become finicky as in an abstraction!
                                        (... but lately
I'm always lethargic ...    the last heavy sweetness
through the wine ...)
                            Who dwells alone
                            Except at night
(... basted the shackles the temporal music the spit)
    Southwest lost doubloons rest, no comforts drift on
dream smoke
                    (my dream    the big earth)
On the green a white boy goes    to not
Forget    Released by night (which is not to imply
Clarity    The logic is not The Boats    and O, I am not
    alone


TONY HARRISON

## *On Not Being Milton*

*for Sergio Vieira & Armando Guebuza (Frelimo)*


Read and committed to the flames, I call
these sixteen lines that go back to my roots
my *Cahier d'un retour au pays natal,*
my growing black enough to fit my boots.

The stutter of the scold out of the branks
of condescension, class and counter-class

thickens with glottals to a lumpen mass
of Ludding morphemes closing up their ranks.
Each swung cast-iron Enoch of Leeds stress
clangs a forged music on the frames of Art,
the looms of owned language smashed apart!

Three cheers for mute ingloriousness!

Articulation is the tongue-tied's fighting.
In the silence round all poetry we quote
Tidd the Cato Street conspirator who wrote:

*Sir, I Ham a very Bad Hand at Righting.*


PAUL MARIANI

## Hopkins in Ireland

*For the Jesuit community at Boston College*

Above the bluebleak priest the brightblue fisher
    hovers.
The priest notes the book upon the table, the
    lamp beside the book.
A towering Babel of papers still to grade, and
    that faraway look
as once more the mind begins to wander. Ah, to
    creep beneath the covers

of the belled bed beckoning across the room. He
    stops, recovers,
takes another sip of bitter tea, then winces as he
    takes another look
at the questions he has posed his students and
    the twists they took
to cover up their benighted sense of Latin. The
    fisher hovers

like a lit match closer to him. The windows have all
    been shut against
the damp black Dublin night. After all these years,
    his collar chokes
him still, in spite of which he wears it like some
    outmoded mark
of honor, remembering how his dear Ignatius must
    have sensed
the same landlocked frustrations. Again he lifts his
    pen. His strokes
lash out against the dragon din of error. The fisher
    incandesces in the dark.

BILLY COLLINS

## American Sonnet

We do not speak like Petrarch or wear a hat like
    Spenser
and it is not fourteen lines
like furrows in a small, carefully plowed field

but the picture postcard, a poem on vacation,
that forces us to sing our songs in little rooms
or pour our sentiments into measuring cups.

We write on the back of a waterfall or lake,
adding to the view a caption as conventional
as an Elizabethan woman's heliocentric eyes.

We locate an adjective for the weather.
We announce that we are having a wonderful time.
We express the wish that you were here

and hide the wish that we were where you are,
walking back from the mailbox, your head lowered
as you read and turn the thin message in your
    hands.

A slice of this place, a length of white beach,
a piazza or carved spires of a cathedral
will pierce the familiar place where you remain,

and you will toss on the table this reversible display:
a few square inches of where we have strayed
and a compression of what we feel.

BERNADETTE MAYER

### Sonnet

You jerk you didn't call me up
I haven't seen you in so long
You probably have a fucking tan
& besides that instead of making love tonight
You're drinking your parents to the airport
I'm through with you bourgeois boys
All you ever do is go back to ancestral comforts
Only money can get—even Catullus was rich but

Nowadays you guys settle for a couch
By a soporific color cable t.v. set
Instead of any arc of love, no wonder
The G.I. Joe team blows it every other time

Wake up! It's the middle of the night
You can either make love or die at the hands of
                    the Cobra Commander

To make love, turn to page 121.
To die, turn to page 172.

RONALD WALLACE

### Broken Sonnet

He always wanted to be one of those guys
who knew how to fix things that were broken,
instead of what he was: one of those guys

who broke things that were fixed. What expertise
could he claim as his own? What small token
of manhood? The tools of the trades were a
    foreign tongue:
*torque, resistance, grain, flow, calibration,*
drained him like a faulty valve or coupling.

Which may explain why he became a poet
and not a plumber, mechanic, carpenter, or
    technician.
But the language warped and buckled when he
    wrote it.
His best lines never made the right connection.
And nothing ever seemed quite level or true.

SANDRA MCPHERSON

### Sonnet for Joe

When I tell you I would rather you describe a
    clock than time,
that the essence of your ocean sentiments is
    not the ocean,
I'm wondering if you would live if your feet got
    tangled in seaweed.
Write me the superstructure of water.

And now you drop your face. I see my mistake.
    You did not write
to contend. So it was the ocean in four dry lines
like seaweed from Japanese groceries that thickens
    and plumps
when ladled in water. Look, you don't even like it

when I give you some copies of ocean poems. You
    detest the sea
and its marketable herring, its common tuna,
    and starfish
always losing their legs. Think of the man

who fell from his fishing boat in the fog off
    Alaska. He heard the motor
slowly *trup*ping away, its cargo of vain fish
    under its wing. Think of
his widow who detests the sea, who lives beside
    it, who writes now to her friend.

BRAD LEITHAUSER

## Post-Coitum Tristesse: A Sonnet

Why
do
you
sigh,
roar,
fall,
all
for
some
hum-
drum
come
—mm?
Hm ...

KARL KIRCHWEY

## from *Two Tidal Sonnets*

### 1. Ludovisi Throne

The Queen of Love was born out of the tide
(so legend tells), and learned those rhythms
    first,
cut static from the foam of mackerel-sided
swells, all creation in her like a thirst.
Apparently she was fond of the smell
of brine, fond of small swarming birds and
    flowers.
She had no memory of pain at all,

but felt the distance of remembered pleasures.
Valved like a conch, her smile archaic, she
moved with a single salt imperative
toward the shore, her perfect nudity
a weight to make the rainbowed shell's lip dive
and tremble gladly underneath her feet,
desire still just a vague unease—the slight
asymmetry of new sharp breasts a girl
gracefully stoops to dress in pleats of wool.

# THE SONNET
# AROUND THE WORLD

The sonnet is a fixed form that nonetheless leaves room for a great deal of improvisation. It is adaptable to different languages and meters, different kinds of argument. It can proceed through its fourteen lines with a great deal of resolve and certainty, or it can hesitate and seem formally unresolved until the very final line. It can declare its subject or keep it hidden for as long as possible. Its subject matter can be high or low, occasional or permanent. It can engage and invert its long erotic history, or it can turn away from that history altogether.

We offer here a small sampling of sonnets from around the world. These are examples of the enduring power—the peculiar richness—of the sonnet tradition.

# THE SONNET AROUND THE WORLD

*I pursue a form . . .*

—RUBÉN DARÍO, *Profane Prose and Other Poems* (1896)

The sonnet has always traveled well. It is a powerful form that began in the halls of power. It was created in a circle of fourteen legal officials (notaries) at the royal court of Frederick II, the Holy Roman Emperor and King of Sicily. There are fifty-eight surviving Sicilian sonnets, twenty-six of them written by Giacomo da Lentino, who is generally given credit for inventing the form. *Il Notaro* (as Dante refers to him in the *Purgatorio*) was part of a small group of poet-lawyers who developed the sonnet as an argumentative form, a love poem that makes a case.

The poet Guittone d'Arezzo took the Sicilian court poem and adapted it to the teeming world of the Tuscan city-states. He codified the rhyme scheme (*abbaabba*) and wrote 246 sonnets on a wide variety of subjects. The new sonnet excited the early Italian writers of the *dolce stil nuovo* ("sweet new style"), who recognized its discursive power even as they infused it with a deeper musicality. Dante Alighieri and Guido Cavalcanti both emerged from this circle.

Dante is the first major practitioner of the sonnet form, and *La Vita Nuova (The New Life)* is the world's first sonnet sequence. These twenty-five sonnets are surrounded by a prose commentary in which Dante explains the formal structure of each poem. He explains the circumstances—the emotional pressure—that led to each poem. The poems themselves express his passionate but distant devotion for Beatrice Portinari, whom he first saw when he was nine years old and never knew personally. She is his earthly ideal.

Dante's greatest heir was another Florentine exile, Francesco Petrarch (or Petrarca in Italian), who perfected the form that bears his name in a series of poems addressed to a young woman he identified as Laura (most likely Laurette de Noves). Laura is a distant but real presence in Petrarch's *Canzoniere.* Petrarch applied logic to the emotions in his ingenious sonnets of passionate desire, unrequited love, and spiritual longing. These sonnets would subsequently influence all of European love poetry.

The Petrarchan sonnet created an unprecedented vogue throughout Europe. In the fifteenth and sixteenth centuries, the sonnet made its way to France, Spain, Portugal, Poland, and the Netherlands. It later traveled to Germany, Scandinavia, and Russia. It also continued to be a useful form in Italy—from Torquato Tasso and Michelangelo Buonarroti to Gabriele D'Annunzio and Eugenio Montale. To give a sense of its tremendous popularity: by one estimate, there were more than three hundred thousand sonnets produced in Western Europe during the Elizabethan era. Most of them were amatory.

There have been great sonneteers in all the major European languages. The sonnet has its own internal history in each country. For example, the French poet Joachim du Bellay wrote the first non-Italian sonnet cycle, *L'Olive,* and the form was used prominently by Pierre de Ronsard (*Les Amours*), the master of the Pléiade poets, and Louise Labé, who established a tradition that would later be revived by Théophile Gautier and Charles Baudelaire. The French sonnet became a form of great romantic modernity in the hands of Gérard de Nerval, Stéphane Mallarmé, Arthur Rimbaud, and Paul Valéry.

In Spain, Juan Boscán's sonnets led to the sonnets of the major Golden Age poets, especially Luis de Góngora, Lope de Vega, Francisco Gómez de Quevedo, and Sor Juana Inés de la Cruz. The Spanish introduced the sonnet into Portugal, where it reached a peak in the work of Luis de Camões. Later, the Nicaraguan poet

Rubén Darío, who was a bridge between the poetry of Spain and the Americas, turned it into a significant symbolist form. He influenced the major Spanish Civil War poets, such as Antonio Machado, Miguel Hernández, and Federico García Lorca, whose *Sonnets of Dark Love* have an unprecedented homoerotic power, and the key Latin American poets, such as César Vallejo, Jorge Luis Borges, and Pablo Neruda, whose book *100 Love Sonnets* shows the continued vitality of the form as a love poem.

The sonnet, which became popular in Germany through the work of G. R. Weckherlin, reached prominence during the romantic period in the work of Johann Wolfgang von Goethe, August Wilhelm von Schlegel, Paul von Heyse, and others. They established a tradition that would reach fruition in Rainer Maria Rilke's *Sonnets to Orpheus.*

The sonnet has a strong lineage in Poland, where Adam Mickiewicz made it his own, and in Russia, where Aleksandr Pushkin turned it into a foundational Russian form in *Eugene Onegin.* It has had a strong life in Holland, Denmark, and Sweden. It has its own history in a country such as South Africa. It has traveled to the Middle East—there are fine sonnets in both Hebrew and Arabic—and to countries such as China, South Korea, and Vietnam, where it is an exotic form.

The sonnet is a fixed form that nonetheless leaves room for a great deal of improvisation. It is adaptable to different languages and meters, different kinds of argument. It can proceed through its fourteen lines with a great deal of resolve and certainty, or it can hesitate and seem formally unresolved until the very final line. It can declare its subject or keep it hidden for as long as possible. Its subject matter can be high or low, occasional or permanent. It can engage and invert its long erotic history, or it can turn away from that history altogether. It can turn to political and historical subjects, to mythology. It always seems to keep its sense of immediacy.

The sonnet can be highly traditional (antimodernist movements in poetry often begin with the recovery of sonnet form) or wildly experimental, as in the poetry of Raymond Queneau, whose work *Cent mille milliards de poèmes* (*One Hundred Million*

*Million Poems*) consists of ten sonnets, which can be cut up by every single line and recombined into one hundred trillion different poems. Reading twenty-four hours a day, it would take two hundred million years to read them all.

We offer here a small sampling of sonnets from around the world. These are examples of the enduring power—the peculiar richness—of the sonnet tradition.

GUIDO CAVALCANTI (ADAPTED BY EZRA POUND)

## Sonnet IX

I am reduced at last to self compassion,
For the sore anguish that I see me in;
At my great weakness; that my soul hath been
Concealed beneath her wounds in such a fashion:

Such mine oppression that I know, in brief,
That to my life ill's worst starred ills befall;
And this strange lady on whose grace I call
Maintains continuous my stour of grief,

For when I look in her direction,
She turns upon me her disdeigning eyen
So harshly that my waiting heart is rent

And all my powers and properties are spent,
Till that heart lieth for a sign ill-seen,
Where Amor's cruelty hath hurled him down.


DANTE ALIGHIERI (TRANS. DANTE GABRIEL ROSSETTI)

## *from* La Vita Nuova (The New Life)

The thoughts are broken in my memory,
    Thou lovely Joy, whene'er I see thy face;
    When thou art near me, Love fills up the space,
Often repeating, "If death irk thee, fly."
My face shows my heart's colour, verily,
    Which, fainting, seeks for any leaning-place;
    Till, in the drunken terror of disgrace,
The very stones seem to be shrieking, "Die!"
It were a grievous sin, if one should not
    Strive then to comfort my bewildered mind
        (Though merely with a simple pitying)
For the great anguish which thy scorn has wrought
    In the dead sight o' the eyes grown nearly blind,
        Which look for death as for a blessed thing.

FRANCESCO PETRARCH (ADAPTED BY SIR THOMAS WYATT)
### *"I find no peace, and all my war is done"*

I find no peace, and all my war is done,
I fear, and hope. I burn, and freeze like ice.
I fly above the wind, yet can I not arise.
And naught I have, and all the world I season.
That loseth nor locketh holdeth me in prison,
And holdeth me not, yet can I 'scape nowise:
Nor letteth me live nor die at my devise,
And yet of death it giveth me occasion.
Without eyen I see, and without tongue I 'plain;
I desire to perish, and yet I ask health;
I love another, and thus I hate myself;
I feed me in sorrow, and laugh at all my pain.
  Likewise displeaseth me both death and life,
  And my delight is causer of this strife.


MICHELANGELO BUONARROTI
(TRANS. JOHN FREDERICK NIMS)
### *"My lady, these eyes see vividly—far, near"*

My lady, these eyes see vividly—far, near—
your radiant face, wherever it is—here, there.
Where eyes can go, however, our feet forbear,
forbidden to bring hands, arms to rendezvous.
  The soul, intelligence uncorrupt and true,
can, thanks to the eye, aspire to your beauty's height,
since free to fly, not flesh-bound. No such flight
is permitted, even for love, to bodies here.
  Our bodies, so mortal, cloddish, without wings,
can't follow the least of angels in their zone.
Eyes, only, exult and revel in all they do.
  Lady, if you've such power in celestial things
as here on earth, make all of me eye alone,
all eye, to delight, the whole of me, in you.

VITTORIA COLONNA (TRANS. ABIGAIL BRUNDIN)

## *from* Sonnets for Michelangelo

1

Since my chaste love for many years
kept my soul aflame with the desire for fame, and it
   nourished
a serpent in my breast so that now my heart
   languishes
in pain turned towards God, who alone can help me,
   let the holy nails from now on be my quills,
and the precious blood my pure ink,
my lined paper the sacred lifeless body,
so that I may write down for others all that he
   suffered.
   It is not right here to invoke Parnassus or Delos,
for I aspire to cross other waters, to ascend
other mountains that human feet cannot climb
   unaided.
   I pray to the sun, which lights up the earth and the
heavens, that letting forth his shining spring
he pours down upon me a draught equal to my great
   thirst.

JOACHIM DU BELLAY (ADAPTED BY ANTHONY HECHT)

## *"Heureux qui, comme Ulysse,*
## *a fait un Beau Voyage . . ."*

Great joy be to the sailor if he chart
The Odyssey or bear away the Fleece
Yet unto wisdom's laurel and the peace
Of his own kind come lastly to his start.
And when shall I, being migrant, bring my heart
Home to its plots of parsley, its proper earth,
Pot hooks, cow dung, black chimney bricks whose
   worth
I have not skill to honor in my art.

My home, my father's and grandfather's home.
Not the imperial porphyry of Rome
But slate is my true stone, slate is my blue.
And bluer the Loire is to my reckoning
Than Caesar's Tiber, and more nourishing
Than salt spray is the breathing of Anjou.

LUÍS DE CAMÕES (TRANS. WILLIAM BAER)

## Reader

As long as Fortune dangled in my sight
the hope of happiness, my wishful schemes
for lasting love and all my youthful dreams
compelled me to lift my pen and write.
But Love, afraid I might prove indiscreet
and reveal her unpleasant truth, ingeniously
obscured my mind and cruelly tormented me,
trying to keep my pen from exposing her deceit.
But *you*, whom Love has also subjugated
to her fickle will, if you should come across
my verses, this little book of diverse
songs, conceived in experience, created
in truth, remember: the more you've loved and
    lost,
the better you'll comprehend my verse.

LUIS DE GÓNGORA (TRANS. EDITH GROSSMAN)

## Sonnet LXXXII (Amorous)

Lovers! The sweet mouth tempting you to taste
of a liquor distilled among white pearls,
to turn from the sacred libation poured
for Jupiter by Ida's comely youth,
    touch it not if you value life, for
there, between her inviting scarlet lips
is Love, with deadliest poison armed,
like a serpent lurking among the blooms.
    Do not be deceived; roses that you say

have fallen, fragrant and pearly with dew,
from the purple-hued bosom of the Dawn
   are the apples of Tantalus. Be warned:
they will flee the very one they tempt;
poison is all that will be left of love.

LOPE DE VEGA (TRANS. EDITH GROSSMAN)

### Instant Sonnet

   Violante orders me to write a sonnet,
I've never been so pressed in my life before.
Fourteen verses, they say, are in a sonnet:
I haven't even tried and I have four.

   I thought I'd never find those fourteen lines
and here I'm halfway through another quatrain,
I only have to get to that first tercet
and then no line can ever hold me back.

   And now I'm at the start of tercet one.
It seems I started out on the right foot
because with the third line here's the conclusion.

   I've begun tercet two. I do believe
I'm coming to the end of thirteen verses;
see if there are fourteen: the sonnet's done.

SOR JUANA INÉS DE LA CRUZ (TRANS. EDITH GROSSMAN)

### Sonnet 145

*In which she attempts to refute the praises of a portrait of
the poet, signed by truth, which she calls passion*

This thing you see, a bright-colored deceit,
displaying all the many charms of art,
with false syllogisms of tint and hue
is a cunning deception of the eye;

   this thing in which sheer flattery has tried
to evade the stark horrors of the years
and, vanquishing the cruelties of time,

to triumph over age and oblivion,
   is vanity, contrivance, artifice,
a delicate blossom stranded in the wind,
a failed defense against our common fate;
   a fruitless enterprise, a great mistake,
a decrepit frenzy, and rightly viewed,
a corpse, some dust, a shadow, mere nothingness.


JOHANN WOLFGANG VON GOETHE (TRANS. DAVID LUKE)

## Nature and Art

Nature and Art, they go their separate ways,
It seems; yet all at once they find each other.
Even I no longer am a foe to either;
Both equally attract me nowadays.

Some honest toil's required; then, phase by phase,
When diligence and wit have worked together
To tie us fast to Art with their good tether,
Nature again may set our hearts ablaze.

All culture is like this: the unfettered mind,
The boundless spirit's mere imagination,
For pure perfection's heights will strive in vain.

To achieve great things, we must be self-confined:
Mastery is revealed in limitation
And law alone can set us free again.


GIUSEPPE BELLI (TRANS. MILLER WILLIAMS)

## Night of Terror

You're not going back out, as mad as you are?
Look, I don't like the way you're acting tonight.
Jesus! What is it? What have you got under there?
Holy Virgin, you're looking for a fight!

Pippo, my darling, you're not in any shape
To be out there carousing around town.

Pippo, listen to me, for pity's sake.
Okay, give me the knife. Just put it down.

You're not going out. I'm not yours anymore
The minute you leave. Cut me, go ahead.
There's no way you're going through that door.

Look at our sleeping angel. What a surprise
Not to find his father beside his bed
Smiling at him when he opens his eyes.

ALEKSANDR PUSHKIN (TRANS. BABETTE DEUTSCH)

### *from* Eugene Onegin

**VII**

The art of verse, that lofty pleasure,
He never mastered, never knew
Trochaic from iambic measure,
In spite of all we tried to do.
Theocritus and Homer bored him;
If true delight you would afford him
You'd give him Adam Smith to read.
A deep economist, indeed,
He talked about the wealth of nations;
The state relied, his friends were told,
Upon its staples, not on gold—
This subject filled his conversations.
His father listened, frowned, and groaned,
And mortgaged all the land he owned.

GÉRARD DE NERVAL (TRANS. DANIEL HOFFMAN)

### *The Disinherited*

I am the unconsoled, the widowed one,
The Prince of Acquitaine whose tower is ruined;
My only *star* is dead; my lute, attuned
To the Heavens, bears *Melancholy's crepe-black sun.*

You, in the midnight of the tomb my solace,
Give back Posilipo, the Italian sea,
The *flower* that in my grief helped to assuage me,
And the arbor where the grape and rose embrace . . .

Am I Eros, or Phoebus? Lusignon, Biron?
The queen's kiss has left my cheek afire.
I've dreamed in the grotto where the siren swims . . .

And twice, in triumph, have crossed Acheron
And alternately pluck on Orpheus' lyre
The sighings of the saint, the nymph's wild hymns.

CHARLES BAUDELAIRE (TRANS. RICHARD HOWARD)

## *Correspondences*

The pillars of Nature's temple are alive
and sometimes yield perplexing messages;
forests of symbols between us and the shrine
remark our passage with accustomed eyes.

Like long-held echoes, blending somewhere else
into one deep and shadowy unison
as limitless as darkness and as day,
the sounds, the scents, the colors correspond.

There are odors succulent as young flesh,
sweet as flutes, and green as any grass,
while others—rich, corrupt and masterful—

possess the power of such infinite things
as incense, amber, benjamin and musk,
to praise the senses' raptures and the mind's.

STÉPHANE MALLARMÉ (TRANS. LOUIS SIMPSON)

## The Tomb of Poe

At last the Poet, changed by eternity
Into Himself, goads with a naked sword
The century, dismayed that it ignored
In that amazing voice, death's victory.

Like the vile hydra, leaping up to see
An angel give the tribe the purer word,
They shouted that the charm had been procured
From some dark potion, mixed illicitly.

You are hated by heaven and earth, O grief,
If our art cannot sculpt a bas-relief
For the tomb of Poe, so that dazzling granite,

Calm block fallen from some dark disaster,
At least may stand forever as a limit
To black flights of Blasphemy in the future.


PAUL VERLAINE (TRANS. NORMAN R. SHAPIRO)

## Night Scene

Night. Rain. Spires, empty-windowed turrets, jutting;
A distant, lifeless Gothic city, cutting
Sharp silhouettes against a sallow sky.
The plain. A gibbet, corpses hanging high,
Withered and wizened, swinging, raven-pecked,
Dancing weird nighttime jigs, while wolves collect,
Ravenous, foraging upon their feet.
Against a background, outlined, incomplete—
Bramble-twined chaos, murky mass—left, right,
A bush, a briar, pushing its ghostly height.
And there, marching three prisoners—ashen faces,
Barefoot—a squad of halberdiers: their maces,
Stiff as portcullis spikes, rise from the plain,
Glistening athwart the javelins of the rain.

ARTHUR RIMBAUD (TRANS. F. SCOTT FITZGERALD)

## Voyelles

A black, E white, I red, U green, O blue, vowels
Some day I'll tell you where your genesis lies;
A—black velvet swarms of flies
Buzzing above the stench of voided bowels,
A gulf of shadow; E—where the iceberg rushes
White mists, tents, kings, shady strips;
I—purple, spilt blood, laughter of sweet lips
In anger—or the penitence of lushes;
U—cycle of time, rhythm of seas,
Peace of the paws of animals and wrinkles
On scholars' brows, strident tinkles;
O—the supreme trumpet note, peace
Of the spheres, of the angels. O equals
X-ray of her eyes; it equals sex.


RUBÉN DARÍO

(TRANS. WILL DERUSHA AND ALBERTO ACEREDA)

## "I pursue a form that my style does not find"

I pursue a form that my style does not find,
a bud of thought that seeks to be a rose;
it announces itself with a kiss that alights on my lips
in the impossible embrace of the Venus de Milo.

Green palms adorn the white peristyle;
the stars have predicted for me the vision of the
        Goddess;
and the light reposes in my soul as the bird
of the moon reposes on a tranquil lake.

And I find nothing but the word that gets away,
the melodic initiation that flows from the flute,
and the ship of sleep that sails into space;

and under the window of my Sleeping Beauty,
the continuous sob of the fountain's jet
and the great white swan's neck questioning me.

PAUL VALÉRY (TRANS. RICHARD WILBUR)

## Helen

It is I, O Azure, come from the caves below
To hear the waves clamber the loudening shores,
And see those barks again in the dawn's glow
Borne out of darkness, swept by golden oars.

My solitary hands call back the lords
Whose salty beards beguiled my finger-tips;
I wept. They sang the prowess of their swords
And what great bays fled sternward of their ships.

I hear the martial trumpets and the deep-
Sea conches cry a cadence to the sweeps;
The oarsmen's chantey holds the storm in sway;

And high on the hero prows the Gods I see,
Their antique smiles insulted by the spray,
Reaching their carved, indulgent arms to me.

RAINER MARIA RILKE (TRANS. W. D. SNODGRASS)

## An Archaic Torso of Apollo

We will not ever know his legendary head
Wherein the eyes, like apples, ripened. Yet
His torso glows like a candelabra
In which his vision, merely turned down low,

Still holds and gleams. If this were not so, the curve
Of the breast could not so blind you, nor this smile
Pass lightly through the soft turn of the loins
Into that center where procreation flared.

If this were not so, this stone would stand defaced,
    maimed,
Under the transparent cascade of the shoulder,
Not glimmering that way, like a wild beast's pelt,

Nor breaking out of all its contours
Like a star; for there is no place here
That does not see you. You must change your life.

ALFONSINA STORNI (TRANS. KAY SHORT)

### To My Lady of Poetry

I throw myself here at your feet, sinful,
my dark face against your blue earth,
you the virgin among armies of palm trees
that never grow old as humans do.

I don't dare look at your pure eyes
or dare touch your miraculous hand:
I look behind me and a river of rashness
urges me guiltlessly on against you.

With a promise to mend my ways through your
divine grace, I humbly place on your
hem a little green branch,

for I couldn't have possibly lived
cut off from your shadow, since you blinded me
at birth with your fierce branding iron.

CÉSAR VALLEJO
(TRANS. ROBERT BLY AND JOHN KNOEPFLE)

### Black Stone Lying on a White Stone

I will die in Paris, on a rainy day,
on some day I can already remember.
I will die in Paris—and I don't step aside—
perhaps on a Thursday, as today is Thursday, in
    autumn.

It will be a Thursday, because today, Thursday,
    setting down
these lines, I have put my upper arm bones on

wrong, and never so much as today have I found
    myself
with all the road ahead of me, alone.

    César Vallejo is dead. Everyone beat him,
although he never does anything to them;
they beat him hard with a stick and hard also

    with a rope. These are the witnesses:
the Thursdays, and the bones of my arms,
the solitude, and the rain, and the roads . . .


ILYAS FARHAT
(TRANS. SALMA KHADRA JAYYUSI AND JOHN HEATH-STUBBS)

## My Burned Suit

I put on my new suit, the wind and fire
Observing this, maliciously conspire
And then the wind, just for a merry lark,
Picks up from the train smoke one small spark,
A little spark, hot from the engine's coal,
And casts it on my suit and burns a hole
In that fine serge in which I took such pride
And like a tunnel's entrance it gaped wide.
Pointing this out to God I thus made free:
"You liberally clothe the forest tree
Yet you allow my new suit to be burned
If I had been a bough, when spring returned,
You would renew me. But I'll have to sweat
And moil and toil another suit to get."


JORGE GUILLÉN (TRANS. RICHARD WILBUR)

## The Horses

Shaggy and heavily natural, they stand
Immobile under their thick and cumbrous manes,
Pent in a barbed enclosure which contains,
By way of compensation, grazing-land.

Nothing disturbs them now. In slow increase
They fatten like the grass. Doomed to be idle,
To haul no cart or wagon, wear no bridle,
They grow into a vegetable peace.

Soul is the issue of so strict a fate.
They harbor visions in their waking eyes,
And with their quiet ears participate
In heaven's pure serenity, which lies
So near all things—yet from the beasts concealed.
Serene now, superhuman, they crop their field.

EUGENIO MONTALE (TRANS. JONATHAN GALASSI)

## "The bangs that hide your childlike forehead"

The bangs that hide your childlike forehead—
don't disturb them with your hand.
They too speak of you, along my way
they're all the sky, the only light
beyond the jades you wear around your wrist,
the curtain your condoning hangs
across the roar of sleep,
the wing on which you fly,
transmigratory Artemis, unscathed
among the wars of the stillborn; and if now
those depths get flocked with airy down
it's you who've marbled them, come down
in one fell swoop, and your unquiet brow
gets melded with the dawn, eclipses it.

FEDERICO GARCÍA LORCA
(TRANS. JOHN K. WALSH AND FRANCISCO ARAGON)

## "O secret voice of dark love!"

O secret voice of dark love!
O bleeting without fleece! O wound!
O needle of gall, sunken camellia!
O current without sea, city without walls!

O immense night of sure profile,
celestial mountain tall with anguish!
O dog in the heart, beleaguered voice,
borderless silence, ripened lily!

Away from me, simmering voice of ice,
and lose me not among the weeds
where flesh and heaven moan, leaving no fruit.

Forsake the hard ivory of my head,
take pity on me, break my pain!
For I am love, for I am nature!

JORGE LUIS BORGES (TRANS. ALAN S. TRUEBLOOD)

## A Poet of the Thirteenth Century

He looks over the laborious drafts
of that first sonnet (still to be so called),
the random scribbles cluttering the page—
triads, quatrains promiscuously scrawled.
Slowly he smoothes down angularities,
then stops. Has some faint music reached his
 sense,
notes of far-off nightingales relayed
out of an awesome future ages hence?
Has he realized that he is not alone
and that Apollo, unbelievably arcane,
has made an archetype within him sing—
one crystal-clear and eager to absorb
whatever night conceals or day unveils:
labyrinths, mazes, enigmas, Oedipus King?

RAYMOND QUENEAU (TRANS. STANLEY CHAPMAN)

## from 100,000,000,000,000 Poems

At five precisely out went La Marquise
Since Elgin left his nostrils in the stone
The showman gargles fire and sword with ease

That suede ferments is not at all well known
Old Galileo's Pisan offerings
The North Wind bites into his architrave
Such merchandise a melancholy brings
Till firemen come with hose-piped tidal wave
The peasant's skirts on rainy days she'd tress
And starve the snivelling baby like a dog
Poor Yorick comes to bury not address
We'll suffocate before the epilogue
Where no one bothered how one warmed one's
    bum
The best of all things to an end must come


PABLO NERUDA (TRANS. STEPHEN TAPSCOTT)

### *from* Cien sonetos de amor

## LXXXIX

When I die, I want your hands on my eyes:
I want the light and wheat of your beloved hands
to pass their freshness over me once more:
I want to feel the softness that changed my destiny.

I want you to live while I wait for you, asleep.
I want your ears still to hear the wind, I want you
to sniff the sea's aroma that we loved together,
to continue to walk on the sand we walk on.

I want what I love to continue to live,
and you whom I love and sang above everything
    else
to continue to flourish, full-flowered:

so that you can reach everything my love directs
    you to,
so that my shadow can travel along in your hair,
so that everything can learn the reason for my
    song.

MIGUEL HERNÁNDEZ (TRANS. ROBERT BLY)

## *"You threw me a lemon, oh it was sour"*

You threw me a lemon, oh it was sour,
with a warm hand, that was so pure
it never damaged the lemon's architecture.
I tasted the sourness anyway.

With that yellow blow, my blood moved
from a gentle laziness into an anguished
fever, for my blood felt the bite
from a long and firm tip of a breast.

Yet glancing at you and seeing the smile
which that lemon-colored event drew from you,
so far from my dishonorable fierceness,

my blood went to sleep in my shirt,
and the soft and golden breast turned
to a baffling pain with a long beak.

ANA ENRIQUETA TERÁN (TRANS. MARCEL SMITH)

## *"Subtle in your fourteen lines surge"*

Subtle in your fourteen lines surge
girl and woman I was, made up,
poised to be me now, an ancient,
reply to weathers you foresee.

You shut yourself in fourteen lines
to go on with her, through some mad
drive to remain, a yet wet page
where scrubbed and chaste you hone yourself,

unpawn self in the first tercet
of valorous tongue, fierce lancet
into tightness thrust and taken

full face on, O! shaft that gives life.
I give all words in noiseless light
to live, head high, in a sonnet.

## A Pity. We Were Such a Good Invention

They amputated
Your thighs off my hips.
As far as I'm concerned
They are all surgeons. All of them.

They dismantled us
Each from the other.
As far as I'm concerned
They are all engineers. All of them.

A pity. We were such a good
And loving invention.
An airplane made from a man and wife.
Wings and everything.
We hovered a little above the earth.

We even flew a little.

## Sonnet

Don't worry, it will come! You're drawing near,
you're getting warm! For the word which is to end
the poem more than the first word will be near
your death, which won't be stopping along the way.

Don't think that it will doze off under the
     branches,
or pause to catch its breath while you are writing.
Even when you drink of the mouth which
     quenches
the deepest thirst, that soft mouth with its sweet

cries, even when you so make fast the knot
of your four arms that you can move no more
caught in the smoldering darkness of your hair,

it's coming, God knows how, towards both of you,
far off or here already, but don't worry,
it's coming: from one word to the next you age.

DAHLIA RAVIKOVITCH
(TRANS. CHANA BLOCH AND ARIEL BLOCH)

## Clockwork Doll

I was a clockwork doll but then
that night I turned round and around
and fell on my face, cracked on the ground,
and they tried to piece me together again.

Then once more I was a proper doll
and all my manner was nice and polite.
But I'd become damaged goods that night,
an injured twig poised for a fall.

And then I went out to dance at the ball
but they cast me aside with the dogs and the cats
though all my steps were measured and true.

And my hair was golden, my eyes were blue,
and my dress was the color of flowers and all,
and a sprig of cherries was tacked to my hat.

LAM THI MY DA
(TRANS. MARTHA COLLINS AND THUY DINH)

## Night Harvest

White circles of conical hats have come out
Like the quiet skies of our childhood
Like the wings of storks spread in the night
White circles evoking the open sky

The golds of rice and cluster-bombs blend together
Even delayed-fuse bombs bring no fear
Our spirits have known many years of war
Come, sisters, let us gather the harvest

Each of us wears her own small moon
Glittering on a carpet of gold rice
We are the harvesters of my village
Twelve white hats bright in the long night

We are not frightened by bullets and bombs in the air
Only by dew wetting our lime-scented hair

# TEN QUESTIONS FOR
# A SONNET WORKSHOP

*Why fourteen lines?*

Fourteen lines has been the set length of the sonnet for hundreds of years. No one knows precisely why this prescribed number, this prede-termined length, has worked so well over time. The sonnet has crossed national boundaries and changed languages, and yet the number of lines remains constant. "Fourteen," Robert Burns exclaims, "What magic myst'ries in that number lie!"

# Ten Questions for a Sonnet Workshop

1. What are the characteristics of the traditional sonnet?
2. Why fourteen lines?
3. What is a Petrarchan sonnet?
4. What is the turn or *volta* in the Petrarchan sonnet?
5. What is a Shakespearean sonnet?
6. What is the purpose of the couplet in the Shakespearean sonnet?
7. Why iambic pentameter?
8. Why rhyme?
9. Can there be an unrhymed sonnet?
10. Can a sonnet be more (or less) than fourteen lines?

1. What are the characteristics of the traditional sonnet?
   - Fourteen lines.
   - A structure based on either the Petrarchan or Shakespearean models.
   - A turn in the poem, or *volta*.
   - A characteristic meter, usually iambic pentameter.
   - A customary rhyme scheme.

2. Why fourteen lines?
   Fourteen lines has been the set length of the sonnet for hundreds of years. No one knows precisely why this prescribed number, this predetermined length, has worked so well over

time. The sonnet has crossed national boundaries and changed languages, and yet the number of lines remains constant. "Fourteen," Robert Burns exclaims, "What magic myst'ries in that number lie!"

First codified in the thirteenth century, fourteen lines proved to be the ideal length for the sonnet. It has turned out to be a highly useful convention. It is practical—a liberating limitation. It may also be archetypal. The fourteen-line sonnet, especially in its Italian incarnation, may have a basis in nature, in natural forms, or in mathematics. It may have something to do with classical harmonies and proportions. It has a kind of architectural solidity. It creates a space that is compressed but ample. The sonnet—and the length has something important to do with this—is intense enough for passion, wide enough for thought. It can hold and extend— it can monumentalize—a moment.

Fourteen lines is a key feature of the traditional sonnet, but it is not a sufficient one. There are fourteen-line poems that are not sonnets and there are sonnets that are not fourteen lines long. A poem needs additional qualities and characteristics to be called a sonnet. Above all, it needs a structure.

### 3. What is a Petrarchan sonnet?

The Petrarchan sonnet, as its name suggests, was developed in Italy and modeled on the most famous sonneteer of all time, Francesco Petrarch (1304–1374). The Petrarchan sonnet, which is sometimes referred to as the "Italian" sonnet, is a bipartite invention, a two-part argument. It is an asymmetrical form that invites a two-part division of thought. It has a logical basis that has been connected to the syllogism.

The first eight lines—the octave—tend to raise an issue, suggest a problem, create a conflict. The first four lines establish the subject. The second four lines complicate it.

The last six lines—the sestet—develop that subject. They respond to the issue, or comment on the problem, or try to resolve the conflict. Together, the three parts (two quatrains and a sestet) create a whole.

The first eight lines rhyme *abbaabba*. The last six lines rhyme either *cdecde* or *cdeced* or *cdcdee*. The change in rhyme between the octave and the sestet signals a change in subject matter in the two parts of the poem.

Petrarch created a forensic instrument that seemed especially suitable to the love poem. The Petrarchan sonnet started its life as a love poem with a spiritual base, though over the centuries poets expanded the subject matter to include every sort of topic. Whatever its subject matter, the Petrarchan sonnet is an immensely useful and satisfying form. It creates a feeling of immediacy. Yet it also gives enough room for an idea (or a feeling) to be worked out.

*Example*

Here the nineteenth-century Irish poet John Kells Ingram (1823–1907) applies the Petrarchan sonnet to the ordeal of nationalism. Though love of country rather than of a woman is involved, the powerful Petrarchan template holds good: its frustrated love, its passionate address to an unattainable beloved, its fierce idealization.

## National Presage

Unhappy Erin, what a lot was thine!
Half-conquer'd by a greedy robber band;
Ill govern'd with now lax, now ruthless hand;
Misled by zealots, wresting laws divine
To sanction every dark or mad design;
Lured by false lights of pseudo-patriot league
Through crooked paths of faction and intrigue;
And drugg'd with selfish flattery's poison'd wine.
Yet, reading all thy mournful history,
Thy children, with a mystic faith sublime,
Turn to the future, confident that Fate,
Become at last thy friend, reserves for thee,
To be thy portion in the coming time,
They know not what—but surely something great.

Notice how the poem begins as a pained address to Ireland herself, a personified being ("Unhappy Erin"). The first eight lines, which rhyme *abbaacca*, constitute a single unit.

The enveloping rhymes (*thine/divine/design/wine*) help to bind the argument. The line of reasoning closes on the phrase *poison'd wine*. The list makes the country's fate seem hopeless.

But then the poem rhetorically pivots on the word *Yet*. It swerves and builds a rousing message in the last six lines. It speaks to Ireland's suffering in the first eight lines, but then turns and recognizes its great promise in the last six lines.

The poem sets out to overcome its own obstacle. This is an exact embodiment of the emotional logic—the very movement—of the Petrarchan sonnet.

4. What is the turn or *volta* in the Petrarchan sonnet?

The Petrarchan sonnet is a form that turns. From its inception, the fourteen-line poem has contained a basic turn, or what in Italian is called a *volta*. The first eight lines create an argument or establish a proposition. They command the reader's attention. They take the stage as an idea or a concept. They establish a base. Then, all of a sudden, the poem shifts. It takes a turn. This is the *volta*.

The turn can take the form of an answer to a question, or the solution to a problem. The *volta* is the essence of the sonnet. The reader is spun around, shaken, shifted in ways that deepen the subject. The *volta* alters perception. It gives the sonnet its capacity to change, to shift, and also to expand its voice. The turn, which often pivots on a logical term (*for, yet, then*), can also provide a great deal of emotional intensity.

Remember, for instance, the turning point in Keats's signature sonnet, "On first looking into Chapman's Homer." "Then felt I like some watcher of the skies," he asserts, "When a new planet swims into his ken." The turn creates a sense of excited breakthrough. It enacts a feeling of wonderment.

*Example*

Wordsworth's Italian sonnet, "It is a beauteous evening, calm and free," illustrates the rhetorical turn or *volta* in a strikingly literal way. The poem is a walk. In the first eight lines, Wordsworth describes an evening infused with a sense of natural divinity. The octave creates a holy sense of solitude, a feeling of sacred communion with the night.

> It is a beauteous evening, calm and free;
> The holy time is quiet as a nun
> Breathless with adoration; the broad sun
> Is sinking down in its tranquility;
> The gentleness of heaven is on the Sea:
> Listen! The mighty Being is awake,
> And doth with his eternal motion make
> A sound like thunder—everlastingly.

But then, suddenly, this quiet poem changes direction. It becomes exclamatory. In the space between the octave and the sestet, the speaker turns to address his daughter: "Dear Child! dear Girl!" This almost suggests a physical turn in her direction. He is not alone after all. He has been walking alongside his daughter all along.

> Dear Child! dear Girl! that walkest with me here,
> If thou appear'st untouched by solemn thought,
> Thy nature is not therefore less divine:
> Thou liest in Abraham's bosom all the year;
> And worshipp'st at the Temple's inner shrine,
> God being with thee when we know it not.

The turn in this poem is highly expressive. It signals a change in sentiment. The first eight lines express a feeling of the way that God inheres in nature. But the last six lines turn to the way that a child intuitively, unconsciously, and quite naturally experiences God directly. She doesn't think about nature, she is herself like nature.

5. What is a Shakespearean sonnet?

   The Shakespearean sonnet, as its name suggests, was developed in England and modeled on the greatest dramatic poet of all time, William Shakespeare (1564–1616). The Shakespearean sonnet, which is sometimes referred to as the "English" sonnet, is a highly determined formal structure. It is a symmetrical form—a four-part invention—that invites a four-fold division of thought or feeling.

The Shakespearean sonnet consists of three four-line stanzas—*quatrains*—and a final two-line stanza—a *couplet.* It shows a stepped progress through the first twelve lines that then leads to a conclusion—a finale—in the rhyming couplet at the end. It rhymes *abab cdce efef gg.*

Like Petrarch, Shakespeare created a forensic instrument that also seemed especially suitable to the love poem. The Shakespearean sonnet started its life as an earthy and argumentative erotic poem, but over the centuries poets also vastly expanded its subject matter. It is a logical form that nonetheless breaks more often than the Petrarchan form. It is more open to changes in tone and voice. It has room to develop an idea, but it can also create staccato outbursts of emotion, which are them summarized in the couplet at the end.

*Example*

Sir Walter Ralegh rigorously follows the logic of the English sonnet in this chilling poem addressed to his son, which was probably written in the Tower of London. "Sir Walter Ralegh to His Son" is a closely reasoned poem. It employs a dark wit and a clear argumentative structure.

## Sir Walter Ralegh to His Son

Three things there be that prosper up apace
And flourish, whilst they grow asunder far,
But on a day, they meet all in one place,
And when they meet, they one another mar;
And they be these: the wood, the weed, the wag.
The wood is that which makes the gallow tree;
The weed is that which strings the hangman's bag;
The wag, my pretty knave, betokeneth thee.
Mark well, dear boy, whilst these assemble not,

Green springs the tree, hemp grows, the wag is wild,
But when they meet, it makes the timber rot,
It frets the halter, and it chokes the child.
   Then bless thee, and beware, and let us pray
   We part not with thee at this meeting day.

Note how the first four lines establish the basic proposition of the poem—here are three quite different and otherwise unrelated things, fine alone, but hazardous together.

The second four lines then name those seemingly innocent things (*the wood, the weed, the wag*), defining their dark potential use. The wag is a mischievous boy, a youth. The *wag*, he tells his son, whom he affectionately calls "my pretty knave," *betokeneth thee*; that is, gives a sign to you.

The third quatrain addresses the son directly and warns him to keep the tree, the hemp, and the wag apart. The father frets that just as the wood and the weed may provide the material for hanging (a gallows, a rope), so might his son's waggery, his mischievous nature, get him permanently strung up.

The final rhyming couplet, which is signaled by the logical *Then*, concludes the poem with a blessing, a dark warning, and a prayer.

6. What is the purpose of the couplet in the Shakespearean sonnet?

The Shakespearean sonnet concludes with a rhyming couplet. After three rhyming quatrains, that couplet stands alone as a formal unit. This is one of the key distinguishing features of the English form.

One of the characteristics of the sonnet is its ability to be a sound chamber. Sometimes the volume is up; sometimes down. Because it is an intact unit, the couplet is one of the most memorable aspects of the Shakespearean sonnet. The formal structure sets up an expectation that requires a convincing conclusion.

The couplet brings the poem to a powerful resolution. Often it operates as a proposition, and thus begins: *For* or *So* or *If* or *And yet* or *Therefore*. The logic, which often seems syllogistic, has a strong emotional force. Think of Shakespeare's decisive concluding lines:

> For thy sweet love remembered such wealth brings
> That then I scorn to change my state with kings.
> (Sonnet 29)

> So, till the judgement that yourself arise,
> You live in this, and dwell in lovers' eyes.
> (Sonnet 55)

> If this be error and upon me proved,
> I never writ, nor no man ever loved.
> (Sonnet 116)

> And yet, by heaven, I think my love as rare
> As any she belied with false compare.
> (Sonnet 130)

> Therefore I lie with her and she with me,
> And in our faults by lies we flattered be
> (Sonnet 138)

The couplet at the end of a Shakespearean sonnet is usually witty and self-conscious. It is slightly louder than the rest of the poem. It is reflexive and has an aphoristic quality. It is also the place where the poet decides the poem: demanding, asserting, sometimes thwarting or reversing, usually resolving the argument. This gives it a rhetorical power, a poignant finality, a rapt conclusiveness.

7. Why iambic pentameter?
   The sonnet may have derived from the word *sonetto* ("a little song"), but it developed into a form that is actually closer to speech than to song itself. It is characteristically spoken, not sung. It is meant for reading and can be read silently as well as aloud. It tends to follow the most common meter of the language in which it is written. In English this is iambic pentameter.

Iambic pentameter is the standard line in English. *Iambic* refers to the particular pattern of stresses and unstressed syllables, and *pentameter* refers to the number of stress units (otherwise known as *feet*) in the line. An iamb is a short stress followed by a long one. The pentameter line consists of five feet. Therefore, iambic pentameter has five iambs, which is ten syllables. Shelley's question at the end of "Ode to the West Wind"—"If Winter comes, can Spring be far behind?"—is a characteristic iambic pentameter line. It creates a rising and falling rhythm.

A poem in iambic pentameter sets up a fixed metrical pattern. That pattern creates a series of rhythmic expectations. The individual iambic pentameter line, then, is often strongest when it is meaningfully varied. Take, for instance, the opening two lines of a well-known sonnet by John Donne:

Batter my heart, three-personed God; for you
As yet but knock, breathe, shine, and seek to mend;

Notice how Donne immediately starts the poem on an aggressive note by reversing the first iamb. The word *Batter* kicks it off on a strong stress rather than a weak one. Donne then jams six strong stresses into the second ten-syllable line. The rhythm of these two lines dramatizes the speaker's passionate address.

The basic iambic pentameter line is substantial enough to hold a thought in a poised and complete way before folding into the next sound, the next idea. It can be end-stopped and sufficient unto itself, but it is also well suited to enjambment. It makes room for complex sounds, ideas, and rhymes. It creates enough space to build an argument.

*Example*

This sonnet, by the British poet Charlotte Mew, develops a premature elegy for her own death. She imagines herself perishing on the ocean. But it is an imaginary perishing. The poem is rhythmically carried by a well-modulated iambic pentameter rhythm.

## Péri en Mer

*(Cameret)*

One day the friends who stand about my bed
   Will slowly turn from it to speak of me
Indulgently, as of the newly dead,
   Not knowing how I perished by the sea,
That night in summer when the gulls topped white
   The crowded masts cut black against a sky
Of fading rose—where suddenly the light
   Of Youth went out, and I, no longer I,
Climbed home, the homeless ghost I was to be.
   Yet as I passed they sped me up the heights—
Old seamen round the door of the Abri
   De la Tempête. Even on quiet nights
   So may some ship go down with all her lights
Beyond the sight of watchers on the quay!

Mew establishes a regular iambic rhythm in the first four lines. She then dramatically interrupts that rhythm in line five with the three stresses in a row of *gulls topped white*. The poem's complicated maneuver—from imagined death to the reality of its fiction—is accomplished by the metrics of the lines, five through nine, with their changing moods, odd tenses, and dropped syntax. There's also an important stress reversal on the word *Even* in line twelve to signal the end of the poem.

    The rhythm of this powerful poem enacts its subject matter, how the living poet becomes *the homeless ghost I was to be*.

### 8. Why rhyme?

Rainer Maria Rilke called rhyme "a goddess of secret and ancient coincidences." He said, "she comes as happiness comes, hands filled with an achievement that is already in flower."

    Rhyme has the joyousness of discovery, of hidden relations uncovered, as if by accident. Rhyme is a form of relationship and connection, of encounter and metamorphosis. It creates a partnership between words, lines of poetry, feeling, and ideas.

Rhyme foregrounds the sounds of words as words. It functions as a marker signaling the end of a rhythmic unit. It is mnemonic.

The traditional sonnet has a *rhyme scheme* (a characteristic pattern of rhymes), which embodies the emergence, the delivery, of meaning in a poem. It is an abstraction blooded.

There are two rhymes in the first quatrains of the Petrarchan sonnet (*abbaabba*), which creates a great tightness of form. The rhymes help to bind the argument. There is more liberty in the final six lines, which can rhyme in three different ways (*cdecde* or *cdeced* or *cdcdee*). This strategically gives the poet more room to resolve the argument.

The Shakespearean sonnet has many more rhymes, since the rhymes can change each stanza (*abab cdcd efef gg*). Italian is much richer in rhymes than English, and the Shakespearean form enables a greater range of rhymes. The rhyme scheme enacts the logical development of the Shakespearean sonnet. It carries in its body the rhetorical argument of love. It concludes with a couplet that binds the poem together.

*Example*

In this scathing critique of wartime patriotism, Siegfried Sassoon turns up the volume of his criticism, and the aphorisms that are the engine of it, with direct rhyme. He sets up a poem that uses a Shakespearean rhyme scheme in the first eight lines (*ababcdcd*) and a Petrarchan one in the last six lines (*efgefg*).

## Glory of Women

You love us when we're heroes, home on leave,
Or wounded in a mentionable place.
You worship decorations; you believe
That chivalry redeems the war's disgrace.
You make us shells. You listen with delight,
By tales of dirt and danger fondly thrilled.
You crown our distant ardours while we fight,
And mourn our laurelled memories when we're killed.

You can't believe that British troops "retire"
When hell's last horror breaks them, and they run,
Trampling the terrible corpses—blind with blood.
    O German mother dreaming by the fire,
    While you are knitting socks to send your son
    His face is trodden deeper in the mud.

Any good rhyming poem suggests a relationship between sound and sense, and invites a consideration of words linked together by rhyme. There is a sharp conjunction here of "mentionable place" in line two and "war's disgrace" in line four. The word *delight* (line five) rhymes ironically with the word *fight* (line seven), just as the word *thrilled* rhymes, a little horrifically, with the word *killed* (line eight). These are full rhymes, precisely matched vowels, and they create a powerful sound studio for Sassoon's rage.

9. Can there be an unrhymed sonnet?
    There have been many poems that have been characterized as sonnets—by poets and their readers—without rhyming. Rhyming is a key element of the traditional sonnet, but it is not the only element. Without rhyme, a poem needs to establish other elements that characterize it as a sonnet. It must gain something crucial by setting up the formal expectation that it *is* a sonnet.

    There are purists who believe that only metrical, fourteen-line rhyming poems should be considered sonnets. But others take a more liberal view of the form. There is something at the core of the sonnet that may transcend the technique of any one constituent element, such as traditional meter or rhyme. There can be a sonnet in free verse just as there can be an unrhymed sonnet. It is an internal structural principle—emotional, intellectual—that characterizes the sonnet.

    The nontraditional sonnet usually maintains two elements of the sonnet form. What usually marks a poem as a sonnet is an argumentative structure. A sonnet tends to objectify a conflict. A poem engages the sonnet tradition by making a case or taking up the characteristic subject matter of the traditional sonnet. It engages and echoes the tradition, sometimes by trying to refute it. One might say that it creates a sonnet experience.

*Example*

This sonnet by the British poet Simon Armitage considers a relationship that has survived a decade. He employs the image of the woodland flower, the harebell, closed into a book the way the connection between two people may be closed into convention.

This sonnet is reflective and argumentative. It is divided into four stanzas (three, four, four, three). It clearly turns with the eighth line *A decade on, now we astound ourselves.* The tone is contemporary, breezy, conversational.

"In Our Tenth Year" has a strong iambic pentameter rhythm that helps bind the poem together and echoes the sonnet tradition in English. The poem is also evidently working off a muted Petrarchan idea, suggesting itself as a pewter version of the old gilded romantic melodies. It is structured as an unrhymed sonnet.

## In Our Tenth Year

This book, this page, this harebell laid to rest
between these sheets, these leaves, if pressed still
    bleeds
a watercolour of the way we were.

Those years, the fuss of such and such a day,
this disagreement and its final word,
your inventory of names and dates and times,
my infantries of tall, dark, handsome lies.

A decade on, now we astound ourselves;
still two, still twinned but doubled now with love
and for a single night apart, alone,
how sure we are, each of the other half.

This harebell holds its own. Let's give it now
in air, with light, the chance to fade, to fold.
Here, take it from my hand. Now, let it go.

10. Can a sonnet be more (or less) than fourteen lines?
Yes, decidedly. The core sonnet is fourteen lines long. That is
its essential shape, its basic identity. Yet there have always been
meaningful variations on the format. There have been sub-
stantial alternatives.

The sonnet originated in English as a short love lyric.
The word *sonet* was originally used to describe almost any
short poem. It was really only in the sixteenth century that
the English-language sonnet became codified as a fourteen-
line poem.

The sonnet is a form with variations. The early Italian
poets came up with a kind of double sonnet, a twenty-line
poem that consists of two sextets followed by two quatrains.
It is analogous to the traditional sonnet. Dante used this
structure to great effect in two key poems in *La Vita Nuova*
*(The New Life)*. So, too, John Milton invented the "caudated"
or "tailed" sonnet form in English. He based his twenty-line
polemical poem "On the New Forcers of Conscience under
the Long Parliament" (a sonnet with a so-called tail) on an
Italian Renaissance model.

Poets have tried to vary the length of the sonnet while
keeping some of its essential qualities. It is only useful to name
a poem a "sonnet" if it keeps some intrinsic aspect of the son-
net structure.

The relationship between the octave and the sestet in the
Petrarchan sonnet—the 8:6 ratio—has especially fascinated
many poets. It has been both reduced and expanded. For
example, Gerard Manley Hopkins's "curtal sonnet," which is
ten-and-a-half lines long, consists of three-fourths of a
Petrarchan sonnet. It is shrunk proportionately. On the other
side, W. H. Auden expanded the sonnet form in the propor-
tion 12:9 in a poem of his sonnet sequence "The Quest."

Poets have also toyed with the symmetry of the sonnet.
Shakespeare himself reduced one sonnet to twelve lines (Son-

net 126). Herbert ("A Wreath") and Keats ("Nature withheld Cassandra in the skies") did the same. In his sequence *Modern Love*, George Meredith expanded the traditional sonnet to sixteen lines, four symmetrical quatrains. Both Tennyson ("The Kraken") and Frost ("Hyla Brook") wrote fifteen-line sonnets.

The poet who writes a sonnet of different lengths will always have to answer the question: what makes this poem a sonnet? The poem itself should suggest the answer to that question.

## Example

Dante Alighieri, the most significant early practitioner of the sonnet form before Petrarch, included two twenty-line sonnets in *La Vita Nuova (The New Life)* (c. 1293). Here is Dante Gabriel Rossetti's skillful metrical rendition of the second one:

> Death, alway cruel, Pity's foe in chief,
> Mother who brought forth grief,
>   Merciless judgment and without appeal!
>   Since thou alone hast made my heart to feel
>   This sadness and unweal,
> My tongue upbraideth thee without relief.
>
> And now (for I must rid thy name of ruth)
> Behoves me speak the truth
>   Touching thy cruelty and wickedness:
>   Not that they be not known; but ne'ertheless
>   I would give hate more stress
> With them that feed on love in very sooth.
>
> Out of this world thou hast driven courtesy,
>   And virtue, dearly prized in womanhood;
>   And out of youth's gay mood
> The lovely lightness is quite gone through thee.
>
> Whom now I mourn, no man shall learn from me
>   Save by the measures of these praises given.

Whoso deserves not Heaven
May never hope to have her company.

Dante interspersed prose commentaries with the lyrics in
*The New Life*, and this is his self-conscious explanation of his
"sonetto":

*This poem is divided into four parts. In the first I address
Death by certain proper names of hers. In the second,
speaking to her, I tell the reason why I am moved to
denounce her. In the third, I rail against her. In the
fourth, I turn to speak to a person undefined, although
defined in my own conception. The second part com-
mences here, "Since thou alone"; the third here, "And now
(for I must)"; the fourth here, "Whoso deserves not."*

Dante conceived of his sonnet as a four-part structure. He
crossed stanzas to apply a rigorous logic—a cool scapular
thought—to his subject, Death. He was a poet of passionate
reason, who employed human feeling to contest an inhuman
foe. This, too, is one of the hallmarks—the legacies—of the
early sonnet. On a couple of significant occasions, that son-
net was twenty lines long.

# THE SONNET
# UNDER THE LAMP:

## A History of Comments
## on a Form

# THE SONNET UNDER THE LAMP:
# A HISTORY OF COMMENTS ON A FORM

Then have you Sonnets: some think that all Poems (being short) may be called Sonnets, as indeed it is a diminutive word derived of *Sonare*, but yet I can best allow to call those Sonnets which are of fourteen lines, every line containing ten syllables. The first twelve do rhyme in staves of four lines by cross meter, and the last two rhyming together do conclude the whole.

—George Gascoigne, "Certain Notes of Instruction Concerning the Making of Verse or Rhyme in English" (1575)

Other sorts of Poetry almost have we none, but that lyrical kind of Songs and Sonnets: which, Lord, if he gave us so good minds, how well it might be employed, and with how heavenly fruit, both private and public, in singing the praises of the immortal beauty, the immortal goodness of that God who giveth us hands to write and wits to conceive; of which we might well want words, but never matter; of which we could turn our eyes to nothing, but we should ever have new budding occasions. But truly many of such writings as come under the banner of unresistible love; if I were a Mistress, would never persuade me they were in love; so coldly they apply fiery speeches, as men that had rather read lovers' writings, and so caught up certain swelling phrases, which hang together like a man which once told me the wind was at Northwest, and by South, because he would be sure to name wind enough—than that in truth they feel those passions, which easily (as I think) may be bewrayed by that same forcibleness, or *Ener-*

*gia* (as the Greeks call it), of the writer. But let this be a sufficient though short note, that we miss the right use of the material point of Poesy.

> —**Sir Philip Sidney**, *An Apology for Poetry* (c. 1583)

For compendious praising of any books, or the authors thereof, or any arguments of other histories, where sundry sentences and change of purpose are required, use Sonnet verse, of fourteen lines, and ten feet in every line. The example whereof I need not to show you, in respect I have set down two in the beginning of this treatise.

> —**King James VI of Scotland**, *A Short Treatise on Verse* (1584)

Sometimes, because Love commonly wears the livery of Wit, he will be an *Inamorato Poeta*, and sonnet a whole quire of paper in praise of Lady Swine-snout, his yellow-faced mistress, and wear a feather of her rainbeaten fan for a favour, like a fore-horse.

> —**Thomas Nashe**, *Pierce Penniless His Supplication to the Devil*
> (1592)

PROTEUS: But you, Sir Thurio, are not sharp enough;
You must lay lime to tangle her desires
By wailful sonnets, whose composed rhymes
Should be full-fraught with serviceable vows.

> —**William Shakespeare**, *The Two Gentlemen of Verona*, III, ii, 67
> (c. 1592)

He [Jonson] cursed Petrarch for redacting verses into sonnets; which he said were like that tyrant's bed, where some who were too short were racked, others too long cut short.

> —**William Drummond**, *Conversations of Ben Jonson with William*
> *Drummond of Hawthornden* (1619)

> We'll build in sonnets pretty rooms;
> As well a well wrought urn becomes
> The greatest ashes, as half-acre tombs

—**John Donne**, "The Canonization" *Songs and Sonets* (1635)

The Spanish proverb informs me, that he is a fool which cannot make one sonnet, and he is mad which makes two.

—**John Donne**, "To my very true and very good friend Sir Henry Goodyere" in *Letters to Severall Persons of Honour* (1651)

The Sonnets, a Species of Poetry so entirely disus'd, that it seems to be scarce known among us at this time.

—**John Hughes**, "Remarks on the Shepherd's Calendar, etc." in *The Works of Mr. Edmund Spenser* (1715)

*Sonnet.* n.s. [*sonnet*, French; *sonetto*, Italian]

1. A short poem consisting of fourteen lines, of which the rhymes are adjusted by a particular rule. It is not very suitable to the English language, and has not been used by any man of eminence since Milton.

2. A small poem.

> Let us into the city presently,
> To sort some gentlemen well skill'd in musick;
> I have a *sonnet* that will serve the turn.     *Shakespeare.*

*Sonnetteer.* n.s. [*sonnetier*, French; from sonnet.]
A small poet, in contempt.

> Assist me, some extempore god of rhime; for I am sure I shall turn *sonneteer.*     *Shakespeare, Love's Labour's Lost.*

> There are as many kinds of gardening as of poetry: your makers of parterres and flower gardens are epigrammatists and *sonnetteers* in this art.     *Spectator.*

What woful stuff this madrigal would be,
In some starv'd hackney *sonnetteer* or me?
But let a lord once own the happy lines,
How the wit brightens! how the style refines!     *Pope.*

—**Samuel Johnson**, *A Dictionary of the English Language* (1755)

Quaintness, obscurity, and tautology are to be regarded as the constituent parts of this exotick species of composition. . . . I am one of those who should have wished it to have expired in the country where it was born. . . . [A sonnet is] composed in the highest strain of affectation, pedantry, circumlocution, and nonsense.

—**George Steevens**, from "Sonnets" in *The Plays and Poems of William Shakespeare* (1821)

Perhaps in brilliancy of imagery, quickness of thought, variety and fertility of allusion, and particularly in touches of pastoral painting, Shakespeare is superior [to Spenser]. But he is more incorrect, indigested, and redundant: and if Spenser has too much learning, Shakespeare has too much conceit. It may be necessary however to read the first one hundred & twenty six sonnets of our divine dramatist as written by a lady: for they are addressed with great fervency yet delicacy of passion, and with more of fondness than friendship, to a beautiful youth.

—**Thomas Warton**, *A History of English Poetry: An Unpublished Continuation* (c. 1782)

Miss Hannah More . . . had expressed a wonder that the poet, who had written "Paradise Lost," should write such poor Sonnets:— "Milton, Madam, was a genius that could cut a colossus from a rock, but could not carve heads upon cherrystones."

—**James Boswell**, *The Life of Samuel Johnson* (1791)

The sonnet will ever be cultivated, by those who write on tender and pathetic subjects.

—**William Preston**, *The Poetical Works* (1793)

The Sonnet then is a small poem, in which some lonely feeling is developed.

> —**Samuel Taylor Coleridge**, Introduction to "A Sheet of Sonnets"
> (1796)

Sophisticated sonnets are so common, for every rhapsody of rhyme, from six lines to sixty comes under that denomination, that the eye frequently turns from this species of poem with disgust. Every school-boy, every romantic scribbler, thinks a sonnet a task of little difficulty. From this ignorance in some, and vanity in others, we see the monthly and diurnal publications abounding with ballads, odes, elegies, epitaphs, and allegories, the non-descript ephemera from the heated brains of self-important poetasters, all ushered into notice under the appellation of SONNET!

> —**Mary Robinson**, Preface to *Sappho and Phaon* (1796)

One of the three Books I have with me is Shakespear's Poems: I neer found so many beauties in the sonnets—they seem to be full of fine things said unintentionally—in the intensity of working out conceits—Is this to be borne?

> —**John Keats**, Letter to J. H. Reynolds (November 22, 1817)

> There's doubtless something in domestic doings,
>     Which forms, in fact, true love's antithesis;
> Romances paint at full length people's wooings,
>     But only give a bust of marriages;
> For no one cares for matrimonial cooings,
>     There's nothing wrong in a connubial kiss:
> Think you, if Laura had been Petrarch's wife,
> He would have written sonnets all his life?

> —**George Gordon, Lord Byron**, *Don Juan*, Canto III, 8
> (1818–1824)

The great object of the Sonnet seems to be, to express in musical numbers, and as it were with undivided breath, some occasional thought or personal feeling, 'some fee-grief due to the poet's breast.' It is a sigh uttered from the fulness of the heart, an involuntary aspiration born and dying in the same moment.

—**William Hazlitt**, "On Milton's Sonnets" in *Table-Talk; Or, Original Essays* (1821)

I used to think [the sonnet] egregiously absurd, though the greatest poets since the revival of literature have written in it. Many years ago my sister happened to read to me the sonnets of Milton, which I could at that time repeat; but somehow or other I was singularly struck with the style of harmony, and the gravity, and republican austerity of those compositions.

—**William Wordsworth**, Letter to Walter Savage Landor (April 20, 1822)

He [Milton] caught the sonnet from the dainty hand
Of Love, who cried to lose it; and he gave
The notes to Glory. . . .

—**Walter Savage Landor**, "To Lamartine President of France" in *The Last Fruit off an Old Tree* (1853)

Every mood of mind can be indulged in a sonnet; every kind of reader appealed to. You can make love in a sonnet, you can laugh in a sonnet, you can lament in it, can narrate or describe, can rebuke, can admire, can pray.

—**Leigh Hunt**, "An Essay On the Desirableness of Cultivating the Sonnet" in *The Book of the Sonnet* (1867)

For the concise expression of an isolated poetic thought—an intellectual or sensuous "wave" keenly felt, emotionally and rhythmically—the sonnet would seem to be the best medium, the means apparently prescribed by certain radical laws of melody and harmony, in other words, of nature; even as the swallow's wing is the best for rapid volant wheel and shift, as the heron's for mounting by wide gyrations, as that of the kite or the albatross for sustained suspension.

—William Sharp, "The Sonnet: Its Characteristics and History" (1887)


The reason why the sonnet has never been so effective or successful in England as in Italy I believe to be this: it is not so long as the Italian sonnet; it is not long enough, I will presently say how. Now in the form of any work of art the intrinsic measurements, the proportions, that is, of the parts to one another and to the whole, are no doubt the principal point, but still the extrinsic measurements, the absolute quantity or size goes for something. Thus supposing in the Doric Order the Parthenon to be the standard of perfection, then if the columns of the Parthenon have so many semidiameters or modules to their height, the architrave so many, and so on these will be the typical proportions. But if a building is raised on a notably greater scale it will be found that these proportions for the columns and the rest are no longer satisfactory, so that one of two things—either the proportions must be changed or the Order abandoned. Now if the Italian sonnet is one of the most successful forms of composition known, as it is reckoned to be, its proportions, inward and outward, must be pretty near perfection. The English sonnet has the same inward proportions, 14 lines, 5 feet to the line, and the rhymes and so on may be made as in the strictest Italian type. Nevertheless it is notably shorter and would therefore appear likely to be unsuccessful, from want not of comparative but of absolute length.

—Gerard Manley Hopkins, Letter to Richard Watson Dixon (October 29, 1881)


Life has been your art. You have set yourself to music. Your days are your sonnets.

—Oscar Wilde, *The Picture of Dorian Gray* (1891)

It may, perhaps, interest the collectors of literary curiosities to learn that no less than 3,000 livres is said to have been given by Richelieu to the poet Achillini for the latter's sonnet on the taking of La Rochelle; and that the still larger sum of 30,000 livres was presented by Henry IV. to Philippe Desportes for the sonnet of *Diane and Hippolyte.*

—**Samuel Waddington,** "The Sonnet: Its History and Composition" in *English Sonnets by Living Writers* (1888)

The English language is comparatively poor in rhymes, and most English poets, when they have to rhyme more than two or three words together, betray their embarrassment. They betray it, for instance, when they write sonnets after the strict Petrarchan rule: the poetical inferiority of most English sonnets, if compared with what their own authors have achieved in other forms of verse, is largely though not entirely the result of this difficulty. Milton is embarrassed by it; Wordsworth, though probably the best of our sonneteers, is pitiably embarrassed, and driven to end the noblest of his sonnets with a wretched tag about 'titles manifold;' Rossetti, our most determined workman in this line, dissimulates his embarrassment by inventing, for the purpose of sonnet-writing, a jargon in which every word is so unnatural that the words which form the rhymes are no more unnatural than the rest and so give rise to no special wonder.

—**A. E. Housman,** "Swinburne" (1910)

These are no sonnets for an idle hour. It is only when the emotions illumine the perceptive powers that we see the reality. It is in the light born of this double current that we look upon the face of the mystery unveiled.

—**Ezra Pound,** *The Sonnets and Ballate of Guido Cavalcanti* (1912)

To create a form is not merely to invent a shape, a rhyme or rhythm. It is also the realization of the whole appropriate content of this rhyme or rhythm. The sonnet of Shakespeare is not merely such and such a pattern, but a precise way of thinking and feeling.

> —T. S. Eliot, "The Possibility of a Poetic Drama" in *The Sacred Wood: Essays on Poetry and Criticism* (1920)

I have discovered the most exciting, the most arduous literary form of all, the most difficult to master, the most pregnant in curious possibilities. I mean the advertisement. . . . It is far easier to write ten passably effective Sonnets, good enough to take in the not too inquiring critic, than one effective advertisement that will take in a few thousand of the uncritical buying public.

> —Aldous Huxley, "Advertisement" in *On the Margin* (1923)

To me all sonnets say the same thing of no importance.

> —William Carlos Williams, *The Wedge* (1944)

Never in this world did I expect to praise a living writer because of his sonnets, but these have been a revelation to me. For years I have been stating that the sonnet form is impossible to us, but Moore, by destroying the rigidities of the old form and rescuing the form itself intact . . . has succeeded in completely altering my opinion. The sonnet, I see now, is not and has never been a form at all in any fixed sense other than that incident upon a certain turn of the mind. It is the extremely familiar dialogue unit upon which all dramatic writing is founded: a statement, then a rejoinder of a sort, perhaps a direct reply, perhaps a variant of the original—but a comeback of one sort or another—which Dante and his contemporaries had formalized for their day and language.

> —William Carlos Williams, "Merrill Moore's Sonnets,"
> Introduction to *Sonnets from New Directions*, by Merrill Moore
> (1938)

Probably, more nonsense has been talked and written, more intellectual and emotional energy expended in vain, on the sonnets of

Shakespeare than on any other literary work in the world. Indeed, they have become the best touchstone I know of for distinguishing the sheep from the goats, those, that is, who love poetry for its own sake and understand its nature, from those who only value poems either as historical documents or because they express feelings or beliefs of which the reader happens to approve.

—**W. H. Auden**, "Shakespeare's Sonnets" (1964)

## The Sonnet

*Remembering Louise Bogan*

The Sonnet, she told the crowd of bearded
        youths, their hands exploring
                rumpled girls,
                is a sacred

vessel: it takes a civilization
        to conceive its shape or know
                its uses. The kids
                stared as though

a Sphinx now spake the riddle of
        a blasted day. . . .

—**Daniel Hoffman**, *The Center of Attention* (1974)

A sentimental aphorism is even more a surprise than a hard-boiled sonnet.

—**Mason Cooley**, *City Aphorisms, Fifth Selection* (1988)

[The sonnet] is the first lyric form since the fall of the Roman Empire intended not for music or performance but for silent reading. As such, it is the first lyric of self-consciousness, or of the self in conflict. . . . The new form was quickly understood as a new way of thinking about mankind. Emotional problems, especially

problems in love, needed no longer merely be expressed or per-
formed: they might now actually be resolved, or provisionally
resolved, through the logic of a form that turned expression
inward . . .

—Paul Oppenheimer, *The Birth of the Modern Mind: Self,*
  *Consciousness, and the Invention of the Sonnet* (1989)


Of all the forms, the sonnet seems most available to poets for
deconstruction.

—Mona Van Duyn, *Firefall* (1992)

# *Appendices*

## SUGGESTIONS FOR FURTHER READING

Auden, W. H. "Shakespeare's Sonnets." In *Forewords and Afterwords*, selected by Edward Mendelson, 88–108. New York: Random House, 1973.

Baer, William, ed. *Sonnets: 150 Contemporary Sonnets*. Evansville, IN: University of Evansville Press, 2005.

Barnstone, Willis. *Six Masters of the Spanish Sonnet: Essays and Translations*. Carbondale, IL: Southern Illinois University Press, 1993.

Baudelaire, Charles. *Les Fleurs du Mal: The Complete Text of the Flowers of Evil*. Translated by Richard Howard. Boston: David R. Godine, 1982.

Bender, Robert M., and Charles L. Squier, eds. *The Sonnet: An Anthology; A Comprehensive Selection of British and American Sonnets from the Renaissance to the Present*. New York: Washington Square Press, 1987.

Bermann, Sandra L. *The Sonnet Over Time: A Study in the Sonnets of Petrarch, Shakespeare, and Baudelaire*. Chapel Hill: University of North Carolina Press, 1988.

Berryman, John. "The Sonnets." In *Berryman's Shakespeare: Essays, Letters, and Other Writings*, edited by John Haffenden, 285–91. New York: Farrar, Straus and Giroux, 1999.

Betjeman, John, and Charles Tennyson, eds. *A Hundred Sonnets*. London: R. Hart-Davis, 1960.

Bloom, Harold, ed. *Shakespeare's Sonnets: Modern Critical Interpretations*. New York: Chelsea House Publishers, 1987.

Booth, Stephen, ed. *Shakespeare's Sonnets*. New Haven, CT: Yale University Press, 2000.

Bromwich, David, ed. *American Sonnets*. New York: The Library of America, 2007.

Browning, Elizabeth Barrett. *Sonnets from the Portuguese.* Edited by Fannie Ratchford, with notes by Deoch Fulton. New York: P. C. Duschnes, 1950.

Bullock, Walter. "The Genesis of the English Sonnet Form." *PMLA* 38, no. 4 (December 1923), 729–44.

Burpee, Lawrence J., ed. *A Century of Canadian Sonnets.* Toronto, Canada: The Musson Book Company, 1910.

Cruttwell, Patrick. *The English Sonnet.* London: Longmans, Green & Co., 1966.

Curran, Stuart. *Poetic Form and British Romanticism.* New York: Oxford University Press, 1986.

Dante Alighieri. *The New Life.* Translated by Dante Gabriel Rossetti. Preface by Michael Palmer. New York: New York Review of Books, 2002.

Donow, Herbert S., ed. *The Sonnet in England and America: A Bibliography of Criticism.* Westport, CT: Greenwood Press, 1982.

Edmondson, Paul, and Stanley Wells. *Shakespeare's Sonnets.* New York: Oxford University Press, 2004.

Evans, Maurice, and Roy J. Booth, eds. *Elizabethan Sonnets.* Revised ed. London: Phoenix, 2003.

Feldman, Paula R., and Daniel Robinson, eds. *A Century of Sonnets: The Romantic-Era Revival, 1750–1850.* New York: Oxford University Press, 1999.

Ferry, Anne. *The "Inward" Language: Sonnets of Wyatt, Sidney, Shakespeare, and Donne.* Chicago: University of Chicago Press, 1983.

Fineman, Joel. *Shakespeare's Perjured Eye: The Invention of Poetic Subjectivity in the Sonnets.* Berkeley: University of California Press, 1986.

Fuller, John, ed. *The Oxford Book of Sonnets.* New York: Oxford University Press, 2000.

———. *The Sonnet.* London: Methuen, 1972.

Fussell, Paul. "Structural Principles: The Example of the Sonnet." In *Poetic Meter and Poetic Form,* revised ed., 109–26. New York: Random House, 1979.

Grossman, Edith, ed. and trans. *The Golden Age: Poems of the Spanish Renaissance.* Introduction by Billy Collins. New York: W. W. Norton, 2006.

Heale, Elizabeth. *Wyatt, Surrey, and Early Tudor Poetry.* New York: Longman, 1998.

Hecht, Anthony. "The Sonnet: Ruminations on Form, Sex, and History." *Antioch Review* 55, no. 2 (Spring 1997), 134–48.

Hollander, John, ed. *Sonnets: From Dante to the Present.* New York: Alfred A. Knopf, 2001.

Hunt, Leigh, and Samuel Adams Lee, eds. *The Book of the Sonnet.* Boston: Roberts Brothers, 1867.

Kallich, Martin, Jack C. Gray, and Robert M. Rodney, eds. *A Book of the Sonnet: Poems and Criticism.* New York: Twayne, 1973.

Keats, John. *The 64 Sonnets*. Introduction by Edward Hirsch and notes by Gary Hawkins. Philadelphia: Paul Dry Books, 2004.

Kitchin, Laurence, trans. *Love Sonnets of the Renaissance*. London: Forest Books, 1990.

Lever, J. W. *The Elizabethan Love Sonnet*. London: Methuen, 1956.

————, ed. *Sonnets of the English Renaissance*. London: Athlone Press, 1974.

Levin, Phillis, ed. *The Penguin Book of the Sonnet: 500 Years of a Classic Tradition in English*. New York: Penguin, 2001.

Main, David M., ed. *A Treasury of English Sonnets*. New York: R. Worthington, 1881.

Millay, Edna St. Vincent. *Collected Sonnets of Edna St. Vincent Millay*. Revised and expanded ed. New York: Harper & Row, 1988.

Milton, John. *Milton's Sonnets*. Edited by E. A. J. Hongmann. New York: St. Martin's Press, 1966.

Neruda, Pablo. *100 Love Sonnets: Cien sonetos de amor*, translated by Stephen Tapscott. Austin: University of Texas Press, 1986.

Nye, Robert, ed. *The Faber Book of Sonnets*. London: Faber and Faber, 1976.

Oppenheimer, Paul. *The Birth of the Modern Mind: Self, Consciousness, and the Invention of the Sonnet*. New York: Oxford University Press, 1989.

Page, Geoff, ed. *The Indigo Book of Modern Australian Sonnets*. Charnwood, Aus.: Ginninderra Press, 2003.

Paterson, Don, ed. *101 Sonnets: From Shakespeare to Heaney*. London: Faber and Faber, 1999.

Petrarca, Francesco. *Petrarch's Lyric Poems: The Rime Sparse and Other Lyrics*. Edited and translated by Robert M. Durling. Cambridge, MA: Harvard University Press, 1976.

————. *The Poetry of Petrarch*. Edited and translated by David Young. New York: Farrar, Straus and Giroux, 2004.

Peterson, Houston, ed. *The Book of Sonnet Sequences*. London and New York: Longmans, Green and Co., 1929.

Phelan, J. P. *The Nineteenth-Century Sonnet*. Basingstoke, UK, and New York: Palgrave MacMillan, 2005.

Post, Jonathan F. S., ed. *Green Thoughts, Green Shades: Essays by Contemporary Poets on the Early Modern Lyric*. Berkeley: University of California Press, 2002.

Ransom, John Crowe. "Shakespeare at Sonnets." In *The World's Body*, 270–303. London and New York: Charles Scribner's Sons, 1938.

Rilke, Rainer Maria. *Sonnets to Orpheus*. Translated by Edward Snow. New York: North Point Press, 2004.

Shakespeare, William. *The Sonnets and A Lover's Complaint*. Edited by John Kerrigan. New York: Penguin, 1999.

Sharp, William. "The Sonnet: Its Characteristics and History." In *Studies and Appreciations*. Vol. II of *Selected Writings of William Sharp*, edited by Mrs. William Sharp. New York: Duffield and Co., 1912.

Sidney, Sir Philip. *The Defense of Poesie, Astrophil and Stella, and Other Writings.* Edited by Elizabeth Porges Watson. Boston: Charles E. Tuttle Co., 1997.

Smith, Barbara Herrnstein. *Poetic Closure: A Study of How Poems End.* Chicago: University of Chicago Press, 1968.

Spiller, Michael R. G. *The Development of the Sonnet: An Introduction.* London and New York: Routledge, 1992.

Vendler, Helen. *The Art of Shakespeare's Sonnets.* Cambridge, MA: Harvard University Press, 1999.

Wagner, Jennifer Ann. *A Moment's Monument: Revisionary Poetics and the Nineteenth-Century English Sonnet.* Madison, WI, and Teaneck, NJ: Fairleigh Dickinson Press, 1996.

White, Gertrude M., and Joan G. Rosen. *A Moment's Monument: The Development of the Sonnet.* New York: Charles Scribner's Sons, 1972.

# BIOGRAPHIES

**John Quincy Adams (1767–1848)** was born in the North Parish of Braintree, Massachusetts, now called Quincy. He was the eldest son of Abigail Smith and John Adams. He went on various diplomatic missions with his father and graduated from Harvard College in 1787. Adams was married to Louisa Johnson; they had four children. He was the sixth president of the United States (1825–1829), and is one of the few presidents to have published poetry in his lifetime. His works include *Dermot MacMorrogh, or The Conquest of Ireland* (1832), an epic poem, and *Poems of Religion and Society* (1848).

*Poems of Religion and Society: With Notices of his Life and Character by John Davis and T. H. Benton* (repr. 2006); *Writings of John Quincy Adams,* Vol. VII, *1820–1823,* ed. Worthington Chauncey Ford (1917)

**Léonie Adams (1899–1988)** was born in Brooklyn, New York, and educated at Barnard College. She was married to the critic William Troy and taught at Columbia University, among other places. In the 1920s she published two books of poetry and held a Guggenheim Fellowship. She then did not publish her own poetry for another twenty-five years, during which time she was appointed Consultant in Poetry to the Library of Congress (poet laureate). She shared the Bollingen Prize with poet Louise Bogan for her book *Poems: A Selection* (1954).

*Those Not Elect* (1925); *High Falcon & Other Poems* (1929)

James Agee (1909–1955) was born in Knoxville, Tennessee, and attended Harvard College. *Permit Me Voyage* (1934), his only collection of poetry, was published in the Yale Series of Younger Poets. *Death in the Family* (1957), an autobiographical novel published after his death, won the Pulitzer Prize. He was also a film critic (*Agee on Film*), journalist (*Time, Fortune, The New Yorker*), essayist (*Let Us Now Praise Famous Men*), and screenwriter (*The African Queen*).

*The Collected Poems of James Agee*, ed. Robert Fitzgerald (1968); *Let Us Now Praise Famous Men, A Death in the Family, & Shorter Fiction*, ed. Michael Sragow (2005)

William Allingham (1824–1889) was born in Ballyshannon, Donegal, Ireland. He left school at fourteen and began working in the local bank where his father was then manager. Editor of *Fraser's Magazine* in the 1870s, he was best known for his novel in verse, *Laurence Bloomfield in Ireland* (1864), and is remembered for his short lyrics influenced by the tradition of Border ballads. In 1874 he married Helen Paterson, who is known as a watercolorist. *William Allingham: A Diary* (1907) contains reminiscences of Tennyson, Carlyle, and other famous contemporaries.

*The Poems of William Allingham*, ed. John Hewitt (1967)

Julia Alvarez (1950–) was born in New York City. For the first ten years of her life she lived in the Dominican Republic, her parents' home country. Educated at Connecticut College, Middlebury College, and Syracuse University, she was awarded the PEN Oakland–Josephine Miles Award for her novel *How the García Girls Lost Their Accents* (1991) and has received grants from the National Endowment for the Arts and the Ingram Merrill Foundation.

*Homecoming: New and Collected Poems* (1996); *Something to Declare* (1998); *The Woman I Kept to Myself: Poems* (2004)

Yehuda Amichai (1924–2000) was born in Würzburg, Germany, and immigrated to Palestine with his family in 1935. Amichai fought with the British army in World War II and in three Israeli wars. He was among the first Israeli poets to select vernacular Hebrew as his chosen language for poetry. His work has been translated into thirty-seven languages. He was the recipient of numerous awards, including the Israel Prize, his country's highest honor. He is commonly regarded as the major Israeli poet of his time.

*Yehuda Amichai: A Life in Poetry*, trans. Benjamin and Barbara Harshav (1994); *The Selected Poetry of Yehuda Amichai*, trans. Chana Bloch and Stephen Mitchell (1996); *Open Closed Open*, trans. Chana Bloch and Chana Kronfeld (2000)

**Alan Ansen** (1922–2006) was born in Brooklyn, New York, grew up on Long Island, and was educated at Harvard College. Longtime secretary to W. H. Auden, Ansen served as the model for fictional characters in Jack Kerouac's *On the Road* and William Burroughs's *Naked Lunch.* His published poetry consisted of *Disorderly Houses* (1961) and *Contact Highs: Selected Poems 1957–1987* (1989). He spent the last years of his life in Athens, Greece.

*The Table Talk of W. H. Auden,* ed. Nicholas Jenkins (1989)

**Matthew Arnold** (1822–1888) was born in Laleham-on-Thames, England, and educated at Balliol College, Oxford. While vacationing in Switzerland in 1848, he fell in love with "Marguerite," to whom he addressed many poems, but left her and in 1851 married the daughter of a judge. He then began working as a government inspector of schools, a position he held for thirty-five years. He was elected Professor of Poetry at Oxford in 1858. Most of his late work was in prose, and his social and literary criticism was both celebrated and influential in Victorian England.

*The Poems of Matthew Arnold,* ed. Kenneth Allott (1965); *The Letters of Matthew Arnold,* ed. Cecil Y. Lang (1996)

**John Ashbery** (1927–) was born in Rochester, New York, and educated at Harvard College. He lived for ten years in Paris and worked as an art reviewer. *Self-Portrait in a Convex Mirror* (1975) won the Pulitzer Prize, the National Book Award, and the National Book Critics Circle Award. Among his many other awards are the Ruth Lilly Poetry Prize and the Frost Medal, as well as fellowships from the Academy of American Poets, the Guggenheim Foundation, and the MacArthur Foundation. He has lived in New York City since 1965. He teaches at Bard College.

*Selected Poems* (1985); *Flow Chart* (1991); *Hotel Lautréamont* (1992); *A Worldly Country* (2007)

**W. H. Auden** (1907–1973) was born in York, England, and educated at Christ Church, Oxford. Poems that Auden wrote at Oxford were handprinted by his friend Stephen Spender in *Poems* (1928). He traveled widely in Germany, Iceland, Spain, and China, and immigrated to the United States in 1939. He became an American citizen in 1946. He collaborated on verse plays with his friends Christopher Isherwood and Louise MacNeice, and on libretti with the poet Chester Kallman, with whom he lived for more than twenty years. He was Professor of Poetry at Oxford from 1956 to 1961. He was awarded the Pulitzer Prize (1948), the Bollingen Prize (1953), the National Book Award (1956), and the National Medal for Literature (1967).

*Selected Essays* (1964); *The English Auden: Poems, Essays and Dramatic Writings, 1927–1939,* ed. Edward Mendelson (1977); *Collected Poems,* ed. Edward Mendelson (2007)

**Philip Ayres** (1638–1712) was born in Northamptonshire, England, and educated at St. John's College, Oxford. Involved in various diplomatic missions to the Continent, Ayres was chiefly known as a translator from the Latin and Italian. His *Lyric Poems* (1687), which included sonnets by Petrarch and Torquato Tasso, was a popular publication and went into five editions.

*Lyric Poems: Made in Imitation of the Italians* (1687); *Minor Poets of the Caroline Period*, Vol. II, ed. George Saintsbury (1906)

**David Baker** (1954–) was born in Bangor, Maine, and educated at Central Missouri State University and the University of Utah. He has been the recipient of a grant from the National Endowment for the Arts and a Guggenheim Fellowship. He is the poetry editor of the *Kenyon Review* and teaches at Denison University, where he directs the creative writing program.

*Treatise in Touch: Selected Poems* (1995); *Heresy and the Ideal: On Contemporary Poetry* (2000); *Midwest Eclogue: Poems* (2005); *Radiant Lyre: Essays on Lyric Poetry*, coed. with Ann Townsend (2007)

**John Codrington Bampfylde** (1754–1796) was born in Devon, England, and educated at Cambridge University. Bampfylde wrote only one book, *Sixteen Sonnets* (1778), and Robert Southey called his sonnets "some of the most original in our language." Bampfylde spent a term in a mental institution in his later years.

*The Poems of John Bampfylde*, ed. Roger Lonsdale (1988)

**George Barker** (1913–1991) was born in Loughton, Essex, England, and attended Regent Street Polytechnic in London. His first book of poems was published in 1935, his *Collected Poems* in 1987, and his posthumous *Street Ballads* in 1992. After many years of living abroad in Japan, the United States, and Italy, he returned to England and lived in Norfolk until his death.

*Selected Poems*, ed. Robert Fraser (1995)

**Barnabe Barnes** (1569–1609) was born in Yorkshire, England, and educated at Brasenose College, Oxford. Barnes was a prolific writer of verse. In addition to *Parthenophil and Parthenophe* (1593), he also wrote *A Divine Centurie of Spirituall Sonnets* (1595) and an anti-popish tragedy *The Divils Charter: a Tragœdie Conteining the Life and Death of Pope Alexander the Sixt* (1607).

*The Devil's Charter*, ed. Jim C. Pogue (1980)

**Richard Barnfield** (1574-1620) was born in Norbury, Staffordshire, England, and educated at Brasenose College, Oxford. He wrote three books before the age of twenty-five: *The Affectionate Shepherd* (1594),

*Cynthia* (1595), and *The Encomion of Lady Pecunia: Or, the Praise of Money* (1598).

    *Sonnets* (2001); *Poems of Richard Barnfield*, ed. George Klawitter (2005)

**Willis Barnstone** (1927–) was born in Lewiston, Maine, and educated at Bowdoin College, Columbia University, and Yale University. A Fulbright Professor, Guggenheim Fellow, and Pulitzer Prize finalist, as well as a recipient of the Emily Dickinson Award and the W. H. Auden Award, Barnstone is Distinguished Professor Emeritus of Comparative Literature and of Spanish and Portuguese at Indiana University.

    *The Secret Reader: 501 Sonnets* (1996); *We Jews and Blacks: Memoir With Poems* (2004); *ABC of Translation* (2007)

**Charles Baudelaire** (1821–1867) was born in Paris, France. His first publication was *Le Salon de 1845*. He earned renown as a critic of modern art and as a translator of Edgar Allan Poe. He published one volume of poems during his lifetime, *Les Fleurs du mal* (1857). The book was extremely controversial in its time, though it was later recognized as a masterpiece of nineteenth-century French literature. His *Petits poèmes en prose* (1869) was one of the first experiments in prose poetry. Near the end of his life, Baudelaire went to Brussels, where he hoped to earn money by lecturing, but his hopes foundered, his health collapsed, and he was taken back to Paris, where he soon died.

    *The Painter of Modern Life and Other Essays*, ed. and trans. Jonathan Mayne (1964); *Les Fleurs du Mal*, trans. Richard Howard (1982); *Complete Poems*, trans. Walter Martin (3rd ed. 2007)

**James K. Baxter** (1926–1972) was born in Dunedin, New Zealand, and educated at Quaker schools in England and New Zealand before attending the University of Otago and the University of Victoria at Wellington. He was a member of the Wellington group of writers and edited the Wellington magazine *Numbers* from 1954 to 1960. After a long battle with alcoholism, he became a Roman Catholic in 1958. He was a prolific writer and social commentator who became a prominent figure in the 1960s counterculture and established a religious community at Jerusalem on the Whanganui River.

    *Beyond the Palisade* (1944); *Collected Poems*, ed. J. E. Weir (1980)

**Aphra Behn** (1640–1689) was born in Wye, near Canterbury, England, but accounts vary and different opinions exist about her date of birth, her parentage, her religion, and even her given name. She seems to have visited Surinam with her family in her youth, returned to England when the colony was handed over to the Dutch, and been married briefly to a Dutch merchant. Behn wrote novels and poems, but she was primarily a playwright and thought to be one of the most prolific dramatists of the Restoration era. She was one of the first English women to support herself through writing.

*Love-Letters Between a Noble-man and His Sister* (1684); *Oroonoko, The Rover, and Other Works*, ed. Janet Todd (1999)

**Joachim du Bellay (1522–1560)** was born at the Château de la Turmelière in Anjou, France, and studied law at Poitiers. His friendship with Ronsard led him to the Collège de Coqueret, Paris. A leader of La Pléiade, a group that encouraged the study of classics and the use of the French language for literary expression, his works included sonnets, satires on literary conventions, and a manifesto of poetic principles.

*Poems*, ed. H. W. Lawton (1961); *The Regrets: With, The Antiquities of Rome, Three Latin Elegies, and The Defense and Enrichment of the French Language*, ed. and trans. Richard Helgerson (2006)

**Giuseppe Belli (1791–1863)** was born in Rome, Italy, and grew up in impoverished circumstances. He is known for his poetry in Romanesco, the Roman dialect. Between 1830 and 1839, he wrote over two thousand sonnets, which serve as a significant record of the lives of ordinary people during nineteenth-century papal Rome. There is a monument to him in Trastevere from "The People of Rome."

*Roman Sonnets*, trans. Harold Norse (1960); *Sonnets of Giuseppe Belli*, trans. Miller Williams (1981)

**Stephen Berg (1934–)** was born in Philadelphia, Pennsylvania, and educated at the University of Pennsylvania, Boston University, the University of Indiana, and the State University of Iowa. A founding editor of the *American Poetry Review* and the recipient of grants from the National Endowment for the Arts and the Guggenheim Foundation, Berg is professor of English at The University of the Arts in Philadelphia.

*New and Selected Poems* (1992); *The Steel Cricket: Versions 1958–1997* (1997); *The Elegy on Hats* (2005)

**Ted Berrigan (1934–1983)** was born Edmund Joseph Michael in Providence, Rhode Island. He served in the army (1954–1957) and then attended the University of Tulsa. Berrigan taught at a variety of universities, including the University of Iowa. An editor and art critic, he was twice married to poets, Sandy Berrigan and Alice Notley. Active in the poetry scene in Chicago, he moved to New York in the sixties and associated with a range of poets and painters. His innovative volume of poems *The Sonnets* (1964) experimented with formal structure.

*The Collected Poems of Ted Berrigan*, ed. Alice Notley, Anselm Berrigan, and Edmund Berrigan (2005)

**Wendell Berry** (1934–) was born in Newcastle, Kentucky, and attended the University of Kentucky at Lexington. A Wallace Stegner Fellow at Stanford University, his awards include a Guggenheim Fellowship and grants from the Lannan Foundation and the National Endowment for the Arts. He is an influential environmental advocate and lives on a working farm along the Ohio River in Kentucky.

*The Selected Poems of Wendell Berry* (1998); *Window Poems* (2007); *The Art of the Commonplace: The Agrarian Essays of Wendell Berry*, ed. Norman Wirzba (2002)

**John Berryman** (1914–1972) was born John Smith Jr. in rural Oklahoma. At the age of ten, his father committed suicide; his mother later married John Berryman, who adopted her sons. He was educated at Columbia University and earned a scholarship to Clare College, Cambridge. He taught at Princeton, Harvard, the University of Iowa, and the University of Minnesota. His works include *Homage to Mistress Bradstreet* (1956); *77 Dream Songs* (1964), which was awarded a Pulitzer Prize; and *Love and Fame* (1970). He committed suicide by leaping from a bridge over the Mississippi River.

*The Dream Songs* (1969); *The Freedom of the Poet* (1976); *Collected Poems, 1937–1971*, ed. Charles Thornbury (1989); *Selected Poems*, ed. Kevin Young (2004)

**Frank Bidart** (1939–) was born in Bakersfield, California, and educated at the University of California, Riverside, and Harvard University, where he became a close friend of Elizabeth Bishop and Robert Lowell. Bidart's many honors include the Lila Wallace–Reader's Digest Writer's Award, the Morton Dauwen Zabel Award (given by the American Academy of Arts and Letters), and the Bollingen Prize. He teaches at Wellesley College.

*Golden State* (1973); *In the Western Night: Collected Poems, 1965–90* (1990); *Desire* (1997)

**Elizabeth Bishop** (1911–1979) was born in Worcester, Massachusetts, and educated at Vassar College. A frequent contributor to *The New Yorker*, Bishop traveled widely and lived in Key West, Florida, and later in Brazil for ten years. After returning to the United States, she taught at Harvard University from 1970 to 1979. She won the Pulitzer Prize for *North and South: A Cold Spring* (1969), the National Book Award for *Complete Poems* (1969), and the National Book Critics Circle Award for *Geography 111* (1976).

*The Complete Poems, 1927–1979* (1983); *The Collected Prose*, ed. Robert Giroux (1984); *One Art: Letters*, ed. Robert Giroux (1994); *Edgar Allan Poe and the Juke-Box: Uncollected Poems, Drafts, and Fragments*, ed. Alice Quinn (2006)

**William Blake** (1757–1827) was born in London, England. He did not attend school but was apprenticed as an engraver to the Society of Antiquaries. Blake illustrated the works of many writers, including John Milton and Mary Wollestonecraft, as well as his own daring *Songs of Innocence* (1789) and *Songs of Experience* (1794). In 1728 he married Catherine Boucher. From the 1820s he devoted himself exclusively to pictorial art. He was a visionary who created his own complex mythology of human history and suffering.

*Poetry and Prose*, ed. David V. Erdman, commentary Harold Bloom (1965)

**Edmund Blunden** (1896–1974) was born in London, England, and educated at The Queen's College, Oxford. He served in the Royal Sussex Regiment of the British army in World War I and is especially noted for *Undertones of War* (1928). In 1922 he won the prestigious Hawthornden Prize. He spent two periods working in Japan and the Far East. He was a fellow at Merton College, a cultural adviser in Tokyo, a professor of English literature at the University of Hong Kong, and Professor of Poetry at Oxford.

*Edmund Blunden: A Selection of His Poetry and Prose*, ed. Kenneth Hopkins (1950)

**Wilfrid Scawen Blunt** (1840–1922) was born in Sussex, England, and educated at Stonyhurst College and St. Mary's College, Oscott. A foe of British imperialism, he traveled extensively throughout the Middle East and India and was imprisoned in 1888 for his support of Irish causes. His poetry includes *Sonnets and Songs by Proteus* (1875).

*The Secret History of the English Occupation of Egypt: Being a Personal Narrative of Events* (1907); *The Poetical Works of Wilfrid Scawen Blunt* (2 vols., 1914)

**Louise Bogan** (1897–1970) was born in Livermore Falls, Maine. She attended Boston University for one year before leaving school to marry. In 1919, newly single, she moved to New York City to pursue writing. She was the poetry reviewer for *The New Yorker* from 1931 until 1969. She served as the Poetry Consultant to the Library of Congress from 1945 to 1946. She published translations and several key critical studies including *Achievement in American Poetry 1900–1950*.

*The Blue Estuaries: Poems, 1923–1968* (1968); *What the Woman Lived: Selected Letters of Louise Bogan, 1920–1970*, ed. Ruth Limmer (1973); *A Poet's Prose: Selected Writings of Louise Bogan*, ed. Mary Kinzie (2005)

**Jorge Luis Borges** (1899-1986) was born in Buenos Aires, Argentina, and educated in Europe. Director of the National Library of Buenos Aires from 1955 to 1973, he was awarded the degree of Doctor of Letters from both Columbia and Oxford Universities. His increasing blindness did not diminish his literary output, and he received various literary awards over the course of his career, including the International Publishers' Prize, the

Jerusalem Prize, and the Alfonso Reyes Prize. *Ficciones*, a collection of stories published in 1944, established him as a prose fabulist and drew international attention. He is one of the foremost Spanish-language literary figures of the twentieth century.

*Collected Fictions*, trans. Andrew Hurley (1999); *Selected Non-Fictions*, ed. Eliot Weinberger, trans. Esther Allen, Suzanne Jill Levine, and Eliot Weinberger (1999); *Selected Poems*, ed. Alexander Coleman (1999); *This Craft of Verse*, ed. Calin-Andrei Mihailescu (2000)

**Edgar Bowers (1924–2000)** was born in Rome, Georgia, and educated at the University of North Carolina and Stanford University, where he studied under the poet Yvor Winters. He received two Guggenheim Fellowships and a Bollingen Prize for *For Louis Pasteur: Selected Poems* (1989). Bowers held teaching appointments at Duke University, Harpur College, and, for over thirty years, the University of California, Santa Barbara.

*Collected Poems* (1997)

**William Lisle Bowles (1762–1850)** was born at King's Sutton, Northamptonshire, England, and educated at Trinity College, Oxford. A clergyman, he received substantial acclaim for his first book, *Fourteen Sonnets* (1789). In 1806 he published a highly critical and controversial edition of the work of Alexander Pope.

*The Poetical Works of William Lisle Bowles, Canon of St. Paul's Cathedral, and Rector of Bremhill*, ed. Rev. George Gilfillan (1855)

**Mark Alexander Boyd (1563–1601)** was born in Ayrshire, Scotland and spent his life as a soldier of fortune, fighting in religious wars in France. He published poetry in both Latin and English, and wrote occasionally in Scots, in which he created his most noted sonnet.

*Scottish Love Poems: A Personal Anthology*, ed. Antonia Fraser (new ed. 1995)

**Elizabeth Brewster (1922–)** was born in Chipman, New Brunswick, Canada, and received degrees from Radcliffe College, the University of Toronto, and Indiana University. Made a member of the Order of Canada in 2001, she is professor emeritus at the University of Saskatchewan.

*Collected Poems of Elizabeth Brewster* (2 vols. 2003); *Bright Centre* (2005)

**R. F. Brissenden (1928–1991)** was born in Wentworth, New South Wales, Australia. Educated at the Universities of Sydney and Leeds, he taught for much of his life in Canberra. An editor, critic, essayist, writer of thrillers, and poet, Brissenden was a uniquely influential figure in the growth of Australian literature.

*The Oxford Book of Australian Light Verse*, coed. Philip Grundy (1991); *Suddenly Evening: The Selected Poems of R. F. Brissenden*, ed. David Brooks (1993)

**Rupert Brooke (1887–1915)** was born in Rugby, England, and educated at King's College, Cambridge. As a young man, he traveled to France, Germany, the United States, Canada, and the South Seas. He was commissioned into the navy shortly after his twenty-seventh birthday and participated in the retreat from Antwerp in 1914. He is chiefly known for his *War Sonnets*, which were composed in the winter of 1914–1915 in Dorset. Remembered for his good looks and romantic air, he died of dysentery and blood poisoning on a troopship bound for Gallipoli.

*The Poetical Works of Rupert Brooke*, ed. Geoffrey Keynes (1946)

**Gwendolyn Brooks (1917–2000)** was born in Topeka, Kansas, raised in Chicago, Illinois, and educated at Wilson Junior College. She ran workshops for underprivileged youths and taught poetry at a number of universities, including the City College of New York. She succeeded Carl Sandburg as Poet Laureate of Illinois and served as Consultant in Poetry to the Library of Congress from 1985 to 1986. *Annie Allen* (1949) received the Pulitzer Prize. Among her many awards were more than seventy-five honorary degrees from colleges and universities around the country.

*A Street in Bronzeville* (1945); *Selected Poems* (1963); *The Near-Johannesburg Boy, and Other Poems* (1986); *The Essential Gwendolyn Brooks*, ed. Elizabeth Alexander (2005)

**George Mackay Brown (1921–1996)** was born in Stromness in the Orkney Islands, Scotland, where he lived for most of his life and which influenced much of his literary imagery. From his youth, he was affected by tuberculosis. He was a prolific poet, essayist, and fiction writer. He also coauthored two libretti with composer Peter Maxwell Davies. His autobiography, *For the Islands I Sing: An Autobiography* (1997), was published shortly after his death.

*The Collected Poems of George Mackay Brown*, ed. Archie Bevan and Brian Murray (2005)

**Sterling Brown (1901–1989)** was born in Washington, D.C., and educated at Williams College and Harvard University. He taught at Howard University for nearly fifty years. His collection *Southern Road* (1932) was a critical success, but he did not publish another book of poems until *The Last Ride of Wild Bill, and Eleven Narrative Poems* (1975). Brown remained an active essayist, critic, and scholar and published several invaluable works in the study of African American culture, including *The Negro in American Fiction* (1937) and *Negro Poetry and Drama* (1937).

*The Collected Poems of Sterling A. Brown*, ed. Michael S. Harper (1980)

**Elizabeth Barrett Browning (1806–1861)** was born near Durham, England. She studied Greek and Latin at home and began publishing poetry at the age of fourteen. She was plagued with bad health for most of her life. In 1846, without her father's knowledge, she married the poet Robert Browning and eloped with him to Italy. Her book of love poems *Sonnets from the Portuguese* (1850) continues to be one of the most popular sonnet sequences ever written. She is also known for her verse novel *Aurora Leigh* (1857).

  *The Letters of Robert Browning and Elizabeth Barrett Barrett, 1845–1846* (2 vols. 1899); *The Complete Works of Elizabeth Barrett Browning,* ed. Charlotte Porter and Helen A. Clarke (1900); *Aurora Leigh: Authoritative Text, Backgrounds and Contexts, Criticism,* ed. Margaret Reynolds (1996)

**Robert Browning (1812–1889)** was born in Camberwell, near London, England, and attended London University. In 1846 he eloped with Elizabeth Barrett to Florence, Italy. After her death in 1861, he returned to London. Browning's early work was received poorly, but his fortunes changed with the publication of *Dramatis Personae* (1864), followed by the immensely popular *The Ring and the Book* (1868). He is especially known for his dramatic monologues. His collected poems were published in sixteen volumes between April 1888 and July 1889. He died on the day that his last work, *Asolando,* was published. He is buried in Poets' Corner in Westminster Abbey.

  *Robert Browning's Poetry,* ed. James F. Loucks (1979); *The Essential Browning,* selected Douglas Dunn (1990); *The Major Works,* ed. Adam Roberts (2005)

**Mary Bryan (fl. 1815–1829)** was raised in rural Bristol, England. Bryan was an impoverished widow and the mother of six young children when her *Sonnets and Metrical Tales* was published in 1815. She corresponded for nearly a decade with Sir Walter Scott, who encouraged her to write her novel *Longhollow: A Country Tale* (1829) before she lost her sight to a degenerative eye disease.

  *Sonnets and Metrical Tales* (1815)

**Robert Burns (1759–1796)** was born into a farming family near Alloway in Ayrshire, Scotland. He was one of seven children and largely self-taught. His first book, *Poems, Chiefly in the Scottish Dialect* (1786), was immediately popular. He wrote in both English and Scots, a vernacular form of English spoken by Scottish country people, and his subject matter was often drawn from Scottish folktales and legends. He devoted his last years to collecting Scottish folk songs as part of a project to preserve Scottish culture and national identity. He achieved sufficient fame in his lifetime to be considered the national poet of Scotland.

*The Essential Burns*, ed. Robert Creeley (1989); *Robert Burns: Selected Poems*, ed. Donald A. Low (1996)

**George Gordon, Lord Byron (1788–1824)** was born near Aberdeen, Scotland, and inherited his title when he was ten years old. He was educated at Harrow School and Trinity College, Cambridge. He embarked on a two-year tour of Portugal, Spain, Malta, and Greece and, in 1812, became an overnight celebrity with the publication of the first part of *Childe Harold's Pilgrimage*. After an affair with his half-sister and the collapse of his marriage, he was forced to leave England in 1816. He followed the poet Percy Shelley to Geneva and Italy and then proceeded on to Greece. He died of fever in Missolonghi, Greece, where he had been taking part in the struggle for Greek independence.

*The Essential Byron*, ed. Paul Muldoon (1989); *Byron: A Self-Portrait; Letters and Diaries 1798–1824*, ed. Peter Quennell (1990); *Selected Poems*, ed. Susan J. Wolfson and Peter J. Manning (2006)

**Luís de Camões (1524–1580)** was born in Lisbon or Coimbra, Portugal. Only a few facts concerning his life can be verified. He evidently spent time in Coimbra and, given his erudition, may have attended the University of Coimbra before returning to Lisbon. He was often at court and reputedly fell in love with Caterina de Ataíde, who became the inspiration for much of his love poetry. In 1547 he became a common soldier and lost his left eye fighting against the Moors. In 1556 he was appointed the Trustee for the Dead and Absent in Macao, China, but was dismissed from his post and suffered one misadventure after another. He died in poverty. Regarded as one of the greatest Portuguese writers, he is known for his lyric poetry and for his great epic poem *Os Lusíadas* (1572), which earned him international recognition.

*Luís de Camões, Epic & Lyric*, ed. L. C. Taylor, trans. Keith Bosley (1990); *Selected Sonnets*, ed. and trans. William Baer (2005)

**Thomas Carew (c. 1595–1640)** was born in West Wickham, Kent, England, and educated at Merton College, Oxford, and the law school of the Middle Temple. He belonged to the school of the Cavalier Poets, a group adhering to the Royalist cause of Charles I and basing their poems on classical models. Carew also wrote a noted elegy for John Donne. His collection *Poems* was published in 1640.

*The Poems of Thomas Carew*, ed. Arthur Vincent (1899); *The Cavalier Poets: An Anthology*, ed. Thomas Crofts (1995)

**Hayden Carruth (1921–)** was born in Waterbury, Connecticut, and educated at the University of North Carolina at Chapel Hill and the University of Chicago. Carruth won the National Book Critics Circle Award for *Collected Shorter Poems 1946–1991* (1992) and the National Book Award for *Scrambled Eggs and Whiskey* (1996). He lived for many years in northern Vermont, and now lives in upstate New York.

*Collected Shorter Poems, 1946–1991* (1992); *Collected Longer Poems* (1993); *Selected Essays and Reviews* (1996); *Reluctantly: Autobiographical Essays* (1998)

**Guido Cavalcanti (c. 1255–1300)** was born in Florence, Italy. He was both a mentor and friend to Dante Alighieri and an essential member of the Tuscan poets now known as the *Dolce Stil Novo*. Much of his writing is concerned with the philosophy of love. In 1300 he was sent into exile in Sarzana but soon decided to return to Florence. He died of fever on his journey home. After Dante, he is considered the greatest Italian poet in early Italian literature.

*The Complete Poems*, trans. Marc A. Cirigliano (1992); "Cavalcanti Poems," in *Translations*, Ezra Pound (1963)

**Blaise Cendrars (1887–1961)** was the pseudonym of Fréderic Sauser, who was born in Le Chaux-de-Fonds, Neuchâtel, Switzerland. He ran away from home at the age of fifteen. He traveled widely through China, Russia, and the Middle East before settling in France and adopting French citizenship. He fought with the French Foreign Legion at the Somme and lost his right arm in battle. An important member of the Montparnasse artists' community between the two world wars, Cendrars eventually abandoned poetry for fiction in order to make enough money on which to live.

*Selected Writings of Blaise Cendrars*, ed. Walter Albert (1966); *Complete Poems / Blaise Cendrars*, trans. Ron Padgett (1992)

**George Chapman (1559–1634)** was born in Hitchin, Hertfordshire, England. He may have attended Oxford but took no degree. A successful playwright, he was also a translator from the classical languages, publishing versions of Juvenal, Virgil, and Hesiod. His celebrated translation of Homer prompted Keats's sonnet "On First Looking Into Chapman's Homer."

*Chapman's Homer: The Iliad*, ed. Allardyce Nicoll (1998); *Plays and Poems*, ed. Jonathan Hudston (1998); *Chapman's Homer: The Odyssey*, ed. Allardyce Nicoll (2000)

**Geoffrey Chaucer (c. 1340–1400)** was possibly born in London, England (his birthplace is uncertain) to a middle-class merchant family. He entered military service in 1359, was captured at the siege of Reims, and eventually ransomed. In 1365 he married Philioppa Roet, sister-in-law of John of Gaunt, the uncle and adviser of King Richard II. He was granted an annuity in the royal household and went on to hold various positions at court. He made many diplomatic missions to Europe, where he encountered works by Spanish, French, and Italian authors. He lived through several plagues, and served as a tax controller, a justice of the peace, and a member of Parliament for the county of Kent. His *Canterbury Tales*, an unfinished group of tales by members of a company of pilgrims, helped establish vernacular English as a viable medium for poetry.

*Complete Works*, ed. Walter W. Skeat (1967)


**Eiléan Ní Chuilleanáin (1942–)** was born in Cork, Ireland, and educated at University College Cork and Oxford University. A founding editor of the magazine *Cyphers*, she has published six books of poetry and won the Patrick Kavanagh Prize.

*The Second Voyage: Poems* (1977); *Irish Women: Image and Achievement; Women in Irish Culture from Earliest Times*, ed. Eiléan Ní Chuilleanáin (1985); *The Magdalene Sermon* (1989); *The Brazen Serpent* (1994)


**Amy Clampitt (1920–1994)** was born in New Providence, Iowa, and educated at Grinnell College. She moved to New York City and worked for many years for Oxford University Press as a freelance editor. She published her first poetry collection, *The Kingfisher*, when she was sixty-three years old. Her awards included a Guggenheim Fellowship (1982) and a MacArthur Fellowship (1992). She died at her second home in Lenox, Massachusetts.

*Predecessors, Et Cetera: Essays* (1991); *The Collected Poems of Amy Clampitt* (1997); *Love, Amy: The Selected Letters of Amy Clampitt*, ed. Willard Spiegelman (2005)


**John Clare (1793–1864)** was born in Helpstone, Northamptonshire, England, where he received little formal schooling. He worked on the land as a gardener and field hand, and in 1822 published his immensely successful first book, *Poems Descriptive of Rural Life and Scenery*, which was marketed as the work of a "Northamptonshire Peasant." Clare moved from his birthplace to a cottage provided by a patron four miles away, and he struggled with poverty and mental illness, spending much of his life in asylums. He had a strong sense of place and is best known for his trenchant antipastoral nature poems. There is a memorial to him in the Poets' Corner of Westminster Abbey.

*John Clare By Himself*, ed. Eric Robinson and David Powell (1996); *"I Am": The Selected Poetry of John Clare*, ed. Jonathan Bate (2003); *The Shepherd's Calendar*, ed. Tim Chilcott (2006)


**Tom Clark (1941–)** was born in Chicago, Illinois, and educated at the Universities of Michigan, Cambridge, and Essex. He was poetry editor of *The Paris Review* from 1963 to 1973, and also known as a biographer of twentieth-century writers. He has taught since 1987 at New College of California.

*Light and Shade: New and Selected Poems* (2006)

**Henri Cole** (1956–) was born in Fukoku, Japan, raised in Virginia, and educated at the College of William and Mary, the University of Wisconsin at Milwaukee, and Columbia University. The executive director of the Academy of American Poets from 1982 to 1988, his awards include the Kingsley Tufts Poetry Award for *Middle Earth* (2003), a Guggenheim Fellowship, and the Rome Prize. He has taught at many colleges and universities; he is currently on the faculty of Ohio State University.

*Middle Earth: Poems* (2003); *The Visible Man* (2005); *Blackbird and Wolf* (2007)

**Samuel Taylor Coleridge** (1772–1834) was born in Ottery St. Mary, a rural village in Devon, England. He was educated at Christ's Hospital School, London, and Jesus College, Cambridge. At Cambridge he met Robert Southey, with whom he planned to start a utopian community. In 1794 he married Sara Fricker, Southey's sister. The next year he met William and Dorothy Wordsworth in Somerset. In 1798 he and Wordsworth published *Lyrical Ballads*, a work that marks a revolutionary turning point in English literature. Coleridge was an enormously influential critic and philosopher —the younger Romantics held him in the greatest esteem—but his later life was marred by opium addiction. He spent his last years in the care of a London clergyman.

*Biographia Literarari, Or, My Literary Life and Opinions*, ed. James Engell and W. Jackson Bate (1993); *The Complete Poems*, ed. William Keach (1997)

**Billy Collins** (1941–) was born in New York City and educated at Holy Cross College and the University of California at Riverside, where he earned his PhD in Romantic poetry. His books include *Questions About Angels* (1991), *The Art of Drowning* (1995), and *Picnic, Lightning* (1998). He has received grants from the Guggenheim Foundation and the National Endowment for the Arts. He served two terms as Poet Laureate Consultant in Poetry to the Library of Congress. His volumes of poetry have been bestsellers.

*Sailing Alone Around the Room: New and Selected Poems* (2001); *Nine Horses: Poems* (2002); *The Trouble with Poetry and Other Poems* (2005)

**Vittoria Colonna** (1492–1547) was born in Marino, near Rome, into an aristocratic family. Colonna is remembered for passionate correspondences in letters and verse with her imprisoned husband, nobleman Francesco Ferrante d'Avalos. She lived in convents after his death and had a deep friendship with Michelangelo. Her literary output consisted mainly of sonnets in the Petrarchan vein. She is the most published and lauded woman writer of early sixteenth-century Italy.

*Sonnets for Michelangelo: A Bilingual Edition*, ed. and trans. Abigail Brundin (2005)

Jane Cooper (1924–2007) was born in Atlantic City, New Jersey, raised in Jacksonville, Florida, and educated at Vassar College, the University of Wisconsin, and the University of Iowa. She has spent most of her adult life in New York City and taught for many years at Sarah Lawrence College. She has received fellowships from the Guggenheim Foundation, the Ingram Merrill Foundation, and the National Endowment for the Arts. From 1995 to 1997 she was State Poet of New York. She died from complications due to Parkinson's disease.

*The Flashboat: Poems Collected and Reclaimed* (2000)

William Cowper (1731–1800) (pronounced "Cooper") was born in Great Berkhamsted, Hertfordshire, England, and was trained to be a lawyer. Severe depression intervened, and he found consolation in evangelical Christianity. An extremely popular poet in his lifetime, he wrote a series of moral satires and translated Homer's and Milton's Greek and Latin poems in later years.

*Selected Poems*, ed. Nick Rhodes (1984); *The Centenary Letters*, ed. Simon Malpas (2000)

Hart Crane (1899–1933) was born in Garretsville, Ohio, and raised in Cleveland. When his parents divorced, Crane went to New York City without finishing high school. Between 1918 and 1923, he moved back and forth between New York and Cleveland, working for his father's candy company and various advertising agencies. His first collection of poems, *White Buildings*, appeared in 1926. His modern epic poem *The Bridge* was published in 1930. He went to Mexico on a Guggenheim Fellowship, and on the return voyage to the United States he committed suicide by jumping into the sea.

*Complete Poems and Selected Letters*, ed. Langdon Hammer (2006)

Sor Juana Inés de la Cruz (1648–1695) was born Juana de Asbaje y Ramirez in San Miguel Nepantla, near Mexico City. She was intellectually precocious and taken to the vice-regal court in the capital while still very young. She entered the Convent of San Jeronimo (*Sor* is her religious title) as a teenager, apparently to avoid marrying and continue her studies. Her celebrated poem "Reply to Sister Filotea of the Cross" (1691) defends a woman's right to knowledge. She died while caring for other nuns during an epidemic. She is often regarded as the greatest lyric poet of the colonial period.

*The Sonnets of Sor Juana Inés de la Cruz in English Verse*, trans. Carl W. Cobb (2001); *Sor Juana Inés de la Cruz: Selected Writings*, trans. Pamela Kirk Rappaport (2005)

Countee Cullen (1903–1946) was born Countee LeRoy Porter in Louisville, Kentucky. He was abandoned at birth and raised in a Methodist parsonage. Educated at New York University and Harvard University, he began publishing at a very early age. A leading figure of the Harlem Renaissance, Cullen spent much of his life teaching in New York City schools, at which time he was recognized as the greatest African American writer. In addition to his five collections of poems, he also published a novel about life in Harlem, edited an anthology of African American poetry, translated Euripides, and wrote two children's books.

*Color* (1925); *The Black Christ & Other Poems* (1929); *My Soul's High Song: The Collected Writings of Countee Cullen, Voice of the Harlem Renaissance*, ed. Gerald Early (1991)

**E. E. Cummings (1894–1962)** was born in Cambridge, Massachusetts, and educated at Harvard University. In the early 1920s he lived in New York City and Paris. His imprisonment in a French detention center during World War I inspired his novel *The Enormous Room* (1922). After the war he divided his time between Greenwich Village and rural Connecticut. He is known for his paintings as well as his experiments in poetry. He remains enduringly popular among young readers, and his awards and honors include two Guggenheim Fellowships, a Ford Foundation grant, and the Bollingen Prize.

*Complete Poems, 1904–1962*, ed. George J. Firmage (rev. ed. 1994)

**J. V. Cunningham (1911–1985)** was born in Cumberland, Maryland. He faced severe financial hardship in his youth, until Yvor Winters invited him to attend Stanford University. He went on to hold teaching appointments at the University of Chicago, the University of Virginia, Harvard University, and Brandeis University. He was a Renaissance scholar as well as a master of the plain style in poetry. He received fellowships from the Academy of American Poets, the Guggenheim Foundation, and the National Endowment for the Arts.

*The Collected Essays of J. V. Cunningham* (1976); *The Poems of J. V. Cunningham*, ed. Timothy Steele (1997)

**Samuel Daniel (1562–1619)** was born in Taunton, Somerset, England, and educated at Magdalen Hill, Oxford. He wrote in a variety of genres, from the sonnet sequence to the neoclassical tragedy. In 1592 he published his own edition of "Delia," a key sequence of sonnets, which was reprinted many times. His *Defense of Rhyme* (1602?) is a crucial treatise of the Elizabethan era. He spent the last part of his life working on a prose history, *The Collection of the Historie of England* (1612–1618).

*Samuel Daniel: Selected Poetry and A Defense of Rhyme*, ed. Geoffrey G. Hiller and Peter L. Groves (1998)

**Dante Alighieri (1265–1321)** was born into a noble family in Florence, Italy, and received a thorough education in classical and Christian literature. In his youth he fought for his city as a cavalryman and pursued a political career but was later banished by his enemies. After wandering for many years, he settled in Ravenna. The masterpiece of Dante's youth, *La Vita Nuova* (*The New Life*; c. 1293), celebrated his love for Beatrice, the girl who was to become his lifelong muse, and mourned her tragic early death. He is everywhere known for the *Commedia*, his three-part epic vision of the afterlife (*Inferno, Purgatorio, Paradisio*), which is known today as the *La Divina Commedia* (*The Divine Comedy*). He began it in 1307 and finished it just before his death.

> *The Divine Comedy*, trans. John Ciardi (1977); *Dante's Lyric Poems*, trans. Joseph Tusiani (1992); *The Inferno of Dante: A New Verse Translation*, trans. Robert Pinsky (1994); *Purgatorio: A New Verse Translation*, trans. W. S. Merwin (2000); *The New Life*, trans. Dante Gabriel Rossetti (2002)

**Rubén Darío (1867–1916)** was born in Metapa, Nicaragua, now renamed Ciudad Darío in his honor. He began writing poems by the age of twelve and was known as "El Niño Poeta" ("the poet child"). His first mature work, *Azul . . .* (1888), brought him transatlantic recognition. He traveled widely throughout South America and Europe. He was happily married to Rafaela Contreras, who died tragically in 1892, and unhappily married to Rosario Murillo, who pursued him across two decades and two continents. His strong advocacy of the Spanish language created a new flowering of literary activity for which he was called "the father of modernism."

> *Selected Poems of Rubén Darío*, ed. and trans. Alberto Acerada and Will Derusha (2001); *Selected Writings / Rubén Darío*, ed. Ilan Stavans, trans. Andrew Hurley, Greg Simon, and Steven F. White (2005)

**Donald Davie (1922–1995)** was born in Barnsley, Yorkshire, England, and brought up in "the industrially ravaged landscape" of the West Riding. He was educated at St. Catherine's College, Cambridge. He taught at many universities in England, Ireland, and the United States. Davie was an influential critic and commentator committed to the ethics of plain writing, often associating himself with the moral perspective of F. R. Leavis. His critical books include *Purity of Diction in English Verse* (1952) and *Articulate Energy: An Inquiry Into the Syntax of English Poetry* (1995). He also edited *The New Oxford Book of Christian Verse* (1981).

> *Collected Poems* (1990)

**Sir John Davies (1569–1626)** was born in Wiltshire, England. He attended The Queen's College, Oxford, studied law, and, serving the government of Queen Elizabeth I, became the attorney general in Ireland at a time of unrest. His best-known work appears in his "epigrammes" and sonnets, and he published a collection, *Nosce Teipsum*, in 1599.

> *The Poems of Sir John Davies*, ed. Robert Krueger (1975)

**Cecil Day-Lewis (1904–1972)** was born in Ballintubbert, Ireland, and educated at Wadham College, Oxford. He was Professor of Poetry at Oxford (1951–1956), and he supplemented his income by writing numerous detective novels under a pseudonym. He later worked as a publishing executive in London and was named Poet Laureate in 1968. Day-Lewis is noted for his lyric and political poetry, which became edged in the pessimism and protest of the 1930s. His critical book *The Poetic Image* (1947) gathered together his Clark Lectures at Cambridge University and influenced the climate of postwar British poetry.

*The Chatto Book of Modern Poetry, 1915–1955*, coed. John Lehmann (1956); *The Complete Poems of C. Day-Lewis* (1992)

**Edwin Denby (1903–1983)** was born in Tientsin, China. He dropped out of Harvard College and spent the 1920s and '30s traveling as a choreographer and dancer in Europe. An influential dance critic, he had a small output as a poet, and his book of poems *In Public, In Private* was not published until 1948. He composed a number of sonnet sequences.

*The Complete Poems*, ed. Ron Padgett (1986); *Dance Writings & Poetry*, ed. Robert Cornfield (1998)

**Peter Dickinson (1927– )** was born in Livingstone, Northern Rhodesia (now Zambia). His family moved back to England and he was educated at Eton College and King's College, Cambridge. He is chiefly known as a prolific writer of detective novels and children's stories, winning the Whitbread Book Award for his children's book *Tulku* (1979) and the Crime Writers Association Gold Dagger Award for *Skin Deep* (1968).

*Water: Tales of the Elemental Spirits*, with Robin McKinley (2002)

**W. S. Di Piero (1945– )** was born in Philadelphia, Pennsylvania, and educated at St. Joseph's College and San Francisco State University. He is a translator and essayist on visual art and film and their relation to poetry, and his writings on both media have been collected in *Shooting the Works: On Poetry and Pictures* (1996). He has received a Guggenheim Fellowship and a Lila Wallace–Reader's Digest Writer's Award. He teaches at Stanford University.

*Out of Eden: Essays on Modern Art* (1991); *Chinese Apples: New and Selected Poems* (2007)

**John Donne (1572–1631)** was born in London, England. His father was an ironmonger and his mother a devout Catholic. He studied at Oxford without taking a degree. He worked as a political secretary to Sir Thomas Egerton, the Lord Keeper, but was dismissed when his secret marriage to Anne More, Lady Egerton's niece, was revealed. The marriage blocked his career as a courtier. After many years of seeking patrons and positions, he took orders in the Church of England. Two years later his wife died. He became dean of St. Paul's Cathedral in 1621. He was celebrated as the foremost preacher of his time in England. His poems circulated in manuscript and very few of them were published in his lifetime.

*The Complete Poetry of John Donne*, intro., notes, and variants John T. Shawcross (1967); *The Essential Donne*, ed. Amy Clampitt (1969)

**Lord Alfred Douglas (1870–1945)** was born in Lancing, Sussex, England, and educated at Magdalen College, Oxford. The son of the Marquess of Queensberry—or "Bosie," as he was known—he is remembered chiefly for his relationship with Oscar Wilde, which caused an enormous scandal. Later in life, he married a woman, claimed he was never a homosexual, reverted to Catholicism, and ran through much of his inheritance. A collected volume of his sonnets was published in 1935.

*The Complete Poems of Lord Alfred Douglas, Including the Light Verse* (1928); *The Autobiography of Lord Alfred Douglas* (1929)

**John Dovaston (1782–1854)** was born in Shropshire, England, and educated at Christ Church, Oxford. After working briefly as a newspaper theater critic, he inherited his father's estate and thereafter pursued his life as a writer and naturalist. An ornithologist and amateur scientist, Dovaston wrote sonnets based on the fables and folklore of rural Shropshire and the Welsh Borders.

*Bewick to Dovaston: Letters 1824–1828*, ed. Gordon Williams (1968); *Letters from Lambeth: The Correspondence of the Reynolds Family with John Freeman Milward Dovaston, 1808–1815*, ed. Joanna Richardson (1981)

**Rita Dove (1952–)** was born in Akron, Ohio, and educated at Miami University, the University of Iowa, and the Universität Tübingen in Germany. Dove won the Pulitzer Prize for *Thomas and Beulah* (1986) and served as Poet Laureate Consultant in Poetry from 1993 to 1995. Her verse play *The Darker Face of the Earth* has been staged in many major theaters. She is Commonwealth Professor of English at the University of Virginia at Charlottesville.

*Selected Poems* (1993); *American Smooth: Poems* (2004)

**Michael Drayton (1563–1631)** was born in Hartsill, Warwickshire, England. As a youth he became page to Sir Henry Goodeere of Polesworth, who oversaw Drayton's education. Drayton's religious verse, odes, sonnets, and satires were extremely influential. Among his books was a vast but incomplete topographical poem on England, *Poly-Olbion*. He lived most of his adult life in London and is buried in Westminster Abbey.

*The Complete Works of Michael Drayton, Now First Collected*, Vol. 1, *Polyolbion* (2001); *The Complete Works of Michael Drayton, Now First Collected*, Vol. 2, *Polyolbion* (2001); *The Complete Works of Michael Drayton, Now First Collected*, Vol. 3, *Polyolbion, and The Harmony of the Church* (2001)

**William Drummond of Hawthornden (1585–1649)** was born in Hawthornden, Midlothian, Scotland, and educated at Edinburgh University. He studied law in France and became laird of Hawthornden at the age of twenty-four. He was a keen correspondent and exchanged letters with his friends Ben Jonson and Michael Drayton. His book *Flowers of Sion* (1623) is often considered the finest collection of seventeenth-century Scottish religious poetry. His poems were collected, edited, and published by John Milton's nephew in 1656.

*The Poems of William Drummond of Hawthornden: With Life*, ed. Peter Cunningham (1833)

**Carol Ann Duffy (1955–)** was born in Glasgow, Scotland, and educated at Liverpool University, where she read philosophy. An acclaimed poet and playwright, she has received the Whitbread Award for *Mean Time* (1993), a Lannan Literary Award, the Forward Poetry Prize, and the T. S. Eliot Prize for *Rapture* (2005). She lives in Manchester and serves as creative director of the Writing School at Manchester Metropolitan University.

*Selling Manhattan* (1987); *Meeting Midnight* (1999); *New Selected Poems* (2004)

**Paul Laurence Dunbar (1872–1906)** was born in Dayton, Ohio, to parents who were escaped slaves. Without studying at college, he published his first book, *Oak and Ivy* (1893), which brought him into literary circles. Dunbar gained international literary fame for his 1896 volume of poems, *Lyrics of a Lowly Life* (1896). In 1898 he married the poet Alice Ruth Moore (later Dunbar-Nelson) and lived with her in Washington, D.C. By the turn of the century he was the most celebrated black writer in the United States. He died of tuberculosis.

*The Collected Poetry of Paul Laurence Dunbar*, ed. Joanne M. Braxton (1993); *The Complete Stories of Paul Laurence Dunbar*, ed. Gene Andrew Jarrett and Thomas Lewis Morgan (2005)

**Robert Duncan (1919–1988)** was born Edward Howard Duncan Jr. in Oakland, California. His biological mother died giving birth to him, and he was adopted by a couple who practiced theosophy. He spent two years at the University of California, Berkeley, and taught at Black Mountain College. A lifelong occultist who spent most of his life in San Francisco and lived with the artist Jess Collins, he is identified with Beat culture, the San Francisco Renaissance, and the Black Mountain poets.

*Selected Poems: Revised and Enlarged*, ed. Robert J. Betholf (1997); *The Letters of Robert Duncan and Denise Levertov*, ed. Robert J. Bertholf and Albert Gelpi (2003); *Ground Work*, ed. Robert J. Berthoff and James Maynard (2006)

**Douglas Dunn** (1942–) was born in Inchinnan, Renfrewshire, Scotland. He was educated at the Scottish School of Librarianship and the University of Hull, where he worked as a librarian under Philip Larkin. Dunn is a professor of English at the University of St. Andrews.

*Elegies* (1985); *New Selected Poems 1964–1999* (2003)

**Thomas Edwards** (1699–1757), a barrister who studied at Lincoln's Inn, retired from practicing law to write poetry. One of his sonnets tells us that all four of his brothers and sisters died before him. He is best known for his controversial attack on William Warburton's 1747 edition of Shakespeare's plays. In 1739 he bought an estate in Buckhinghamshire, where he resided until his death.

*The Sonnets of Thomas Edwards (1765, 1780)*, intro. Dennis G. Donovan (repr. 1974)

**T. S. Eliot** (1888–1965) was born in St. Louis, Missouri, and educated at Harvard University, the Sorbonne, and Oxford University. He moved permanently to England in his late twenties and worked in the international department at Lloyd's Bank before joining the publishing firm Faber and Faber, where he remained for the rest of his life. *The Waste Land*, which he mostly wrote while hospitalized for a nervous breakdown, was published in 1922. In the same year he founded the review *The Criterion*. In 1927 Eliot took British citizenship and joined the Church of England. One of the most influential literary critics of the twentieth century, he considered *Four Quartets* (1935–1943) his greatest work. In 1948 he was awarded the Nobel Prize in Literature.

*The Complete Poems and Plays* (1969); *Selected Prose of T. S. Eliot*, ed. Frank Kermode (1975); *Inventions of the March Hare: Poems 1909–1917*, ed. Christopher Ricks (1996)

**Ebenezer Elliott** (1781–1849) was born to a radical family in Masborough, Yorkshire, England. His childhood was plagued by ill health and difficulties at school, but he found solace in the natural world. In 1831 he published "Corn Law Rhymes," protesting the injustice of the Corn Laws, and he was internationally known thereafter for his strong political opinions.

*The Splendid Village: Corn Law Rhymes; and Other Poems* (1834)

**Ralph Waldo Emerson** (1803–1886) was born in Boston, Massachusetts, and educated at Harvard College and Harvard Divinity School. He was ordained as a junior pastor at Boston's Second Church, but soon left the church because of profound doubts about organized religion. From 1835 on, he earned his living as a secular lecturer, his true profession until old age, and his essays are foundational in American philosophy. He married

Liddian Jackson. He helped found the literary magazine *The Dial*. The Transcendentalist circle that formed around him included the writers Henry David Thoreau and Margaret Fuller. He is buried in Sleepy Hollow Cemetery, Concord, Massachusetts.

*Essays: First and Second Series*, ed. Joel Porte (1990); *Collected Poems and Translations*, ed. Harold Bloom and Paul Kane (1994)

**William Empson (1906–1984)** was born in Yorkshire, England, and educated at Magdalene College, Cambridge. During the 1930s he held lectureships at national universities in Tokyo and Peking. Returning to England in 1939, he worked for the BBC as its Chinese editor from 1942 to 1946. In 1947 he returned to his post in Peking and stayed until 1952. In 1953 he was appointed to the Chair of English Literature at Sheffield University, which he held until his retirement in 1971. He is known for deeply engaging the multiple layers of language in his highly influential prose works, such as *Seven Types of Ambiguity* (1930), which he published when he was only twenty-four, *Some Versions of Pastoral* (1935), and *The Structure of Complex Words* (1951). He was knighted in 1979 and died in London in 1984.

*The Complete Poems of William Empson*, ed. John Haffenden (2001)

**Gavin Ewart (1916–1995)** was born in London, England and educated at Christ's College, Cambridge. Ewart contributed to Geoffrey Grigson's *New Verse* at the age of seventeen and later served in World War II. The editor of *The Penguin Book of Light Verse* (1980), he received the Michael Braude Award for Light Verse in 1991.

*Selected Poems 1933–1993* (1996)

**Frederick William Faber (1814–1863)** was born in Calverley, Yorkshire, England, into a family of Anglican divines. He was educated at Balliol College, Oxford. A follower of John Henry Newman, Faber founded a religious community known as Wilfridians. He converted to Catholicism in 1845 and wrote extensively on the spiritual life. He wrote many hymns that are still sung today.

*Faber, Poet and Priest: Selected Letters by Frederick William Faber, 1833–1863*, ed. Raleigh Addington (1974)

**Ruth Fainlight (1931–)** was born in New York City but has lived in England since the age of fifteen. She studied for two years at the Birmingham and Brighton Colleges of Arts and Crafts. Her work includes fiction, translations, and libretti as well as poetry. She is married to the writer Alan Sillitoe.

*Selected Poems* (1987); *This Time of Year* (1993)

**Ilyas Farhat (1893–1980)** was born in Kafr Shima, Lebanon, and immigrated to Brazil in 1910, at the age of seventeen. A formal poet, he is well known among Arab readers for the intense nationalism of his poetry. His first volume of poems, *Quatrains* (1925), originally called *Ruba'iyyat Farhat*, was followed by *Diwan Farhat* (1932), which appeared in four volumes: *Spring, Summer, Autumn,* and *Winter.*

*Modern Arabic Poetry: An Anthology,* ed. Salma Khadra Jayyusi (1987)

**Kenneth Fields** (1939–) was born in Texas and grew up in San Luis Obispo, California. He was educated at Stanford University. He was a student of Yvor Winters, with whom he edited *Quest for Reality: An Anthology of Short Poems in English* (1969). He is now a professor of English and creative writing at Stanford.

*Sunbelly* (1973); *Classic Rough News* (2005)

**Giles Fletcher, the Elder** (c. 1546–1611) was born in Cranbrook, Kent, England, and educated at King's College, Cambridge. He was a Member of Parliament and ambassador to Russia (1588). Fletcher was known in his time for his sonnet sequence *Licia* (1593). He was the father of the poets Phineas Fletcher and Giles Fletcher the Younger.

*The English Spenserians: The Poetry of Giles Fletcher, George Wither, Michael Drayton, Phineas Fletcher, and Henry More,* ed. William B. Hunter Jr. (1977)

**Robert Francis** (1901–1987) was born in Upland, Pennsylvania, and educated at Harvard College. He lived much of his life in a small house in Amherst, Massachusetts, that he named "Fort Juniper." He won the Shelley Memorial Award in 1939. Winner of the Rome Prize, Francis wrote poems that were often quiet, edged pastorals of New England and rural life.

*Collected Poems, 1936–1976* (1976)

**Robert Frost** (1874–1963) was born in San Francisco, where he lived for eleven years. He attended Dartmouth and Harvard Colleges but never graduated. In 1912 he moved with his wife and four children to England, where he published his first two books, *A Boy's Will* (1913) and *North of Boston* (1914). He returned to the United States in 1915 and, over the years, held a variety of teaching appointments. His poems are rooted in New England, where he lived on a number of different farms. He won the Pulitzer Prize four times. He read his poem "The Gift Outright" at John F. Kennedy's presidential inauguration, an honor indicating his status as one of America's most celebrated and popular poets.

*Collected Poems, Prose, and Plays,* ed. Richard Poirier and Mark Richardson (1995)

**Margaret Fuller** (1810–1850) was born in Cambridge, Massachusetts, and received a rigorous classical education from her father. Along with her friend Ralph Waldo Emerson, with whom she coedited *The Dial*, Fuller became a leader of the Transcendentalist movement. She was an early feminist activist; her tract *Woman in the Nineteenth Century* (1845) remains a classic feminist text. She was also one of the first female journalists and was the first to work at a major newspaper. She had a son with the Italian revolutionary Giovanni Ossoli. All three died on a boat taking them back from Italy to America.

*The Portable Margaret Fuller*, ed. Mary Kelley (1994)

**George Gascoigne (c. 1539–1577)** was born in Cardington, Bedfordshire, England, and educated at Trinity College, Cambridge. A lawyer and Member of Parliament, he also served as a soldier of fortune. Gascoigne wrote a short but noted critical thesis defining the length of the sonnet.

*A Hundreth Sundrie Flowres, from the Original Edition of 1573*, ed. Bernard M. Ward and Ruth Lloyd Miller (2nd ed. 1975)

**Sandra Gilbert (1936–)** was born in New York City and educated at Cornell University, New York University, and Columbia University. Acclaimed as both a poet and influential feminist critic, she wrote, with longtime collaborator Susan Gubar, *The Madwoman in the Attic: The Woman Writer and the Nineteenth-Century Literary Imagination* (1979), which was a finalist for the Pulitzer Prize and the National Book Critics Circle Award. Winner of the American Book Award for *Kissing the Bread: New and Selected Poems 1969–1999* (2000), she is a professor emerita of English at the University of California, Davis.

*Belongings* (2005); *Death's Door: Modern Dying and the Ways We Grieve* (2006)

**Allen Ginsberg (1926–1997)** was born in Newark, New Jersey, and educated at Columbia University, where he began the friendships and associations that resulted in the grouping known as the Beat Generation. In 1954 he moved to San Francisco. His first book of poetry, *Howl and Other Poems* (1956), which was banned for obscenity, was a radical focus of new energies in American poetry. It made him world-famous. Thereafter he was active in radical politics, traveled widely, and studied Tibetan Buddhism and western mystics. He cofounded and directed the Jack Kerouac School of Disembodied Poetics at the Naropa Institute in Colorado. In later years he became a Distinguished Professor at Brooklyn College.

*Collected Poems, 1947–1980* (1984)

**Dana Gioia (1950–)** was born in Hawthorne, California, and educated at Stanford and Harvard Universities. Gioia retired from a corporate career to pursue writing full-time. He has served as the chairman of the National Endowment for the Arts since 2003. Gioia has published several prose books and three volumes of poetry, one of which, *Interrogations at Noon: Poems* (2001), won the American Book Award.

*Daily Horoscope* (1986); *The Gods of Winter* (1991); *Can Poetry Matter?: Essays on Poetry and American Culture* (1992)

**Louise Glück** (1943– ) was born in New York City and educated at Sarah Lawrence College and Columbia University. Glück's first collection, *Firstborn*, was published in 1968. She has won the Pulitzer Prize, the National Book Critics Circle Award, and the Bollingen Prize. A former Poet Laureate Consultant in Poetry to the Library of Congress, she teaches at Yale University and lives in Cambridge, Massachusetts.

*Proofs & Theories: Essays on Poetry* (1994); *The First Four Books of Poems* (1995); *Vita Nova* (1999); *Averno* (2006)

**Johann Wolfgang von Goethe** (1749–1832) was born in Frankfurt am Main, Germany. At sixteen he studied law at Leipzig University (1765–1768). He practiced law in Frankfurt and Wetzlar and published his first novel, *The Sorrows of Young Werther*, in 1824. He was the leading figure in the Sturm und Drang movement. In 1775 he was welcomed by Duke Karl August into the court at Weimar, where he worked in several governmental offices. Released from day-to-day activities, he remained general supervisor of the arts and director of the court theaters. His scientific research was wide-ranging. He spent more than fifty years composing the two-part dramatic poem and masterpiece *Faust*, which was finished when he was eighty-one. Goethe is said to have been the last true Renaissance man and the most prolific and esteemed writer in German history.

*Selected Poems*, ed. Christopher Middleton (1983); *Selected Poetry*, trans. David Luke (1999)

**Luis de Góngora** (1561–1627) was born in Córdoba, Spain, and educated at the University of Salamanca. He was ordained a priest in 1617 but was also known for his devotion to cards, clothes, and carriages. He spent the last years of his life in Madrid, where he sometimes engaged in bitter literary feuds with his contemporaries. Góngora's folk ballads, lyrics, and sonnets achieved popular success, but he is remembered primarily as the creator of Gongorismo, a style characterized by its use of Latinized vocabulary, complex metaphor, and classical and mythological allusion.

*Selected Poems of Luis De Góngora*, trans. John Dent-Young (2007)

**Paul Goodman** (1911–1972) was born in New York City and educated at the City College of New York and the University of Chicago, where he was trained in philosophy. A social critic and activist, he was a cofounder of the New York Institute for Gestalt Therapy. He published novels, essays, books on urban design and politics, and more than one hundred short stories, and is best remembered for *Growing up Absurd: Problems of Youth in the Organized System* (1960).

*Collected Poems*, ed. Taylor Stoehr (1973); *Crazy Hope and Finite Experience: Final Essays of Paul Goodman*, ed. Taylor Stoehr (1994)

**Alan Gould** (1949–) was born in London, of a British father and Icelandic mother. He has lived in Australia since 1966. Gould received degrees from the Australian National University and the Canberra College of Advanced Education. He is a former member of the Literature Board of the Australia Council. He has published essays, fiction, and poetry.

*The Past Completes Me: Selected Poems, 1973–2003* (2005)

**Robert Graves** (1895–1985) was born in Wimbledon, England, and educated at St. John's College, Oxford. During his service with the Royal Welsh Fusiliers in World War I, Graves was injured at the Battle of the Somme. He later penned *Goodbye to All That* (1929), his classic account of his wartime experiences. With his second wife, poet Laura Riding, he lived in Egypt, London, Majorca, and Pennsylvania. He returned to Majorca with his third wife, Beryl Hodge, and lived there for the remainder of his life. Graves served as a Professor of Poetry at Oxford University from 1961 to 1966. In addition to his poetry, Graves is widely known for his critical works, such as *The White Goddess: A Historical Grammar of Poetic Myth* (1948, 1966), and his fiction, which includes *I, Claudius* and *Claudius, the God* (both 1934).

*Complete Poems*, ed. Beryl Graves and Dunstan Ward (3 vols. 1995–1999)

**Thomas Gray** (1716–1771) was born in London, England. He studied at Peterhouse College, Cambridge, but left before taking a degree when an inheritance made him financially independent. Gray refused the Poet Laureateship in 1757. He was appointed Regius Professor of Modern History at Cambridge in 1768. His "Elegy Written in a Country Churchyard" (1750) remains a touchstone of English poetry.

*The Poems of Thomas Gray, William Collins, Oliver Goldsmith*, ed. Roger H. Lonsdale (1969)

**Fulke Greville, Lord Brooke** (1554–1628) was born at Beauchamp Court, Warwickshire, England, and educated at Jesus College, Cambridge. A contemporary of Sir Philip Sidney, Greville held several important governmental positions, including Treasurer of the Navy and Chancellor of the Exchequer. He wrote an autobiographical sonnet sequence, *Cælica*, that was published posthumously in 1633.

*The Prose Works of Fulke Greville, Lord Brooke*, ed. John Gouws (1986); *Selected Poems*, ed. Neil Powell (1990)

**Jorge Guillén** (1893–1984) was born in Valladolid, Spain, and educated at the University of Madrid and the University of Granada. He was awarded the Premio Miguel de Cervantes (Cervantes Prize) in 1976, the highest literary honor of the Spanish-speaking world. He was exiled in 1939 after the Spanish Civil War and taught Spanish at Wellesley College in Massachusetts. After the death of Franco, Guillén returned to his native country. He died in Málaga.

*Cantico: A Selection,* ed. Norman Thomas di Giovanni (1965); *Guillén on Guillén: The Poetry and the Poet,* trans. Reginald Gibbons (1979); *Our Air / Nuestro Aire,* trans. Carl W. Cobb (1997)

**Louise Imogen Guiney (1861–1920)** was born in Roxbury, Massachusetts (now part of Boston), and educated at the Convent of the Sacred Heart in Elmhurst, Rhode Island. To help support her family, she began contributing to various newspapers and magazines. Guiney edited editions of work by Matthew Arnold, Henry Vaughn, and James Clarence Mangan. She moved in England in 1901 and lived there the rest of her life.

*A Roadside Harp: A Book of Verses* (1893); *Happy Ending* (rev. ed. 1927)

**Thom Gunn (1929–2004)** was born in Gravesend, Kent, England, and educated at Trinity College, Cambridge, and Stanford University. He lived in San Francisco from 1954 until the end of his life. His books include *Fighting Terms* (1954), *The Sense of Movement* (1957), and *The Man with the Night Sweats* (1992), a collection memorializing friends and loved ones who had died of the AIDS pandemic. He received fellowships from the Guggenheim and MacArthur foundations. Gunn's work achieved a highly original compact between formal and conversational poems, mirrored by his dual identities as both a British and American poet.

*Collected Poems* (1994); *Shelf Life: Essays, Memoirs, and an Interview* (1994); *Boss Cupid* (2000)

**Ivor Gurney (1890–1937)** was born in Gloucester, England, and studied music at the Royal College of Music. He was posted to the front during World War I, when he was gassed at Ypres and sent home. He suffered a nervous breakdown the following year. He suffered from schizophrenia and spent the last fifteen years of his life in the City of London Mental Hospital. He wrote hundreds of songs as well as instrumental music. Two books of poems were published in his lifetime, *Severn and Somme* (1917) and *War's Embers* (1919).

*Poems of Ivor Gurney, 1890–1937,* intro. Edmund Blunden (1973)

**Marilyn Hacker (1942–)** was born in New York City and educated at New York University and the Art Students League of New York. She has won many awards for her poetry including the Lamont Poetry Selection of the Academy of American Poets and the National Book Award, both for *Presentation Piece* (1975). She was the editor of the *Kenyon Review* from 1990 to 1994. She teaches in New York and lives part of each year in Paris.

*Selected Poems, 1965–1990* (1994); *Winter Numbers: Poems* (1994); *Squares and Courtyards* (2000)

**Kimiko Hahn** (1955–) was born in Mount Kisco, New York, and educated at the University of Iowa and Columbia University. In her poems, Hahn draws on the energies and abrasions in her own past and heritage. Winner of an American Book Award, she teaches at Queens College, City University of New York.

*Mosquito & Ant: Poems* (1999); *The Narrow Road to the Interior* (2006)

**Thomas Hardy** (1840–1928) was born in Higher Bockhampton, Dorset, England, the area he made famous as "Wessex" in his work. He was educated at King's College, Oxford. Early in his life, Hardy practiced as an architect before turning to writing. He did a short stint in London but returned to Dorset, where he lived for the rest of his life. Better known as a novelist in his lifetime, he has become increasingly influential as a poet since his death. Hardy wrote some of the most celebrated novels in the English language including *Tess of the d'Urbervilles* (1891) and *Jude the Obscure* (1895). He published no verse until the publication of his final novel, *The Well-Beloved* (1897), but then devoted the last thirty years of his life to poetry.

*Poems of Thomas Hardy*, ed. Claire Tomalin (2006)

**Tony Harrison** (1931–) was born in Leeds, England, and read classics at the University of Leeds. He spent four years in northern Nigeria and a year teaching in Prague before turning to England to become the first Northern Arts Fellow at the Universities of Newcastle-upon-Tyne and Durham. He received the Whitbread Poetry Award for *The Graze of the Gorgons* (1992). He is well known for his verse plays, many of which he also directed, as well as for his adaptations of works by Molière, Racine, and others.

*Selected Poems* (2nd ed. 1987); *V. and Other Poems* (1990)

**Gwen Harwood** (1920–1995), née Gwendoline Nessie Foster, was born in Taringa, Queensland, and educated in Brisbane, Australia. She moved to Tasmania after her marriage to the linguist William Harwood in 1945, where she developed her lifelong interest in the works of the philosopher Ludwig Wittgenstein. Her first volume of poems, *Poems*, was published in 1963, followed by a second installment in 1968. As well as a poet, Harwood was a musician and librettist.

*A Steady Storm of Correspondence: Selected Letters of Gwen Harwood 1943–1995*, ed. Gregory Kratzmann (2001); *Collected Poems, 1943–1995*, ed. Gregory Kratzmann and Alison Hoddinott (2003)

**Robert Hayden** (1913–1980) was born in Detroit, Michigan, attended Detroit State College (renamed Wayne State University), and continued his education at the University of Michigan. He was a fellow of the American Academy of Poets, Consultant in Poetry to the Library of Congress, and a professor of English at the University of Michigan. He received two Hopwood Awards, the Grand Prize for Poetry at the First World Festival of Negro Arts, and the Russell Loines Award from the National Institute of Arts and Letters.

*Collected Prose*, ed. Frederick Glaysher (1984); *Collected Poems*, ed. Frederick Glaysher (1985)

**Seamus Heaney (1939–)** was born in Mossbawn, County Derry, Northern Ireland, and educated at Queen's University, Belfast. He later moved to the Irish Republic. He has taught at the University of California, Berkeley, and Harvard University. In 1989 he was elected Professor of Poetry at Oxford University. A distinguished critic and translator, he received Whitbread Book of the Year Award for his version of *Beowulf*. In 1995 he received the Nobel Prize in Literature. He lives in Dublin.

*The Government of the Tongue* (1988); *The Redress of Poetry* (1995); *Open Ground: Poems 1966–1996* (1998); *District and Circle* (2006)

**Anthony Hecht (1923–2004)** was born in New York City. After graduating from Bard College in 1944, Hecht joined the U.S. Army and served in both Europe and Japan. He wrote seven books of poems, including *The Hard Hours* (1967), which received the Pulitzer Prize in 1968. He also wrote several volumes of essays and criticism, among them a book-length study of W. H. Auden called *The Hidden Law*. He received the Bollingen Prize in Poetry (1983), the Eugenio Montale Award (1984), the Wallace Stevens Award (1997), and the Robert Frost Medal (2000).

*Collected Earlier Poems* (1990); *Collected Later Poems* (2003)

**Edward, Lord Herbert of Cherbury (1583–1648)** was born at Eyton, in Shropshire, England, and educated at University College, Oxford. The elder brother of the celebrated Metaphysical poet George Herbert, Edward Herbert wrote history and criticism. He also served as ambassador to France, where he was a popular figure. His most noted work is his Latin philosophical treatise *De Veritate* (1624).

*The Autobiography of Edward, Lord Herbert of Cherbury*, ed. Will H. Dircks (1888)

**George Herbert (1593–1633)** was born in Montgomery, Wales, and educated at Trinity College, Cambridge. A Member of Parliament whose sponsors fell out of favor, Herbert took orders and served for much of his life in a tiny parish as rector of Bemerton, near Salisbury. In 1629 he married his stepfather's cousin Jane Danvers, and they adopted his two orphaned nieces. His close friend Nicholas Ferrar published his poems with the title *The Temple: Sacred Poems and Private Ejaculations* (1633).

*George Herbert and the Seventeenth-Century Religious Poets: Authoritative Texts, Criticism,* ed. Mario A. Di Cesare (1978); *The Essential Herbert,* ed. Anthony Hecht (1987); *Complete English Poems,* ed. John Tobin (1991)

**Miguel Hernández (1910–1942)** was born in Orihuela, Spain, to a poor family. He was largely self-taught and heavily influenced by the poets of the Spanish Golden Age. He moved to Madrid, where he met Federico García Lorca and Pablo Neruda, among others. At the age of twenty-three he published his first book, *Perito en lunas* (*Lunar Expert;* 1933). He had a wife and son, and he wrote much of his heartbreaking poetry while imprisoned for his anti-fascist sympathies, before dying of tuberculosis in jail.

*The Selected Poems of Miguel Hernández,* ed. and trans. Ted Genoways (2001)

**Robert Herrick (1591–1674)** was born in London, England, and educated at St. John's College, Cambridge. He belonged to the school of poetry known as the Cavalier Poets, so named because of their Royalist adherence during the English Civil War. He was ordained a priest in 1623, acted as a chaplain on the Duke of Buckingham's expedition to the Isle of Rhe, and was given the position of dean priory in Devon, which he took up in 1630. He produced over twenty-five hundred compositions. He spent his last years in rural quiet after the restoration of the monarchy.

*The Complete Poetry of Robert Herrick,* ed. J. Max Patrick (2nd ed. 1968)

**Geoffrey Hill (1932–)** was born in Bromsgrove, Worcestershire, England, and educated at Keble College, Oxford. He taught at the University of Leeds and then at Cambridge, before moving to the United States in 1988 to teach at Boston University. His first book of poems, *For the Unfallen,* appeared in 1959. A winner of the Whitbread and Hawthornden Prizes, he is a fellow of the American Academy of the Arts and Sciences.

*New and Collected Poems, 1952–1992* (1994); *Canaan* (1996); *The Orchards of Syon* (2002); *Without Title* (2006)

**Daniel Hoffman (1923–)** was born in New York City and educated at Columbia University. W. H. Auden chose *An Armada of Thirty Whales* (1954), his first collection, for the Yale Series of Younger Poets. His honors include the Arthur Rense Prize from the American Academy of Arts and Letters, a Guggenheim Fellowship, and a grant from the National Endowment for the Humanities. Hoffman served as Consultant in Poetry to the Library of Congress (poet laureate) from 1973 to 1974.

*Beyond Silence: Selected Shorter Poems, 1948–2003* (2003); *Makes You Stop and Think: Sonnets* (2005)

**Hugh Holland (1563–1633)** was born in Denbigh, Wales, and educated at Westminster School, where he was distinguished for his classical scholarship. He traveled widely, visiting Rome and Jerusalem, and then retired to Oxford. Later he lived in London after spending some years at the Inns of Court. Holland was a friend and contemporary of Ben Jonson. His chief claim to fame is his sonnet praising Shakespeare, which appeared in the prefatory material to the First Folio in 1623. He is buried at Westminster Abbey.

*Pancharis: the first Booke. Containing the Preparation of the Love between Owen Tudyr and the Queene, long since intended to her Maiden Majestie and now dedicated to the Invincible James* (1603); *Parthenia* (1611)

**John Hollander (1929–)** was born in New York City and educated at Columbia University and Indiana University Bloomington. He is the author of eighteen books of poetry and eight books of criticism, including the award-winning *Rhymes Reason: A Guide to English Verse* (1981). He has also edited or coedited twenty-two collections, among them *The Oxford Anthology of English Literature*. His many awards include a Guggenheim Fellowship, a MacArthur Fellowship, and the Bollingen Prize. He is Sterling Professor Emeritus of English at Yale University.

*Melodious Guile: Fictive Pattern in Poetic Language* (1988); *Selected Poetry* (1993); *Tesserae: And Other Poems* (1993); *The Work of Poetry* (1997)

**A. D. Hope (1907–2001)** was born in Cooma, New South Wales, Australia, and educated at Sydney University and University College, Oxford. He later returned to Australia and published his first collection of poetry, *The Wandering Islands*, in 1955. He taught English at the University of Melbourne from 1945 to 1965 and at Canberra University College from 1965 to 1968, when he retired. Hope's work is formalist, satiric, and unswerving in its attention to sexual malaise and social estrangement. He was made a member of the Order of the British Empire.

*Collected Poems, 1930–1965* (1966)

**Gerard Manley Hopkins (1844–1889)** was born in Stratford, Essex, England, and educated at Balliol College, Oxford. He converted to Catholicism in 1866, became a novitiate of the Society of Jesuits two years later, and was ordained in 1877. He served as a parish priest and a teacher of Classics. In 1884 he was appointed to the Chair of Greek at University College Dublin. Very little of his poetry was published during his lifetime. The poet Robert Bridges, his lifelong friend, brought out an edition of his work in 1918.

*Poems of Gerard Manley Hopkins*, ed. W. H. Gardner and N. H. MacKenzie (4th ed. 1970); *The Collected Works of Gerard Manley Hopkins*, Vol. IV, *Oxford Essays and Notes 1863–1868*, ed. Lesley Higgins (2006)

**Henry Howard, Earl of Surrey (1517–1547)**, also known as "Surrey," was born in Hunsdon, Hertfordshire, England, to a family related to the English kings. He was brought up at Windsor and given the title "Earl of

Surrey" in 1524. He was both a solider and a poet. With Thomas Wyatt, Surrey brought the sonnet form from Italy to England, and he introduced the use of blank verse in his 1557 translation of the *Aeneid.* For imagined acts of treason, Henry VIII had him imprisoned and then executed at the age of thirty.

*Poems,* ed. Emrys Jones (1964)

**Langston Hughes (1902–1967)** was born in Joplin, Missouri. After his parents separated, Hughes lived at first with his grandmother in Kansas and then with his mother and stepfather in Illinois. He attended Columbia University but dropped out after a year and traveled to Africa and France. He moved to Washington, D.C., in 1925 and the next year published his collection of poetry *The Weary Blues* to great acclaim. He received a BA from Lincoln University in Pennsylvania. In addition to poetry, he wrote fiction, drama, screenplays, essays, and autobiography. Hughes is famous for his years in New York City, where was a central figure in the Harlem Renaissance.

*I Wonder As I Wander: An Autobiographical Journey* (1956); *The Collected Poems of Langston Hughes,* ed. Arnold Rampersad (1994)

**T. R. Hummer (1950–)** was born in Macon, Mississippi, and educated at the University of Southern Mississippi and the University of Utah. He is the recipient of a Guggenheim Fellowship and a National Endowment for the Arts Fellowship, among other awards, and has edited numerous magazines including the *Kenyon Review, Cimarron Review, New England Review,* and the *Georgia Review.* He is currently director of the writing program at Arizona State University.

*Bluegrass Wasteland: Selected Poems* (2005); *The Muse in the Machine: Essays on Poetry and the Anatomy of the Body Politic* (2006)

**David Humphreys (1752–1818)** was born in Derby, Connecticut, and educated at Yale University. He served as a colonel and aide-de-camp to George Washington and then as the American minister to Portugal and Spain. His interests in poetry and regional background made him one of "The Hartford Wits," a group of American writers centered around Yale University at the end of the eighteenth century. He is reputed to have written the first genuine sonnet by an American poet. He wrote twelve irregular sonnets in all. He died in New Haven, Connecticut.

*Miscellaneous Works* (1804)

**Leigh Hunt (1784–1859)** was born James Henry Leigh Hunt in Southgate, Middlesex, England, to American parents who had fled the Revolutionary War because of their Loyalist sympathies. He was educated at Christ's Hospital. As a young man, his wide circle of poets and reformers included Percy

Bysshe Shelley, Lord Byron, William Hazlitt, and John Keats. In 1813 Hunt and his brother were prosecuted and imprisoned for two years for attacks on the Prince Regent in their political journal *The Examiner*. A prolific poet, playwright, and critic, Hunt is chiefly remembered as an influential editor and journalist as well as a generous mentor and friend. He died in Putney.

*Selected Writings*, ed. David Jesson-Dibley (1990)

**John Kells Ingram** (1823–1907) was born in Templecarne, County Donegal, Ireland, and educated at Trinity College, Dublin, where he later became become a professor of oratory and Greek, librarian, and administrator. He wrote celebrated nationalist poems in honor of the dead of the rebellion of 1798, was an advocate of home rule for Ireland, and wrote widely on trade and labor issues.

*A History of Political Economy* (1888)

**Philippe Jaccottet** (1925–) was born in Moudon, Switzerland, and educated at the University of Lausanne. He spent seven years in Paris, where he worked for the publisher Mermod, and then married the artist Anne-Marie Haesler and moved to Grignan, in Haute Provence, where he has lived ever since. He has published definitive translations of, among others, Hölderlin, Rilke, Ungaretti, Leopardi, and Musil. He was awarded the Goncourt / Adrien Bertrand poetry prize for his work in 2003.

*Words in the Air: A Selection of Poems*, trans. Derek Mahon (1998)

**James I of England** (1566–1625) was the only child of Mary, Queen of Scots, and Henry, Lord Darnley. He was the King of England and Scotland (the latter as James VI). He was also a sometime poet, who wrote most of his poetry before acceding to the English throne in 1603. His first book was *The Essays of a Prentice in the Divine Art of Poesy* (1584). His sonnets reflect his admiration for William Shakespeare and Sir Philip Sidney.

*The Poems of James VI of Scotland*, ed. James Craigie (2 vols. 1955–1958)

**Robinson Jeffers** (1887–1962) was born in Pittsburgh, Pennsylvania, and educated at the University of Pittsburgh and Occidental College, as well as in Germany and Switzerland. During the 1920s, he moved to the Pacific coast of California, which became the emblem and source of his poetry. He lived with his wife, Una, and their twin sons in a stone tower that he built with his own hands in Carmel. *The Selected Poetry of Robinson Jeffers* was published in 1931.

*The Collected Poetry of Robinson Jeffers*, ed. Tim Hunt (3 vols. 1988 –2001); *The Wild God of the World: An Anthology of Robinson Jeffers*, ed. Albert Gelpi (2003)

**Denis Johnson** (1949–) was born in Munich, Germany; raised in Tokyo, Manila, and Washington, D.C.; and educated at the University of Iowa. He is known for his edgy fiction as well as his poetry. He has received a Guggenheim Fellowship, the Whiting Writers' Award, and the Academy Award for Literature from the American Academy of Arts and Letters. He lives in northern Idaho.

*The Incognito Lounge: And Other Poems* (1982); *The Veil: Poems* (1987); *The Throne of the Third Heaven of the Nations Millennium General Assembly: Poems Collected and New* (1995)

**Helene Johnson** (1906–1995) was born in Boston, Massachusetts. She attended Columbia University but did not graduate. Together with her cousin, the writer Dorothy West, she moved to Harlem and was an important figure in the Harlem Renaissance. Her poems mostly appeared in journals, such as the NAACP's *Crisis* and *Challenge: A Literary Quarterly*. Johnson's poems were typically bold, rhetorical, and celebratory of urban life and the vitality of Harlem.

*This Waiting for Love: Helene Johnson, Poet of the Harlem Renaissance*, ed. Verner D. Mitchell (new ed. 2006)

**James Weldon Johnson** (1871–1938) was born in Jacksonville, Florida, and educated at Atlanta University. Johnson worked in education and collaborated on songwriting with his brother before entering the U.S. consular service in South America. A dedicated activist with the NAACP and a figure in the Harlem Renaissance, he anonymously published his controversial autobiography, *The Autobiography of an Ex-Colored Man* (1912). His pathbreaking anthology, *The Book of American Negro Poetry*, was published in 1922.

*Writings*, ed. William L. Andrews (2004)

**Anna Maria Jones** (1748–1829) was born Anna Maria Shipley, daughter of Jonathan Shipley, Dean of Winchester and Bishop of St. Asaph. She was a family friend of Benjamin Franklin, with whom she corresponded. Her literary career began in Calcutta, where she moved with her husband Sir William Jones, a pioneer in comparative linguistics. She published a book of poems and then returned to England because of illness.

*The Poems of Anna Maria Jones* (1793)

**Ben Jonson** (1572–1637) was born in London, England, and educated at Westminster School. He was a soldier in the Low Countries and married Anne Lewis. He was an actor and playwright whose plays were often performed: *Every Man in His Humour* (1598), *Volpone* (1606), *The Alchemist* (1910). He was paralyzed by a stroke in 1628 and appointed chronologer of the City of London, a sinecure. He is buried in Westminster Abbey.

*The Complete Poetry of Ben Jonson*, ed. William B. Hunter Jr. (1963); *The Complete Masques*, ed. Stephen Orgel (1969)

**June Jordan (1936–2002)** was born in New York City to Jamaican immigrants and educated at Barnard College. She won many awards including a Rockefeller Foundation grant and a National Endowment for the Arts fellowship. She taught at the University of California, Berkeley, where she founded Poetry for the People.

*Some of Us Did Not Die: New and Selected Essays of June Jordan* (2002); *Directed by Desire: The Collected Poems of June Jordan*, ed. Jan Heller Levi and Sara Miles (2005)

**Donald Justice (1925–2004)** was born and raised in Miami, Florida. He was educated at the Universities of Miami, North Carolina, and Iowa, where his teachers included Robert Lowell, John Berryman, and Karl Shapiro. He taught at the Iowa Writers' Workshop, the University of Florida, Gainesville, and elsewhere. He received numerous awards, including the Pulitzer Prize in 1980 and the Bollingen Prize in 1991.

*The Sunset Maker: Poems, Stories, a Memoir* (1987); *A Donald Justice Reader: Selected Poetry and Prose* (1991); *New & Selected Poems* (1995)

**Patrick Kavanagh (1904–1967)** was born in Inniskeen, County Monaghan, Ireland. He left school at the age of thirteen to go to work. He published his own magazine called *Kavanagh's Weekly*. His books include *"Ploughman" and Other Poems* (1936); the epic poem *The Great Hunger* (1942), a landmark in Irish poetry; and the autobiographical novel *Tarry Flynn* (1948). He was a hugely popular poet in Ireland.

*Collected Prose* (1967); *The Complete Poems*, ed. Peter Kavanagh (1984)

**John Keats (1795–1821)** was born in Moorfield, London, and educated at Enfield Private School. In 1811 he was apprenticed to a surgeon, completing his professional training at Guy's Hospital in 1816. He abandoned this career in favor of poetry and published *Poems* (1817) and *Endymion* (1818). He nursed his brother Tom, who died of tuberculosis, and fell in love with Fanny Brawne, a relationship that was never fulfilled. In 1819 he composed many of his greatest poems, including "The Eve of St. Agnes," "La Belle Dame Sans Merci," and "Lamia"; the famous odes "Ode to Psyche," "Ode to a Nightingale," "Ode on a Grecian Urn," "Ode on Melancholy," and "To Autumn"; and the fragment "The Fall of Hyperion." He traveled to Italy to try to recover from tuberculosis but died in Rome, where he is buried.

*Letters of John Keats*, ed. Robert Gittings (1970); *Complete Poems*, ed. Jack Stillinger (1982); *The 64 Sonnets*, ed. Edward Hirsch (2004)

**Weldon Kees (1914–1955)** was born in Beatrice, Nebraska, and educated at Doane College, the University of Missouri, and the University of Nebraska. Kees worked for the Federal Writers' Project in Lincoln, Nebraska. After moving to New York, he worked as a photographer, painter, jazz pianist, and filmmaker. He wrote fiction as well as poetry. In 1955 Kees's car was found near the Golden Gate Bridge, but it has never been determined whether he committed suicide or simply chose to disappear. His body was never found.

*Weldon Kees and the Midcentury Generation: Letters, 1935–1955,* ed. Robert Knoll (1986); *The Collected Poems of Weldon Kees,* ed. Donald Justice (rev. ed. 1992)

**Galway Kinnell (1927–)** was born in Providence, Rhode Island, and educated at Princeton University and the University of Rochester. He has been a Guggenheim Fellow, a MacArthur Fellow, and the state poet of Vermont. His *Selected Poems* (1980) received both the Pulitzer Prize and the National Book Award. He has published several books of translations, including the poetry of François Villon and Rainer Maria Rilke. For many years he was the Erich Maria Remarque Professor of Creative Writing at New York University. He is a chancellor of the Academy of American Poets and lives in Vermont.

*Body Rags: Poems* (1968); *The Book of Nightmares* (1971); *A New Selected Poems* (2000); *Strong Is Your Hold* (2006)

**Thomas Kinsella (1928–)** was born in Dublin, Ireland, and educated at University College Dublin. He served for many years in the Irish Civil Service and later taught at Southern Illinois University and Temple University. He owns and manages the Peppercanister Press. In addition to writing poetry, he has translated extensively from the Irish.

*The Táin,* trans. Thomas Kinsella (1969); *An Duanaire, 1600–1900: Poems of the Dispossessed / curtha I láthairag Seán Ó Tuama,* trans. Thomas Kinsella (1981); *The Dual Tradition: An Essay on Poetry and Politics in Ireland* (1995); *The Collected Poems, 1956–1994* (1996)

**Karl Kirchwey (1956–)** was born in Boston, Massachusetts, and educated at Yale University and Columbia University. For thirteen years he served as the director of the 92nd Street Y Unterberg Poetry Center in New York City. He is director of the creative writing program at Bryn Mawr College in Pennsylvania.

*At the Palace of Jove: Poems* (2002); *The Happiness of This World: Poems and Prose* (2007)

**Carolyn Kizer (1925–)** was born in Spokane, Washington, and educated at Sarah Lawrence College, Columbia University, and the University of Washington, where she studied with the poet Theodore Roethke. Kizer served as the first director of literary programs at the National Endowment for the Arts. Her awards include an Academy Award from the American Academy of Arts and Letters, the Frost Medal, the John Masefield Memorial Award, and the Theodore Roethke Memorial Foundation Poetry Prize. Her 1984 volume *Yin* won the Pulitzer Prize.

*Proses: On Poems and Poets* (1993); *Cool, Calm and Collected: Poems 1960–2000* (2001)

**Bill Knott (1940–)** was born in Gratiot County, Michigan. An autodidact, he published his landmark first collection *The Naomi Poems* (1968) under the pseudonym "St. Giraud." He has subsequently published more than eleven volumes of poetry. He has received a Guggenheim Fellowship and teaches at Emerson College in Boston, Massachusetts.

*Selected and Collected Poems* (1977); *Laugh at the End of the World: Collected Comic Poems 1969–1999* (2000); *The Unsubscriber* (2004)

**Kenneth Koch (1925–2002)** was born in Cincinnati, Ohio, and educated at Harvard College and Columbia University. He was a key figure in what became known as the New York School of poets, which included his friends Frank O'Hara, James Schuyler, and John Ashbery. He published numerous books about teaching and writing poetry, including the landmark volumes *Wishes, Lies, and Dreams* (1970) and *Rose, Where Did You Get That Red?* (1973). He received a Guggenheim Fellowship and won the Bollingen Prize, the Bobbit Library of Congress Poetry Prize, and the first annual Phi Beta Kappa Poetry Award. He taught at Columbia University for almost forty years.

*The Art of Poetry: Poems, Parodies, Interviews, Essays, and Other Work* (1996); *The Collected Poems of Kenneth Koch* (2005)

**Stanley Kunitz (1905–2006)** was born in Worcester, Massachusetts, and educated at Harvard University. He served as Consultant in Poetry to the Library of Congress and for many years taught in the graduate writing program at Columbia University. He received a Guggenheim Fellowship, a National Medal of Arts, and the Frost Medal from the Poetry Society of America. He also received the Pulitzer Prize and the National Book Award. He founded Poets House in New York City and the Fine Arts Work Center in Provincetown, Massachusetts. He lived in both places with his wife, the painter Elise Asher. He died at the age of one hundred.

*A Kind of Order, a Kind of Folly: Essays and Conversations* (1975); *The Collected Poems* (2000); *The Wild Braid*, with Genine Lentine (2005)

**Walter Savage Landor (1775–1864)** was born in Warwick, England, and educated at Trinity College, Oxford. He lived in Italy from 1815 to 1835 and from 1857 until his death. Landor was an essayist and linguist, chiefly noted for his series *Imaginary Conversations* (1824–1853), which invented conversations between historical characters. He died in Florence and is buried in the Protestant Cemetery.

*Selections from the Imaginary Conversations of Walter Savage Landor,* ed. Alphonso G. Newcomer (1899); *Walter Savage Landor: Selected Poetry and Prose,* ed. Keith Hanley (1981)

**Philip Larkin (1922–1985)** was born in Coventry, England, and educated at St. John's College, Oxford. He served for many years as the librarian of Hull University. He first made his name as a member of The Movement, a group of postwar poets anthologized in Robert Conquest's *New Lines* (1956). He published two novels, *Jill* (1946) and *A Girl in Winter* (1947); a book on jazz; and four volumes of poetry: *The North Ship* (1945), *The Less Deceived* (1955), *The Whitsun Weddings* (1964), and *High Windows* (1974). He also edited *The Oxford Book of Twentieth-Century English Verse* (1973).

*Collected Poems,* ed. Anthony Thwaite (1988)

**Emma Lazarus (1849–1887)** was born in New York City to a prominent Jewish family that had lived in America since at least the eighteenth century. She was educated by private tutors at home and proved to be precocious in languages. A translator of Jewish poets into English, Lazarus is best known for her 1883 sonnet "The New Colossus," which appears on the plaque at the base of the Statue of Liberty. Moved by the expulsion of Russian and Eastern European Jews, she was an early advocate for Jewish refugees in New York.

*Selected Poems,* ed. John Hollander (2005)

**Edward Lear (1812–1888)** was born in Highgate, near London, England, the twentieth child of a large family. He was educated primarily at home by his elder sisters. At the age of fifteen he began working as an illustrator, at which he excelled throughout his life. An epileptic, he developed a reputation for popularizing the limerick and nonsense poems.

*The Complete Nonsense of Edward Lear,* ed. Holbrook Jackson (new ed. 2001)

**Eugene Lee-Hamilton (1845–1907)** was born in France to English parents. He was educated in France and Germany and at Oriel College, Oxford, afterwards entering the diplomatic service. The writer Vernon Lee was his half-sister. He married the writer Annie E. Holdsworth in 1898. His books include *Imaginary Sonnets* (1888), which adapted the dramatic monologue to the sonnet form, and *Sonnets of the Wingless Hours* (1894). He died in Florence.

*Selected Poems of Eugene Lee-Hamilton (1845–1907): A Victorian Craftsman Rediscovered,* ed. MacDonald P. Jackson (2002)

David Lehman (1948–) was born in New York City and educated at Columbia University. The editor of *The Oxford Book of American Poetry* (2006), he is the series editor for the annual *Best American Poetry* volumes. His honors include fellowships from the Guggenheim Foundation, the Ingram Merrill Foundation, and the National Endowment for the Arts. He teaches at The New School and New York University.

*The Last Avant-Garde: The Making of the New York School of Poets* (1998); *The Evening Sun: A Journal in Poetry* (2002); *When a Woman Loves a Man: Poems* (2005)

Brad Leithauser (1953–) was born in Detroit, Michigan, and educated at Harvard College and Harvard Law School. The recipient of fellowships from the MacArthur Foundation and the Guggenheim Foundation, he has written fiction as well as poetry. Leithauser is married to the poet Mary Jo Salter and teaches at Mount Holyoke College in Massachusetts.

*Hundreds of Fireflies* (1982); *Darlington's Fall* (2003); *Curves and Angles: Poems* (2006)

Phillis Levin (1954–) was born in Paterson, New Jersey, and educated at Sarah Lawrence College and Johns Hopkins University. The recipient of several awards including a Guggenheim fellowship, she taught English and creative writing at the University of Maryland from 1989 to 2001. She currently teaches at Hofstra University.

*Mercury* (2001); *The Penguin Book of the Sonnet: 500 Years of a Classic Tradition in English,* ed. Phillis Levin (2001); *May Day* (2008)

Philip Levine (1928–) was born in Detroit, Michigan, and educated at Wayne University and the University of Iowa, where he studied with John Berryman. He is the author of sixteen collections of poetry. His books include *The Names of the Lost* (1975), which won the Lenore Marshall Poetry Prize; *Ashes: Poems New and Old* (1979), which won the National Book Critics Circle Award and the American Book Award; *What Work Is* (1991), which won the National Book Award; and *The Simple Truth* (1994), which won the Pulitzer Prize. He has received the Ruth Lilly Poetry Prize, the Harriet Monroe Memorial Prize, the Frank O'Hara Prize, and two Guggenheim Fellowships.

*They Feed They Lion* (1972); *New Selected Poems* (1991); *The Bread of Time: Toward an Autobiography* (1994); *Breath* (2004)

Janet Lewis (1899–1998) was born in Chicago, Illinois, and educated at the University of Chicago. She spent time in Paris before contracting tuberculosis, which forced her to return to the United States. She spent five years in a New Mexico sanitarium before moving to Los Altos, California. She was married to the poet and critic Yvor Wintersand taught creative writing at Stanford University. Lewis also wrote a libretto based on her best-selling novel *The Wife of Martin Guerre* (1941).

*Indians in the Woods* (1922); *Poems Old and New, 1918–1978* (1981); *Morning Devotion: A Poem* (1995)

**Anne Locke (1533–1607)**, also known as Anne Vaughn Lock, was born in London. Around 1551, she married Henry Lock(e). A correspondent of John Knox, she was a poet of serious Protestant convictions, who joined the exiled Protestant community in Geneva, and only returned to England after Elizabeth's ascension to the throne. After the death of her husband, she married Edward Dering. Locke wrote the first sonnet sequence in English, *A Meditation of a Penitent Sinner* (1560).

*A Meditation of a Penitent Sinner: Anne Locke's Sonnet Sequence with Locke's Epistle*, ed. Kel Morin-Parsons (1997); *The Collected Works of Anne Vaughan Lock*, ed. Susan Felch (1999)

**Mary Locke (fl. 1791–1816)** was orphaned at an early age and raised by an uncle, who left her a considerable fortune. She began contributing poetry to periodicals in 1791. After her marriage to William Mister in 1808, she published books for children under the name Mary Mister.

*Mungo, the Little Traveler* (1811); *Tales from the Mountains* (1811); *The Adventures of a Doll* (1816)

**Thomas Lodge (c. 1558–1625)** was born in London, England, the son of a lord mayor of England and his wife. He was educated at Trinity College, Oxford. Trained as a lawyer, he instead took up literature, traveling widely and writing fiction and historical romances. Later in life he returned to Catholicism and became a noted medical doctor.

*Noble English from Thomas Lodge to John Milton*, ed. Henry Newbolt (2004); *Elizabethan Sonnet Cycles*, with Giles Fletcher, ed. Martha Foote Crow (2006)

**Henry Wadsworth Longfellow (1807–1882)** was born in Portland, Maine, and educated at Bowdoin College, where Nathaniel Hawthorne was a fellow student. From 1835 to 1854 he was a professor of modern languages at Harvard, and thereafter he devoted himself entirely to writing. His books *Evangeline* (1843) and *The Song of Hiawatha* (1855) were immensely popular. His translations of Dante and other poets were collected in *The Poets and Poetry of Europe* (1845). In 1835 his first wife suffered a miscarriage and died. In 1861 he was badly injured in a fire that burned his second wife to death. He lived for most of his life in Cambridge, Massachusetts.

*Poems and Other Writings*, ed. J. D. McClatchy (2000)

**Michael Longley (1939–)** was born in Belfast, Ireland, to English parents and educated at Trinity College, Dublin, where he studied classics. Considered one of the central poets of his generation, he won the Whitbread Poetry Prize for *Gorse Fires* (1991) and the Hawthornden Prize for *The Weather in Japan* (2000). He lives in Belfast.

*Collected Poems* (2006)

**Federico García Lorca (1898–1936)** was born in the village of Fuente Vaqueros, an Andalusian village west of Granada, Spain, and educated at the Residence of Students in Madrid, where his classmates were Luis Buñuel and Salvador Dalí. He wrote five books of poems in the 1920s and became famous for *Romancero gitano* (*Gypsy Ballads*; 1928), which drew heavily from folk traditions. He spent a year in New York and wrote *Poeta en Nueva York* (*Poet in New York*; 1929–1930), which was published after his death. A playwright as well as a poet, he participated in the Second Republic and organized a theater troupe that traveled through the Spanish countryside. He was killed at the age of thirty-eight by right-wing partisans at the beginning of the Spanish Civil War.

*Collected Poems*, ed. Christopher Maurer (1991); *The Selected Poems of Federico García Lorca*, Francisco García Lorca and Donald M. Allen (2005)

**Richard Lovelace (1618–1657)** was born in Lovelace Place, Bethersden, England, to a wealthy family and educated at Gloucester Hall, Oxford. Lovelace, a Royalist, belonged to the Cavalier Poets. His most celebrated lyrics were written during his times of imprisonment in 1642 and 1648. His generous support of the Stuart cause ruined him financially, and from 1648 until his death he suffered a miserable existence in London.

*The Poems of Richard Lovelace*, ed. C. H. Wilkinson (repr. 1992); *Ben Jonson and the Cavalier Poets*, ed. Hugh MacLean (1975)

**Robert Lowell (1917–1977)** was born in Boston, Massachusetts, and educated at Harvard College and Kenyon College, where he studied with John Crowe Ransom. He was a conscientious objector during World War II, and a forceful opponent of the Vietnam War. He was married to Jean Stafford, Elizabeth Hardwick, and Caroline Blackwood. His interrogation of his family legacy and his personal struggle with manic depression created the foundation for *Life Studies* (1959) and the books that followed it. He taught at Harvard University and received the Pulitzer Prize twice—once for *Lord Weary's Castle* (1947) and once for *The Dolphin* (1974).

*Collected Prose*, ed. Robert Giroux (1987); *Collected Poems*, ed. Frank Bidart and David Gewanter (2003); *The Letters of Robert Lowell*, ed. Saskia Hamilton (2005)

**Malcolm Lowry (1909–1957)** was born in Wallasey, Cheshire, England, and educated at St. Catharine's College, Cambridge, where he wrote his first novel, *Ultramarine* (1933), which was published the same year that he married his first wife, Jan Gabrial. They divorced in 1940, after which

Lowry married Margerie Bonner. Starting in 1936 and while moving between Mexico, the United States, and Canada, he worked on his second novel, *Under the Volcano* (1947), which is considered one of the great fictional works of the twentieth century. He suffered from alcoholism. The coroner attributed his death to "misadventure."

*Selected Poems of Malcolm Lowry*, ed. Earle Birney (1962); *The Voyage that Never Ends: Fictions, Poems, Fragments, Letters*, ed. Michael Hofmann (2007)

**Louis MacNeice (1907–1963)** was born in Belfast, Ireland, and educated at Merton College, Oxford. With his first book, *Blind Fireworks* (1929), MacNeice established himself as a witty formalist and maverick poet. He was a close friend of the other political poets of the thirties, such as Stephen Spender, W. H. Auden, and Cecil Day-Lewis. *Autumn Journal, a Poem* (1939), his signature meditation on identity and history, is considered his finest work.

*Collected Poems of Louis MacNeice*, ed. E. R. Dodds (2nd ed. 1979); *Selected Poems of Louis MacNeice*, ed. Michael Longley (1990)

**Derek Mahon (1941–)** was born in Belfast, Ireland, and educated at Trinity College, Dublin. Mahon is a leading poet in the generation of Northern Irish poets who were first published in the mid-to-late 1960s and came to international prominence in the 1970s with the escalating Troubles. Renowned as a translator as well as a poet, he lives in Kinsale, County Cork.

*Collected Poems* (1999); *Harbour Lights* (2005); *Adaptations* (2006)

**Stéphane Mallarmé (1842–1898)** was born in Paris, France. He did not do well in school, except in languages, but began writing poetry at an early age. He married Marie Gerhard in London. He made his living as a provincial schoolteacher and taught English in Tournon, Besancon, Avignon, and Paris from 1864 until his retirement in 1893. The major progenitor of the Symbolist movement, he was famous for holding salons where writers such as W. B. Yeats, Rainer Maria Rilke, Paul Valéry, and Stefan George were often in attendance.

*Collected Poems*, trans. Henry Weinfield (1994); *Collected Poems and Other Verse*, trans. E. H. and A. M. Blackmore (2006)

**Paul Mariani (1940–)** was born in New York City and educated at Manhattan College, Colgate University, and the City University of New York. He has written biographies of Hart Crane, Robert Lowell, John Berryman, William Carlos Williams, and Gerard Manley Hopkins, and has won fellowships from the Guggenheim Foundation and the National Endowment for the Arts. He teaches at Boston College in Massachusetts.

*Salvage Operations: New & Selected Poems* (1990); *God and the Imagination: On Poets, Poetry, and the Ineffable* (2002); *Deaths & Transfigurations: Poems* (2005)

**R. A. K. Mason** (1905–1971) was born in Auckland, New Zealand. Mason's polished and important early poems are credited with helping to establish the tradition of poetry in New Zealand that began in the twenties. His first book, *The Beggar* (1924), was published when he was nineteen. By the age of thirty-five, he was substantially finished with poetic composition and turned to political and trade union activism.

*Collected Poems* (1962)

**William Matthews** (1942–1997) was born in Cincinnati, Ohio, and educated at Yale University and the University of North Carolina. Matthews taught widely and was president of the Associated Writing Programs and the Poetry Society of America. A Guggenheim Fellow and winner of the Ruth Lilly Prize as well as a fellowship from the National Endowment for the Arts, he won the National Book Critics Circle Award for *Time & Money* (1996).

*Search Party: Collected Poems*, ed. Sebastian Matthews and Stanley Plumly (2004)

**Bernadette Mayer** (1945–) was born in Brooklyn, New York, and educated at the New School for Social Research. From 1972 to 1974, Mayer and conceptual artist Vito Acconci edited the journal *0 to 9*. With her husband, the writer Lewis Walsh, she edited United Artists Press. Her books include *The Golden Book of Words* (1978) and *The Bernadette Mayer Reader* (1992). She lives in New York City.

*Sonnets* (1989); *Two Haloed Mourners: Poems* (1998); *Scarlet Tanager* (2005)

**James McAuley** (1917–1976) was born in Lakemba, near Sydney, Australia, and educated at Sydney University. He served in the militia for the Australian army before turning to editing and teaching. Together with musician Richard Connolly, he produced the most significant collection of Australian Catholic hymnody to date.

*New and Selected Poems* (2005)

**J. D. McClatchy** (1945–) was born in Bryn Mawr, Pennsylvania, and educated at Georgetown and Harvard Universities. He is the author of five books of poems and two collections of essays. He has written many texts for musical settings, including eight opera libretti, which have been performed in opera houses around the world. He has received the Witter Bynner Poetry

Prize of the American Academy of Arts and Letters and fellowships from the Guggenheim Foundation and the National Endowment for the Arts. He edits the *Yale Review* and lives in Stonington, Connecticut.

*Ten Commandments: Poems* (1998); *The Vintage Book of Contemporary American Poetry*, ed. J. D. McClatchy (1990); *Hazmat* (2002)

**Phyllis McGinley** (1905–1978) was born in Ontario, Oregon, and educated at the University of Utah. Writing in formal meters and always using rhyme, McGinley wrote well-crafted light verse that made her a popular and widely quoted poet in her lifetime. Her subjects were daily objects and events, family life, and humorous occasions. She won the Pulitzer Prize for her collection *Times Three: Selected Verse from Three Decades with Seventy New Poems* (1960).

*One More Manhattan* (1937); *Stones from a Glass House: New Poems* (1946); *Saint-Watching* (1969)

**Medbh McGuckian** (1950–) was born in Belfast, Ireland, and educated at Queen's University, Belfast. McGuckian's first collection, *The Flower Master*, was published in 1982. She has held residencies at many colleges and universities and currently lectures in creative writing at the Seamus Heaney Centre for Poetry at Queen's University.

*On Ballycastle Beach* (1988); *Marconi's Cottage* (1991); *Selected Poems: 1978–1994* (1997); *Shelmalier* (1998)

**Claude McKay** (1889–1948) was born in Jamaica, where he served as a police officer before publishing two books of poetry. He then immigrated to the United States, where he studied at the Tuskegee Institute and Kansas State College. He also edited the radical newspaper *The Liberator*. McKay was a prominent writer of fiction, nonfiction, and poetry. His most important book was *Harlem Shadows* (1922).

*Complete Poems*, ed. William J. Maxwell (2004)

**Sandra McPherson** (1943–) was born in San Jose, California, and educated at San Jose State University and the University of Washington, where she studied with Elizabeth Bishop. Much of her poetry could be described as tracking her own biography through its focus on the natural world. She has served as the poetry editor of the *Antioch Review* and the *California Quarterly* and teaches now at the University of California, Davis.

*The God of Indeterminacy: Poems* (1993); *The Spaces Between Birds: Mother/Daughter Poems, 1967–1995* (1996); *A Visit to Civilization* (2002)

**Paula Meehan** (1955–) was born in Dublin, Ireland, and educated at Trinity College, Dublin, and Eastern Washington University. She has been a writer-in-residence at University College Dublin and Trinity College. She lives in Dublin.

*The Man Who Was Marked by Winter* (1991); *Pillow Talk* (1994)

**George Meredith (1828–1909)** was born in Portsmouth, England. His formal schooling ended at the age of seventeen. Meredith worked in journalism and publishing and was widely noted for such novels as *The Egoist* (1879) and *Diana of the Crossways* (1885). He is also remembered for his sonnet sequence *Modern Love* (1862), a largely fictive account of the breakup of a marriage. Its sonnets are sixteen lines long, an asymmetric version of the form, which became known as the Meredithian sonnet.

*Selected Poems of George Meredith*, ed. Graham Hough (1962)

**William Meredith (1919–2007)** was born in New York City and educated at Princeton University. He taught at Connecticut College from 1955 to 1983. He served as Consultant in Poetry to the Library of Congress (poet laureate) from 1978 to 1980. He won the Pulitzer Prize for *Partial Accounts* (1988) and the National Book Award for *Effort at Speech* (1997).

*Effort at Speech: New and Selected Poems* (1997)

**James Merrill (1926–1995)** was born in New York City and educated at Amherst College. His father, Charles Merrill, was a founding partner of the Merrill Lynch investment firm. His financial independence enabled him to devote himself to writing. He spent long periods of his life in Greece, but in later years divided his time between Key West, Florida, and Stonington, Connecticut. He was awarded the National Book Award for *Nights and Days* (1966) and the Pulitzer Prize for *Divine Comedies* (1977). His fifteenth book of poems, *A Scattering of Salts*, appeared posthumously in 1995.

*A Different Person: A Memoir* (1993); *Collected Poems*, ed. J. D. McClatchy and Stephen Yenser (2001); *Collected Prose*, ed. J. D. McClatchy and Stephen Yenser (2004); *The Changing Light at Sandover*, ed. J. D. McClatchy and Stephen Yenser (2006)

**W. S. Merwin (1927–)** was born in New York City and raised in Union City, New Jersey, and Scranton, Pennsylvania. He was educated at Princeton University, where he studied with John Berryman and R. P. Blackmur. From 1949 to 1956, he traveled through Europe, working first as a tutor and then as a translator for the BBC. He has translated Latin, Greek, French, Spanish, Italian, Chinese, and Japanese poetry into English. His many honors include the Pulitzer Prize for *The Carrier of Ladders* (1970) and the National Book Award for *Migration: New and Selected Poems* (2005). For many years he has lived in Hawaii.

*The First Four Books of Poems* (1975); *The Second Four Books of Poems* (1993); *East Window: The Asian Translations* (1998)

**Charlotte Mew (1869–1928)** was born in London, England, to a family that became impoverished after the death of Mew's father. Mew took on any odd writing jobs she could find to support her mother and siblings. Her central collection *The Farmer's Bride* was not published until 1916. Despite the recognition she received from such luminaries as John Masefield, Thomas Hardy, and Virginia Woolf, she died by her own hand, a victim of severe depression.

*Collected Poems and Selected Prose*, ed. Val Warner (1997)

**Michelangelo Buonarroti (1475–1564)** was born in Caprese, Tuscany. He was apprenticed to Domenico Ghirlandaio and later to a sculptor, Bertoldo. He worked on the Sistine Chapel ceiling between 1508 and 1512. His other major works include the *Bacchus*, the first *Pietà*, and the sculpture *David*. The most celebrated Renaissance painter, sculptor, and architect, he wrote poetry in a variety of forms and received much attention for sonnets that addressed same-sex desire.

*The Sonnets of Michelangelo*, trans. Elizabeth Jennings (1961); *The Complete Poems of Michelangelo*, trans. John Frederick Nims (1998)

**Josephine Miles (1911–1985)** was born in Chicago, Illinois, and lived most of her life in California. She was educated at the University of California, Los Angeles, and the University of California, Berkeley, where she spent her entire academic career. She was the first woman to be tenured in the English department at Berkeley and became a well-known scholar of the conventions of grammar and vocabulary in literature. She received fellowships from the National Endowment for the Arts and the Guggenheim Foundation. She suffered from lifelong arthritis and died of pneumonia in Berkeley, California.

*Collected Poems, 1930–83* (1983)

**Edna St. Vincent Millay (1892–1950)** was born in Rockland, Maine, and educated at Vassar College. After graduating in 1917, she moved to New York's Greenwich Village and published her first book, *Renascence and Other Poems*. After traveling in Europe from 1921 to 1923, she married Eugen Boissevain and bought the farm Steepletop in Austerlitz, New York. She won the Pulitzer Prize in 1923.

*A Few Figs from Thistles* (1920); *Collected Sonnets of Edna St. Vincent Millay* (1941); *Selected Poems*, ed. J. D. McClatchy (2003)

**John Milton (1608–1674)** was born in London, England, and educated at Christ's College, Cambridge. From 1632 until 1638, he lived in his parents' house and studied privately. Later he supported himself as a tutor. He was immensely learned and mastered Hebrew, Greek, Latin, Italian, French, and other modern languages, including Dutch. He was married three times. A vigorous polemicist for Cromwell, Milton wrote a powerful prose of advocacy. In 1652 he lost his sight. Nonetheless, his greatest poetry was composed after the age of fifty-seven. He completed *Paradise Lost* in 1663 (1667), and *Paradise Regained* and *Samson Agonistes* were published together in 1671. A monument to Milton rests in Poets' Corner at Westminster Abbey.

*The Complete Poetry and Essential Prose of John Milton*, ed. William Kerrigan, John Rumrich, and Stephen M. Fallon (2007)

**Susan Mitchell (1944–)** was born in New York City and educated at Wellesley College and Georgetown University. She has received fellowships from the National Endowment for the Humanities, the Lannan Foundation, the Guggenheim Foundation, and the Fine Arts Work Center in Provincetown, Massachusetts, where her career as a poet began. She lives in Boca Raton, Florida, where she teaches in the creative writing program at Florida Atlantic University.

*The Water Inside the Water* (1983); *Rapture: Poems* (1992); *Erotikon: Poems* (2000)

**John Montague (1929–)** was born in Brooklyn, New York, and reared on the family farm in County Tyrone, Ireland. He was educated at University College Dublin. He was the Paris correspondent for the *Irish Times*. His best-known volume of poems, *The Rough Field* (1972), brings together the particular burden of place in Ireland with a wide and reflective meditation on identity and political allegiance. In 1998 he became the first occupant of the Irish Chair of Poetry. He lives in Cork, Ireland.

*Collected Poems* (1995)

**Eugenio Montale (1896–1981)** was born in Genoa, Italy. His formal education was cut short by poor health. Much of his early poetry describes the Cinque Terre on the Tuscan coast, where he spent summers throughout his youth. He lived in Florence from 1927 until 1948, when he moved to Milan to join the staff of *Il Corrierre della Sera*, Italy's leading newspaper. His three books, *Cuttlefish Bones*, *The Occasions*, and *The Storm, Etc.*, hold substantial significance in twentieth-century Italian literature. He was an important translator, a voluminous writer of prose, and a talented amateur painter. He was awarded the Nobel Prize for Literature in 1975.

*Collected Poems: 1920–1954*, trans. Jonathan Galassi (1998); *Selected Poems*, ed. David Young (2004)

**Marianne Moore (1887–1972)** was born in Kirkwood, Missouri, raised in Carlisle, Pennsylvania, and educated at Bryn Mawr College. In 1918 she moved to New York City. She lived all her life with her mother, first in New Jersey, then in Greenwich Village, and finally in Brooklyn. Her first collection of poetry, *Poems* (1921), was published in England. She worked variously as a teacher, a secretary, and a librarian, and edited *The Dial* from 1925 to 1929. Her many honors included the Bollingen Prize, the National Book Award, the Pulitzer Prize, and the National Medal for Literature.

*The Complete Poems of Marianne Moore* (1967); *The Selected Letters of Marianne Moore*, ed. Bonnie Costello (1997); *The Poems of Marianne Moore*, ed. Grace Schulman (2003)

**Merrill Moore (1903–1957)** was born in Columbia, Tennessee, and educated at Vanderbilt University, where he studied medicine and was a member of the Fugitive group of poets. He practiced psychiatry in Boston and became an expert in the fields of alcoholism and suicide. He was a prolific sonneteer.

*M: One Thousand Autobiographical Sonnets* (1938); *Verse-Diary of a Psychiatrist: New Sonnets* (1954); *Experimental Sonnets* (1956)

**Edwin Morgan (1920–)** was born in Glasgow, Scotland. He began his education at the University of Glasgow before serving in World War II. Morgan is associated with the Scottish Renaissance and considered one of the most influential Scottish writers of the twentieth century. He was named the first Glasgow Poet Laureate in 1999.

*New Selected Poems* (2000); *Cathures: New Poems, 1997–2001* (2002)

**Howard Moss (1922–1987)** was born in New York City and educated at the University of Wisconsin. He published twelve volumes of poetry and three books of criticism. He was the poetry editor of *The New Yorker* magazine for almost forty years. He was awarded the National Book Award for poetry for his *Selected Poems* in 1972.

*New Selected Poems* (1985); *Minor Monuments: Selected Essays* (1986)

**Edwin Muir (1887-1959)** was born in the Orkney Islands. In 1901 his family moved to Glasgow. Within five years, both of his parents and two of his brothers had died. He left school at the age of eleven and worked in several factories and law offices. In 1919 he moved to London and started a literary career. From 1921 until 1956 he and his wife, Willa Muir, moved between Europe, England, and Scotland, eventually settling in Cambridgeshire, England. He wrote a noted *Autobiography* (1954) and served as the Charles Eliot Norton Professor at Harvard University from 1955 to 1956.

*Scottish Journey* (1935); *The Complete Poems of Edwin Muir*, ed. Peter Butter (1991)

**Paul Muldoon** (1951–) was born in County Armagh, Northern Ireland, and educated at Queen's University, Belfast. Muldoon's honors include a Guggenheim Fellowship, the T. S. Eliot Prize, and the Irish Literature Prize from the *Irish Times*. He won the Pulitzer Prize for *Moy Sand and Gravel* (2002). He held the chair of Professor of Poetry at Oxford University for a five-year term, from 1999 to 2004, and he is an Honorary Fellow of Hertford College, Oxford. He teaches at Princeton University and has lived in the United States since 1987.

*Poems, 1968–1998* (2001); *The End of the Poem: Oxford Lectures* (2006); *Horse Latitudes* (2006)

**Les Murray** (1938–) was born in Nabiac, on the north coast of New South Wales, Australia, and educated at the University of Sydney. In 1974 he devoted himself to his writing full-time, and in 1986 he moved from Sydney to live with his family in his native valley. His book *Subhuman Redneck Poems* (1996) received the United Kingdom's T. S. Eliot Prize. He edited *The New Oxford Book of Australian Verse* (1986).

*The Rabbiter's Bounty: Collected Poems* (1991); *Poems the Size of Photographs* (2002); *The Biplane Houses: Poems* (2006)

**Philip Neilsen** (1949–) was born in Brisbane, Queensland, Australia. He is the former chair of the Queensland Writers Centre and was a member of the Literature Board of the Australia Council. The author of ten books, Neilsen currently serves as the creative director of the Kelvin Grove Urban Village Sharing Stories public history project.

*Imagined Lives: A Study of David Malouf* (rev. ed. 1996); *The Sting in the Wattle*, ed. Philip Neilsen (1993)

**Marilyn Nelson** (1946–) was born in Cleveland, Ohio, and educated at the University of California, Davis; the University of Pennsylvania; and the University of Minnesota. She has twice been a finalist for the National Book Award. Her other honors include a Guggenheim Fellowship and two fellowships from the National Endowment for the Arts. She served as Poet Laureate of Connecticut from 2001 to 2006. *Carver: A Life in Poems* (2001) was named a Newbery Honor Book.

*The Cachoeira Tales and Other Poems* (2005)

**Howard Nemerov** (1920–1991) was born in New York City and educated at Harvard College. He was the brother of photographer Diane Arbus. During World War II he served in the Royal Canadian Air Force and later in the U.S. Army. He was appointed Consultant in Poetry to the Library of Congress (poet laureate) from 1963 to 1964 and from 1988 to 1990. *The Collected Poems of Howard Nemerov* (1977) was awarded the Pulitzer Prize and the National Book Award. He served as Distinguished Poet in Residence at Washington University in St. Louis from 1969 until his death.

*The Collected Poems of Howard Nemerov* (1977); *The Selected Poems of Howard Nemerov*, ed. Daniel Anderson (2003)

**Pablo Neruda** (1904–1973) was born in Parral, in central Chile, and educated at the Instituto Pedagógico in Santiago and the University of Chile. At the age of twenty he published *Twenty Love Poems and A Song of Despair* (1924), a book that made him famous throughout Latin America. He was elected senator in 1945, joining the Communist Party of Chile, but went into hiding to avoid arrest for his participation in protests against the Chilean dictatorship. He lived underground for two years before secretly leaving Chile in 1949. Neruda was awarded the International Peace Prize in 1950, the Stalin Peace Prize in 1953, a Doctorate in Literature from Oxford University in 1965, and the Nobel Prize in Literature in 1971. He is among the most widely translated poets in the world.

*The Poetry of Pablo Neruda*, ed. Ilan Stavans (2003); *I Explain a Few Things: Selected Poems*, ed. Ilan Stavans (2007)

**Gérard de Nerval** (1808–1855) was born Gérard Labrunie in Paris, France, and educated at the Collège Charlemagne. His translations of Goethe's *Faust* (1828–1840) gained him access early on to influential French literary circles. His work preceded Symbolist and Surrealist movements. He was famous for parading his pet lobster on the end of a blue ribbon around Paris. He suffered from severe mental illness and committed suicide, hanging himself from a window grating. He is buried in Père Lachaise Cemetery in Paris.

*Selected Writings*, trans. Richard Sieburth (1999); *Aurélia*, trans. Monique DiDonna (2001)

**Alice Notley** (1945–) was born in Bisbee, Arizona, and educated at Barnard College and the University of Iowa. Notley married the poet Ted Berrigan, and they lived and worked together in Chicago and New York City. She is often associated with the New York School of poets. She later moved to Paris. Winner of the *Los Angeles Times* Book Prize in poetry, Notley is also the author of a book of essays on poetry, *Coming After* (2005).

*Grave of Light: New and Selected Poems, 1970–2005* (2006)

**Frank O'Hara** (1926–1966) was born in Baltimore, Maryland, and grew up in Massachusetts. He studied at Harvard College, where he majored in music and began his association with John Ashbery, and at the University of Michigan. He was at the center of what became known as the New York School of poets. He worked at the Museum of Modern Art in New York and was a catalyst in both the painting and poetry worlds until his early death in a car accident.

*In Memory of My Feelings: A Selection of Poems*, ed. Bill Berkson (1967); *The Collected Poems of Frank O'Hara*, ed. Donald Allen (1971)

**Alicia Ostriker** (1937–) was born in Brooklyn, New York, and educated at Brandeis University and the University of Wisconsin. Since 1965 she has taught at Rutgers University. Ostriker's books of poetry include *The Crack in Everything* (1996), which won both the Paterson Poetry Prize and the San Francisco State Poetry Center Award. She is also a noted critic, whose works include *Stealing the Language: The Emergence of Women's Poetry in America* (1986).

*Poems Selected and New, 1968–1998* (1998); *No Heaven* (2007)

**Wilfred Owen** (1893–1918) was born in Oswestry, Shropshire, England, and educated at the University of London. Owen served in the British army during World War I. He wrote extensively on antiwar themes while recuperating from shell shock; he returned to battle in 1918 and was killed just one week before the war ended. He is remembered as the finest poet of World War I.

*The Collected Poems of Wilfred Owen*, ed. C. Day-Lewis (1963); *Collected Letters*, ed. Harold Owen and John Bell (1967)

**Geoff Page** (1940–) was born in Grafton, New South Wales, Australia, and educated at the University of New England. Page has published four verse novels and edited an anthology of sonnets. He has taught at Edith Cowan University and Narrabundah College and has lectured worldwide about Australian poetry.

*Selected Poems* (1991); *A Reader's Guide to Contemporary Australian Poetry* (1995); *The Indigo Book of Modern Australian Sonnets*, ed. Geoff Page (2003); *Agnostic Skies* (2006)

**Michael Palmer** (1943–) was born in New York City and educated at Harvard College. He has translated work from French, Russian, and Portuguese and frequently collaborated with painters and dancers. His honors include two grants from the National Endowment for the Arts, a Guggenheim Fellowship, the Shelley Memorial Prize, and the 2006 Wallace Stevens Award. He lives in San Francisco.

*The Lion Bridge: Selected Poems, 1972–1995* (1998); *The Promises of Glass* (2000); *Company of Moths* (2005)

**Dorothy Parker** (1893–1967) was born in Long Branch, New Jersey. While her formal education ended at age fourteen, she went on to write for *Vanity Fair, Vogue,* and *The New Yorker* before becoming a screenwriter in Los Angeles. She was best known for her ferocious, biting wit and as a founding member of what became known as the Algonquin Round Table.

*The Poetry and Short Stories of Dorothy Parker* (1994); *The Portable Dorothy Parker*, ed. Marion Meade (rev. ed. 2006)

**Kenneth Patchen** (1911–1972) was born in Niles, Ohio, and educated at the University of Wisconsin. Patchen's first collection, *Before the Brave*, was published in 1936 and widely noticed. He suffered a permanent spinal injury, and a botched surgery disabled him for life. He and his wife settled in California, where he became a major influence on the Beat poets. He was also the author of a noted novel, *The Memoirs of a Shy Pornographer* (1945).

*The Collected Poems of Kenneth Patchen* (1968)

**George Peele** (1558?–1597?) was born in London, England, and educated at Christ Church, Oxford. He was chiefly noted for his plays, including *The Arraignment of Paris* (1584). He was also known for his poems, one of which is the sonnet that ends his blank verse poem "Polyhymnia" (1590).

*The Works of George Peele*, ed. A. H. Bullen (2 vols. 1888)

**Francesco Petrarch** (1304–1374) was born in Arezzo, Italy. He was brought up in Provence and studied law at Montpellier and Bologna. In 1330 he entered the service of Cardinal Giovanni Colonna. At Avignon in 1327 he first saw Laura, who inspired his great vernacular poetry. In 1341 he was crowned laureate of Rome. Petrarch is popularly called the "father of humanism." He was prodigiously learned and wrote mostly in Latin, although he is remembered for his Italian poetry, including *Canzoniere* (*Book of Songs*) and *Trionfi* (*Triumphs*). He is revered for his perfection of the sonnet form.

*Canzoniere: Selected Poems*, ed. and trans. Anthony Mortimer (2002); *The Poetry of Petrarch*, trans. David Young (2004)

**Robert Pinsky** (1940–) was born in Long Branch, New Jersey, and educated at Rutgers and Stanford Universities. From 1997 to 2000 he served as the Poet Laureate Consultant in Poetry to the Library of Congress, where he founded the Favorite Poem Project. He has received an American Academy of Arts and Letters Award, the William Carlos Williams Award, and a Guggenheim Fellowship. His translation *The Inferno of Dante* (1994) received the *Los Angeles Times* Book Prize in poetry. He teaches at Boston University and lives in Cambridge, Massachusetts.

*The Inferno of Dante: A New Verse Translation*, trans. Robert Pinsky (1994); *The Figured Wheel: New and Collected Poems 1966–1996* (1996); *The Sounds of Poetry: A Brief Guide* (1998); *Gulf Music* (2007)

**Sylvia Plath** (1932–1963) was born in Boston, Massachusetts, and educated at Smith College and Newnham College, Cambridge, where she met her husband, the poet Ted Hughes. They married in 1956. In 1958 she attended Robert Lowell's verse-writing seminar at Boston University, where she met Anne Sexton. Her first volume of poetry, *The Colossus*, was published in 1960. In 1963, following the dissolution of her marriage, she suffered her second severe bout of depression and committed suicide. Her second book, *Ariel*, was published after her death, in 1965. Her *Collected Poems* posthumously received the Pulitzer Prize.

*The Collected Poems*, ed. Ted Hughes (1981); *The Journals of Sylvia Plath*, ed. Frances McCullough with Ted Hughes (1982); *Ariel: The Restored Edition; A Facsimile of Plath's Manuscript, Reinstating Her Original Selection and Arrangement* (2004)

**Edgar Allan Poe (1809–1849)** was born in Boston, Massachusetts, and raised in Virginia. He was orphaned in 1811 and then raised by John Allan, a Richmond merchant, who later disowned him. He joined the army and attended West Point but was expelled. His literary career took him to Baltimore, Richmond, Philadelphia, and New York but never provided a sufficient living. He married his cousin Virginia when she was thirteen years old. In 1845 she died of tuberculosis at the age of twenty-five. Poe is considered the founding spirit of American romanticism. He invented the detective story and is internationally known for his gothic short stories.

*Essays and Reviews*, ed. G. R. Thompson (1984); *Poetry and Tales*, ed. Peter F. Quinn (1984); *Poems and Poetics*, ed. Richard Wilbur (2003)

**Marie Ponsot (1921–)** was born Marie Birmingham in New York City and educated at St. Joseph's College for Women in Brooklyn and Columbia University. She has taught at many colleges and universities, including Queens College in New York, where she retired in 1991. *The Bird Catcher* (1998) won the National Book Critics Circle Award, and her other honors include a grant from the National Endowment for the Arts, the Delmore Schwartz Memorial Poetry Award, and the Frost Medal.

*Springing: New and Selected Poems* (2002)

**Ezra Pound (1885–1972)** was born in Hailey, Idaho, and raised in a suburb of Philadelphia, Pennsylvania. He was educated at Hamilton College and the University of Pennsylvania, where he became lifelong friends with William Carlos Williams and was briefly engaged to H.D. (Hilda Doolittle). In 1908 he moved to London, where he met many influential writers, including W. B. Yeats, for whom he worked as a secretary. He launched the movement of Imagism, and his reputation was established by the publication of *Hugh Selwyn Mauberley: Life and Contacts* (1920). He had a son with his wife, Dorothy Shakespear, and a daughter with his mistress, Olga Rudge. He settled in Rapallo, Italy. During World War II he made a series of pro-Fascist and anti-Semitic radio broadcasts that led to his indictment for treason. He was sentenced to St. Elizabeth's Hospital for the Criminally Insane in Washington, D.C. He was released in 1958 and returned to Italy. *Translations* (enlarged ed. 1963); *The Cantos of Ezra Pound* (new ed. 1996); *Literary Essays*, ed. T. S. Eliot (1954); *Collected Early Poems of Ezra Pound*, ed. Michael John King (1976)

**Aleksandr (Sergeyevich) Pushkin (1799–1837)** was born in Moscow, Russia. He learned Russian from household serfs and French from tutors and governesses. He spent his teenage years at the Lyceum in Tsarskoye Selo (now Pushkin, near St. Petersburg). He lived most of his life in St. Petersburg. In 1811 he married Natalia Goncharova, who bore him five children. He was kept under close watch by the court and suffered from financial worries. He was fatally wounded in a duel with George d'Anthès. The first writer to employ the vernacular, Pushkin is revered as Russia's greatest and most influential poet.

*The Poems, Prose, and Plays of Pushkin*, ed. Avrahm Yarmolinsky (1943); *Eugene Onegin: A Novel in Verse*, trans. Vladimir Nabokov (2-vol. rev. ed. 1975); *The Bronze Horseman and Other Poems*, trans. D. M. Thomas (1982)

**Raymond Queneau (1903–1976)** was born in Le Havre, Normandy, France, and educated at the Sorbonne. He is associated with the development of the Surrealist movement. He worked for the Gallimard publishing house, becoming director of the *Encyclopédie de la Pléiade*. Queneau wrote in virtually every field, from film scripts to essays, fiction, poetry, and miscellaneous nonfiction. He is remembered for his incorporation of slang into literary works and for his manipulation or parody of traditional forms.

*One Hundred Million Million Poems*, trans. John Crombi (1983); *Oulipo Compendium*, ed. Harry Matthews and Alastair Brotchie (1998)

**Ann Radcliffe (1764–1823)** was born Ann Ward in London, England. She married William Radcliffe, a journalist and editor. In 1794 Radcliffe's celebrated gothic novel *The Mysteries of Udolpho* was published. She was recognized as a master of gothic fiction and, especially after the publication of *The Mysteries of Udolpho*, became a source of subject matter and strong intellectual influence for later writers such as Jane Austen and Charlotte Brontë.

*The Mysteries of Udolpho: A Romance*, ed. Jacqueline Howard (2001); *Women's Writing, 1778–1838: An Anthology*, ed. Fiona Robertson (2001)

**Kathleen Raine (1908–2003)** was born in London, England, and raised in Northumberland. Raine studied science at Girton College, Cambridge, where she was drawn into poetic activity. She eventually married another poet, Charles Madge. Her first volume, *Stone and Flower*, appeared in 1943. She wrote criticism and published it widely, and was a noted scholar of William Blake and W. B. Yeats.

*Autobiographies* (1991); *The Collected Poems of Kathleen Raine* (2000); *Blake and Antiquity* (new ed. 2002)

**Sir Walter Ralegh (c. 1552–1618)** was born in Devon, England, and educated at Oriel College, Oxford. He was an adventurer, courtier, soldier, and sailor. He embarked on several voyages to colonize the New World and founded the first colony in Virginia. He was a favorite of Queen Elizabeth but fell afoul of James I, who imprisoned him in 1603. He was a prisoner in the Tower of London for thirteen years, where he wrote some of his finest poems as well as *The History of the World* (1614). He was beheaded on false charges for treason at the age of sixty-eight.

*The Letters of Sir Walter Ralegh*, ed. Joyce Youings and Agnes Latham (1999); *The Poems of Sir Walter Ralegh: A Historical Edition*, ed. Michael Rudick (1999); *Sir Walter Ralegh: The Poems, with Other Verse from the Court of Elizabeth I*, ed. Martin Dodsworth (1999)

**John Crowe Ransom (1888–1974)** was born in Pulaski, Tennessee, and educated at Vanderbilt University and Christ Church, Oxford, where he was a Rhodes Scholar. After teaching at Vanderbilt, where he presided over the Fugitives, he moved to Kenyon College in 1937. There he founded the *Kenyon Review*, which he edited until 1959. He was a key member of the Southern Agrarians and a founder of the practice of New Criticism.

*Beating the Bushes: Selected Essays 1941–1970* (1972); *Selected Poems* (rev. ed. 1991)

**Dahlia Ravikovitch (1936–2005)** was born in Ramat Gan, near Tel Aviv, Israel, and educated at Kibbutz Geva and the Hebrew University of Jerusalem. In addition to her poetry, Ravikovitch wrote children's books and short stories. She was awarded the Israel Prize for Literature in 1998, and she was regarded as one of Israel's foremost women poets.

*A Dress of Fire*, trans. Chana Bloch (1976); *The Window: New and Selected Poems*, trans. Chana Bloch and Ariel Bloch (1989); *All the Poems Till Now* (1995)

**Lizette Woodworth Reese (1856–1935)** was born in Waverly, Maryland. She began her teaching career the year she left high school and taught English in the Baltimore public schools for forty-five years. Although she was a popular writer in her time, today she is largely unknown except for her sonnet "Tears."

*The Selected Poems of Lizette Woodworth Reese* (1926); *A Victorian Village, Reminiscences of Other Days* (1929)

**Adrienne Rich** (1929-) was born in Baltimore, Maryland, and educated at Radcliffe College. The year she graduated, her first book, *A Change of World* (1951), was published in the Yale Series of Younger Poets. *Diving into the Wreck* (1973) won the National Book Award and *The School Among the Ruins* (2004) won the National Book Critics Circle Award. Among her other honors are a Guggenheim Fellowship, the Ruth Lilly Poetry Prize, the Lenore Marshall Poetry Prize, and the Bollingen Prize. She refused the National Medal of Art in 1967 for political reasons. She is one of the foundational voices of the women's movement.

*Of Woman Born: Motherhood as Experience and Institution* (1976); *Collected Early Poems, 1950–1970* (1993); *What is Found There: Notebooks on Poetry and Politics* (1993); *The Fact of a Doorframe: Selected Poems 1950–2001* (new ed. 2002)

**Rainer Maria Rilke** (1875–1926) was born in Prague and educated at Charles University (Prague) and the University of Munich. His nomadic existence led him through Germany, Russia, Spain, Italy, France, and finally Switzerland. He lived in Paris for twelve years and for a time acted as secretary to the sculptor Auguste Rodin. At Worpswede he met and married the painter Clara Westoff. They had one daughter. He published *The Book of Hours* (1906), *New Poems* (1907), and *The Notebooks of Malte Laurids Brigge* (1907). After publishing his last two works, *Duino Elegies* (1923) and *Sonnets to Orpheus* (1923), he received international attention. He died of leukemia.

*The Selected Poetry of Rainer Maria Rilke*, ed. and trans. Stephen Mitchell (1982); *New Poems (1907)*, trans. Edward Snow (1984); *New Poems (1908): The Other Part*, trans. Edward Snow (1987); *The Essential Rilke*, trans. Galway Kinnell and Hannah Liebmann (1999); *Sonnets to Orpheus*, trans. Willis Barnstone (2004)

**Arthur Rimbaud** (1854–1891) was born in Charleville, France. He was a brilliant student but ran away from home often. At sixteen he wandered the French countryside and ended up in Paris, where he lived as a vagabond until he was noticed by Paul Verlaine, who took Rimbaud home to live with him and his wife. He and Verlaine became lovers. Their stormy affair lasted for eighteen months and took them through three countries. Rimbaud was a volatile prodigy who wrote all of his poetry in less than five years and established a remarkable reputation by the age of nineteen, the year he stopped writing. He took jobs in African towns as a colonial tradesman, but his travels left him sick and exhausted. He died in Marseilles at the age of thirty-seven.

*Complete Works*, trans. Paul Schmidt (1975); *Rimbaud Complete*, ed. and trans. Wyatt Mason (2002); *Rimbaud: Complete Works, Selected Letters; A Bilingual Edition*, trans. Wallace Fowlie (rev. ed. 2005)

**Robin Robertson** (1955– ) was born in Scone, Perthshire, Scotland. Robertson lives in London, where he is the poetry and fiction editor at Jonathan Cape. He is the winner of two Forward Poetry Prizes and is considered one of Scotland's foremost poets.

*A Painted Field* (1997); *Slow Air* (2002); *Swithering* (2006)

**Edwin Arlington Robinson** (1869–1935) was born in Head Tide and raised in Gardiner, Maine, which he renamed "Tilbury Town" in his work. He studied for two years as a special student at Harvard College. He lived most of his life in poverty until Theodore Roosevelt, who liked Robinson's book *The Children of the Night*, arranged for his sinecure at the New York Customs House. Robinson's *Collected Poems* (1921) was awarded the first Pulitzer Prize for poetry; he won a second Pulitzer with *The Man Who Died Twice* (1924) and a third with *Tristram* (1927). He died in New York City.

*Collected Poems of Edward Arlington Robinson* (1929); *Selected Letters of Edwin Arlington Robinson* (1940); *The Essential Robinson*, ed. Donald Hall (1994); *Selected Poems*, ed. Robert Faggen (1997)

**Mary Robinson** (c. 1756–1800) was born to a schoolteacher and a sea captain. During an ill-fated early marriage, Robinson lived in a debtor's prison with her husband and daughter. She later found fame on the stage. She is also known for her affair with the Prince of Wales, who later became King George IV. Her books include the best-selling novel *Walsingham* (1797), the collection of poems *Lyrical Tales* (1800), and an autobiography (1801).

*Mary Robinson: Selected Poems*, ed. Judith Pascoe (2000)

**Theodore Roethke** (1908–1963) was born in Saginaw, Michigan, and educated at the University of Michigan. His German-born family operated greenhouses, which later figured prominently in his work. In 1935 he was hospitalized for the first of several breakdowns. From 1947 until his death, Roethke taught at the University of Washington. He was awarded the Pulitzer Prize for *The Waking* (1954). He also received two Guggenheim Fellowships, the Bollingen Prize, the Shelley Memorial Award, and two National Book Awards. He died in Bainbridge, Washington.

*Collected Poems* (1966); *On the Poet and His Craft: Selected Prose*, ed. Ralph J. Mills Jr. (1965); *Selected Letters*, ed. Ralph J. Mills Jr. (1968); *Selected Poems*, ed. Edward Hirsch (2005); *Straw for the Fire: From the Notebooks of Theodore Roethke, 1943–63*, ed. David Wagoner (2nd ed. 2006)

**Christina Rossetti** (1830–1894) was born in London, England, and educated at home by her mother. She was the sister of the poet Dante Gabriel Rossetti. Her early work was published under the pseudonym Ellen Alleyne. She lived a retiring life, punctuated by periods of illness. Her

*Monna Innominata* is a sonnet series on unhappy love. She published four volumes of poetry, two books for children, and a collection of stories. Her work encompasses poems of fantasy, verses for young people, and religious poetry. It was largely neglected after her death, but recent years have seen a resurgence of interest in her life and verse.

> *Poems and Prose*, ed. Jan Marsh (1994)

**Dante Gabriel Rossetti (1828–1882)** was born in London and educated at King's College School and the Royal Academy Antique School. He was the brother of Christina Rossetti. A painter as well as a poet, he was a founding member, with Holman Hunt, John Everett Millais, and others, of the Pre-Raphaelite Brotherhood, an influential movement that founded its aesthetic ideals on the art of the early Italian Renaissance. In 1860 he married his model, Elizabeth Siddal, who committed suicide two years later. He buried a number of his poems with her, which were later exhumed and published as *The House of Life* (1870).

> *Selected Poems and Translations*, ed. Clive Wilmer (1991); *Collected Writings*, ed. Jan Marsh (1999)

**Kay Ryan (1945–)** was born in San Jose, California, and educated at the University of California, Los Angeles. Her honors include the Ruth Lilly Poetry Prize, an Ingram Merrill Award, and fellowships from the Guggenheim Foundation and the National Endowment for the Arts.

> *Say Uncle: Poems* (2000); *The Niagara River: Poems* (2005)

**Muriel Rukeyser (1913–1980)** was born in New York City and educated at Vassar College, where she founded the *Student Review* (along with Elizabeth Bishop, Eleanor Clark, and Mary McCarthy) but never graduated. Her debut collection, *Theory of Flight* (1935), won the Yale Younger Poets prize. She taught at Sarah Lawrence College and the California Labor School in Berkeley. Dedicated to progressive politics throughout her life, she was also active in the antiwar movement during the 1960s.

> *The Collected Poems* (1978); *A Muriel Rukeyser Reader*, ed. Jan Heller Levi (1994)

**Mary Jo Salter (1954–)** was born in Grand Rapids, Michigan, and educated at Harvard College and New Hall, Cambridge. She has been an editor at the *Atlantic Monthly* and *The New Republic*. Salter is a coeditor of *The Norton Anthology of Poetry*. She is married to the writer Brad Leithauser and teaches at Mount Holyoke College.

> *Unfinished Painting: Poems* (1989); *Sunday Skaters: Poems* (1994); *A Kiss in Space: Poems* (1999)

**George Santayana (1863–1952)** was born Jorge Agustín Nicolás Ruiz de Santayana in Spain. Although a Spanish citizen, he was raised in the United

States and wrote in English. Educated at Harvard University, he later taught there for many years; his students included Gertrude Stein, Wallace Stevens, and T. S. Eliot. In 1894 he published *Sonnets and Other Verses*, his first of over twenty books. He is principally known as a philosopher. He lived for eight years in Spain, forty years in Boston, and forty years in Europe. He died in Rome.

*The Complete Poems of George Santayana: A Critical Edition*, ed. William G. Holzberger (1979)

**Sherod Santos (1948–)** was born in Greenville, South Carolina, and educated at the University of California and the University of Utah. He has received awards from the Guggenheim Foundation and the National Endowment for the Arts. He is married to the poet Lynn McMahon and teaches at the University of Missouri, Columbia.

*The City of Women: A Sequence of Poems and Prose* (1993); *The Perishing* (2003); *Greek Lyric Poetry: A New Translation* (2005)

**Siegfried Sassoon (1886–1967)** was born in Kent, England, and attended Clare College, Cambridge. He moved between his family's country estate and fashionable literary circles in London. Sassoon's devastating verses on World War I, in which he served with conspicuous bravery but increasing despair and disgust, made him a leader of the protest poetry of that war. His war poems were published in two volumes, *The Old Huntsman* (1917) and *Counter-Attack* (1918), which are unsparing in their critique of official hypocrisy and the delusions of a public patriotism.

*Collected Poems 1908–1956* (1961)

**Delmore Schwartz (1913–1966)** was born in Brooklyn, New York, and educated at New York University. He is a key member of the Middle Generation of American writers, which includes his friends John Berryman, Robert Lowell, and Saul Bellow, who modeled the title character of *Humboldt's Gift* on him. Schwartz was a gifted prodigy who published short fiction and essays as well as poetry. He also struggled with mental illness and alcoholism. He won the Bollingen Prize for *Summer Knowledge* in 1959.

*Summer Knowledge: New and Selected Poems, 1938–1958* (1959); *The Selected Essays of Delmore Schwartz*, ed. Donald A. Dike and David H. Zucker (1970)

**Frederick Seidel (1936–)** was born in St. Louis, Missouri, and educated at Harvard College. His books include *Going Fast* (1998), a finalist for the 1999 Pulitzer Prize in poetry, and *Ooga-Booga* (2006), a finalist for the National Book Critics Circle Award. He received the 2002 PEN/Voelker Award for Poetry. He lives in New York City.

*Poems, 1959–1979* (1980); *My Tokyo: Poems* (1993); *The Cosmos Trilogy* (2003)

**Anna Seward (1742–1809)** was born in Eyam, Derbyshire, and grew up in Lichfield, Staffordshire, England. She authored the novel *Louisa* (1784) and became a member of a literary circle that included William Hayley, Erasmus Darwin, and Richard Lovell Edgeworth. In her day, she was called "The Swan of Lichfield." She wrote elegies and sonnets. Sir Walter Scott, her literary executor, edited her work.

*The Swan of Lichfield: Being a Selection from the Correspondence of Anna Seward*, ed. Hesketh Pearson (1936); *The Swan at Lichfield: The Lichfield Poems of Anna Seward (1742–1809)*, ed. Margaret Williams (1994)

**Anne Sexton (1928–1974)** born in Newton, Massachusetts. She attended Garland Junior College for one year and married Alfred Muller Sexton II at the age of nineteen. She had two daughters. She was hospitalized throughout her life for mental breakdowns. One of her doctors encouraged her to pursue an interest in poetry, and she enrolled in a workshop with Robert Lowell at Boston University. Her first collection, *To Bedlam and Part Way Back*, was published in 1960. She won the Pulitzer Prize for *Live or Die* (1967). She committed suicide in 1974.

*The Complete Poems* (1981); *Anne Sexton: A Self-Portrait in Letters*, ed. Linda Gray Sexton and Lois Ames (2004)

**William Shakespeare (1564–1616)** was born in Stratford-upon-Avon, England. He probably attended the Stratford grammar school but received no university education. He married Anne Hathaway in 1582 and had three children with her. For most of his career, he was an actor, shareholder, and principal playwright of the most important theatrical company of his time. His tragic masterpieces—*Hamlet, Othello, King Lear, Macbeth*, and *Antony and Cleopatra*—were composed in rapid succession after the turn of the century. Shakespeare's sonnets were first published in 1609. He apparently retired to Stratford around 1610.

*Shakespeare's Sonnets*, ed. Katherine Duncan-Jones (1987); *The Sonnets and A Lover's Complaint*, ed. John Kerrigan (2000)

**Karl Shapiro (1913–2000)** was born in Baltimore, Maryland, and attended the University of Virginia and Johns Hopkins University. He became Consultant in Poetry to the Library of Congress in 1946. He was editor of *Poetry* (1950–1956) and *The Prairie Schooner* (1956–1966). His second book of poems, *V-Letter and Other Poems*, was awarded the Pulitzer Prize in 1945. He also received the Bollingen Prize in 1969.

*Collected Poems 1940–1978* (1978); *The Wild Card: Selected Poems, Early and Late*, ed. Stanley Kunitz and David Ignatow (1998); *Selected Poems*, ed. John Updike (2003)

**Percy Bysshe Shelley (1792–1821)** was born in Sussex, England, and educated at University College, Oxford, where he was expelled for refusing to recant his pamphlet *The Necessity of Atheism*. In 1811 he married sixteen-year-old Harriet Westbrook. In 1813 he abandoned Harriet and moved to London, where he came under the influence of William Godwin. He fell in love with Godwin's daughter, Mary Wollstonecraft Godwin, future author of *Frankenstein*, and they eloped to Europe. Byron joined them in Switzerland and followed them to Italy. In 1819 he published *The Cenci* and in 1820 his renowned drama *Prometheus Unbound*. Shortly afterward he wrote many of his most celebrated lyrics. He drowned while sailing on the Gulf of Spezia.

*The Complete Poetry of Percy Bysshe Shelley*, ed. Donald H. Reiman and Neil Fraistat (2 vols. 2000–2004)

**Sir Philip Sidney (1554–86)** was born at Penshurst, in Kent, England, and educated at Shrewsbury School and Christ Church, Oxford. He was a zealous Protestant. In 1576 he became friendly with Walter Devereux, the first Earl of Essex, and Penelope, his daughter, to whom Sidney addressed the series of sonnets known as *Astrophil and Stella* (1591). He married the daughter of the courtier Sir Francis Walsingham and was knighted in 1583. Legendary as the quintessential English gentlemen, he was made governor of Flushing, an English possession, and fought for Protestantism in the Low Countries. He died of gangrene from a wound in his leg.

*The Poems of Sir Philip Sidney*, ed. William A. Ringler Jr. (1962); *An Apology for Poetry; or The Defence of Poesy*, ed. Geoffrey Shepherd (1965)

**Charles Simic (1938–)** was born in Belgrade, in former Yugoslavia, and moved with his family to the United States in 1953. They lived in and around Chicago until 1958. After service with the U.S. Army, he graduated from New York University. His book *The World Doesn't End* (1989) was awarded the Pulitzer Prize. He has received a Guggenheim Fellowship, a MacArthur Fellowship, and the Wallace Stevens Award. He is the Poet Laureate Consultant in Poetry to the Library of Congress and lives in New Hampshire.

*The Uncertain Certainty: Interviews, Essays, and Notes on Poetry* (1985); *Selected Poems, 1963–1983* (rev. ed. 1990); *The Voice at 3:00 A.M.: Selected Late and New Poems* (2003); *My Noiseless Entourage* (2005)

**Burns Singer (1928–1964)** was born in New York City and raised in Glasgow, Scotland. He loved both English and zoology but abandoned his studies after the suicide of his mother. After four years as a successful marine biologist, he became a freelance journalist in London. He was married to the American psychologist Marie Battle and remained an American citizen. His one volume of poems, *Still and All*, and his classic study of the British fishing industry, *Living Silver*, both appeared in 1957. He died of a heart attack in Plymouth at the age of thirty-six.

*The Collected Poems of Burns Singer*, ed. W. A. S. Keir (1970)

**Tom Sleigh** (1953–) was born in Mount Pleasant, Texas, and educated at the California Institute of the Arts, Evergreen State College, and Johns Hopkins University. He has received grants from the Guggenheim Foundation, the National Endowment for the Arts, and the Fine Arts Work Center in Provincetown. He teaches in the creative writing program at Hunter College in Manhattan.

*Interview with a Ghost: Essays* (2006); *Space Walk* (2007)

**Charlotte Smith** (1749–1806) was born in London, England. At the age of fifteen, she was contractually married to Benjamin Smith, the son of a wealthy merchant who soon lost everything. She began to write and publish poems to earn money while imprisoned with her husband for debt. Her book *Elegiac Sonnets* (1894) was an immediate success. Well known in her time as a novelist, she was a popular and widely read sonneteer.

*The Poems of Charlotte Smith*, ed. Stuart Curran (1993)

**Dave Smith** (1942–) was born in Portsmouth, Virginia, and educated at the University of Virginia, Southern Illinois University, and Ohio University. He has written more than twenty-five books. His many awards include Guggenheim, National Endowment for the Arts, and Lyndhurst fellowships. He taught for many years at Louisiana State University, where he coedited the *Southern Review*. He is the Elliot Coleman Professor of Poetry and chairman of the Writing Seminars at Johns Hopkins University.

*The Wick of Memory: New and Selected Poems, 1974–2000* (2000); *Little Boats, Unsalvaged: Poems, 1992–2004* (2005); *Hunting Men: Reflections on a Life in American Poetry* (2006)

**Elizabeth Smither** (1941–) was born in New Plymouth, New Zealand, where she still lives and works as a librarian. She was educated at Massey University and the Victoria University of Wellington. She has published twelve collections of poetry as well as novels, short stories, and a collection of journals. Her volume of selected poems, *The Tudor Style*, was published in 1993. She was New Zealand's Te Mata Poet Laureate.

*The Sea Between Us* (2003); *Different Kinds of Pleasure* (2006)

**W. D. Snodgrass** (1926–) was born in Wilkinsburg, Pennsylvania. He began studies at Geneva College before being drafted during World War II. He then went on to receive an MFA from the University of Iowa Writers' Workshop, where he studied with Robert Lowell. His first collection, *Heart's Needle* (1959), won the Pulitzer Prize in 1960. His other honors include an Ingram Merrill Award and fellowships from the Academy of American Poets, the Ford Foundation, and the Guggenheim Foundation.

*To Sound Like Yourself: Essays on Poetry* (2002); *Not for Specialists: New and Selected Poems* (2006)

**Robert Southey (1774–1843)** was born in Bristol, England, and educated at Westminster School and Balliol College, Oxford. Southey was a popular Romantic poet associated with the "Lake Poets," including his friends William Wordsworth and Samuel Taylor Coleridge, with whom he had an early political and writing partnership. His sequence "Poems on the Slave Trade" expresses his passionate objections to slavery. In 1813 he was appointed Poet Laureate.

*Robert Southey: Poetical Works, 1793–1810,* ed. Lynda Pratt with Tim Fulford and Daniel Roberts (5 vols. 2004)

**Edith Speers (1949–)** was born in British Columbia, Canada, and educated at Simon Fraser University, where she studied biochemistry before moving to Australia in 1974. She manages Esperance Press in Dover, Tasmania. She was awarded the Centenary Medal for community service in 2001.

*By Way of a Vessel* (1986); *Four Quarters: Poetry* (2001)

**Stephen Spender (1909–1995)** was born in London, England, and educated at University College, Oxford, where he was a friend and contemporary of Christopher Isherwood, W. H. Auden, and Louis MacNeice. Like Auden, Spender was a frequent visitor to Spain in 1937. He briefly joined the Communist Party, and his book *Poems* (1933) shows his commitment to politics. Spender later became disillusioned with extreme left activism. He was coeditor of the journals *Horizon* and *Encounter.* His autobiography, *World Within World* (1951), chronicles his growth and regrowth as a poet. He was knighted in 1983.

*New Collected Poems,* ed. Michael Brett (2004)

**Edmund Spenser (c. 1552–1599)** was born in London, England, and educated at Merchant Taylors' School and Pembroke Hall, Cambridge, where he was a "poor scholar." He served as secretary to several prominent men. He published *The Shepheardes Calender* in 1579 with a dedication to Sir Philip Sidney. Spenser lived for some years in Ireland, where he worked as a civil servant and acquired extensive lands. He began work on *The Faerie Queene* in 1579, intending to publish it in twelve books. He completed only six before he died, publishing the first three books in 1590 and the next three in 1596. He died in London.

*Edmund Spenser's Poetry: Authoritative Texts, Criticism,* ed. Hugh Maclean and Anne Lake Prescott (3rd ed. 1993)

**William Stafford (1914–1993)** was born in Hutchinson, Kansas, and educated at the University of Kansas and the University of Iowa. Stafford published his first collection, *Traveling Through the Dark* (1962), at the age of forty-eight; it won the National Book Award. He served as Consultant in Poetry to the Library of Congress (poet laureate) in 1975. He taught at Lewis and Clark College for over thirty years.

*The Way It Is: New & Selected Poems* (1998); *The Answers Are Inside the Mountains: Meditations on the Writing Life*, ed. Paul Merchant and Vincent Wixon (2003)

**George Starbuck (1931–1996)** was born in Columbus, Ohio, raised in Illinois and California, and educated at the University of Chicago and other schools. His first collection, *Bone Thoughts* (1960), was selected for the Yale Series of Younger Poets. A witty and formal poet, he referred to his sonnets as SLABS for Standard Length And Breadth Sonnets. He was twice married and had five children. He directed the writing programs at the University of Iowa and Boston University. He died in Tuscaloosa, Alabama.

*Bone Thoughts* (1960); *The Works: Poems Selected from Five Decades*, ed. Elizabeth A. Meese and Kathryn Starbuck (2003)

**C. K. Stead (1932–)** was born in Auckland, New Zealand, and educated at the University of Auckland and the University of Bristol. A critic, editor, and novelist, Stead was a professor of English at the University of Auckland for almost twenty years. He was made a Commander of the Order of the British Empire in 1985 for services to New Zealand literature, and he was elected a fellow of the Royal Society of Literature in 1995. He received the prestigious Creative New Zealand Michael King Writers' Fellowship in 2005.

*Straw Into Gold: Poems New & Selected* (1997); *The Writer at Work: Essays* (2000)

**Gerald Stern (1925–)** was born in Pittsburgh, Pennsylvania, and educated at the University of Pittsburgh. He served in the air corps and then taught in many colleges, most notably at the University of Iowa Writers' Workshop. His volume of poems *Lucky Life* (1977) was the Lamont Poetry Selection of the Academy of American Poets. His other books of poetry include *This Time: New and Selected Poems* (1998), which won the National Book Award. In 2006 he was elected a Chancellor of the Academy. He lives in Lambertville, New Jersey.

*Leaving Another Kingdom: Selected Poems* (1990); *What I Can't Bear Losing: Notes from a Life* (2003); *Everything Is Burning: Poems* (2005)

**Wallace Stevens (1879–1955)** was born in Reading, Pennsylvania, and educated at Harvard College. He entered New York Law School, gained admission to the New York State bar, and practiced, unsuccessfully, in New York. He then joined the legal staff of an insurance firm and eventually became a vice president of the Hartford Accident and Indemnity Company. His first collection of poetry, *Harmonium* (1923), was one of the great debuts in American poetry. He received the National Book Award twice, once for *The Auroras of Autumn* (1951) and once for *The Collected Poems of Wallace*

*Stevens* (1955), which also won the Pulitzer Prize. He died in Hartford, Connecticut.

   *Letters of Wallace Stevens*, ed. Holly Stevens (repr. 1996); *Collected Poetry and Prose*, ed. Frank Kermode and Joan Richardson (1997)

**Susan Stewart** (1952–) was born in York, Pennsylvania, and educated at Dickinson College, Johns Hopkins University, and the University of Pennsylvania. She is the author of four books of poems, including *Columbarium* (2003), which won the National Book Critics Circle Award. She has also written several books of literary and art criticism, including *Poetry and the Fate of the Senses*, which received the Phi Beta Kappa 2002 Christian Gauss Award for Literary Criticism. Both a Guggenheim and a MacArthur Fellow, she is a professor of English at Princeton University.

   *The Forest (1995); The Open Studio: Essays on Art and Aesthetics* (2005)

**Trumbull Stickney** (1874–1904) was born in Geneva, Switzerland. His parents traveled widely and he grew up in many cities and countries. Stickney was educated at Harvard College and then at the Université Paris Sorbonne, where he received his doctorate. He published his first book, *Dramatic Verses*, in Boston in 1902. He died there of a brain tumor at the age of thirty.

   *The Poems of Trumbull Stickney*, ed. Amberys R. Whittle (1972)

**Alfonsina Storni** (1892–1938) was born in Sala Capriasca, Switzerland, and raised in Argentina. She was forced to abandon her studies at an early age. She lived most of her life in Buenos Aires and divided her time between writing poems and teaching. She published eleven books in her lifetime and wrote numerous articles and essays on women's rights. She received the first Municipal Poetry Prize and the second National Literature Prize in 1920 for her book *Languidez*. Isolated and suffering from breast cancer, Storni committed suicide near Mar del Plata, Argentina.

   *Selected Poems*, ed. Marion Freeman, trans. Marion Freeman, Mary Crow, Jim Normington, and Kay Short (1987)

**Mark Strand** (1934–) was born on Canada's Prince Edward Island and was educated at Antioch College; Yale University, where he studied to be a painter; and the University of Iowa. He has taught at the University of Utah, Johns Hopkins University, the University of Chicago, and Columbia University. He is a noted translator and anthologist and has written short stories, books for children, and art criticism, including a study of Edward Hopper. His honors include the Bollingen Prize, a Guggenheim Fellowship, a MacArthur Fellowship, and the Pulitzer Prize. He is a former Poet Laureate Consultant in Poetry to the Library of Congress and lives in New York City.

*Selected Poems* (1980); *The Making of a Poem: A Norton Anthology of Poetic Forms*, coed. with Eavan Boland (2000); *Man and Camel: Poems* (2006)

**Sir John Suckling (1609–1642)** was born in Whitton, Middlesex, England. He matriculated at Trinity College, Cambridge, in 1623 but left without taking a degree in 1626. A Cavalier poet and dramatist, Suckling's writing was lyrical, fanciful, and occasionally profane. He was known as a gamester and is credited with having invented the game of cribbage. He supported the cause of Charles I, was knighted in 1630, and became a member of the Long Parliament.

*The Works of Sir John Suckling*, ed. Thomas Clayton and L. A. Beaurline (2 vols. 1971)

**Algernon Charles Swinburne (1837–1909)** was born in London, England, but spent most of his boyhood on the Isle of Wight. He was educated at Balliol College, Oxford, where he became friends with Dante Gabrel Rossetti, Edward Burne-Jones, and William Morris. He joined the Pre-Raphaelite movement and coined the phrase "art for art's sake." His second book, *Atalanta in Calydon* (1865), revealed his mastery of form and won him great renown at an early age. Swinburne's masochistic tendencies, his chronic epilepsy, and his severe alcoholism brought him close to death in 1878, but he was nursed back to health by Theodore Watts-Dunton, who cared for him for the next thirty years.

*Major Poems and Selected Prose*, ed. Jerome McGann and Charles Sligh (2004)

**John Addington Symonds (1840–1893)** was born in London, England, and educated at Balliol College, Oxford. Robert Louis Stevenson described Symonds "as the best of talkers." A major figure in the underground homosexual world of Victorian England, Symonds wrote much poetry and nonfiction, including *Renaissance in Italy*, which was published in seven volumes between 1875 and 1886.

*The Memoirs of John Addington Symonds*, ed. Phyllis Grosskurth (1984)

**Dorothea Tanning (1910–)** was born in Galesburg, Illinois. After studying briefly at the Art Institute of Chicago, she moved to New York City and learned about art by going to galleries. She later moved to Paris and lived there for twenty-eight years. Influenced by Surrealism, she became the fourth wife of the German painter Max Ernst in 1946 and was herself a noted painter and printmaker. She started to write poetry in her old age and has published one collection.

*Between Lives: An Artist and Her World* (2001); *A Table of Content: Poems* (2004)

**Allen Tate** (1899–1979) was born in Winchester, Kentucky, and attended Vanderbilt University, where, along with Robert Penn Warren and John Crowe Ransom, he became part of the Southern Fugitives. He edited *The Fugitive* and *The Sewanee Review,* and wrote biographies of Stonewall Jackson and Jefferson Davis. He was Consultant in Poetry to the Library of Congress (poet laureate) from 1944 to 1945. He taught for many years at the University of Minnesota. He died in Nashville, Tennessee.

    *Essays of Four Decades* (1968); *Collected Poems* (1970)

**Sara Teasdale** (1884–1933) was born in St. Louis, Missouri, and educated privately. She became part of Harriet Monroe's *Poetry* magazine circle in Chicago, though after she married Ernst Filsinger in 1914, she moved to New York City. Her books include *Sonnets to Duse, and Other Poems* (1907), *Rivers to the Sea* (1915), and *Love Songs* (1917), which won the Columbia University Poetry Society Prize, later named the Pulitzer Prize for poetry. She divorced in 1929 and lived the remainder of her life as a semi-invalid. She committed suicide in 1933. Her final collection, *Strange Victory*, appeared posthumously the same year.

    *Collected Poems of Sara Teasdale* (1967)

**Alfred, Lord Tennyson** (1809–1892) was born in Somersby, England, and educated at Trinity College, Cambridge. His early poems, such as "Mariana" and "The Kraken," are some of his most loved, and he published *Poems, Chiefly Lyrical* in 1830. He was plagued by melancholia through most of his later life. He was stricken by the death of his college friend Arthur Hallam and thereafter composed his masterpiece *In Memoriam,* which he wrote over a period of seventeen years. When it was finally published in 1850, it brought him great public recognition and enough money to marry Emily Sellwood. He succeeded William Wordsworth as Poet Laureate in 1850.

    *The Poems of Tennyson,* ed. Christopher Ricks (1969)

**Ana Enriqueta Terán** (1918–) was born in Valera, in the state of Trujillo, Venezuela. She has published more than a dozen collections of poetry. She served as her country's cultural attaché in Argentina during the Peron era. She has lived in New York and traveled widely in Europe. She was named Doctora Honoris Causa by the University of Carabobo and in 1989 was awarded her country's highest literary honor, the Premio Nacional de Literatura. She is widely considered Venezuela's greatest poet, but her work, only recently translated, is virtually unknown to the English-speaking world.

    *The Poetess Counts to 100 and Bows Out: Selected Poems,* trans. Marcel Smith (2003)

**Lam Thi My Da** (1949–) was born in Le Thuy District, Quang Binh Province, in central Vietnam, and educated at the Writer's College in Vietnam and Gorky University in Moscow. The author of poetry and several childrens' books, she has twice been awarded honors from the Vietnamese Writers' Association.

*Green Rice: Poems*, trans. Martha Collins and Thuy Dinh (2005)

**Dylan Thomas (1914–1953)** was born in Swansea, Wales, and educated at the Swansea Grammar School. He left school in 1931 to embark on a literary career and published his first book, *18 Poems*, when he was twenty. He worked as a broadcaster, prose writer, poet, and lecturer. He traveled and gave readings widely in the United Kingdom, Europe, and the United States. His most famous work, *Under Milk Wood*, was recorded in New York before his death. He died from alcoholism in a New York hospital.

*The Collected Prose of Dylan Thomas* (1969); *The Poems of Dylan Thomas*, ed. Daniel Jones (rev. ed. 2003)

**Edward Thomas (1878–1917)** was born in London, England, and educated at Lincoln College, Oxford. He worked hard as a freelancer to support his family and began writing poetry in 1914 at the behest of his friend Robert Frost, who strongly encouraged him. The next year he enlisted as a private soldier in the British army and was killed in France on Easter Monday of 1917. Thomas's *Poems* (1917) was published under his pseudonym, Edward Eastaway. *Last Poems* (1918) and *Collected Poems* (1920) appeared under his own name. His wife Helen published two memoirs of their life together.

*The Poems of Edward Thomas* (2003)

**Mary Tighe (1772–1810)**, née Blackford, was born in Dublin, Ireland. At twenty-one she contracted what proved to be an unhappy marriage to her cousin Henry Tighe. In 1805 she published her epic poem *Pysche; or, The Legend of Love*, which gained her wide visibility. John Keats was one of her great admirers. After her death, her reputation became obscured.

*The Collected Poems and Journals of Mary Tighe*, ed. Harriet Kramer Linkin (2005)

**Frederick Goddard Tuckerman (1821–1873)** was born in Boston, Massachusetts, and educated at Harvard College and Harvard Law School. In the late 1840s he retired from the law and devoted himself to the study of botany, astronomy, and poetry on his family estate in Greenfield, Massachusetts. He began writing poems after the early death of his wife and published only one collection in his lifetime, *Poems* (1860).

*Complete Poems*, ed. N. Scott Momaday (1965)

**John Updike (1932–)** was born in Shillington, Pennsylvania, and educated at Harvard College. He spent a year at the Ruskin School of Drawing and

Fine Art in Oxford. From 1955 to 1957 he was a member of the staff of *The New Yorker*. He has four children and has lived in Massachusetts since 1957. A renowned American writer, he has won every major literary prize, including the National Book Award and the Pulitzer Prize. His writing includes fiction, poetry, literary and art criticism, memoir, and short stories.

*Collected Poems, 1953–1993* (1993); *Americana and Other Poems* (2001); *Terrorist* (2006)

**Constance Urdang (1922–1996)** was born in New York City and educated at Smith College and the University of Iowa. Urdang worked as a military intelligence analyst for the U.S. Department of the Army and taught at several universities. She was married to the poet Donald Finkel for forty years. Her honors included a grant from the National Endowment for the Arts and the Delmore Schwartz Memorial Poetry Award.

*Only the World* (1983); *Alternative Lives* (1990)

**Jean Valentine (1934–)** was born in Chicago, Illinois, and educated at Radcliffe College. She won the Yale Younger Poets prize for her first collection, *Dream Barker and Other Poems* (1965). Her volume of new and collected poems received the National Book Award in 2004. She has lived for most of her life in New York City.

*Door in the Mountain: New and Collected Poems, 1965–2003* (2004)

**Paul Valéry (1871–1945)** was born in Sète, France, and studied law at Montpelier before going to Paris in 1892. He published a few small pieces but then stopped writing poetry for fifteen years. In 1917 the poem "La jeune parque," which he had been working on for years, made him famous. By 1923 he was able to turn completely to literature, in particular to the investigation of philosophical problems. Five volumes of critical essays appeared between 1924 and 1944. He was elected to the Académie in 1925, and from 1937 until his death in Paris he held the specially created chair of poetry at the Sorbonne.

*Selected Writings of Paul Valéry* (1964); *Paul Valery: An Anthology*, selected by James R. Lawler (1977)

**César Vallejo (1892–1938)** was born in the mountain community of Santiago de Chuco, Peru, and educated at Trujillo University. His first book, *Los heraldos negros* (*The Black Heralds*), appeared in 1919. While visiting his hometown, he was unfairly imprisoned for one hundred and five days, an experience that embittered him. In 1922 he published *Trilce* and the next year left Peru for good. He settled in Paris, met the artist Georgette Philipart, whom he married, and became fervently committed to social justice. He made three trips to Russia and founded the Peruvian Socialist

Party with other expatriates. He was deeply involved with the Spanish Civil War and wrote *España, aparte de mí este cáliz* (*Spain, Take This Cup From Me*; 1939). He died on Good Friday.

    *Neruda and Vallejo: Selected Poems*, ed. Robert Bly, trans. Robert Bly, John Knoeple, and James Wright (1971); *The Complete Poetry*, ed. and trans. Clayton Eshleman (2007)

**Mona Van Duyn** (1921–2004) was born in Waterloo, Iowa, and educated at Northern Iowa University and the University of Iowa. In 1943 she married Jarvis Thurston. *To See, To Take* (1970) won the National Book Award and *Near Changes* (1990) received the Pulitzer Prize. She was also awarded a Guggenheim Fellowship, the Bollingen Prize, the Hart Crane Memorial Poetry Award, and the Ruth Lilly Poetry Prize. She was the Poet Laureate Consultant in Poetry to the Library of Congress from 1992 to 1993.

    *If It Be Not I: Collected Poems, 1959–1982* (1993)

**Lope de Vega** (1562–1635) was born in Madrid, Spain. He studied at the University of Alcalá. He had many love affairs and two marriages. He took part in the Invincible Armada, served as secretary to different noblemen, and was ordained a priest in 1614. An extremely prolific playwright and poet, Vega's accomplishments were second only to those of Miguel de Cervantes. Vega is revered as the most influential dramatist of Spain's Golden Age. He wrote more than two thousand plays and is credited for establishing the genre of the *comedia*. His poetry collections include *Rimas humanas* (1602) and *Rimas sacras* (1614). He wrote an estimated three thousand sonnets.

    *Three Spanish Golden Age Plays*, trans. Gwynne Edwards (2005); *The Golden Age: Poems of the Spanish Renaissance*, trans. Edith Grossman (2006)

**Paul Verlaine** (1844–1896) was born in Metz, France, and educated at the lycée in Paris. He then entered the civil service. He was married to Mathilde Mauté and had a son with her, but abandoned the relationship for a stormy affair with Arthur Rimbaud. It ended when Verlaine shot Rimbaud and injured him in the wrist. He spent eighteen months in jail. Afterward Verlaine converted to Catholicism. His last years were marred by alcoholism and poverty. Elected "Prince of Poets" by his peers, Verlaine, who was first associated with the Parnassian poets, came to be considered one of the most influential Symbolists of the nineteenth century.

    *One Hundred and One Poems*, trans. Norman R. Shapiro (1999); *Selected Poems*, trans. Martin Sorrell (1999)

**Jones Very** (1813–1880) was born in Salem, Massachusetts, and educated at Harvard College, where he was appointed a tutor in Greek. In 1837 he had a mystical revelation and began writing sonnets, which he declared were communicated to him by the Lord. In 1838 he resigned from Harvard and entered an asylum. He published one volume of prose and poetry, *Essays and Poems* (1839), which was admired by the Transcendentalists, though it never gained a widespread fame or readership.

   *Jones Very: The Complete Poems*, ed. Helen R. Deese (1993)

**Ellen Bryant Voigt (1943–)** was born in Danville, Virginia, and educated at Converse College and the University of Iowa. The recipient of Guggenheim and National Endowment for the Arts fellowships, she developed the nation's first low-residency creative writing program at Goddard College. She also founded the low-residency program at Warren Wilson College. She was the Vermont State Poet from 1999 to 2003 and lives in Marshfield, Vermont.

   *The Flexible Lyric* (1999); *Messenger: New and Selected Poems, 1976–2006* (2007)

**Derek Walcott (1930–)** was born in the town of Castries in St. Lucia, one of the Windward Islands in the Lesser Antilles. After studying at the University of the West Indies, Jamaica, he moved to Trinidad, where he and his twin brother established a theater company. Walcott's breakthrough came with *In a Green Night: Poems 1948–1960* (1962). For many years he has divided his time between the West Indies, where he has a home, and Boston University, where he teaches literature and creative writing. He is the author of thirteen collections of poetry, seven collections of plays, and a book of essays. He was awarded the Nobel Prize in Literature in 1992.

   *Collected Poems, 1948–1984* (1986); *Omeros* (1990); *Selected Poems*, ed. Edward Baugh (2007)

**Ronald Wallace (1945–)** was born in Cedar Rapids, Iowa, and educated at the College of Wooster and the University of Michigan. Wallace teaches at the University of Wisconsin–Madison, where he codirects the creative writing program. His book *The Uses of Adversity* (1998) is a collection of one hundred sonnets.

   *Quick Bright Things: Stories* (2000); *Long for This World: New and Selected Poems* (2003)

**Sylvia Townsend Warner (1893–1978)** was born in Harrow on the Hill, England, and educated privately at home. She was an accomplished musicologist and a prolific writer, who published widely in England and the United States, where she was a favorite of *The New Yorker*. Her novels include *Lolly Willowes* (1926), *Mr. Fortune's Maggot* (1927), and *The True Heart* (1929). She lived in rural Norfolk and in Dorset with her partner Valentine Ackland, who died in 1969.

*Selected Poems* (1985); *The Element of Lavishness: The Letters of Sylvia Townsend Warner and William Maxwell 1938–1978*, ed. Michael Steinman (2003)

**Robert Penn Warren** (1905–1989) was born in Guthrie, Kentucky, and educated at Vanderbilt University, where he was the youngest member of the Fugitives; the University of California; and New College, Oxford, where he was a Rhodes Scholar. He taught at Vanderbilt University, Louisiana State University, the University of Minnesota, and Yale University. He coauthored *Understanding Poetry* (1938), which heavily influenced New Criticism. His celebrated novel *All The King's Men* (1946) dealt with Southern politics and won the Pulitzer Prize. He became the only writer to win Pulitzers for both fiction and poetry; *Promises: Poems 1956–1958* (1957) and *Now and Then* (1979) also won Pulitzer Prizes. A MacArthur Fellow, he served as the Consultant in Poetry to the Library of Congress (poet laureate) from 1944 to 1945.

*The Collected Poems of Robert Penn Warren*, ed. John Burt (1998); *Conversations with Robert Penn Warren*, ed. Gloria L. Cronin and Ben Siegel (2005)

**Rosanna Warren** (1953– ) was born in Fairfield, Connecticut, to the writers Eleanor Clark and Robert Penn Warren. She was educated at Yale University, where she studied painting, and Johns Hopkins University, where she received an MA from the Writing Seminars program. Her book *Stained Glass* (1993) won the James Laughlin Award from the Academy of American Poets. Warren's other awards include the Peter I. B. Lavan Younger Poets Award, the Witter Bynner Poetry Prize, and a Guggenheim Fellowship. She teaches at Boston University.

*Each Leaf Shines Separate* (1984); *Departure* (2003)

**Thomas Warton, the Younger** (1728–1790) was born in Basingstoke, Hampshire, England, and educated at Trinity College, Oxford. Warton's main contribution was to history and literary criticism. He published *The History of English Poetry* in three volumes, bringing them out from 1774 to 1781. He was also Poet Laureate of England from 1785 to 1790. His most highly regarded poems were his sonnets.

*Silver Poets of the Eighteenth Century*, ed. Arthur Pollard (1976); *The Poets Laureate*, Kenneth Hopkins (1954)

**Thomas Watson** (c. 1557–1592) was born in London, England, and possibly educated at Oxford. He first gained fame as a writer of Latin poems. When he began to write in English, he was widely read for his asymmetric sonnets that were eighteen lines long. His posthumous book *The Tears of*

*Fancie, or Love Disdained* (1593) consists of sixty fourteen-line sonnets. He was buried in the Church of St. Bartholomew the Less.

*The Complete Works of Thomas Watson (1556–1592)*, ed. Dana F. Sutton (2 vols. 1997)

**Theodore Watts-Dunton (1832–1914)** was born in St. Ives, Huntingdonshire, England, and educated as a naturalist. Watts-Dunton is now chiefly remembered as caretaker to Algernon Charles Swinburne. He worked as a lawyer and was a close friend of Dante Gabriel Rossetti and Lord Alfred Tennyson.

*The Coming of Love* (1897); *Old Familiar Faces* (1916)

**Ian Wedde (1946–)** was born in Blenheim, New Zealand. He spent his childhood in East Pakistan and England as well as New Zealand. He graduated from the University of Auckland, traveled widely, and lived for a year in Amman, Jordan. He coedited *The Penguin Book of New Zealand Verse*. In addition to poetry, he has also published novels, short stories, and a substantial body of literary and art criticism. From 1994 to 2004, he served as Concept Leader Humanities at the Museum of New Zealand Te Papa Tongarewa.

*Tales of Gotham City* (1984); *Making Ends Meet: Essays & Talks 1992–2004* (2005)

**Jane West (1758–1852)**, née Ilife, was born in London, England. She was entirely self-educated and began to write poetry at the age of thirteen. She was married to Thomas West, a yeoman farmer of Northamptonshire, and had three children. A novelist and playwright as well as a poet, West was a political conservative who nonetheless argued for expanded education for women.

*The Advantages of Education, or, the History of Maria Williams: A Tale for Misses and Their Mammas* (2 vols. 1793); *Alicia de Lacy: An Historical Romance* (4 vols. 1814)

**John Brooks Wheelwright (1897–1940)** was born in Boston, Massachusetts, to a family with a Brahmin background. He studied at Harvard College and later associated with avant-garde poets in New York City. A fierce Trotskyite, he was purged from the Socialist Party in 1937 and then helped to found the Socialist Workers Party. His sonnet sequence *Mirrors of Venus* was published in 1938.

*Collected Poems of John Wheelwright*, ed. Alvin H. Rosenfeld (1972)

**Walt Whitman (1819–1885)** was born on Long Island and raised in Brooklyn, New York. He left school at the age of eleven and worked as an office boy, a printer's apprentice, and an itinerant schoolteacher before establishing himself as a journalist and editor. In 1855 he published the first edition of *Leaves of Grass*, which he continued to revise and republish throughout his life. During the Civil War he worked as an unofficial nurse to Northern and Southern soldiers in Washington, D.C. After the war he became a clerk in the Indian Bureau of the Department of the Interior, but was dismissed on the grounds that *Leaves of Grass* was immoral. His other books include *Drum-Taps* (1865) and *Specimen Days* (1882). He spent the last nineteen years of his life in Camden, New Jersey.

*Poetry and Prose*, ed. Justin Kaplan (1996)

**John Greenleaf Whittier (1807–1892)** was born into a Quaker family near Haverhill, Massacusetts. He received little formal education. Whittier was an outspoken abolitionist, and he wrote many patriotic poems as well. His book *Snow-Bound* (1866) made him famous. He was editor of the *New England Weekly Review* and helped found the *Atlantic Monthly*. The seven-volume Riverside edition of his works, *The Writings of John Greenleaf Whittier*, was published from 1888 to 1889.

*Complete Writings of John Greenleaf Whittier* (7 vols. 1894); *Selected Poems*, ed. Brenda Wineapple (2004)

**Richard Wilbur (1921–)** was born in New York City and educated at Amherst College and Harvard University. He succeeded Robert Penn Warren as Consultant in Poetry to the Library of Congress (poet laureate). He is known not only for his poetry but also for his elegant translations from the French. *Things of This World* (1957) won the National Book Award and the Pulitzer Prize. He won a second Pulitzer Prize for *New and Collected Poems* in 1989. He has also won the Bollingen Prize and the Gold Medal for Poetry from the American Academy of Arts and Letters.

*The Beautiful Changes and Other Poems* (1947); *Things of This World: Poems* (1956); *The Catbird's Song: Prose Pieces, 1963–1995* (1997); *Collected Poems 1943–2004* (2004)

**Ella Wheeler Wilcox (1850–1919)** was born in Johnstown, Wisconsin. She was educated at home and spent one unhappy year at the University of Wisconsin. She started writing poetry at an early age and was known in her home state by the time she graduated from high school. Wilcox practiced Theosophy with her husband, and both had an extremely strong interest in the concept of life after death. Her collection *Poems of Passion* (1883), which was initially rejected because of its erotic content, sold 60,000 copies in two years. She wrote forty-six books and remained an extremely popular poet during her lifetime.

*Collected Poems of Ella Wheeler Wilcox* (1924); *The Best of Ella Wheeler Wilcox*, ed. Lady Lalique L'Endell (1971)

**Oscar Wilde (1854–1900)** was born in Dublin, Ireland, and educated at Trinity College, Dublin, and Magdalen College, Oxford. He was a disciple of Walter Pater and the leading spokesman for Aestheticism. He married Constance Lloyd and they had two sons. He lectured in America, published *The Picture of Dorian Gray* (1891), and wrote the plays that made his reputation, including *The Importance of Being Earnest* (1895). His relationship with Alfred Douglas led to his trial on charges of homosexuality, then illegal in Britain. He was sentenced to two years hard labor for the crime of sodomy. Two remarkable works, *The Ballad of Reading Gaol* (1898) and *De Profundis* (1949), were the outcome of the scandal and imprisonment that ended his career. He died in Paris and is buried in Père Lachaise cemetery.

    *The Complete Works of Oscar Wilde*, Vol. 1, *Poems and Poems in Prose*, ed. Karl Beckson (2000)

**C. K. Williams (1936–)** was born in Newark, New Jersey, and educated at Bucknell University and the University of Pennsylvania. His books of poetry include *Flesh and Blood* (1987), which received the National Book Critics Circle Award; *Repair* (1999), which won the Pulitzer Prize; and *The Singing* (2003), which garnered the National Book Award. Williams teaches at Princeton University and lives part of the year in France.

    *Poems, 1963–1983* (1988); *Collected Poems* (2006)

**Miller Williams (1930–)** was born in Hoxie, Arkansas, and educated at the University of Arkansas. He wrote the inaugural poem for Bill Clinton's second-term presidential inauguration. Among his many honors are the Amy Lowell Poetry Traveling Fellowship and the Rome Prize. He teaches at the University of Arkansas, and is the founding director of University of Arkansas Press.

    *Some Jazz a While: Collected Poems* (1999)

**William Carlos Williams (1883–1963)** was born in Rutherford, New Jersey. In 1906 he earned an MD from the University of Pennsylvania, where he became a lifelong friend of Ezra Pound and met H.D. (Hilda Doolittle). Williams studied pediatrics in Leipzig for a year and then returned to Rutherford, where he practiced general medicine for the rest of his life. He married Florence ("Flossie") Herman and they had two sons. Williams called for a distinctly American art, which he fulfilled in such books as *Spring and All* (1923); *In the American Grain* (1925), an essay collection; and *Paterson* (1946–1958), his five-volume epic. He received the Gold Medal for Poetry, the Bollingen Prize, and the Pulitzer Prize, which he was awarded posthumously for his last book, *Pictures from Brueghel* (1962).

    *Autobiography* (1951); *Selected Essays* (1954); *The Collected Poems of William Carlos Williams*, Vol. I, *1909–1939*, ed. A. Walton Litz and Christopher MacGowan (1986); *The Collected Poems of William Carlos Williams,* Vol. II, *1939–1962,* ed. Christopher MacGowan (1988)

**Yvor Winters (1900–1968)** was born in Chicago, Illinois. While studying at the University of Chicago, he was diagnosed with tuberculosis and relocated to Santa Fe, New Mexico, for his health. All his early poems were written at a sanitarium. He attended the University of Colorado and in 1926 married the poet and novelist Janet Lewis. He received his PhD from Stanford University, where he remained for the rest of his writing and teaching life. Winters became well known as an essayist and critic; his criticism emphasized the moral content of art. His honors include a National Institute of Arts and Letters Award as well as a Guggenheim Fellowship. His *Collected Poems* was published in 1952.

*In Defense of Reason* (1947); *Collected Poems* (rev. ed. 1960); *Selected Poems,* ed. Thom Gunn (2003)

**David Wojahn (1953– )** was born in St. Paul, Minnesota, and educated at the University of Minnesota and the University of Arizona. He has published seven books of poems and coedited the *Collected Poems* of his late wife, Lynda Hull. He has received fellowships from the Guggenheim Foundation and the National Endowment for the Arts, among others. He teaches at Virginia Commonwealth University.

*Interrogation Palace: New and Selected Poems, 1982–2004* (2006)

**William Wordsworth (1770–1850)** was born in Cockermouth, England, and educated at St. John's College, Cambridge. Wordsworth visited France as a young man and was strongly influenced by the euphoria of the French Revolution. He fell in love with Annette Vallon, but shortly after their daughter was born, he went back to England and did not return for many years, over which time they grew estranged. In 1795 he received a legacy and settled down in Racedown, Dorset, with his beloved sister, Dorothy. In 1798 he and Samuel Taylor Coleridge published *Lyrical Ballads,* possibly the most important single book of poems since the Renaissance. That same year he began his autobiographical masterpiece *The Prelude,* which he completed in 1805 but revised throughout his life. Over fifty years he wrote more than five hundred sonnets. In 1802 he married Mary Hutchinson. In 1843 he succeeded Robert Southey as Poet Laureate.

*The Major Works: Including The Prelude,* ed. Stephen Gill (2000); *Selected Poetry,* ed. Mark Van Doren and David Bromwich (2002)

**James Wright (1927–1980)** was born in Martins Ferry, Ohio. He served with the U.S. Army in Japan. Afterward he attended Kenyon College, where he studied under John Crowe Ransom, and later continued his studies at the

University of Washington, where he studied with Theodore Roethke. He went on to teach at the University of Minnesota, Macalester College, and Hunter College. His *Collected Poems* (1971) was awarded the Pulitzer Prize.

*The Branch Will Not Break* (1963); *Shall We Gather at the River* (1968); *This Journey* (1982); *Above the River: The Complete Poems* (1990)

**Judith Wright** (1915–2000) was born in Armidale, New South Wales, in a remote part of Australia. She lived so far from the nearest school that the department of education prepared a correspondence course for her until she was twelve years of age. Later she attended the University of Sydney. In addition to her poetry, she wrote short stories, essays, and books for children. She was active in both the antiwar and the conservationist movement in Australia.

*Phantom Dwelling* (1985); *Collected Poems 1942–1985* (1994)

**Mary Wroth** (1586–1651) was born into an aristocratic family. She was the niece of Sir Philip Sidney. Her arranged marriage to Sir Robert Wroth was unhappy, and after his death she had two children by her lover and cousin, William Herbert, third Earl of Pembroke. Her sonnet sequence *Pamphilia to Amphilanthus* was appended to her prose romance *The Countess of Mountgomery's Urania* (1621), the first long work of fiction by an English woman. This bold work caused a scandal because of its thinly veiled allusions to well-known figures in the Jacobean court.

*The Poems of Lady Mary Wroth*, ed. Josephine A. Roberts (1983); *The First Part of the Countess of Montgomery's Urania*, ed. Josephine A. Roberts (1995); *The Second Part of the Countess of Montgomery's Urania*, ed. Suzanne Gossett, Janel M. Mueller, and Josephine A. Roberts (1999)

**Thomas Wyatt** (1503–1542) was born at Allingham Castle, Kent, England, and educated at St. John's College, Cambridge. He married Elizabeth Brooke but soon separated from her. He held various positions at court and served on diplomatic missions in France, Spain, and Italy. Wyatt served as a courtier and was knighted in 1535. He was twice imprisoned. His second imprisonment has sometimes been connected to the fall of Henry VIII's second wife, Anne Boleyn, who was rumored to have been Wyatt's mistress. He again fell from royal favor in 1541, when he was accused of treason, but regained his status. Three years later his son, Thomas Wyatt ("the younger"), was hanged for treason. Wyatt introduced the Petrarchan sonnet into English. Along with Surrey's, his poems were published by the printer Richard Tottel in *Songs and Sonettes* (1557), an anthology that came to be known as *Tottel's Miscellany*.

*The Poetry of Sir Thomas Wyatt*, ed. E. M. W. Tillyard (1929); *The Essential Wyatt*, ed. W. S. Merwin (1989)

**Elinor Wylie** (1885–1928), née Hoyt, was born in Somerville, New Jersey, to a wealthy and prominent family. Wylie was educated at home and moved in fashionable circles. Her most notable collection of poems is *Nets to Catch the Wind* (1921). After an unhappy marriage to Philip Hichborn, with whom she had a son, she eloped to England with her second husband, Horace Wylie, whom she divorced in 1923. From 1922 until her death, she lived in Greenwich Village. In 1923 she married William Rose Benét, a poet and editor, who edited her *Collected Poems* (1932) and *Collected Prose* (1933), and wrote a study of her work, *The Prose and Poetry of Elinor Wylie* (1934). She also wrote eight novels.

*Collected Poems of Elinor Wylie*, ed. William Rose Benét (1932)

**W. B. Yeats** (1865–1939) was born in Dublin, Ireland, and educated at the Dublin Metropolitan School of Art. He spent his childhood and early manhood in Sligo, where he was influenced by the Irish country people; in Dublin, where he was influenced by the currents of Irish nationalism; and in London, where he met the key poets of his time. He sought to rejuvenate Irish literature and culture, fell in love with Maud Gonne, who persistently refused to marry him, and studied mystical philosophy. He cofounded the Abbey Theatre, worked as a dramatist, and got involved in various public controversies. He married George Hyde-Lees, whose automatic writing stimulated him to work out the system that he developed in *A Vision* (1925, 1937). They had two children. In 1922 he became a senator of the Irish Free State and in the following year was awarded the Nobel Prize in Literature.

*The Poems: A New Edition*, ed. Richard J. Finneran (1983); *The Plays*, ed. David R. Clark and E. Rosalind (2001)

# Permissions Acknowledgments

Mazur. Reprinted by permission of David R. Godine, Publisher, Inc. Copyright 1982 by Charles Baudelaire.

JAMES K. BAXTER, "Jerusalem Sonnets: #10," from *Collected Poems of James K. Baxter*. Reprinted by permission of The James K. Baxter Trust.

JOACHIM DU BELLAY, "Heureux Qui, Comme Ulysse, a Fait un Beau Voyage," from *Collected Earlier Poems* by Anthony Hecht, copyright © 1990 by Anthony E. Hecht. Used by permission of Alfred A. Knopf, a division of Random House, Inc., and Carcanet Press Ltd.

GUISEPPE BELLI, "Night of Terror" reprinted by permission of Louisiana State University Press from *Sonnets of Guiseppe Belli* translated by Miller Williams. Translation copyright © 1981 by Miller Williams.

STEPHEN BERG, "My Bohemian Life," from *Rimbaud Version and Inventions*. Reprinted by permission of Sheep Meadow Press.

TED BERRIGAN, From The Sonnets: #L ("I like to beat people up"); LXXII ("A Sonnet for Dick Gallup") from *The Collected Poems of Ted Berrigan*. Copyright © 2005, Alice Notley. Reprinted by permission of University of California Press.

WENDELL BERRY, "The Venus of Botticelli" from *Entries* by Wendell Berry, copyright © 1994 by Wendell Berry. Used by permission of Pantheon Books, a division of Random House, Inc.

JOHN BERRYMAN, "Sonnets to Chris: #117" from *Collected Poems 1937–1971* by John Berryman Copyright © 1989 by Kate Donahue Berryman. Reprinted by permission of Farrar, Straus and Giroux, LLC, and Faber and Faber Ltd.

FRANK BIDART, "Self-Portrait, 1969" from *In the Western Night: Collected Poems 1965–1990* by Frank Bidart. Copyright © 1990 by Frank Bidart. Reprinted by permission of Farrar, Straus and Giroux, LLC, and Carcanet Press Limited.

ELIZABETH BISHOP, "Sonnet" ("Caught—the bubble...") from *The Complete Poems 1927–1979* by Elizabeth Bishop. Reprinted by permission of Farrar, Straus and Giroux, LLC.

EDMUND BLUNDEN, "Vlamertinghe: Passing the Chateau, July 1917" from *Selected Poems*, 1986. Reprinted by permission of Carcanet Press Limited.

LOUISE BOGAN, "Single Sonnet" from *The Blue Estuaries: Poems 1923–1968* by Louise Bogan. Reprinted by permission of Farrar, Straus and Giroux, LLC.

JORGE LUIS BORGES, "A Poet of the Thirteenth Century," translated by Alan S. Trueblood, from *Selected Poems* by Jorge Luis Borges, edited by Alexander Coleman, copyright © 1999 by Maria Kodama. Used by permission of Viking Penguin, a division of Penguin Group (USA) and by Penguin Group UK.

EDGAR BOWERS, "In the Last Circle," from *Collected Poems* by Edgar Bowers, copyright © 1997 by Edgar Bowers. Used by permission of Alfred A. Knopf, a division of Random House, Inc.

ELIZABETH BREWSTER, "Death by Drowning" by Elizabeth Brewster is reprinted from *Selected Poems* by permission of Oberon Press.

R. F. BRISSENDEN, "Samuel Johnson Talking." Reprinted by permission of Australian National University.

PAUL GOODMAN, From "Sonnets, 1, 3 (Foster excellence. If I do not)" from *Collected Poems* by Paul Goodman. Reprinted by permission Sally Goodman.

ROBERT GRAVES, "In Her Praise" from *Complete Poems in One Volume* by Robert Graves. Reprinted by permission of Carcanet Press Limited.

ALAN GOULD, "An Interrogator's Opening Remarks" by Alan Gould. Reprinted by permission of the author.

THOM GUNN, "High Fidelity" from *Collected Poems* by Thom Gunn. Reprinted by permission of Farrar, Straus and Giroux, LLC, and Faber and Faber Ltd.

JORGE GUILLÉN, "The Horses," translated by Richard Wilbur, from *Collected Poems: 1943–2004*, copyright © 2004 by Richard Wilbur. Reprinted by permission of Harcourt, Inc., and from *New and Collected Poems* by Faber and Faber Ltd.

IVOR GURNEY, "Strange Hells" from *Collected Poems* by Ivor Gurney. Reprinted by permission of Carcanet Press Limited.

MARILYN HACKER, "Fourteen" from *Selected Poems: 1965–1990* by Marilyn Hacker. Copyright © 1994 by Marilyn Hacker. Reprinted by permission of Frances Collins, Literary Agent, and W. W. Norton & Company, Inc.

TONY HARRISON, "On Not Being Milton" from *Selected Poems* by Tony Harrison. Reprinted by permission of Gordon Dickerson.

GWEN HARWOOD, "In the Park" from *Gwen Harwood: Collected Poems 1943–1995* by Gwen Harwood. Reprinted by permission of Penguin Australia.

ROBERT HAYDEN, "Those Winter Sundays." Copyright © 1966 by Robert Hayden from *Collected Poems of Robert Hayden* by Robert Hayden, edited by Frederick Glaysher. Used by permission of Liveright Publishing Corporation.

SEAMUS HEANEY, "Fireside" and "Requiem for the Croppies" from *Opened Ground: Selected Poems 1966–1996* by Seamus Heaney. Copyright © 1998 Seamus Heaney. Reprinted by permission of Farrar, Straus and Giroux, LLC, and from *Door in the Dark* by Faber and Faber Ltd.

ANTHONY HECHT, "Naming the Animals," from *Collected Later Poems* by Anthony Hecht, copyright © 2003 by Anthony Hecht. Used by permission of Alfred A. Knopf, a division of Random House.

MIGUEL HERNANDEZ, "You threw me a lemon," translated by Robert Bly, from *Selected Poems*, edited by Timothy Baland. Copyright © 1972, 1991 by Timothy Baland. Reprinted with the permission of White Pine Press, Buffalo, New York.

DANIEL HOFFMAN, "Violence" reprinted by permission of Louisiana State University Press from *Beyond Silence: Selected Shorter Poems, 1948–2003* by Daniel Hoffman. Copyright © 2003 by Daniel Hoffman.

JOHN HOLLANDER, "'Thirteen' from Powers of Thirteen," from *Selected Poetry* by John Hollander, copyright © 1993 by John Hollander. Used by permission of Alfred A. Knopf, a division of Random House, Inc.

A. D. HOPE, "Pasiphaë" by A.D. Hope. Reprinted by Arrangement with the Licensor, The Estate of A.D. Hope c/o Curtis Brown (Aust) Pty Ltd.

LANGSTON HUGHES, "Christ in Alabama," from The *Collected Poems of Langston Hughes* by Langston Hughes, edited by Arnold Rampersad with David Roessel, Associate Editor, copyright © 1994 by The Estate of Langston Hughes. Used by permission of Alfred A. Knopf, a division of Random House, Inc., and Harold Ober Associates Incorporated.

T. R. HUMMER, "Telepathic Poetics" reprinted by permission of Louisiana State University Press from *Useless Virtues: Poems.* Copyright © 1994 by T.R. Hummer.

PHILIPPE JACCOTTET, "Sonnet," by Philippe Jaccottet, translated by Donald Justice. Reprinted by permission of the estate of Donald Justice.

ROBINSON JEFFERS, "Love the Wild Swan," copyright 1935 and renewed 1963 by Donnan Jeffers and Garth Jeffers, from *Selected Poetry of Robinson Jeffers* by Robinson Jeffers. Used by permission of Random House.

DENIS JOHNSON, "Passengers" from *The Throne of the Third Heaven of the Nations Millennium General Assembly: Poems Collected and New* by Denis Johnson. Copyright © 1969, 1976, 1982, 1987, 1995 by Denis Johnson. Reprinted by permission of HarperCollins Publishers.

HELENE JOHNSON, Reprinted by permission from *This Waiting for Love* by Helene Johnson, edited by Verner D. Mitchell, published by the University of Massachusetts Press, Copyright © 2000 by Abigail McGrath.

JUNE JORDAN, "Sunflower Sonnet Number Two" from *Directed by Desire* by June Jordan. Reprinted by permission of the estate of June Jordan and the Watkins/Loomis Agency.

DONALD JUSTICE, "Mrs. Snow" from *Collected Poems* by Donald Justice, copyright © 2004 by Donald Justice. Used by permission of Alfred A. Knopf, a division of Random House, Inc.

PATRICK KAVANAGH, "Epic" by Patrick Kavanagh is reprinted from *Collected Poems* edited by Antoinette Quinn (Allen Lane 2004) by kind permission of the Trustees of the Estate of the late Katherine B. Kavanagh, through the Jonathan Williams Literary Agency.

WELDON KEES, "For My Daughter" reprinted from *The Collected Poems of Weldon Kees* edited by Donald Justice by permission of the University of Nebraska Press. Copyright 1962, 1975, by the University of Nebraska Press. © renewed 2003 by the University of Nebraska Press.

GALWAY KINNELL, "Blackberry Eating" from *Mortal Acts, Mortal Words* by Galway Kinnell. Copyright © 1980 by Galway Kinnell. Reprinted by permission of Houghton Mifflin Company. All rights reserved.

THOMAS KINSELLA, "Wedding Morning" by Thomas Kinsella. By kind permission of the author, Wake Forest University Press and The Gallery Press, Loughcrew, Oldcastle, County Meath, Ireland from *Collected Poems* (2006).

KARL KIRCHWEY, From "Two Tidal Sonnets: #1 (Ludovisi Throne)" from *Those I Guard*, copyright 1993 by Karl Kirchwey, reprinted by permission of Harcourt, Inc.

CAROLYN KIZER, "Reunion" from *Cool, Calm and Collected: Poems*

the author and The Gallery Press, Loughcrew, Oldcastle, County Meath, Ireland from *Collected Poems* (1999).

STÉPHANE MALLARMÉ, "The Tomb of Poe," by Stephane Mallarme, translated by Louis Simpson. Reprinted by permission of Louis Simpson.

PAUL MARIANI, "Hopkins in Ireland," *Deaths & Transfigurations* By Paul Mariani. © 2005 by Paul Mariani. Used by permission of Paraclete Press, www.paracletepress.com.

R. A. K. MASON, "Sonnet of Brotherhood." Reproduced with permission from *Collected Poems* (Victoria University Press, 1990).

WILLIAM MATTHEWS, "Cheap Seats, the Cincinnati Gardens, Professional Basketball, 1959" from *Time and Money: New Poems by William Matthews.* Copyright © 1995 by William Matthews. Reprinted by permission of Houghton Mifflin Company. All rights reserved.

BERNADETTE MAYER, "Sonnet" by Bernadette Mayer, from *A Bernadette Mayer Reader,* copyright © 1968 by Bernadette Mayer. Reprinted by permission of New Directions Publishing Corp.

JAMES MCAULEY, "Pietà" from *Collected Poems* by James McAuley. Reprinted by permission of HarperCollins Publishers.

J. D. MCCLATCHY, "Kilim, I," from *The Rest of the Way* by J.D. McClatchy, copyright © 1990 by J.D. McClatchy. Used by permission of Alfred A. Knopf, a division of Random House, Inc.

PHYLLIS MCGINLEY, "View from a Suburban Window," copyright 1941 by Phyllis McGinley, from *Times Three* by Phyllis McGinley. Used by permission of Viking Penguin, a division of Penguin Group (USA) Inc.

MEDBH MCGUCKIAN, "Shelmalier" by Medbh McGuckian. By kind permission of the author, Wake Forest University Press, and The Gallery Press, Loughcrew, Oldcastle, County Meath, Ireland from *Shelmalier* (1998).

SANDRA MCPHERSON, "Sonnet for Joe" by Sandra McPherson. Copyright 1973 by Sandra McPherson; first published in *The New Republic* and subsequently in *Radiation* (The Ecco Press, New York, 1973). Reprinted by permission of the author.

PAULA MEEHAN, "Queen" by Paula Meehan. By kind permission of the author and The Gallery Press, Loughcrew, Oldcastle, County Meath, Ireland from *The Man who was Marked by Winter* (1991).

WILLIAM MEREDITH, "The Illiterate" is reprinted from *Effort at Speech: New and Selected Poems* by William Meredith, published by TriQuarterly Books/Northwestern University Press in 1997. Copyright © 1997 by William Meredith. All rights reserved; used by permission of Northwestern University Press and the author.

JAMES MERRILL, "Marsyas," from *Collected Poems* by James Merrill, edited by J.D. McClatchy and Stephen Yenser, copyright © 2001 by the Literary Estate of James Merrill at Washington University. Used by permission of Alfred A. Knopf, a division of Random House, Inc.

W. S. MERWIN, "Sonnet," W.S. Merwin. © 2005 by W.S. Merwin, permission of The Wylie Agency.

JOSEPHINE MILES, "Luncheon 2" from *Collected Poems, 1930–1983*. Copyright by Josephine Miles. Used with permission of the poet and the University of Illinois Press.

EDNA ST. VINCENT MILLAY, "I will put Chaos into fourteen lines" and "Rendezvous" from *Collected Poems*, HarperCollins. Copyright © 1923, 1934, 1939, 1951, 1954, 1962, 1982 by Edna St. Vincent Millay and Norma Millay Ellis. All rights reserved. Used by permission of Elizabeth Barnett, literary executor.

SUSAN MITCHELL, "Boca Raton," p. 84, from *Rapture* by Susan Mitchell. Copyright © 1992 by Susan Mitchell. Reprinted by permission of HarperCollins Publishers.

JOHN MONTAGUE, "She writes #1" by John Montague. By kind permission of the author, Wake Forest University Press and the Gallery Press, Loughcrew, Oldcastle, County Meath, Ireland from *Collected Poems* (1995).

MARIANNE MOORE, "No Swan So Fine" by Marianne Moore. Reprinted with the permission of Scribner, an imprint of Simon & Schuster, Adult Publishing Group, from *The Collected Poems of Marianne Moore* by Marianne Moore. Copyright © 1935 by Marianne Moore; copyright © renewed 1963 by Marianne Moore and T.S. Eliot. All rights reserved. Reprinted by permission of Faber and Faber Ltd.

EDWIN MORGAN, "Sonnets from Scotland: The Coin" from *Collected Poems* (2000) by Edwin Morgan. Reprinted by permission of Carcanet Press Limited.

HOWARD MOSS, "The Snow Weed" from *New Selected Poems* by Howard Moss. Reprinted by permission of the Estate of Howard Moss.

EDWIN MUIR, "Milton" from *Poetry of Edwin Muir: Field of Good and Ill* (1971) by Elizabeth Huberman by Edwin Muir. Reprinted by permission of Oxford University Press, Inc., and Faber and Faber Ltd.

PAUL MULDOON, "The Old Country #1" from *Horse Latitudes* by Paul Muldoon. Copyright © by Paul Muldoon. Reprinted by permission of Farrar, Straus and Giroux, LLC, and Faber and Faber Ltd.

LES MURRAY, "Performance" from *Subhuman Redneck Poems* by Les Murray. Copyright © 1997 by Les Murray. Reprinted by permission of Farrar, Straus and Giroux, LLC, and Carcanet Press Limited.

PHILIP NEILSEN, "Vermouth" by Philip Neilsen. Reprinted by permission of the author.

MARILYN NELSON, "Beauty Shoppe" reprinted by permission of Louisiana State University Press from *The Fields of Praise: Poems* by Marilyn Nelson. Copyright © 1997 by Marilyn Nelson.

HOWARD NEMEROV, "A Primer of the Daily Round" by Howard Nemerov. Reprinted by permission of Margaret Nemerov.

PABLO NERUDA, "#LXXXIX" from *100 Love Sonnets: Cien Sonetos de Amor* by Pablo Neruda, translated by Stephen Tapscott, Copyright © Pablo Neruda 1959 and Fundacion Pablo Neruda, Copyright © 1986 by the University of Texas Press. By permission of the University of Texas Press.

GÉRARD DE NERVAL, "The Disinherited" from *Makes You Stop and Think: Sonnets* (New York: George Braziller, Inc., 2005).

ALICE NOTLEY, "Sonnet" by Alice Notley from *Grave of Light* (Wesleyan

University Press, 2006). © 2006 by Alice Notley and reprinted by permission of Wesleyan University Press.

DONALD ALLEN, "A City Winter, 1," edited by Donald Allen, from *The Collected Poems of Frank O'Hara* by Frank O'Hara, edited by Donald Allen, copyright © 1971 by Maureen Granville-Smith, Administratrix of the Estate of Frank O'Hara. Used by permission of Alfred A. Knopf, a division of Random House, Inc.

ALICIA OSTRIKER, "Sonnet: To Tell the Truth" from *Little Space: Poems Selected and New, 1968–1998,* by Alicia Suskin Ostriker, © 1998. Reprinted by permission of the University of Pittsburgh Press.

GEOFF PAGE, "The Recipe" by Geoff Page from *Darker and Lighter* (Five Islands Press 2001). Reprinted by permission of the author.

MICHAEL PALMER, "Pre-Petrarchan Sonnet" by Michael Palmer, from *The Lion Bridge,* copyright © 1998 by Michael Palmer. Reprinted by permission of New Directions Publishing Corp.

DOROTHY PARKER, "I Shall Come Back" from *The Portable Dorothy Parker* by Dorothy Parker, edited by Marion Meade, copyright 1928, renewed © 1956 by Dorothy Parker. Used by permission of Viking Penguin, a division of Penguin Group (USA) Inc. and from *Enough Rope* (1926) by Pollinger Limited.

KENNETH PATCHEN, "Religion Is That I Love You" by Kenneth Patchen, from *The Collected Poems of Kenneth Patchen,* copyright © 1957 by New Directions Publishing Corp. Reprinted by permission of New Directions Publishing Corp.

ROBERT PINSKY, "Sonnet" from *The Figured Wheel: New and Collected Poems 1966–1996* by Robert Pinsky. Copyright © 1996 by Robert Pinsky. Reprinted by permission of Farrar, Straus and Giroux, LLC, and Orion Books UK.

SYLVIA PLATH, "Conversation Among the Ruins" from *The Collected Poems of Sylvia Plath,* EDITED by TED HUGHES. Copyright © 1960, 1965, 1971, 1981 by the Estate of Sylvia Plath. Editorial material copyright © by Ted Hughes. Reprinted by permission of HarperCollins Publishers and Faber and Faber Ltd.

MARIE PONSOT, "Out of Eden," from *Springing: New and Selected Poems* by Marie Ponsot, copyright © 2002 by Marie Ponsot. Used by permission of Alfred A. Knopf, a division of Random House, Inc.

EZRA POUND, "A Virginal" from *Personae,* copyright © 1926 by Ezra Pound. Reprinted by permission of New Directions Publishing Corp. And from *Collected Shorter Poems* by Ezra Pound. Reprinted by permission of Faber and Faber Ltd.

ALEXANDER PUSHKIN, *From Eugene Onegin: A Novel in Verse:* #7 ("The art of verse, that lofty pleasure"), translated by Babette Deutsch, published by Dover Publications, 1998.

RAYMOND QUENEAU, From *Cent mille milliard de poèmes* (*100,000,000,000,000 Poems*), Sonnet #31804123559959 by Raymond Queneau and translated by Stanely Chapman. © Editions Gallimard, Paris, 1961. Reprinted by permission of Atlas Press, London and Gallimard.

1990 by Linda G. Sexton. Reprinted by permission of Houghton Mifflin Company and Little, Brown Book Group Limited. All rights reserved.

KARL SHAPIRO, "Jew" from *The Wild Card* by Karl Shapiro. Reprinted by permission of Robert Phillips.

CHARLES SIMIC, "History" from *Selected Poems* (New York: George Braziller, 1990) by Charles Simic. Reprinted by permission of George Braziller, Inc., and Faber and Faber Ltd.

BURNS SINGER, "Sonnets for a Dying Man: #XLIX" from *Collected Poems* (2001) by Burns Singer. Reprinted by permission of Carcanet Press Limited.

TOM SLEIGH, From *The Work*, 1. Today ("Today, this moment, speechlessly in pain") from *The Chain* by Tom Sleigh. Reprinted by permission of the author.

DAVE SMITH, "The Spring Poem" reprinted by permission of Louisiana State University Press from *The Wick of Memory: New and Selected Poems 1970–2000* by Dave Smith. Copyright © 2000 by Dave Smith.

ELIZABETH SMITHER, "Visiting Juliet Street" from *The Legend of Marcello Mastroianni's Wife* (Auckland University Press, 1981) by Elizabeth Smither. Reprinted by permission of the author.

W. D. SNODGRASS, "Not any man…No Man" from *Heart's Needle* by W.D. Snodgrass. Reprinted by permission of the author.

EDITH SPEERS, "Love Sonnets: #9" from *Four Quarters* (2001) by Edith Speers. Reprinted by permission of the author.

STEPHEN SPENDER, "Daybreak" from *New Collected Poems* by Stephen Spender © 2004. Reprinted by kind permission of the Estate of Stephen Spender.

WILLIAM STAFFORD, "A Stared Story" copyright 1962, 1998 by the Estate of William Stafford. Reprinted from *The Way It Is: New & Selected Poems* with the permission of Graywolf Press, Saint Paul, Minnesota.

GEORGE STARBUCK, "Sonnet with a Different Letter at the End of Every Line." Reprinted by permission of The University of Alabama Press.

C. K. STEAD, From *Twenty-Two Sonnets* 16 from *Walking Westward* by C.K. Stead. Reprinted by permission of the author.

GERALD STERN, "American Heaven," from *American Sonnets* by Gerald Stern. Copyright © 2002 by Gerald Stern. Used by permission of W. W. Norton & Company, Inc.

WALLACE STEVENS, "The Poem that Took the Place of a Mountain" from *The Collected Poems of Wallace Stevens* by Wallace Stevens, copyright 1954 by Wallace Stevens and renewed 1982 by Holly Stevens. Used by permission of Alfred A. Knopf, a division of Random House, Inc., and by Faber and Faber Ltd.

SUSAN STEWART, "Slaughter": #5 from "Slaughter," *The Forest*, University of Chicago Press, 1995. Reprinted by permission of the author.

ALFONSINA STORNI, "To My Lady of Poetry," translated by Kay Short, from *Selected Poems*, edited by Marion Freeman. Copyright © 1987 by Kay Short. Reprinted with the permission of White Pine Press, Buffalo, New York.

MARK STRAND, "One Winter Night," from *The Continuous Life* by Mark Strand, copyright © 1990 by Mark Strand. Used by permission of Alfred A. Knopf, a division of Random House, Inc.

DOROTHEA TANNING, "Report from the Field" copyright 2004 by Dorothea Tanning. Reprinted from *A Table of Content* with the permission of Graywolf Press, Saint Paul, Minnesota.

ALLEN TATE, "Sonnets at Christmas: #1" ("This is the day of the hour...") from *Collected Poem, 1919–1976* by Allen Tate. Reprinted by permission of Farrar, Straus and Giroux, LLC.

ANA ENRIQUETA TERÁN, "Subtle in Your Fourteen Lines Surge." Teran, Ana Enriqueta; *The Poetess Counts to 100 and Bows Out.* © 2003 Ana Enriqueta Teran. Published by Princeton University Press. Reprinted by permission of Princeton University Press.

LAM THI MY DA, "Night Harvest" from *Green Rice* by Lam Thi My Da. English translation by Martha Collins and Thuy Dinh. Curbstone Press, 2005. Reprinted with permission of Curbstone Press. Distributed by Perseus/Consortium.

DYLAN THOMAS, "When All My Five and Country Senses See" by Dylan Thomas, from *The Poems of Dylan Thomas*, copyright © 1939 by New Directions Publishing Corp. Reprinted by permission of New Directions Publishing Corp. and David Higham Associates.

JOHN UPDIKE, "Love Sonnet," from *Midpoint and Other Poems* by John Updike, copyright © 1969 and renewed 1997 by John Updike. Reprinted by permission of Alfred A. Knopf, a division of Random House, Inc.

CONSTANCE URDANG, From "To Live with a Landscape, 1" ("Take your boulevards, your Locust Street"), from *The Lone Woman and Others* by Constance Urdang. Reprinted by permission of Constance Urdang Estate.

JEAN VALENTINE, "X" by Jean Valentine from *Door in the Mountain: New and Collected Poems, 1965–2003* (Wesleyan University Press, 2004). © 2004 by Jean Valentine and reprinted by permission of Wesleyan University Press.

PAUL VALÉRY, "Paul Valery: Helen" from *Things of This World*, copyright © 1956 and renewed 1984 by Richard Wilbur, reprinted by permission of Harcourt, Inc., and from *New and Collected Poems* by Faber and Faber Ltd.

CÉSAR VALLEJO, "Black Stone Lying on a White Stone," translated by Robert Bly and John Knoepfle. Reprinted by permission of Robert Bly.

MONA VAN DUYN, "Double Sonnet for Minimalists," from *Near Changes* by Mona Van Duyn, copyright © 1990 by Mona Van Duyn. Used by permission of Alfred A. Knopf, a division of Random House, Inc.

PAUL VERLAINE, "Night Scene," by Norman Shapiro. Copyright © 1999 University of Chicago Press. Reprinted by permission of the author.

ELLEN BRYANT VOIGT, [Who said the worst was past, who knew] from *Kyrie* by Ellen Bryant Voigt. Copyright © 1995 by Ellen Bryant Voigt. Used by permission of W. W. Norton & Company, Inc.

DEREK WALCOTT, "Homage to Edward Thomas" from *Collected Poems 1948–1984* by Derek Walcott. Copyright © 1986 by Derek Walcott. Reprinted by permission of Farrar, Straus and Giroux, LLC, and Faber and Faber Ltd.

# Index

---